100.00

U.S. FOREIGN POLICY

U.S. FOREIGN POLICY

A Documentary and Reference Guide

Akis Kalaitzidis and Gregory W. Streich

Documentary and Reference Guides

GREENWOOD

AN IMPRINT OF ABC-CLIO, LLC
Santa Barbara, California • Denver, Colorado • Oxford, England

Library of Congress Cataloging-in-Publication Data

Kalaitzidis, Akis, 1969–
    U.S. foreign policy : a documentary and reference guide / Akis Kalaitzidis and Gregory W. Streich.
        p. cm. — (Documentary and reference guides)
    Includes bibliographical references and index.
    ISBN 978–0–313–38375–5 (hard copy : alk. paper) — ISBN 978–0–313–38376–2 (ebook)
1. United States—Foreign relations—Sources. 2. United States—Foreign relations. I. Streich,
Gregory W. II. Title.
E183.7.K3415   2011
327.73—dc22   2011013522

ISBN: 978–0–313–38375–5
EISBN: 978–0–313–38376–2

15 14 13 12 11   1 2 3 4 5

This book is also available on the World Wide Web as an eBook.
Visit www.abc-clio.com for details.

Greenwood
An Imprint of ABC-CLIO, LLC

ABC-CLIO, LLC
130 Cremona Drive, P.O. Box 1911
Santa Barbara, California 93116-1911

This book is printed on acid-free paper (∞)

Manufactured in the United States of America

CONTENTS

READER'S GUIDE TO THE DOCUMENTS AND SIDEBARS

INTRODUCTION: AMERICAN FOREIGN POLICY: THE THEORETICAL LANDSCAPE

Books about American foreign policy must highlight important debates surrounding important historical events as well as the ultimate goals and conduct of U.S. foreign policy. Some argue that throughout U.S. history, the United States has engaged in an unending quest for power and supremacy which culminated in the articulation of the Bush Doctrine as the official national security statement. Others claim that the United States' primary objective was to dominate the world economically and as such it engaged in an endless battle to reshape and dominate the global economy, especially after World War II and the introduction of the Washington consensus. Still other practitioners and scholars believe that the United States has always been "exceptional" and carries a duty to act in a manner reflecting its role as a world leader. Finally, some consider the United States to be more or less just another superpower (or, perhaps even a "hyper-power") whose position as a superpower will inevitably come to an end. No matter which position readers take, we suggest that in order to judge the merits of these theoretical camps it behooves readers to consider the evidence that each relies upon to make their case.

AMERICAN FOREIGN POLICY IN THE EARLY DAYS—THE REGIONAL ERA

Much ink has been spilled on the early years of the American republic and its foreign policy, primarily because it predates most modern theories of foreign policymaking and as such is hard to categorize. Was America an isolationist nation, a pragmatic nation recognizing its limitations, or a regional bully engaging in local expansionist policies on its way to global dominance? Much of the answer to these questions depends on the choices the reader makes in assigning weight to different events, actors, policies, beliefs, and institutions of the time. We argue that it is probable that a mixture of all these elements explains the early days of U.S. foreign policy and, as such, choose to represent the historical development of U.S. foreign policy as a mixed bag up to the end of World War II. Because U.S.

foreign policymaking has always been influenced by the character of the men that run the country, Walter Russell Mead's categorization of four different schools of thought is useful to our understanding of U.S. foreign policy in its early years. Mead divides foreign policymaking into four ideological categories, each named after a major political contributor: Hamiltonianism, Jeffersonianism, Jacksonianism, and Wilsonianism.

Hamiltonianism is an ideology based on the beliefs of Alexander Hamilton, a founding father of the United States. An avid Anglophile and a strong Federalist, Hamilton exalted the ideas of continental realism (Mead 2001: 100). He also believed in capitalism and uninhibited global trade. For presidents and other actors who take a Hamiltonian view of U.S. foreign policy, the economy should guide American foreign policy because the national interest is interconnected with national economic well-being. Further, international capitalism leads to world peace because it enhances the interconnectedness of nations through trade. For Mead, "Hamiltonians did not have to believe that the United States must either conquer or be conquered in its international relations; they could and did believe that the United States, without neglecting its military forces, was able to seek constructive compromises of mutual benefit in its dealings with foreign powers" (Mead 2001: 105). For such policies to exist, the conduct of trade and the exchange of goods and capital should proceed uninhibited and the U.S. role in the world is to make sure that this is the case. Yet this did not prohibit the United States from enacting the highest tariffs and other barriers to free trade to protect its own national economy and interests during the sixty years that this ideology dominated U.S. foreign policy, from 1865 to 1929 (Mead 2001: 109).

On the other hand, the ideology named after Thomas Jefferson, Jeffersonianism, became the opposition, not only because the two leaders disagreed on a personal and political level in the early years of the republic, but also because their attitudes were diametrically opposed. Jeffersonians believe the United States should stay away from the entangling alliances of Europe, a view first expressed by George Washington and reiterated by Jefferson himself in his inaugural address after the election of 1800. Jefferson had a deep mistrust of centralized government and was skeptical of U.S. elites, including his rival Alexander Hamilton. Jefferson believed that stronger central governments have more ability to oppress the common people, and his followers went as far as to argue that King George III was substituted by King George I upon the election of Washington as president. Jeffersonian figures such as Patrick Henry went as far as refusing to attend the Constitutional Convention in Philadelphia, famously saying he "smelled a rat!" To Jeffersonians, U.S. foreign policy can only be isolationist. If the United States were to pursue an internationalist policy, Jeffersonians worry that the nation would be involved in alliances and costly wars that would, in turn, increase the burden on citizens at the same time as it legitimized the influence of powerful interests such as banking on U.S. foreign policy (Mead 2001: 187). Early on in the history of the United States, Jeffersonians produced several key foreign policy instruments such as the Monroe Doctrine. Famously, John Quincy Adams, in a speech to Congress on July 4, 1821, declared, "Wherever the standard of freedom and Independence has been or shall be unfurled, there will her heart, her benedictions and her prayers be. But she goes not abroad, in search of monsters to destroy. She is the well-wisher to the freedom and independence of all. She is the champion and vindicator only of her own."

A third ideological camp became dominant with the consolidation of the Jeffersonian Democrats (which eventually became the Democratic Party) under the leadership of President Andrew Jackson. A populist and hero of the Battle of New Orleans, Jackson was suspicious of elites and believed in the power of folksy America (Mead 2001: 226–227). Jacksonian values include honor, individualism, and courage and as such it is the most militant and expansionistic of American ideologies to this day. U.S. foreign policy guided by Jacksonianism included wars of expansion and a brief stint in good old European-style imperialism after the Spanish-American war. For Jacksonians, the United States should exhibit fierceness in war: Jackson urged his people to deliberate, but when the time of action arrived, to stop thinking and act. He also urged them to fight for what they believed when he said, "Every good citizen makes his country's honor his own, and cherishes it not only as precious but as sacred. He is willing to risk his life in its defense and is conscious that he gains protection while he gives it."

The last but not least of the four ideological groups to be found in U.S. foreign policy is that of Wilsonianism, which in our day is somewhat similar to idealism. President Woodrow Wilson, a deeply religious man, was convinced of the moral superiority of the United States. He rejected Jeffersonian calls to isolationism and argued that the United States had a moral obligation to help those less fortunate and to advance the American way of life. Wilsonian politicians to this day believe the United States to be blessed by God and as such has the obligation to bring Christianity to the rest of the globe. Internationalism is the only way by which a country accepting this mission can operate, and by President Wilson's administration the United States seems to be changing its attitude toward global affairs. Although briefly interrupted by the one period of time U.S. foreign policy can be called isolationist, Wilsonianism is one of the most pervasive schools of thought in U.S. foreign policymaking in the twentieth century. Opposing the Jacksonian tradition on issues of war, the Wilsonian school seeks to create international institutions for the avoidance of war, such as the League of Nations, Wilson's brain trust, and the expansion of democratic rule all over the world (Mead 2001: 162–166). Although it suffered deeply from the outbreak of World War II and the hostilities which ravaged the globe, Wilsonianism was not eradicated as a foreign policy camp but took a back seat to the realist tradition that dominated the post–World War II era.

Overall, the first century and a half of U.S. history can be considered a "regional era," with the United States fighting to establish itself as a leader in the Western Hemisphere, expand its borders, secure its people, and promote capitalism as its main goals. It would not be until the end of World War II that the United States entered global superpower status and foreign policy becomes dominated by the modern school of "realism" which overshadowed idealism.

FROM IDEALISM TO REALISM—WORLD SUPERPOWER

The regional era was brought to a close by World War I, otherwise known as the War to End All Wars. Clearly the end of that era poses tremendous dilemmas for theorists and practitioners alike who are struggling to deal with the changing status quo.

Martin Hollis and Steve Smith (1990) argue that there were four main conclusions from World War I: "first, war was a senseless act, which could never be a rational tool of state policy; secondly, the 1914–18 war had been the result of leaders becoming caught up in a set of processes that no one could control; thirdly, the causes of war lay in misunderstandings between leaders and in the lack of democratic accountability within the states involved; and fourthly, the underlying tensions which provided the rationale for the conflict could be removed by the spread of statehood and democracy." Given these lessons, "idealism" seems to be a natural for people attempting to create a new order, one in which identity issues such as culture and ethnicity would be taken seriously but not lead to another war. In this respect the study of U.S. foreign policy, importantly from both the theoretical and the practitioner's point of view in developing a theory of international relations, begins with the presentation of President Wilson's Fourteen Points, which directly addressed such issues.

The post–World War I order was unable to prevent the eruption of a new world war which proved even more destructive (Stoessinger 2001). In its wake, the field of international relations changed and a new school of thought became prominent—realism. Realism differed from its predecessor in all respects, but most importantly it rejected idealist utopianism (Carr 2001). Realism proposes to see and analyze the world as it is, not as it ought to be. E. H. Carr's theory of realism was based on three tenets: (1) History is a result of a cause and effect process; (2) theory does not create practice but the other way around; and (3) morality is a product of power, not the other way around (Hollis and Smith 1990). Following in his footsteps, Hans Morgenthau's book *Politics among Nations*, published in 1948, attempted to scientifically analyze international relations for the purpose of understanding the world. His claims became central to what we now call classical realism. Morgenthau's main thesis is that there is an inherently rational way of understanding relations among states that can be achieved by focusing on the interest of states defined in terms of power (Keohane 1986). For the realist camp, international relations are primarily relations among states, and these relations are a quest for power, and there is no single standard of morality in the world.

For realists, elements of power such as military force, economics, population, and natural resources were more attractive because they were more quantifiable, and thus more scientific than issues of identity, religion, and culture. Yet Morgenthau's view of power politics was not itself very scientific, which led to several attempts to develop "systemic" theories of international relations by scholars such as Morton Kaplan (1957), Stanley Hoffmann (1965), and Richard Rosecrance (1963). These attempts led to a more precise definition of the word system, using a levels of analysis approach (Singer 1961) as well as a neo-realist movement which attempted to explain power politics mainly by looking at systemic explanations of international relations such as state behavior in the international system and its constraints. Kenneth Waltz, in *Theory of International Politics*, argues that it is the structure of the international system that defines the behavior of states, and systems have three characteristics: (1) the ordering of units, (2) the functions of units, and (3) their capabilities (Waltz 1979). The difference is then attributed to the third characteristic, which becomes the essential one (Keohane 1986). Yet within any given system one can have only a given set of behaviors, that is, different behaviors for a unipolar system as opposed to a multipolar one (Hollis and Smith 1990). In fact, theorist and practitioner Henry Kissinger notes that at this time there are four international systems that coexist side by side (2001).

During the Cold War the United States was involved in numerous conflicts while avoiding the major one with the Soviet Union. This period has been dubbed "the long peace" (Gaddis 1989). Picking up the superpower mantle from the United Kingdom and getting involved in the Greek civil war, the United States vowed to remain a friend to those who would seek to defend themselves against communism, a position expressed in the Truman Doctrine. In its effort to defend against the expansion of the Soviet Union, the United States adopted a policy of containment and created several Cold War institutions that exist today, such as the Joint Chiefs of Staff and the Central Intelligence Agency (CIA). It also provided for the reconstruction of Europe and Japan. A two-pronged policy of geostrategic imperatives and economic expansionism followed. In Europe the United States spent enormous amounts of money to reconstruct the failing economies on a destroyed continent. The North Atlantic Treaty Organization (NATO) was created in order to provide for security in Europe, and a treaty was signed with Japan that did the same.

Although it seems that the policy of containment largely worked against Soviet aggression in Europe and Japan, other continents and regions of the world were not so lucky. This era became the era of wars by proxy, with upheaval in Southeast Asia, the Middle East, Latin America, and Africa. The two superpowers, attempting to check each other's powers, fueled local wars that killed millions. Starting with a war in the Middle East after the emigration of hundreds of thousands of Jewish survivors of the holocaust to Palestine, the region has not found peace to this day, grappling with the Palestinian question endlessly. Although the United States was not directly involved in this war, its proxy, the newly created state of Israel, defeated its Arab neighbors in war after war, largely thanks to unlimited support from the United States. Yet the United States depended greatly on Arab oil and made several Machiavellian deals with Arab regimes to keep their energy deposits intact and secure the flow of Middle Eastern oil not only to the United States but also to Europe and Japan. It acquiesced to illegitimate Arab monarchs and dictators, going as far to help religious fanatics in Afghanistan to defeat the Soviets, something that came back to haunt the United States in 2001. In Asia, the United States protected South Korea from North Korean aggression, fighting a bloody conflict in 1950, and then picked up where the French forces could not succeed in French Indochina in the 1960s in order to contain the spread of communism.

Vietnam became the darkest hour of the U.S. military. After the United States was defeated, it would take a couple of decades before the U.S. military would be deployed en masse again. The lessons from Vietnam led policymakers to shy away from participation in major wars. Instead, the United States continued an ongoing policy of attempting to control other areas of the world by helping install brutal dictatorships in countries such as Iran, Pakistan, Chile, Brazil, Argentina, Nicaragua, El Salvador, Guatemala, Greece, and Turkey, to name just a few. Overthrowing unfriendly regimes was part of the Cold War business, starting early on with the overthrown of Mohamad Mosadegh, the elected leader of Iran, in favor of pro-U.S. Shah Reza Pahlavi was just the beginning of a 30-year period of activity out of Washington on the global chessboard. Realism demanded the rejection of the constraints of morality on U.S. foreign policy and focusing the State and Defense departments on pursuing policies that would check Soviet ambitions and promote U.S. strategic interests.

The isolationists, the Jeffersonians and their fellow travelers, seem to have disappeared from within the ranks of the U.S. foreign policy establishment.

FROM REALISM TO SUPREMACY—HYPERPOWER

Two major events mark the current foreign policy activities of the United States: (1) the collapse of the Berlin Wall, and (2) the attacks of 9/11/2001. By the end of the 1980s, the United States had started to see the development of liberal institutionalist ideals in government. Raw realism was on the wane and at least one president, Jimmy Carter, made human rights a priority, although short-lived. Theoretically, realism was under assault for its pessimistic view of the world as an anarchic place where each country would do its best to defend itself and where decision makers would do what they could and the weak would suffer what they must, to paraphrase Thucydides. The collapse of the Soviet Union seemed to catch the world by surprise, and in the United States a period of soul searching ensued in foreign policy circles, a period dubbed "the Kennan sweepstakes" (Cox and Stokes 2008).

With the liberal internationalists on the rise, the United States invaded Panama to remove Manuel Noriega from power, and six months later mobilized against Iraqi dictator Saddam Hussein, who invaded Kuwait in 1991. It seemed that dictators who had previously been U.S. clients no longer had a role in American foreign policy and that the United States was enjoying a "unipolar moment" (Krauthammer 1990) in which it could do as it pleased on an unprecedented global scale. The lessons of Vietnam were largely forgotten after the Gulf War against Saddam Hussein, and the United States seemed poised to become a true liberal leader in the world. However, the United States reluctantly got involved in the civil wars that followed the collapse of Yugoslavia, especially in the wars of Bosnia-Herzegovina and Kosovo, and the civil wars of Somalia and Haiti. Leading a community of nations based on international law, the United States brought to justice Serb and Croat war criminals and African dictators and arranged for the restoration for democracy in Haiti. Yet traditionally the United States always faced stiff opposition internally when acting as the conscience of the world, and in the 1990s opponents of the liberal interventionists fought hard to stop U.S. forces from participating in these wars where the United States had nothing tangible to gain. Politicians such as President Bill Clinton had a difficult time convincing the American public that it was in the interests of the United States to be involved in faraway places such as Somalia and Bosnia. The loss of American lives in Somalia and their brutal display on TV produced a backlash against interventionism. When humanitarian intervention was needed during the genocide in Rwanda, the United States shied away, allowing for the systematic killing of nearly a million Tutsis by their ethnic opponents the Hutus.

The second event that marked a change of course in U.S. foreign policy was the attacks of 9/11. On the morning of September 11, 2001, four domestic flights were hijacked by al Qaeda operatives in the United States. Two planes were flown into the World Trade Center towers in New York, the third into the Pentagon, and the fourth crashed in Pennsylvania. Together, these attacks caused the death of thousands of Americans and billions of dollars in economic damages. Al Qaeda, a fundamentalist Islamic terrorist network founded by former ally of the U.S. in Afghanistan in the war against the Soviet forces, claimed responsibility. The United

States entered a Jacksonian moment. Although some of the public pronouncements by President George W. Bush could be seen as part of the same liberal international tradition that guided his father George H.W. Bush's and Bill Clinton's foreign policy, the conduct of U.S. foreign policy changed dramatically. International law and international organizations became unwanted nuances in the global War on Terror; the massive intelligence machine that was built after World War II became even bigger. The United States invaded Iraq, purportedly to stop Saddam Hussein from using or obtaining weapons of mass destruction (WMDs) and using them on the U.S. But it seems the Jacksonian tradition that calls for a fight to the ultimate end was present and the enemies were deemed not worthy, so in a classic unilateralist mode the United States disregarded any suggestions or reservations expressed by its allies and moved to dispense justice in its own way.

Clearly at the height of its power, engaged in two wars at the same time, and ignoring many of the rules it had a hand in creating, the United States is at the apex of another unipolar moment. Some have embraced this moment, suggesting that the lesson of history is that the United States is a "liberal empire" that can benefit the world by continuing to spread its policies around the globe, using force if necessary (Ferguson 2005). Others, however, have described the United States as an "empire" (Johnson 2004, Todd 2002) or "hyperpower" (Vedrine, 2001, Cohen 2004, Chua 2007).

The fact of the matter remains that the United States is currently engaged in two wars in Iraq and Afghanistan while simultaneously conducting intelligence operations in what President Bush called the Global War on Terror. To understand how the United States arrived at this point, and perhaps even to understand lessons of the past that can guide the U.S. into the future, the following chapters present American foreign policy in historical sequence from George Washington to Barack Obama.

REFERENCES

Carr, E. H. (2001) *The Twenty Years' Crisis, 1919–1939: An Introduction to the Study of International Relations*. New York: Palgrave.

Chua, A. (2007) *Day of Empire: How Hyperpowers Rise to Global Dominance—and Why They Fall*. New York: Random House.

Cohen, E. (2004) "History and the Hyperpower," *Foreign Affairs*, 84(4), 49–63.

Cox, M., and Stokes, D. eds. (2008) *US Foreign Policy*. Oxford: Oxford University Press.

Ferguson, N. (2005) *Colossus: The Rise and Fall of the American Empire*. New York: Penguin Books.

Gaddis, J. L. (1989) *The Long Peace: Inquiries in the History of the Cold War*. Oxford: Oxford University Press.

Hoffmann, S. (1965) *The State of War: Essays on the Theory and Practice of International Politics*. New York: Praeger.

Hollis, M., and Smith S. (1990) *Explaining and Understanding International Relations*. Oxford: Oxford University Press.

Johnson, C. (2000) *Blowback: The Cost and Consequences of American Empire*. New York: Henry Holt.

Johnson, C. (2004) *Sorrows of Empire: Militarism, Secrecy, and the End of the Empire*. New York: Henry Holt.

Johnson, C. (2006) *Nemesis: The Last Days of the American Republic*. New York: Henry Holt.

Kaplan, M. (1957) *Systems and Process in International Politics*. New York: Wiley.

Keohane, R., ed. (1986) *Neo-Realism and its Critics*. New York: Columbia University Press.

Kissinger, H. (2001) *Does America Need a Foreign Policy? Towards Diplomacy for the 21st Century*. New York: Simon & Schuster.

Krauthammer C. (1990) "The Unipolar Moment," *Foreign Affairs*, 70(1), 23–33.

Mead, W. R. (2001) *Special Providence: American Foreign Policy and How It Changed the World*. New York: Alfred A. Knopf.

Rosecrance, R. (1963) *Action and Reaction in World Politics*. New York: Little, Brown.

Singer, J. D. (1961) "The Level of Analysis Problem in International Relations," *World Politics*, 14(1), 77–92.

Stoessinger, J. G. (2001) *Why Nations Go to War*. Florence, KY: Wadsworth.

Todd, E. (2003) *After the Empire: The Breakdown of the American Order*. New York: Columbia University Press.

Vedrine, H (2001) *France in the Age of Globalization*. Washington, DC: Brookings Institution Press.

Waltz, K. (1979) *Theory of International Politics*. New York: McGraw Hill.

1

GEORGE WASHINGTON
TO
JAMES MONROE:
THE ORIGINS OF REGIONALISM

INTRODUCTION

At the dawn of the American republic, foreign policy was a highly contentious undertaking. The first issue was establishing the republic after a revolutionary struggle that involved not only the former colonial power, Britain, but its allies and enemies, most importantly France. France's involvement in the American war of independence was vital to secure victory, and thus America's foreign policy challenges started even before the republic itself. The second and most important phase of early American foreign policy was adapting to the belligerent European environment while being young, small, and by comparison very weak. Foreign policy issues came to dominate American politics early on and have had a decisive influence in the development of internal politics as well, such as the political party system and the transition from one president to another. Finally, foreign affairs became increasingly focused on maintaining the growth of the country and thus obsessed with trade and settlement issues.

From the onset of the Revolutionary War, it seemed that the American colonies were attempting the impossible. Revolutionary leader Thomas Paine called it starting the world over again (Herring 2008). It would be a futile action, however, unless the colonies received international support and recognition, which meant developing a plan and diplomatic skills of some note even though no centralized state existed as of yet. Students of American foreign policy are well advised to view this era as a baptism by fire in the city of Paris. One of the first elements of American foreign policy on display, pragmatism, became clear when the colonists attempted to enlist Britain's arch-enemy France in their struggle for independence. The delegation of Americans included John Adams, Thomas Jefferson (the author of the Declaration of Independence), and Benjamin Franklin. Jefferson eventually developed a long-term Francophilia that would ultimately play a great role in his dealings as a member of the first cabinet of the U.S. government, especially vis-à-vis his political opponents Alexander Hamilton and John Adams. Yet it was Benjamin Franklin who stole the show. Extremely well equipped by character to deal with the elite of the city of lights, Franklin took Paris by storm. The women of Paris called him "mon cher papa" (Wood 2004: 177) and crowded around him, helping him appeal to the French public.

This diplomatic mission succeeded and resulted in the Treaty of 1778, a perpetual alliance between the two nations. Treaties such as this have a way of becoming a point of contention when the proverbial shoe is on the other foot, as the first president of the United States, George Washington, found out when war broke between Britain and France in 1793. At the time it was completed, however, it was a genuine success for the American revolutionary effort. With the help of France and illustrious French generals such as Lafayette, the United States was able to conclude a protracted struggle for independence with the Treaty of 1783.

The Treaty of Paris, as it is known, between the warring parties—Britain, the United States, Spain, France, and Holland—established the independence of the 13 American colonies from British rule. The colonies were now sovereign, possessed recognized boundaries, and were free to conduct their affairs as they saw fit. The treaty also made provisions for trade, fishing rights, and commercial activities by the colonies. It also established the accepted routine for finalizing property claims the British crown might have in the United States, appropriate compensation, and, most importantly, the removal of the British army from U.S. soil without further delay or destruction of property, including slaves. The treaty was quickly ratified by the Continental Congress meeting in Annapolis in 1784 so that it could move on to its next issue, the question of expansion and dealing with the Native American peoples, who were completely ignored in this agreement between peoples of European descent.

The first president of the United States clearly understood early on that his country had unrivaled potential but also that it was hard to reach. He understood that colonizing as much as possible of the continent was necessary, having himself been at war with the British Army in the western territory and engaged in land speculation. He also understood that the United States must remain outside of the influence of the great European rivalries in order to achieve that goal. And for that, a policy of neutrality would be necessary. However, the position of the United States in the greater rivalry between France and Britain was precarious. It had an alliance with the French from which it would be hard to extricate itself without causing a crisis. But Washington also watched the belligerent moves of Britain, which threatened a new war that would weaken the United States.

Almost as important were the divisions within his cabinet, which included some of the preeminent members of the American political elite. One was Alexander Hamilton, an Anglophile pushing for the United States to abrogate its 1778 treaty obligations with France and remain neutral, thus favoring Britain. Another was Thomas Jefferson, a Francophile, who stressed that treaty obligations were important for the foreign relations of America and its future. The two men also had different outlooks on political rule. Hamilton favored a strong central authority and a standing army, while Jefferson opposed both. These divisions eventually led to the creation of two political parties.

The more immediate concern was the Native American presence in the Northwest Territory and control of the Mississippi waterways, which pitted the United States against the Spanish. The government, having been partially successful with the Creek Indians, decided that the problem in the Northwest was solvable by military action, an action that failed. The failed campaigns must have given President Washington pause regarding the power of his government and might have been influential in his decision to side with Alexander Hamilton in regard to the war in Europe. The British, meanwhile, did not make things easier by attempting to starve the French into submission and cutting off food supplies from the United States to France, raiding American ships and confiscating their cargo. These issues, along with some lingering ones from the Revolutionary War, were solved by the Jay Treaty, otherwise known as the Treaty of London of 1794. The importance of this treaty cannot be overstated. The reaction to it, however, was one of public outrage and indignation. Jefferson's Republicans vehemently opposed it and took to the streets, even burning effigies of John Jay.

The treaty's domestic importance is that it solidified the two political parties, the Jeffersonian Democratic Republicans (the predecessor of today's Democrats) and the Hamiltonian Federalists. The treaty was clearly very important for the Washington administration because the president was focused on avoiding war, which the treaty did in no uncertain terms. Despite the domestic disagreement surrounding the treaty, it was beneficial for the United States. It increased international trade, which helped the U.S. economy grow, and it kept the United States out of the entanglement of alliances in Europe. It is no surprise that Washington's farewell address to the nation (which was partially written by Hamilton) warns of the insidious wiles of foreign influence and the passionate attachment to permanent alliances, a not-so-veiled reference to the treaty with France and a swipe at Jefferson. President Washington was convinced that such a foreign policy position was the right direction for the United States.

The French, however, were not positively disposed to this U.S. action. Nor were they inclined to entertain the U.S. fears about alliances, or the machinations of Hamilton, a man whose own president described as "the greatest intriguant in the world—a man devoid of every moral principle—and a bastard" (Herring 2008: 89). As the pendulum swung the other way, the French used the same punishment on the U.S. commercial fleet as had the British, raiding ships and confiscating cargoes. A settlement would not come easily, given that France was at the peak of its powers, with Napoleon at its helm. Yet a settlement was achieved, of which President Adams was very proud, that disentangled the United States from the perpetual alliance and gained liberal maritime concessions from Napoleonic France, albeit with the loss of compensation for lost vessels and cargo. Yet again the Jeffersonians dissented, but upon his arrival in the Oval Office, President Jefferson nevertheless ratified the treaty. The long-term interest of the United States had won again.

The change in government from the Federalists to the Republicans, one would have assumed, would bring some changes in foreign policy—in both actions and principles. Indeed, Jefferson had complained about the previous administrations' relationship with the British Empire, and he adopted a more Francophile position, which by the presidency of his friend James Madison became a full-scale war with Britain, the War of 1812. Yet the long-term interests and vision of the United States as a continental nation, one surrounded by oceans and in full control of itself, did not die with Jefferson. The president became famous for strengthening this vision with his shrewd purchase of the Louisiana Territory from Napoleon, admittedly one of the best real estate deals in the history of the world. It was probably fortuitous that colonial powers such as France and Spain were on the wane and could not defend their colonies in the Americas, especially the North American continent.

Whatever the reason, first Napoleon sold Louisiana to Jefferson, and later the Spanish sold Florida, albeit reluctantly and after an invasion led by Andrew Jackson.

Did You Know?

The Louisiana Purchase

With the Louisiana Purchase in 1803, the United States bought from France most of the land between the Rocky Mountains and the Mississippi River. The United States had negotiated with Spain in 1795 to secure access to the Gulf of Mexico via the Mississippi. However, in 1801 President Thomas Jefferson learned that Spain had secretly ceded control of the Louisiana territory to France. Jefferson then instructed Robert Livingston, the American minister to Paris, to negotiate with France to obtain either a port at the mouth of the Mississippi or permanent trading rights in New Orleans. In January 1803, James Monroe was sent to join Livingston with an appropriation of $2 million to buy New Orleans and West Florida, but was secretly told he could offer up to $10 million. While Napoleon had acquired Louisiana from Spain with an eye to building an empire in North America, his plans were threatened first by the Haitian slave revolt, through which Haiti eventually won its independence, and second by an impending war with England. Napoleon was willing to sell the territory to raise money, and on April 11, 1803 Livingston and Monroe were offered all of Louisiana for $15 million—what amounted to four cents per acre for roughly 828,000 square miles of territory, doubling the size of the United States. After the purchase was approved by the U.S. Senate in October 1803, westward expansion soon followed. A territorial government was established in 1804, and in 1812 the state of Louisiana was admitted into the Union.

The Louisiana Purchase was not without critics. First, Monroe and Livingston had exceeded their instructions regarding the purchase price. And second, Jefferson's political opponents, the Federalists, argued that he exceeded his presidential authority because the Constitution made no provision for buying foreign territory.

The Louisiana Purchase was a major step toward the continental dream that founders such as James Madison had for the United States. Nonetheless, the War of 1812 was a draw, and the Americans only proved themselves in battle at sea, while on land they suffered defeat and humiliation. Taking on the British nevertheless satisfied the people who demanded that the European superpowers treat the United States as an equal nation and not as a former colony. Even though the war was not so successful in financial or military terms, the nation emerged from it in a stronger position, and with some memorable victories, such as the Battle of New Orleans. The biggest losers in this war were the Native Americans, who, because of the removal of the Europeans as meddling powers in the continent, could not count on anyone to save them from the rush of settlers, land speculators, and military expeditions that the white man was about to unleash.

If the first four presidents had even the slightest qualms about revealing the expansionist nature of the American polity, the next two completely ignored them, making sure the world understood that the Americans were up to the task of consolidating their continental state. This continuous U.S. expansion was spurred by two revolutions. First, Simón Bolívar and subsequent leaders in South America revolted against Spanish rule in South America. Second, the Greeks revolted against the Ottomans. It seemed that Spanish rule abroad was fast coming to an end and that the United States could benefit by annexing Florida. President Monroe sent Andrew Jackson to quell the Seminole tribe, making the first and most significant step in annexation. Jackson's heavy-handedness, however, embarrassed Monroe, who had to disavow him as well as all knowledge of his actions. Yet the Americans argued that they could not have an armed rebellion at their border.

Monroe's secretary of state and successor, John Quincy Adams, was perhaps the most active secretary of state in the history of the United States. He concluded twelve trade agreements, talked Monroe out of recognizing Greece, exercised caution in his dealings with newly independent Latin American republics, and was the influence behind the Monroe Doctrine.

The revolutionary movements in South America and Greece allowed the United States to claim a sphere of responsibility by arguing that what was around them was their responsibility, while what was in Europe was a European responsibility. To the great dismay of the supporters of the Greek revolution who came to the United States asking for help—the Greek revolution was, as it were, the intellectual child of the American Revolution—John Quincy Adams gave a speech to the House of Representatives arguing against the tremendous wave of sympathy toward the embattled Greeks. Adams said, "Wherever the standard of freedom and Independence has been or shall be unfurled, there will [America's] heart, her benedictions and her prayers be. But she goes not abroad, in search of monsters to destroy. She is the well-wisher to the freedom and independence of all. She is the champion and vindicator only of her own." It was the natural expression of the Monroe Doctrine, which argued that the Western Hemisphere was an American zone of responsibility, while Europe and its system were totally different. Henry Clay, the speaker of the House of Representatives and then secretary of state, argued that the United States sold out its own ideals for trade with the Turks, while Bolívar, thinking about what the doctrine meant for his continent, lamented that it "seemed destined by Providence to plague America with torments in the name of freedom" (Herring 2008: 161).

- **Document: Treaty of 1778** (otherwise known as Treaty of Alliance)
- **Date**: February 6, 1778
- **Significance**: The treaty was a significant boost to the American colonies fighting for their independence from the British Empire. King Louis XVI promised perpetual support for the U.S. insurrection and, in return, he expected the same once the U.S. was an independent nation.
- **Source**: *Treaties and Other International Acts of the United States of America*, Volume 2, Documents 1–40: 1776–1818. Edited by Hunter Miller. Washington: Government Printing Office, 1931.

The most Christian King and the United States of North America, to wit, New Hampshire, Massachusetts Bay, Rhodes island, Connecticut, New York, New Jersey, Pennsylvania, Delaware, Maryland, Virginia, North Carolina, South Carolina, and Georgia, having this Day concluded a Treaty of amity and Commerce, for the reciprocal advantage of their Subjects and Citizens have thought it necessary to take into consideration the means of strengthening those engagements and of rendering them useful to the safety and tranquility of the two parties, particularly in case Great Britain in Resentment of that connection and of the good correspondence which is the object of the said Treaty, should break the Peace with France, either by direct hostilities, or by hindering her commerce and navigation, in a manner contrary to the Rights of Nations, and the Peace subsisting between the two Crowns; and his Majesty and the said united States having resolved in that Case to join their Councils and efforts against the Enterprises of their common Enemy, the respective Plenipotentiaries, impower'd to concert the Clauses & conditions proper to fulfil the said Intentions, have, after the most mature Deliberation, concluded and determined on the following Articles.

ART. 1.
ADVERTISING
If War should break out betwan france and Great Britain, during the continuance of the present War betwan the United States and England, his Majesty and the said united States, shall make it a common cause, and aid each other mutually with their good Offices, their Counsels, and their forces, according to the exigence of Conjunctures as becomes good & faithful Allies.

ART. 2.
The essential and direct End of the present defensive alliance is to maintain effectually the liberty, Sovereignty, and independance absolute and unlimited of the said united States, as well in Matters of Gouvernement as of commerce.

ART. 3.
The two contracting Parties shall each on its own Part, and in the manner it may judge most proper, make all the efforts in its Power, against their common Ennemy, in order to attain the end proposed.

ART. 4.

The contracting Parties agree that in case either of them should form any particular Enterprise in which the concurrence of the other may be desired, the Party whose concurrence is desired shall readily, and with good faith, join to act in concert for that Purpose, as far as circumstances and its own particular Situation will permit; and in that case, they shall regulate by a particular Convention the quantity and kind of Succour to be furnished, and the Time and manner of its being brought into action, as well as the advantages which are to be its Compensation.

ART. 5.

If the united States should think fit to attempt the Reduction of the British Power remaining in the Northern Parts of America, or the Islands of Bermudas, those Countries or Islands in case of Success, shall be confederated with or dependent upon the said united States.

ART. 6.

The Most Christian King renounces for ever the possession of the Islands of Bermudas as well as of any part of the continent of North america which before the treaty of Paris in 1763, or in virtue of that Treaty, were acknowledged to belong to the Crown of Great Britain, or to the united States heretofore called British Colonies, or which are at this Time or have lately been under the Power of The King and Crown of Great Britain.

ART. 7.

If his Most Christian Majesty shall think proper to attack any of the Islands situated in the Gulph of Mexico, or near that Gulph, which are at present under the Power of Great Britain, all the said Isles, in case of success, shall appertain to the Crown of france.

ART. 8.

Neither of the two Parties shall conclude either Truce or Peace with Great Britain, without the formal consent of the other first obtain'd; and they mutually engage not to lay down their arms, until the Independence of the united states shall have been formally or tacitly assured by the Treaty or Treaties that shall terminate the War.

ART. 9.

The contracting Parties declare, that being resolved to fulfil each on its own Part the clauses and conditions of the present Treaty of alliance, according to its own power and circumstances, there shall be no after claim of compensation on one side or the other whatever may be the event of the War.

ART. 10.

The Most Christian King and the United states, agree to invite or admit other Powers who may have received injuries from England to make common cause with them, and to accede to the present alliance, under such conditions as shall be freely agreed to and settled between all the Parties.

ART. 11.

The two Parties guarantee mutually from the present time and forever, against all other powers, to wit, the united states to his most Christian Majesty the present

Possessions of the Crown of france in America as well as those which it may acquire by the future Treaty of peace: and his most Christian Majesty guarantees on his part to the united states, their liberty, Sovereignty, and Independence absolute, and unlimited, as well in Matters of Government as commerce and also their Possessions, and the additions or conquests that their Confederation may obtain during the war, from any of the Dominions now or heretofore possessed by Great Britain in North America, conformable to the 5th & 6th articles above written, the whole as their Possessions shall be fixed and assured to the said States at the moment of the cessation of their present War with England.

ART. 12.

In order to fix more precisely the sense and application of the preceding article, the Contracting Parties declare, that in case of rupture between france and England, the reciprocal Guarantee declared in the said article shall have its full force and effect the moment such War shall break out and if such rupture shall not take place, the mutual obligations of the said guarantee shall not commence, until the moment of the cessation of the present War between the united states and England shall have ascertained the Possessions.

ART. 13.

The present Treaty shall be ratified on both sides and the Ratifications shall be exchanged in the space of six months, sooner if possible.

In faith where of the respective Plenipotentiaries, to wit on the part of the most Christian King Conrad Alexander Gerard royal syndic of the City of Strasbourgh & Secretary of his majestys Council of State and on the part of the United States Benjamin Franklin Deputy to the General Congress from the State of Pensylvania and President of the Convention of the same state, Silas Deane heretofore Deputy from the State of Connecticut & Arthur Lee Councellor at Law have signed the above Articles both in the French and English Languages declaring Nevertheless that the present Treaty was originally composed and concluded in the French Language, and they have hereunto affixed their Seals.

Done at Paris, this sixth Day of February, one thousand seven hundred and seventy eight.

- **Document: The Treaty of Paris**
- **Date:** September 3, 1783
- **Significance:** This treaty ends hostilities between the U.S. and Britain, and the United States comes into existence as an independent nation.
- **Source:** *Treaties and Other International Acts of the United States of America*, Volume 2, Documents 1–40: 1776–1818. Edited by Hunter Miller. Washington: Government Printing Office, 1931.

THE DEFINITIVE TREATY OF PEACE 1783

In the name of the most holy and undivided Trinity.

It having pleased the Divine Providence to dispose the hearts of the most serene and most potent Prince George the Third, by the grace of God, king of Great Britain, France, and Ireland, defender of the faith, duke of Brunswick and Lunebourg, arch-treasurer and prince elector of the Holy Roman Empire etc., and of the United States of America, to forget all past misunderstandings and differences that have unhappily interrupted the good correspondence and friendship which they mutually wish to restore, and to establish such a beneficial and satisfactory intercourse , between the two countries upon the ground of reciprocal advantages and mutual convenience as may promote and secure to both perpetual peace and harmony; and having for this desirable end already laid the foundation of peace and reconciliation by the Provisional Articles signed at Paris on the 30th of November 1782, by the commissioners empowered on each part, which articles were agreed to be inserted in and constitute the Treaty of Peace proposed to be concluded between the Crown of Great Britain and the said United States, but which treaty was not to be concluded until terms of peace should be agreed upon between Great Britain and France and his Britannic Majesty should be ready to conclude such treaty accordingly; and the treaty between Great Britain and France having since been concluded, his Britannic Majesty and the United States of America, in order to carry into full effect the Provisional Articles above mentioned, according to the tenor thereof, have constituted and appointed, that is to say his Britannic Majesty on his part, David Hartley, Esqr., member of the Parliament of Great Britain, and the said United States on their part, John Adams, Esqr., late a commissioner of the United States of America at the court of Versailles,

The signing of the Treaty of Paris on September 3, 1783, officially brought a close to the American Revolution. At the signing of the treaty, the United States also acquired the so-called Western Lands, making the land the exclusive domain of the federal government. As payment for surrendering its claims, Connecticut reserved a tract of three-million acres in the northeastern corner of what is present-day Ohio, known as the Western Reserve. (Library of Congress)

late delegate in Congress from the state of Massachusetts, and chief justice of the said state, and minister plenipotentiary of the said United States to their high mightinesses the States General of the United Netherlands; Benjamin Franklin, Esqr., late delegate in Congress from the state of Pennsylvania, president of the convention of the said state, and minister plenipotentiary from the United States of America at the court of Versailles; John Jay, Esqr., late president of Congress and chief justice of the state of New York, and minister plenipotentiary from the said United States at the court of Madrid; to be plenipotentiaries for the concluding and signing the present definitive treaty; who after having reciprocally communicated their respective full powers have agreed upon and confirmed the following articles.

Article 1:

His Brittanic Majesty acknowledges the said United States, viz., New Hampshire, Massachusetts Bay, Rhode Island and Providence Plantations, Connecticut, New York, New Jersey, Pennsylvania, Maryland, Virginia, North Carolina, South Carolina and Georgia, to be free sovereign and independent states, that he treats with them as such, and for himself, his heirs, and successors, relinquishes all claims to the government, propriety, and territorial rights of the same and every part thereof.

Article 2:

And that all disputes which might arise in future on the subject of the boundaries of the said United States may be prevented, it is hereby agreed and declared, that the following are and shall be their boundaries, viz.; from the northwest angle of Nova Scotia, viz., that angle which is formed by a line drawn due north from the source of St. Croix River to the highlands; along the said highlands which divide those rivers that empty themselves into the river St. Lawrence, from those which fall into the Atlantic Ocean, to the northwesternmost head of Connecticut River; thence down along the middle of that river to the forty-fifth degree of north latitude; from thence by a line due west on said latitude until it strikes the river Iroquois or Cataraquy; thence along the middle of said river into Lake Ontario; through the middle of said lake until it strikes the communication by water between that lake and Lake Erie; thence along the middle of said communication into Lake Erie, through the middle of said lake until it arrives at the water communication between that lake and Lake Huron; thence along the middle of said water communication into Lake Huron, thence through the middle of said lake to the water communication between that lake and Lake Superior; thence through Lake Superior northward of the Isles Royal and Phelipeaux to the Long Lake; thence through the middle of said Long Lake and the water communication between it and the Lake of the Woods, to the said Lake of the Woods; thence through the said lake to the most northwesternmost point thereof, and from thence on a due west course to the river Mississippi; thence by a line to be drawn along the middle of the said river Mississippi until it shall intersect the northernmost part of the thirty-first degree of north latitude, South, by a line to be drawn due east from the determination of the line last mentioned in the latitude of thirty-one degrees of the equator, to the middle of the river Apalachicola or Catahouche; thence along the middle thereof to its junction with the Flint River, thence straight to the head of Saint Mary's River; and thence down along the middle of Saint Mary's River to the Atlantic Ocean; east, by a line to be drawn along the middle of the river Saint Croix, from its mouth in the Bay of Fundy to its source, and from its source directly north to the aforesaid highlands which divide the rivers that fall into the Atlantic Ocean from those which fall into the river Saint Lawrence; comprehending all islands within twenty leagues of any part of the shores of the United States, and lying between lines to be drawn due east from the points where the aforesaid boundaries between Nova Scotia on the one part and East Florida on the other shall, respectively, touch the Bay of Fundy and the Atlantic Ocean, excepting such islands as now are or heretofore have been within the limits of the said province of Nova Scotia.

Article 3:

It is agreed that the people of the United States shall continue to enjoy unmolested the right to take fish of every kind on the Grand Bank and on all the other banks of Newfoundland, also in the Gulf of Saint Lawrence and at all other places in the sea, where the inhabitants of both countries used at any time heretofore to fish. And also that the inhabitants of the United States shall have liberty to take fish of every kind on such part of the coast of Newfoundland as British fishermen shall use, (but not to dry or cure the same on that island) and also on the coasts, bays and creeks of all other of his Brittanic Majesty's dominions in America; and that the American fishermen shall have liberty to dry and cure fish in any of the unsettled bays, harbors, and creeks of Nova Scotia, Magdalen Islands, and Labrador, so long as the same shall remain unsettled, but so soon as the same or either of them shall be settled, it shall not be lawful for the said fishermen to dry or cure fish at such settlement without a previous agreement for that purpose with the inhabitants, proprietors, or possessors of the ground.

Article 4:

It is agreed that creditors on either side shall meet with no lawful impediment to the recovery of the full value in sterling money of all bona fide debts heretofore contracted.

Article 5:

It is agreed that Congress shall earnestly recommend it to the legislatures of the respective states to provide for the restitution of all estates, rights, and properties, which have been confiscated belonging to real British subjects; and also of the estates, rights, and properties of persons resident in districts in the possession on his Majesty's arms and who have not borne arms against the said United States. And that persons of any other decription shall have free liberty to go to any part or parts of any of the thirteen United States and therein to remain twelve months unmolested in their endeavors to obtain the restitution of such of their estates, rights, and properties as may have been confiscated; and that Congress shall also earnestly recommend to the several states a reconsideration and revision of all acts or laws regarding the premises, so as to render the said laws or acts perfectly consistent not only with justice and equity but with that spirit of conciliation which on the return of the blessings of peace should universally prevail. And that Congress shall also earnestly recommend to the several states that the estates, rights, and properties, of such last mentioned persons shall be restored to them, they refunding to any persons who may be now in possession the bona fide price (where any has been given) which such persons may have paid on purchasing any of the said lands, rights, or properties since the confiscation.

And it is agreed that all persons who have any interest in confiscated lands, either by debts, marriage settlements, or otherwise, shall meet with no lawful impediment in the prosecution of their just rights.

Article 6:

That there shall be no future confiscations made nor any prosecutions commenced against any person or persons for, or by reason of, the part which he or they may have taken in the present war, and that no person shall on that account suffer any future loss or damage, either in his person, liberty, or property; and that those who may be in confinement on such charges at the time of the ratification of the treaty in America shall be immediately set at liberty, and the prosecutions so commenced be discontinued.

Article 7:

There shall be a firm and perpetual peace between his Brittanic Majesty and the said states, and between the subjects of the one and the citizens of the other, wherefore all hostilities both by sea and land shall from henceforth cease. All prisoners on both sides shall be set at liberty, and his Brittanic Majesty shall with all convenient speed, and without causing any destruction, or carrying away any Negroes or other property of the American inhabitants, withdraw all his armies, garrisons, and fleets from the said United States, and from every post, place, and harbor within the same; leaving in all fortifications, the American artilery that may be therein; and shall also order and cause all archives, records, deeds, and papers belonging to any of the said states, or their citizens, which in the course of the war may have fallen into the hands of his officers, to be forthwith restored and delivered to the proper states and persons to whom they belong.

Article 8:

The navigation of the river Mississippi, from its source to the ocean, shall forever remain free and open to the subjects of Great Britain and the citizens of the United States.

Article 9:

In case it should so happen that any place or territory belonging to Great Britain or to the United States should have been conquered by the arms of either from the other before the arrival of the said *Provisional Articles* in America, it is agreed that the same shall be restored without difficulty and without requiring any compensation.

Article 10:

The solemn ratifications of the present treaty expedited in good and due form shall be exchanged between the contracting parties in the space of six months or sooner, if possible, to be computed from the day of the signatures of the present treaty. In witness whereof we the undersigned, their ministers plenipotentiary, have in their name and in virtue of our full powers, signed with our hands the present definitive treaty and caused the seals of our arms to be affixed thereto.

Done at Paris, this third day of September in the year of our Lord, one thousand seven hundred and eighty-three.

D. HARTLEY (SEAL)
JOHN ADAMS (SEAL)
B. FRANKLIN (SEAL)
JOHN JAY (SEAL)

- **Document: Treaty of Amity, Commerce and Navigation** (otherwise known as the Jay Treaty of 1794)
- **Date:** November 19, 1794
- **Significance:** The treaty tied up loose ends left over from the War of Independence. It created an emotional outburst against it in the United States, with many viewing it as giving in to the former colonial power.
- **Source:** *Treaties and Other International Acts of the United States of America*, Volume 2, Documents 1–40: 1776–1818. Edited by Hunter Miller. Washington: Government Printing Office, 1931.

JOHN JAY'S TREATY, 1794–1795

Treaty of Amity, Commerce and Navigation

His Britannic Majesty and the United States of America, being desirous, by a treaty of amity, commerce and navigation, to terminate their difference in such a manner, as, without reference to the merits of their respective complaints and pretentions, may be the best calculated to produce mutual satisfaction and good understanding; and also to regulate the commerce and navigation between their respective countries, territories and people, in such a manner as to render the same reciprocally beneficial and satisfactory; they have, respectively, named their Plenipotentiaries, and given them full powers to treat of, and conclude the said treaty, that is to say:

His Britannic Majesty has named for his Plenipotentiary, the Right Honorable William Wyndham Baron Grenville of Wotton, one of His Majesty's Privy Council, and His Majesty's Principal Secretary of State for Foreign Affairs; and the President of the said United States, by and with the advice and consent of the Senate thereof, hath appointed for their Plenipotentiary, the Honorable John Jay, Chief Justice of the said United States, and their Envoy Extraordinary to His Majesty; Who have agreed on and concluded the following articles:

ARTICLE I.

There shall be a firm, inviolable and universal peace, and a true and sincere friendship between His Britannic Majesty, his heirs and successors, and the United States of America; and between their respective countries, territories, cities, towns and people of every degree, without exception of persons or places.

ARTICLE II.

His Majesty will withdraw all his troops and garrisons from all posts and places within the boundary lines assigned by the treaty of peace to the United States. This evacuation shall take place on or before the first day of June, one thousand seven hundred and ninetysix, and all the proper measures shall in the interval be taken by concert between the Government of the United States and His Majesty's Governor-General in America for settling the previous arrangements which may be necessary respecting the delivery of the said posts.

. . .

ARTICLE III.

It is agreed that it shall at all times be free to His Majesty's subjects, and to the citizens of the United States, and also to the Indians dwelling on either side of the said boundary line, freely to pass and repass by land or inland navigation, into the respective territories and countries of the two parties, on the continent of America, (the country within the limits of the Hudson's Bay Company only excepted.) and to navigate all the lakes, rivers and waters thereof, and freely to carry on trade and commerce with each other. But it is understood that this article does not extend to the admission of vessels of the United States into the seaports, harbours, bays or creeks of His Majesty's said territories; nor into such parts of the rivers in His Majesty's said territories as are between the mouth thereof, and the highest port of entry from the sea, except in small vessels trading bona fide between Montreal and Quebec, under such regulations as shall be established to prevent the possibility of any frauds in this respect. Nor to the admission of British vessels from the sea into the rivers of the United States, beyond the highest ports of entry for foreign vessels from the sea.

The river Mississippi shall, however, according to the treaty of peace, be entirely open to both parties; and it is further agreed, that all the ports and places on its eastern side, to whichsoever of the parties belonging, may freely be resorted to and used by both parties, in as ample a manner as any of the Atlantic ports or places of the United States, or any of the ports or places of His Majesty in Great Britain All goods and merchandize whose importation into His Majesty's said territories in America shall not be entirely prohibited, may freely, for the purposes of commerce, be carried into the same in the manner aforesaid, by the citizens of the United States, and such goods and merchandize shall be subject to no higher or other duties than would be payable by His Majesty's subjects on the importation of the same from Europe into the said territories.

. . .

ARTICLE IV.

Whereas it is uncertain whether the river Mississippi extends so far to the northward as to be intersected by a line to be drawn due west from the Lake of the Woods, in the manner mentioned in the treaty of peace between His Majesty and the United States:

. . .

ARTICLE VI.

Whereas it is alleged by divers British merchants and others His Majesty's subjects, that debts, to a considerable amount, which were bona fide contracted before the peace, still remain owing to them by citizens or inhabitants of the United States, and that by the operation of various lawful impediments since the peace, not only the full recovery of the said debts has been delayed, but also the value and security thereof have been, in several instances, impaired and lessened, so that, by the ordinary course of judicial proceedings, the British creditors cannot now obtain, and actually have and receive full and adequate compensation for the losses and damages which they have thereby sustained: It is agreed, that in all such cases, where full compensation for such losses and damages cannot, for whatever reason, be actually obtained, had and received by the said creditors in the ordinary course of justice, the United States will make full and complete compensation for the same to the said creditors: But it is distinctly understood, that this provision is to extend to such losses only as have been occasioned by the lawful impediments aforesaid, and is not to extend to losses occasioned by such insolvency of the debtors or other causes as would equally have operated to produce such loss, if the said impediments had not existed; nor to such losses or damages as have been occasioned by the manifest delay or negligence, or wilful omission of the claimant.

. . .

ARTICLE VII.

Whereas complaints have been made by divers merchants and others, citizens of the United States, that during the course of the war in which His Majesty is now engaged, they have sustained considerable losses and damage, by reason of irregular or illegal captures or condemnations of their vessels and other property, under color of authority or commissions from His Majesty, and that from various circumstances belonging to the said cases, adequate compensation for the losses and damages so sustained cannot now be actually obtained, had, and received by the ordinary course of judicial proceedings; it is agreed, that in all such cases, where adequate compensation cannot, for whatever reason, be now actually obtained, had, and received by the said merchants and others, in the ordinary course of justice, full and complete compensation for the same will be made by the British Government to the said complainants.

. . .

ARTICLE IX.

It is agreed that British subjects who now hold lands in the territories of the United States, and American citizens who now hold lands in the dominions of His Majesty, shall continue to hold them according to the nature and tenure of their respective estates and titles therein; and may grant, sell or devise the same to whom they please, in like manner as if they were natives and that neither they nor their heirs or assigns shall, so far as may respect the said lands and the legal remedies incident thereto, be regarded as aliens.

ARTICLE X.

Neither the debts due from individuals of the one nation to individuals of the other, nor shares, nor monies, which they may have in the public funds, or in the public or private banks, shall ever in any event of war or national differences be sequestered or confiscated, it being unjust and impolitic that debts and engagements contracted and made by individuals having confidence in each other and in their respective Governments, should ever be destroyed or impaired by national authority on account of national differences and discontents.

ARTICLE XI.

It is agreed between His Majesty and the United States of America, that there shall be a reciprocal and entirely perfect liberty of navigation and commerce between their respective people, in the manner, under the limitations, and on the conditions specified in the following articles.

ARTICLE XII.

His Majesty consents that it shall and may be lawful, during the time hereinafter limited, for the citizens of the United States to carry to any of His Majesty's islands and ports in the West Indies from the United States, in their own vessels, not being above the burthen of seventy tons, any goods or merchandizes, being of the growth, manufacture or produce of the said States, which it is or may be lawful to carry to the said islands or ports from the said States in British vessels; and that the said American vessels shall be subject there to no other or higher tonnage duties or charges than shall be payable by British vessels in the ports of the United States; and that the cargoes of the said American vessels shall be subject there to no other or higher duties or charges than shall be payable on the like articles if imported there from the said States in British vessels.

And His Majesty also consents that it shall be lawful for the said American citizens to purchase, load and carry away in their said vessels to the United States, from the said islands and ports, all such articles, being of the growth, manufacture or produce of the said islands, as may now by law be carried from thence to the said States in British vessels, and subject only to the same duties and charges on exportation, to which British vessels and their cargoes are or shall be subject in similar circumstances.

. . .

ARTICLE XIII.

His Majesty consents that the vessels belonging to the citizens of the United States of America shall be admitted and hospitably received in all the seaports and harbors of the British territories in the East Indies.

And that the citizens of the said United States may freely carry on a trade between the said territories and the said United States, in all articles of which the importation or exportation respectively, to or from the said territories, shall not be entirely prohibited. Provided only, that it shall not be lawful for them in any time of war between the British Government and any other Power or State whatever, to export from the said territories, without the special permission of the British Government there, any military stores, or naval stores, or rice.

. . .

ARTICLE XIV.

There shall be between all the dominions of His Majesty in Europe and the territories of the United States a reciprocal and perfect liberty of commerce and navigation.

The people and inhabitants of the two countries, respectively, shall have liberty freely and securely, and without hindrance and molestation, to come with their ships and cargoes to the lands, countries, cities, ports, places and rivers within the dominions and territories aforesaid, to enter into the same, to resort there, and to remain and reside there, without any limitation of time.

. . .

ARTICLE XVII.

It is agreed that in all cases where vessels shall be captured or detained on just suspicion of having on board enemy's property, or of carrying to the enemy any of the articles which are contraband of war, the said vessels shall be brought to the nearest or most convenient port; and if any property of an enemy should be found on board such vessel, that part only which belongs to the enemy shall be made prize, and the vessel shall be at liberty to proceed with the remainder without any impediment.

And it is agreed that all proper measures shall be taken to prevent delay in deciding the cases of ships or cargoes so brought in for adjudication, and in the payment or recovery of any indemnification, adjudged or agreed to be paid to the masters or owners of such ships.

. . .

ARTICLE XXVII.

It is further agreed that His Majesty and the United States, on mutual requisitions, by them respectively, or by their respective Ministers or officers authorized to make the same, will deliver up to justice all persons who, being charged with murder or forgery, committed within the jurisdiction of either, shall seek an asylum within any of the countries of the other, provided that this shall only be done on such evidence of criminality as, according to the laws of the place, where the fugitive or person so charged shall be found, would justify his apprehension and commitment for trial, if the offence had there been committed. The expence of such apprehension and delivery shall be borne and defrayed by those who made the requisition and receive the fugitive.

ARTICLE XXVIII.

It is agreed that the first ten articles of this treaty shall be permanent, and that the subsequent articles, except the twelfth, shall be limited in their duration to twelve years, to be computed from the day on which the ratifications of this treaty shall be exchanged, but subject to this condition.

. . .

Done at London this nineteenth day of November, one thousand seven hundred and ninety four.

GRENVILLE (SEAL)
JOHN JAY (SEAL)

- **Document: President George Washington's Farewell Address**
- **Date:** September 17, 1796
- **Significance:** In his farewell address to the nation, Washington intended to stress unity against factionalism, emphasize the dangers that lay ahead especially through foreign alliances, and to set his administration's record straight.
- **Source:** Library of Congress, Annals of Congress, 4th Congress, pp. 2869–2880, Washington's Farewell Address.

General George Washington bids farewell to his officers at the end of the Revolutionary War. (National Archives)

Friends, And Fellow Citizens

The period for a new election of a citizen to administer the executive government of the United States, being not far distant, and the time actually arrived when your thoughts must be employed in designating the person who is to be clothed with that important trust, it appears to me proper, especially as it may conduce to a more dis- tinct expression of the public voice, that I should now apprise you of the resolution I have formed, to decline being considered among the number of those out of whom a choice is to be made.

I beg you, at the same time, to do me the justice to be assured that this resolution has not been taken without a strict regard to all the considerations appertaining to the relation which binds a dutiful citizen to his country; and that, in withdrawing the tender of service which silence in my situation might imply, I am influenced by no diminution of zeal for your future interest; no deficiency of grateful respect for your past kindness; but am supported by a full conviction that the step is compatible with both.

The acceptance of, and continuance hitherto in, the office to which your suff- rages have twice called me, have been a uniform sacrifice of inclination to the opin- ion of duty, and to a deference for what appeared to be your desire. I constantly hoped that it would have been much earlier in my power, consistently with motives which I was not at liberty to disregard, to return to that retirement from which I had been reluctantly drawn. The strength of my inclination to do this, previous to the last election, had even led to the preparation of an address to declare it to you; but mature reflection on the then perplexed and critical posture of our affairs with foreign nations, and the unanimous advice of persons entitled to my confidence, impelled me to abandon the idea.

I rejoice, that the state of your concerns, external as well as internal, no longer renders the pursuit of inclination incompatible with the sentiment of duty, or propriety; and am persuaded whatever partiality may be retained for my services, that, in the present circumstances of our country, you will not disapprove my determination to retire.

The impressions, with which, I first undertook the arduous trust, were explained on the proper occasion. In the discharge of this trust, I will only say that I have, with good intentions, contributed towards the organization and administration of the government the best exertions of which a very fallible judgment was capable. Not unconscious, in the outset, of the inferiority of my qualifications, experience in my own eyes, perhaps still more in the eyes of others, has strengthened the motives to diffidence of myself; and every day the increasing weight of years admonishes me more and more that the shade of retirement is as necessary to me as it will be welcome. Satisfied that, if any circumstances have given peculiar value to my services, they were temporary, I have the consolation to believe, that while choice and prudence invite me to quit the political scene, patriotism does not forbid it.

In looking forward to the moment, which is intended to terminate the career of my public life, my feelings do not permit me to suspend the deep acknowledgment of that debt of gratitude which I owe to my beloved country for the many honors it has conferred upon me; still more for the steadfast confidence with which it has supported me; and for the opportunities I have thence enjoyed of manifesting my inviolable attachment, by services faithful and persevering, though in usefulness unequal to my zeal. If benefits have resulted to our country from these services, let it always be remembered to your praise, and as an instructive example in our annals, that under circumstances in which the passions, agitated in every direction, were liable to mislead, amidst appearances sometimes dubious, vicissitudes of fortune often discouraging, in situations in which not unfrequently want of success has countenanced the spirit of criticism, the constancy of your support was the essential prop of the efforts, and a guarantee of the plans, by which they were effected. Profoundly penetrated with this idea, I shall carry it with me to my grave, as a strong incitement to unceasing vows that Heaven may continue to you the choicest tokens of its beneficence; that your union and brotherly affection may be perpetual; that the free constitution which is the work of your hands, may be sacredly maintained; that its administration in every department may be stamped with wisdom and virtue; that, in fine, the happiness of the people of these States, under the auspices of liberty, may be made complete, by so careful a preservation and so prudent a use of this blessing, as will acquire to them the glory of recommending it to the applause, the affection, and adoption of every nation which is yet a stranger to it.

Here, perhaps, I ought to stop. But a solicitude for your welfare which cannot end but with my life, and the apprehension of danger natural to that solicitude, urge me, on an occasion like the present, to offer to your solemn contemplation, and to recommend to your frequent review, some sentiments which are the result of much reflection, of no inconsiderable observation, and which appear to me all important to the permanency of your felicity as a people. These will be offered to you with the more freedom, as you can only see in them the disinterested warnings of a parting friend, who can possibly have no personal motive to bias his counsel. Nor can

I forget, as an encouragement to it your indulgent reception of my sentiments on a former and not dissimilar occasion.

Interwoven as is the love of liberty with every ligament of your hearts, no recommendation of mine is necessary to fortify or confirm the attachment. The unity of government which constitutes you one people is also now dear to you. It is justly so: for it is a main pillar in the edifice of your real independence, the support of your tranquility at home, your peace abroad; of your safety; of your prosperity; of that very liberty which you so highly prize. But as it is easy to foresee that, from different causes and from different quarters, much pains will be taken, many artifices employed, to weaken in your minds the conviction of this truth; as this is the point in your political fortress against which the batteries of internal and external enemies will be most constantly and actively (though often covertly and insidiously) directed, it is of infinite moment that you should properly estimate the immense value of your national Union to your collective and individual happiness; that you should cherish a cordial, habitual, and immoveable attachment to it; accustoming yourself to think and speak of it as of the palladium of your political safety and prosperity; watching for its preservation with jealous anxiety; discountenancing whatever may suggest even a suspicion that it can in any event be abandoned; and indignantly frowning upon the first dawning of every attempt to alienate any portion of our country from the rest, or to enfeeble the sacred ties which now link together the various parts.

For this you have every inducement of sympathy and interest. Citizens, by birth or choice, of a common country, that country has a right to concentrate your affections. The name of AMERICAN, which belongs to you in your national capacity, must always exalt the just pride of patriotism, more than any appellation derived from local discriminations. With slight shades of difference, you have the same religion, manners, habits and political principles. You have in a common cause fought and triumphed together; the independence and liberty you possess are the work of joint councils and joint efforts, of common dangers, sufferings, and successes.

But these considerations, however powerfully they address themselves to your sensibility, are greatly outweighed by those which apply more immediately to your interest. Here every portion of our country finds the most commanding motives for carefully guarding and preserving the union of the whole.

The North, in an unrestrained intercourse with the South, protected by the equal Laws of a common government, finds, in the productions of the latter, great additional resources of maritime and commercial enterprise and precious materials of manufacturing industry. The South in the same intercourse, benefitting by the agency of the North, sees its agriculture grow and its commerce expand. Turning partly into its own channels the seamen of the North, it finds its particular navigation invigorated; and while it contributes, in different ways, to nourish and increase the general mass of the national navigation, it looks forward to the protection of a maritime strength, to which itself is unequally adapted. The East, in a like intercourse with the West, already finds, and in the progressive improvement of interior communications, by land and water, will more and more find, a valuable vent for the commodities which it brings from abroad, or manufactures at home. The West derives from the East supplies requisite to its growth and comfort, and what is perhaps of still greater consequence, it must of necessity owe the secure enjoyment of indispensable outlets for its own productions to the weight, influence, and the future maritime strength of the Atlantic side of the Union, directed by an indissoluble community of interest as one Nation. Any other tenure by which the West can hold this essential advantage, whether derived from its own separate strength, or from an apostate and unnatural connection with any foreign power, must be intrinsically precarious.

While, then, every part of our country thus feels an immediate and particular interest in union, all the parts combined cannot fail to find in the united mass of means and efforts greater strength, greater resource, proportionally greater security from external danger, a less frequent interruption of their peace by foreign Nations; and, what is of inestimable value, they must derive from union an exemption from those broils and wars between themselves, which so frequently afflict neighboring countries not tied together by the same government, which their own rivalships alone would be sufficient to produce, but which opposite foreign alliances, attachments, and intrigues would stimulate and imbitter. Hence, likewise, they will avoid the necessity of those overgrown military establishments, which, under any form of government, are inauspicious to liberty, and which are to be regarded as particularly hostile to republican liberty. In this sense it is, that your Union ought to be considered as a main prop of your liberty, and that the love of the one ought to endear to you the preservation of the other.

These considerations speak a persuasive language to every reflecting and virtuous mind, and exhibit the continuance of the UNION as a primary object of patriotic desire. Is there a doubt whether a common government can embrace so large a sphere? Let experience solve it. To listen to mere speculation in such a case were criminal. We are authorized to hope that a proper organization of the whole, with the auxiliary agency of governments for the respective subdivisions, will afford a happy issue to the experiment. It is well worth a fair and full experiment. With such powerful and obvious motives to union, affecting all parts of our country, while experience shall not have demonstrated its impracticability, there will always be reason to distrust the patriotism of those who in any quarter may endeavor to weaken its bands.

In contemplating the causes which may disturb our Union, it occurs as matter of serious concern, that any ground should have been furnished for characterizing parties by geographical discriminations, Northern and Southern, Atlantic and Western; whence designing men may endeavor to excite a belief that there is a real difference of local interests and views. One of the expedients of party to acquire influence, within particular districts, is to misrepresent the opinions and aims of other districts. You cannot shield yourselves too much against the jealousies and heart burnings which spring from these misrepresentations; they tend to render alien to each other those who ought to be bound together by fraternal affection. The inhabitants of our western country have lately had a useful lesson on this head; they have seen, in the negotiation by the Executive, and in the unanimous ratification by the Senate, of the treaty with Spain, and in the universal satisfaction at that event, throughout the United States, a decisive proof how unfounded were the suspicions propagated among them of a policy in the general Government and in the Atlantic States unfriendly to their interests in regard to the Mississippi; they have been witnesses to the formation of two treaties, that with Great Britain, and that with Spain, which secure to them everything they could desire, in respect to our foreign relations, towards confirming their prosperity. Will it not be their wisdom to rely for the preservation of these advantaged on the UNION by which they were procured? Will they not henceforth be deaf to those advisers, if such there are, who would sever them from their brethren and connect them with aliens?

To the efficacy and permanency of your Union, a government for the whole is indispensable. No alliances, however strict, between the parts can be an adequate substitute; they must inevitably experience the infractions and interruptions which all alliances in all times have experienced. Sensible of this momentous truth, you have improved upon your first essay, by the adoption of a constitution of government better calculated than your former for an intimate union, and for the efficacious management of your common concerns. This government, the offspring of our own choice, uninfluenced and unawed, adopted upon full investigation and mature deliberation, completely free in its principles, in the distribution of its powers uniting security with energy, and containing within itself a provision for its own amendment, has a just claim to your confidence and your support. Respect for its authority, compliance with its laws, acquiescence in its measures, are duties enjoined by the fundamental maxims of true liberty. The basis of our political systems is the right of the people to make and to alter their constitutions of government.

But the constitution which at any time exists, till changed by an explicit and authentic act of the whole people, is sacredly obligatory upon all. The very idea of the power and the right of the people to establish government presupposes the duty of every individual to obey the established government.

. . .

Observe good faith and justice towards all nations; cultivate peace and harmony with all. Religion and morality enjoin this conduct; and can it be, that good policy does not equally enjoin it? It will be worthy of a free, enlightened, and, at no distant period, a great nation, to give to mankind the magnanimous and too novel example of a people always guided by an exalted justice and benevolence. Who can doubt that, in the course of time and things, the fruits of such a plan would richly repay any temporary advantages which might be lost by a steady adherence to it? Can it be, that Providence has not connected the permanent felicity of a nation with its virtue? The experiment, at least, is recommended by every sentiment which ennobles human nature. Alas! is it rendered impossible by its vices?

In the execution of such a plan, nothing is more essential than that permanent, inveterate antipathies against particular nations, and passionate attachments for others, should be excluded; and that, in place of them, just and amicable feelings towards all should be cultivated. The nation which indulges towards another an habitual hatred, or an habitual fondness, is in some degree a slave. It is a slave to its animosity or to its affection, either of which is sufficient to lead it astray from its duty and its interest. Antipathy in one Nation against another disposes each more readily to offer insult and injury, to lay hold of slight causes of umbrage, and to be haughty and intractable, when accidental or trifling occasions of dispute occur. Hence frequent collisions, obstinate, envenomed, and bloody contests. The nation, prompted by ill will and resentment sometimes impels to war the government, contrary to the best calculations of policy. The government sometimes participates in the national propensity, and adopts through passion what reason would reject; at other times, it makes the animosity of the nation subservient to projects of hostility instigated by pride, ambition, and other sinister and pernicious motives. The peace often, sometimes perhaps the Liberty, of nations has been the victim.

So likewise, a passionate attachment of one nation for another produces a variety of evils. Sympathy for the favorite nation, facilitating the illusion of an imaginary common interest, in cases where no real common interest exists, and infusing into one the enmities of the other, betrays the former into a participation in the quarrels and wars of the latter, without adequate inducement or justification. It leads also to concessions to the favorite nation of privileges denied to others, which is apt doubly to injure the nation making the concessions: by unnecessarily parting with what ought to have been retained; and by exciting jealousy, ill will, and a disposition to retaliate, in the parties from whom equal privileges are withheld. And it gives to ambitious, corrupted, or deluded citizens (who devote themselves to the favorite nation), facility to betray or sacrifice the interests of their own country, without odium, sometimes even with popularity; gilding, with the appearances of a virtuous sense of obligation, a commendable deference for public opinion, or a laudable zeal for public good, the base of foolish compliances of ambition, corruption, or infatuation.

As avenues to foreign influence in innumerable ways, such attachments are particularly alarming to the truly enlightened and independent patriot. How many opportunities do they afford to tamper with domestic factions, to practice the arts of seduction, to mislead public opinion, to influence or awe the public councils! Such an attachment of a small or weak, towards a great and powerful nation, dooms the former to be the satellite of the latter.

Against the insidious wiles of foreign influence (I conjure you to believe me, fellow-citizens), the jealousy of a free people ought to be constantly awake; since history and experience prove that foreign influence is one of the most baneful foes of republican government.

But that jealousy, to be useful, must be impartial; else it becomes the instrument of the very influence to be avoided, instead of a defence against it. Excessive partiality for one foreign nation, and excessive dislike of another, cause those whom they actuate to see danger only on one side, and serve to veil and even second the arts of influence on the other. Real Patriots, who may resist the intrigues of the favorite, are liable to become suspected and odious; while its tools and dupes usurp the applause and confidence of the people, to surrender their interests.

The great rule of conduct for us, in regard to foreign nations, is, in extending our commercial relations, to have with them as little political connection as possible. So far as we have already formed engagements, let them be fulfilled with perfect good faith. Here let us stop.

Europe has a set of primary interests, which to us have none, or a very remote relation. Hence she must be engaged in frequent controversies, the causes of which are essentially foreign to our concerns. Hence therefore, it must be unwise in us to implicate ourselves, by artificial ties, in the ordinary vicissitudes of her politics, or the ordinary combinations and collisions of her friendships or enmities.

Our detached and distant situation invites and enables us to pursue a different course. If we remain one people, under an efficient government, the period is not far off, when we may defy material injury from external annoyance; when we may take such an attitude as will cause the neutrality we may at any time resolve upon, to be scrupulously respected; when belligerent nations, under the impossibility of making acquisitions upon us, will not lightly hazard the giving us provocation; when we may choose peace or war, as our interest, guided by justice, shall counsel.

Why forego the advantages of so peculiar a situation? Why quit our own to stand upon foreign ground? Why, by interweaving our destiny with that of any part of Europe, entangle our peace and prosperity in the toils of European ambition, rivalship, interest, humor, or caprice?

'Tis our true policy to steer clear of permanent alliances with any portion of the foreign world; so far, I mean, as we are now at liberty to do it; for let me not be understood as capable of patronizing infidelity to existing engagements. I hold the maxim no less applicable to public than to private affairs, that honesty is always the best policy. I repeat it therefore; let those engagements be observed in their genuine sense. But, in my opinion, it is unnecessary and would be unwise to extend them.

Taking care always to keep ourselves, by suitable establishments, on a respectable defensive posture, we may safely trust to temporary alliances for extraordinary emergencies.

Harmony, liberal intercourse with all nations, are recommended by policy, humanity, and interest. But even our commercial policy should hold an equal and impartial hand: neither seeking nor granting exclusive favors or preferences; consulting the natural course of things; diffusing and diversifying by gentle means the streams of commerce, but forcing nothing; establishing with powers so disposed, in order to give trade a stable course, to define the rights of our merchants, and to enable the government to support them, conventional rules of intercourse, the best that present circumstances and mutual opinion will permit, but temporary, and liable to be from time to time abandoned or varied, as experience and circumstances shall dictate; constantly keeping in view, that 'tis folly in one nation to look for disinterested favors from another; that it must pay with a portion of its independence for whatever it may accept under that character; that, by such acceptance, it may place itself in the condition of having given equivalents for nominal favors, and yet of being reproached with ingratitude for not giving more. There can be no greater error than to expect or calculate upon real favors from nation to nation. 'Tis an illusion, which experience must cure, which a just pride ought to discard.

In offering to you, my countrymen, these counsels of an old and affectionate friend, I dare not hope they will make the strong and lasting impression I could wish; that they will control the usual current of the passions, or prevent our nation from running the course which has hitherto marked the destiny of nations. But if I may even flatter myself that they may be productive of some partial benefit, some occasional good; that they may now and then recur to moderate the fury of party spirit, to warn against the mischiefs of foreign intrigue, to guard against the impostures of pretended patriotism; this hope will be a full recompense for the solicitude for your welfare by which they have been dictate. How far in the discharge of my official duties I have been guided by the principles which have been delineated, the public records and other evidences of my conduct must witness to you and to the world. To myself, the assurance of my own conscience is, that I have at least believed myself to be guided by them.

In relation to the still subsisting war in Europe, my proclamation of the 22d of April, 1793, is the index to my plan. Sanctioned by your approving voice, and by that of your representatives in both Houses of Congress, the spirit of that measure has continually governed me, uninfluenced by any attempts to deter or divert me from it. After deliberate examination, with the aid of the best lights I could obtain, I was well satisfied that our country, under all the circumstances of the case, had a right to take, and was bound in duty and interest to take, a neutral position. Having taken it, I determined, as far as should depend upon me, to maintain it, with moderation, perseverance, and firmness.

The considerations which respect the right to hold this conduct, it is not necessary on this occasion to detail. I will only observe that, according to my understanding of the matter, that right, so far from being denied by any of the belligerent powers, has been virtually admitted by all.

Did You Know?

Political Parties and Early American Foreign Policy

Although the founding fathers did not like political parties and George Washington spent a great deal of time in his farewell address warning against the negative aspects of party competition, political parties became the vehicle of mass participation and enfranchisement very soon after the first president's departure. Foreign policy was at the heart of the political debates of the day for both the Federalists and the Anti-Federalists. The first competitive election of 1796 set the benchmark. The Federalist candidate was John Adams, an Anglophile accused of being "champion of Kings, ranks, and titles," who stood against the Anti-Federalist (Democratic-Republican) candidate, Thomas Jefferson, who was accused of being a Francophile, an atheist, and a friend of revolutionary mobs (Cummings 2007: 21). The United States having only recently won independence from the British crown, the charge of being an Anglophile was serious. John Jay had found out how dangerous it was to be labeled an Anglophile two years earlier when he concluded the so-called Jay Treaty, properly named the Treaty of London of 1974. In that treaty the United States and Great Britain had avoided war and settled a number of outstanding issues in the post-Revolutionary era, such as border disputes; compensation for damages during the Revolutionary War, such as ships confiscated and slaves taken; and the delineation of the border with Canada. Upon completion of the treaty, John Jay returned to the United States to find that his political opponents were burning his effigy in town squares. Thomas Jefferson and James Madison strongly opposed the treaty, siding with the French in their revolutionary wars and arguing the United States had an obligation to support France against the British. The Jay Treaty was ratified in 1796 and immediately became a campaign issue between Adams and Jefferson in the election.

The duty of holding a neutral conduct may be inferred, without any thing more, from the obligation which justice and humanity impose on every nation, in cases in which it is free to act, to maintain inviolate the relations of peace and amity towards other nations.

The inducements of interest for observing that conduct will best be referred to your own reflections and experience. With me, a predominant motive has been to endeavor to gain time to our country to settle and mature its yet recent institutions, and to progress without interruption to that degree of strength and consistency which is necessary to give it, humanly speaking, the command of its own fortunes.

Though, in reviewing the incidents of my administration, I am unconscious of intentional error, I am nevertheless too sensible of my defects not to think it probable that I may have committed many errors. Whatever they may be, I fervently beseech the Almighty to avert or mitigate the evils to which they may tend. I shall also carry with me the hope, that my country will never cease to view them with indulgence; and that, after forty-five years of my life dedicated to its service with an upright zeal, the faults of incompetent abilities will be consigned to oblivion, as myself must soon be to the mansions of rest.

Relying on its kindness in this as in other things, and actuated by that fervent love towards it which is so natural to a man who views in it the native soil of himself and his progenitors for several generations, I anticipate with pleasing expectation that retreat in which I promise myself to realize, without alloy, the sweet enjoyment of partaking, in the midst of my fellow citizens, the benign influence of good laws under a free government, the ever favorite object of my heart, and the happy reward, as I trust, of our mutual cares, labors and dangers.

George Washington
United States, 17th September 1796

- **Document:** President James Monroe's Seventh Annual Message to Congress: The Monroe Doctrine
- **Date:** December 12, 1823
- **Significance:** This address sends a clear statement that the Western Hemisphere is considered as the United States' sphere of influence. It signals to European powers that the United States will view European states as having influence over their own sphere of influence, but that European states must recognize and not interfere in the United States' sphere of influence.
- **Source:** Annals of Congress, Senate, 18th Congress, 1st Session, p. 14.

From President,

At the proposal of the Russian Imperial Government, made through the minister of the Emperor residing here, a full power and instructions have been transmitted to the Minister of the United States at St. Petersburgh to arrange, by amicable negotiation, the respective rights and interests of the two nations on the northwest coast of this continent. A similar proposal has been made by His Imperial Majesty to the Government of Great Britain, which has likewise been acceded to. The Government of the United States has been desirous, by this friendly proceeding, of manifesting the great value which they have invariably attached to the friendship of the Emperor, and their solicitude to cultivate the best understanding with his Government. In the discussions to which this interest has given rise, and in the arrangements by which they may terminate the occasion has been judged proper for asserting, as a principle in which the rights and interests of the United States are involved, that the American continents, by the free and independent condition which they have assumed and maintain, are henceforth not to be considered as subjects for future colonization by any European powers. . . .

It was stated at the commencement of the last session that a great effort was then making in Spain and Portugal, to improve the condition of the people of those countries, and that it appeared to be conducted with extraordinary moderation. It need scarcely be remarked, that the result has been, so far, very different from what was then anticipated. Of events in that quarter of the globe, with which we have so much intercourse, and from which we derive our origin, we have always been anxious and interested spectators. The citizens of the United States cherish sentiments the most friendly, in favor of the liberty and happiness of their fellow men on that side of the Atlantic. In the wars of the European powers, in matters relating to

James Monroe, the last of the eighteenth-century revolutionary patriots to lead the nation, served as president during the period known as the Era of Good Feelings. His "Monroe Doctrine" established U.S. hegemony over the Western Hemisphere. (Library of Congress)

themselves, we have never taken any part, nor does it comport with our policy to do so. It is only when our rights are invaded, or seriously menaced, that we resent injuries, or make preparation for our defence. With the movements in this hemisphere, we are, of necessity, more immediately connected, and by causes which must be obvious to all enlightened and impartial observers. The political system of the allied powers is essentially different, in this respect, from that of America. This difference proceeds from that which exists in their respective governments. And to the defence of our own, which has been achieved by the loss of so much blood and treasure, and matured by the wisdom of their most enlightened citizens, and under which we have enjoyed unexampled felicity, this whole nation is devoted. We owe it, therefore, to candor, and to the amicable relations existing between the United States and those powers, to declare, that we should consider any attempt on their part to extend their system to any portion of this hemisphere, as dangerous to our peace and safety. With the existing colonies or dependencies of any European power we have not interfered, and shall not interfere. But with the governments who have declared their independence, and maintained it, and whose independence we have, on great consideration, and on just principles, acknowledged, we could not view any interposition for the purpose of oppressing them, or controlling, in any other manner, their destiny, by any European power in any other light than as the manifestation of an unfriendly disposition towards the United States. In the war between those new governments and Spain we declared our neutrality at the time of their recognition, and to this we have adhered, and shall continue to adhere, provided no change shall occur, which, in the judgement of the competent authorities of this government, shall make a corresponding change, on the part of the United States, indispensable to their security.

The late events in Spain and Portugal, shew that Europe is still unsettled. Of this important fact, no stronger proof can be adduced than that the allied powers should have thought it proper, on any principle satisfactory to themselves, to have interposed, by force, in the internal concerns of Spain. To what extent such interposition may be carried, on the same principle, is a question, to which all independent powers, whose governments differ from theirs, are interested; even those most remote, and surely none more so than the United States. Our policy, in regard to Europe, which was adopted at an early stage of the wars which have so long agitated that quarter of the globe, nevertheless remains the same, which is, not to interfere in the internal concerns of any of its powers; to consider the government *de facto* as the legitimate government for us; to cultivate friendly relations with it, and to preserve those relations by a frank, firm, and manly policy; meeting, in all instances, the just claims of every power; submitting to injuries from none. But, in regard

Did You Know?

Irredentism

Irredentism is a term for one state laying claim to another state's territory, usually for historical reasons or because of ethno-cultural, religious, or linguistic ties. The word comes from the phrase Italia irredenta ("unredeemed Italy"), which came into use in the nineteenth century when Italian nationalists called for the unification of all lands under the control of Austria-Hungary that nevertheless were inhabited by a majority of Italian people. Throughout history, the term has been expressed in terms of claims of the "greater" nation, for example, Greater Albania, which would include Kosovo, or Greater Germany, which (during World War II) would include the Sudetenland and western Poland. The modern notion of the "state" is historically young, having emerged in 1648 with the signing of the Treaty of Westphalia. Drawing the boundaries of modern states resulted in the dispersal of historically defined groups across two or more states. Ever since, when these boundaries are disputed, claims of irredentism often emerge. Too numerous to list here, irredentist claims are said to have caused World War I, World War II, the Balkan Wars, and the Middle East conflict, to name a few. There are several nations in which irredentism is an official policy and even included in the constitution, in what is called "constitutional irredentism." For example, the Chinese constitution states that Taiwan is a part of the People's Republic of China. And until recently, the Irish constitution considered the country to be the entire island, not just the southern part, even though Northern Ireland is part of the United Kingdom.

to these continents, circumstances are eminently and conspicuously different. It is impossible that the allied powers should extend their political system to any portion of either continent, without endangering our peace and happiness: nor can any one believe that our Southern Brethren, if left to themselves, would adopt it of their own accord. It is equally impossible, therefore, that we should behold such interposition, in any form, with indifference. If we look to the comparative strength and resources of Spain and those new governments, and their distance from each other, it must be obvious that she can never subdue them. It is still the true policy of the United States to leave the parties to themselves, in the hope that other powers will pursue the same course.

FURTHER READING

Bemis, S. (1949) *John Quincy Adams and the Foundations of American Foreign Policy.* New York: A. A. Knopf.

Cummings, J. (2007) *Anything for a Vote: Dirty Tricks, Cheap Shots, and October Surprises in U.S. Presidential Campaigns.* San Francisco: Chronicle Books.

Fishman, E., Pederson, W., and Rozell, M. eds. (2001) *George Washington: Foundation of Presidential Leadership and Character.* New York: Praeger.

Herring, G. (2008) *From Colony to Superpower: U.S. Foreign Relations since 1776.* Oxford: Oxford University Press.

Kaplan, L. (1987) *Entangling Alliances with None: American Foreign Policy in the Age of Jefferson.* Kent, OH: Kent State University Press.

White, P. (1970) *The Critical Years: American Foreign Policy, 1793–1823.* New York: Wiley.

Wood, G. S. (2004) *The Americanization of Benjamin Franklin.* New York: Penguin.

Woolery, W. (1971) *The Relation of Thomas Jefferson to American Foreign Policy, 1783–1793.* St. Clair Shores, MI: Scholarly Press.

2

ANDREW JACKSON
TO
ANDREW JOHNSON:
WESTWARD EXPANSIONISM
AND MANIFEST
DESTINY

INTRODUCTION

After the first five presidents, U.S. foreign policy became more aggressively expansionistic and entered what many called the era of manifest destiny. Manifest destiny also reflected the racialization of U.S. domestic and foreign policies by making the assumption that white Americans (that is, those with Anglo-Saxon heritage) were culturally, biologically, and morally superior and as such had a divine mandate to govern allegedly inferior, backward, and uncivilized peoples. In other words, it was the "white man's burden" to rule, and to control, expel, or convert those seen as racially inferior or culturally backward. Finally, in this era the United States employed what is called "gunboat diplomacy," a more aggressive stance coupled with a willingness to deploy U.S. military force against nations that stood in the way of U.S. political, territorial, and economic goals.

This era begins in 1828 with the election of President Andrew Jackson, hero of the Battle of New Orleans. In his electoral campaign Jackson alluded to a return to simpler times and vowed to "ask nothing but what is right, permit nothing that is wrong" (Herring 2008: 165). Influenced by a fear of the mighty British Royal Navy as well as a desire to emulate it, the United States adopted a policy of gunboat diplomacy through which it enforced its wishes upon smaller nations. The British had already set the example in the Opium Wars in China, and the United States sought to follow it. The most important instance, one with serious consequences for the world, was the opening of Japan by Commodore Matthew Perry in 1853. A direct result of Commodore Perry's arrival in Japan was the Treaty of Amity and Commerce, which was signed five years later.

In dealing with China, the United States secured the same commercial rights the British had obtained years earlier; with the Treaty of Wang-hsia in 1844, the United States formally gained access to China, which had previously been opened at gunpoint.

In the meantime the main diplomatic and military focus of the United States remained its southern neighbors, Central America and the Caribbean, especially Cuba. The main strategic objective in Central America was Panama. The United States moved aggressively to acquire rights of passage through the Panama Canal, eventually signing the 1850 Clayton-Bulwer Treaty providing for the joint construction of the canal (which remained a foreign policy issue into the twenty-first century, when the United States ceded control of the Panama Canal Zone to Panama). However, treaty making was not the only way to proceed; there was gunboat diplomacy as well as the extralegal private activity in Central America which would define U.S. foreign policy in the region for more than a hundred years. For example, the United States landed forces in Nicaragua, and in 1855 the fortune-seeker William Walker took the country over, even going so far as reinstituting slavery (Herring 2008: 220).

Although race is typically seen as an explosive domestic issue that ignited the deadliest war the United States has ever fought—the Civil War, 1861–1865—American foreign policy in this era was also greatly shaped by race. Paired, manifest destiny and the racialization of U.S. politics became a deadly combination for Native American nations. European diseases had killed millions of indigenous Americans, but the job was not complete, and hundreds of nations possessed much of the desirable territory that American policymakers sought. Warfare was one option to get what they wanted. They fought the natives with a fierce mania that had its roots in a racial hierarchy which posited whites as superior—Christian and civilized, as opposed to Indians, who were thought to be inherently inferior, heathen, and uncivilized. Such assumptions were expressed by General William T. Sherman, who said: "The more we can kill this year, the less will have to be killed the next war, for the more I see of these Indians the more convinced I am that all have to be killed or be maintained as a species of pauper. Their attempts at civilization are simply ridiculous" (Hunt 1987: 55). Considering that General Sherman was at the highest echelon of the U.S. government and commanded the U.S. Army in the West, it is arguable that this era witnessed a genocide perpetrated by the U.S. government against Native Americans. Andrew Jackson himself was involved in a brutal campaign for the total destruction of the Creeks and Seminoles, even while Florida was not yet part of the United States. Claiming the right to act on the principle of self-defense, Jackson attacked the Spanish in Pensacola and put to death, in Spanish territory no less, two British subjects while expecting the Spanish to fold in the Florida territory so that he could finish controlling the Native Americans who were present (Herring 2008: 148).

Yet warfare was not the only way for white colonists to acquire land. The U.S. government signed a series of treaties with the remnants of native nations and then proceeded to systematically violate them, taking away the Native Americans' lands, expelling them, and even killing them through exposure and starvation. In the words of one governor of Georgia: "Treaties were expedients by which ignorant, intractable, and savage people were induced without bloodshed to yield up what civilized peoples had the right to possess" (Hunt 1987: 53). These policies produced the infamous "Trail of Tears," which was initiated by Jackson but continued under President Martin Van Buren, by which Native Americans were driven from the Southeast to points west of the Mississippi. Thousands of Native Americans from the Seminole, Choctaw, Chickasaw, Muskogee-Creek, and especially the Cherokee nations saw their families die along the way to their new destinations. The Cherokee resisted Jackson's removal policies, even winning a case before the U.S. Supreme Court that affirmed its status as a sovereign domestic nation (*Worcester v. Georgia*, 1832). But the court's decision was ignored by President Jackson, who initiated their removal despite the fact that the Cherokee were among the "Five Civilized Tribes" that modeled their governments after American institutions and even assimilated into white culture.

The Cherokee agreed to westward removal by the 1835 Treaty of New Echota, and the Trail of Tears began in 1838. The Cherokee traveled almost thirteen hundred miles west without sufficient food, water, or medicine; and approximately one-third of them died on the Trail of Tears. The Potowatami nation of Indiana experienced similar hardship along their "Trail of Death." These results were justified by one pro-removal congressman, who stated: "What is history but the obituary of nations?" (Herring 2008: 173). In this manner, manifest destiny rationalized the expulsion, and even the death, of Native Americans in order to make way for what was thought to be the divinely ordained white American territorial acquisition.

Native Americans were not the only ones to suffer at the hands of white American colonists. During this time Mexicans and African-American slaves were treated harshly. Manifest destiny led to the Mexican-American War, which resulted in Mexico losing half its territory to the United States. In the years prior to the war, American colonists had poured into sparsely inhabited regions of Mexico because of its fertile land and lax immigration enforcement by Mexican authorities, who generally

The Treaty of Guadalupe Hidalgo, signed on February 2, 1848, ended the Mexican-American War and granted the United States nearly half of the Republic of Mexico in exchange for $15 million. (Library of Congress)

welcomed the new colonists. Alarmed by the influx of more and more colonists, the Mexican government attempted to curb immigration into Texas and declared slavery illegal in 1829. This led to an armed revolt by American settlers and Mexican dissidents, who won the Battle of San Jacinto in 1836 and declared Texas an independent republic in which slavery was legal. The United States immediately recognized the Republic of Texas; Mexico did not. In addition, territory that would become New Mexico and California was in the sights of the United States.

With the Mexican government weakened and divided, the United States moved to annex Texas in 1845 even though the Mexicans considered the action an act of war. France and Britain did not want the United States to gain this territory and therefore attempted to convince Mexican authorities to recognize the independence of Texas, while the United States, pointing to the Monroe Doctrine, warned against undue interference. President James Polk's heavy-handed diplomacy ensured that the war would take place; Polk told Congress in 1846 that "Mexico has passed the boundary of the United States, has invaded our territory and shed American blood upon American soil" (Polk, May 11, 1846). The United States proceeded to invade Mexico from the north in California and Texas and from the south at Veracruz. The war ended with the Treaty of Guadalupe Hidalgo in 1848, in which the United States emerged victorious in all its aims and Mexico ceded more territory to the United States. As a result of the treaty, the United States increased its territories by 33 percent, acquiring most of the present states of Arizona, New Mexico, California, Colorado, Texas, Nevada, Utah, Kansas, Oklahoma, and Wyoming.

The Mexican-American War ended up being a self-fulfilling prophecy for those who were active believers in manifest destiny and the superiority of the American political system. Having won a decisive military victory in its first major campaign abroad and its first attempt to occupy a foreign territory, the United States considered taking all of Mexico. But the same racial bias that spurred the Americans forward ended up stopping them from conquering all of Mexico. Americans thought that Mexican "blood" would not mix well with their own, and thus decided not to extend their reach (Herring 2008). The United States did, however, purchase more land from a financially strapped Mexican government. In the Gadsen Purchase of 1853, the United States purchased what are now the southern portions of New Mexico and Arizona, land the United States wanted to complete a railroad line to California. President Polk also negotiated the Oregon Treaty with Great Britain, resulting in the acquisition of territory that would eventually become Oregon, Washington, Idaho, and parts of Montana and Wyoming.

This era also saw the origin of the desire to eventually annex Hawaii, which, dominated by white plantation owners and missionaries, proved no match for the ever-increasing American appetite for territorial acquisition. U.S. policymakers desired

Hawaii because it was located halfway between the U.S. mainland and the great Eastern countries of China and Japan. Meanwhile, the British were in the midst of their Opium Wars with China. The 1842 Treaty of Nanking had given the British commercial rights in formerly isolationist China, and the United States followed with the Treaty of Wang-hsia in 1844. Most importantly, in 1853 came Commodore Perry's mission to Japan, which would have tremendous consequences for the Japanese and, in decades to come, for the world. The eventual goal of the United States in the Far East was achieved with the Treaty of Amity and Commerce, also known as the Harris Treaty, in 1858, by which the opening of Japan was completed. This treaty opened Japan up to modern forces which, in turn, would eventually erode its centuries-old social structures.

The strongest example of the racialization of U.S. foreign policy during this era concerned African-American slaves within and around the United States. American foreign policy toward Haiti highlights the central role that race played in foreign policymaking. Having achieved independence at a very high human price, Haiti presented a direct challenge to the "peculiar institution" of slavery, with Haitians not only overthrowing the white yoke but also forbidding slavery in their new nation. In the United States, Haitian independence was considered an abomination by white southerners. The United States refused to recognize the small nation or even to use the word *Haiti*. One U.S. senator from Georgia warned against meeting with "the emancipated slave, his hands yet reeking from the blood of his masters" (Herring 2008: 163). Many in the United States, especially in the South, feared that the United States could fall into the "chaos and negroism" of slave revolts inspired by the Haitian example. By the time President Lincoln reminded the people of the United States of their moral obligations and their international position in a world in which the international slave trade was illegal, it was too late.

During the Civil War, the main concern for the Union was to keep the European powers out of the conflict; a task at which they were successful. The goal of the Confederacy was to involve Britain and France and to enlist them in the Confederate cause. For that, they had a great asset, or so they thought: King Cotton. The southerners banked on the demand for cotton in European factories and thought that European powers would not be able to resist securing the commodity by helping the South. Yet the war ended with the preservation of the Union, and of a United States that would eventually turn its sights abroad to countries such as Cuba, just one of many foreign lands desired by U.S. businesses and political leaders.

- **Document: Clayton-Bulwer Treaty**
- **Date:** April 19, 1850
- **Significance:** Due to the great-power competition over what became the Panama Canal, the United Kingdom and the United States completed a treaty that essentially guaranteed the neutrality of the canal, the safety of its operation, and the nonintervention of the great powers in the region, at least in the form of colonization.
- **Source:** United States Statutes at Large, Volume 9: 29th–31st Congresses, 1845–1851, p. 995. Boston: Little, Brown and Company, 1862.

THE CLAYTON-BULWER TREATY

THE United States of America and her Britannic Majesty, being desirous of consolidating the relations of amity which so happily subsist between them, by setting forth and fixing in a convention their views and intentions with reference to any means of communication by ship canal, which may be constructed between the Atlantic and Pacific Oceans, by the way of the River San Juan de Nicaragua, and either or both of the lakes of Nicaragua or Managua, to any port or place on the Pacific Ocean: the President of the United States has conferred full powers on John M. Clayton, Secretary of State of the United States; and her Britannic Majesty on the Right Honorable Sir Henry Lytton Bulwer, a member of her Majesty's Most Honorable Privy Council, Knight Commander of the Most Honorable Order of the Bath, and Envoy Extraordinary and Minister Plenipotentiary of her Britannic Majesty to the United States, for the aforesaid purpose; and the said plenipotentiaries, having exchanged their full powers, which were found to be in proper form, have agreed to the following articles:

ARTICLE I.

The governments of the United States and Great Britain hereby declare, that neither the one nor the other will ever obtain or maintain for itself any exclusive control over the said ship canal; agreeing that neither will ever erect or maintain any fortifications commanding the same or in the vicinity thereof, or occupy, or fortify, or colonize, or assume or exercise any dominion over Nicaragua, Costa Rica, the Mosquito coast, or any part of Central America; nor will either make use of any protection which either affords or may afford, or any alliance which either has or may have, to or with any State or people, for the purpose of erecting or maintaining any such fortifications, or of occupying, fortifying, or colonizing Nicaragua, Costa Rica, the Mosquito coast, or any part of Central America, or of assuming or exercising dominion over the same; nor will the United States or Great Britain take advantage of any intimacy, or use any alliance, connection, or influence that either may possess, with any State or government through whose territory the said canal may pass, for the purpose of acquiring or holding, directly or indirectly, for the citizens or subjects of the one, any rights or advantages in regard to commerce or navigation through the said canal which shall not be offered on the same terms to the citizens or subjects of the other.

ARTICLE II.

Vessels of the United States or Great Britain traversing the said canal shall, in case of war between the contracting parties, be exempted from blockade, detention, or capture by either of the belligerents; and this provision shall extend to such a distance from the two ends of the said canal as may hereafter be found expedient to establish.

ARTICLE III.

In order to secure the construction of the said canal, the contracting parties engage, that, if any such canal shall be undertaken upon fair and equitable terms, by any parties having the authority of the local government or governments through whose territory the same may pass, then the persons employed in making the said canal, and their property used or to be used for that object, shall be protected, from the commencement of the said canal to its completion, by the governments of the United States and Great Britain, from unjust detention, confiscation seizure, or any violence whatsoever.

ARTICLE IV.

The contracting parties will use whatever influence they respectively exercise with any State, states, or governments, possessing, or claiming to possess, any jurisdiction or right over the territory which the said canal shall traverse, or which shall be near the waters applicable thereto, in order to induce such states or governments to facilitate the construction of the said canal by every means in their power; and furthermore, the United States and Great Britain agree to use their good offices, wherever or however it may be most expedient, in order to procure the establishment of two free ports, one at each end of the said canal.

ARTICLE V.

The contracting parties further engage that, when the said canal shall have been completed, they will protect it from interruption, seizure, or Unjust confiscation, and that they will guarantee the neutrality thereof, so that the said canal may forever be open and free, and the capital invested therein secure. Nevertheless, the governments of the United States and Great Britain, in according their protection to the construction of the said canal, and guaranteeing its neutrality and security when completed, always understand that this protection and guarantee are granted conditionally, and may be withdrawn by both governments, or either government, if both governments, or either government should deem that the persons or company undertaking or managing the same adopt or establish such regulations concerning the traffic thereupon as are contrary to the spirit and intention of this convention, either by making unfair discriminations in favor of the commerce of one of the contracting parties over the commerce of the other, or by imposing oppressive exactions or unreasonable tolls upon passengers, vessels, goods, wares, merchandise, or other articles. Neither party, however, shall withdraw the aforesaid protection and guarantee, without first giving six months notice to the other.

- **Document: Treaty of Wang-hsia**
- **Date:** July 3, 1844
- **Significance:** Having ended the first Opium War, whereby Western imperialists opened China by force to opium, the United States took advantage of its position by signing its first treaty with the Asian power in order to gain unfettered access to the Chinese markets.
- **Source:** United States Statutes at Large, Volume 8: 1778–1845, p. 592. Boston: Little, Brown, and Company, 1867.

TREATY OF PEACE AMITY AND COMMERCE, WITH TARIFF OF DUTIES

The United States of America, and The Ta Tsing Empire, Desiring to establish firm, lasting, and sincere friendship between the two Nations, have resolved to fix, in a manner clear and positive, by means of a treaty or general convention of peace, amity, and commerce, the rules which shall in future be mutually observed in the intercourse of their respective countries: – For which most desirable object, the President of the United States has conferred full powers on their Commissioner Caleb Cushing, Envoy Extraordinary and Minister Plenipotentiary of the United States to China; and the August Sovereign of the Ta Tsing Empire on his Minister and Commissioner Extraordinary Tsiyeng, of the Imperial House, a vice Guardian of the Heir Apparent, Governor-general of the Two Kwang, and Superintendant General of the trade and foreign intercourse of the five ports.

And the said Commissioners, after having exchanged their said full powers, and duly considered the premises, have agreed to the following articles.

ARTICLE I.

There shall be a perfect, permanent, universal peace, and a sincere and cordial amity, between the United States of America on the one part, and the Ta Tsing Empire on the other part, and between their people respectively, without exception of persons or places.

ARTICLE II.

Citizens of the United States resorting to China for the purposes of commerce will pay the duties of import and export prescribed in the Tariff, which is fixed by and made a part of this Treaty. They shall, in no case, be subject to other or higher duties than are or shall be required of the people of any other nation whatever. Fees and charges of every sort are wholly abolished, and officers of the revenue, who may be guilty of exaction, shall be punished according to the laws of China. If the Chinese Government desire to modify, in any respect, the said Tariff, such modifications shall be made only in consultation with consuls or other functionaries thereto duly authorized in behalf of the United States, and with consent thereof. And if additional advantages or privileges, of whatever description, be conceded hereafter by China to any other nation, the United States, and the citizens thereof, shall be entitled thereupon, to a complete, equal, and impartial participation in the same.

ARTICLE III.

The citizens of the United States are permitted to frequent the five ports of Kwangchow, Amoy, Fuchow, Ningpo and Shanghai, and to reside with their families and trade there, and to proceed at pleasure with their vessels and merchandize to and from any foreign port and either of the said five ports, and from either of the said five ports to any other of them. But said vessels shall not unlawfully enter the other ports of China, nor carry on a clandestine and fraudulent trade along the coasts thereof. And any vessel belonging to a citizen of the United States, which violates this provision, shall, with her cargo, be subject to confiscation to the Chinese government.

ARTICLE IV.

For the superintendence and regulation of the concerns of the citizens of the United States doing business at the said five ports, the government of the United States may appoint Consuls, or other officers, at the same, who shall be duly recognized as such by the officers of the Chinese government, and shall hold official intercourse and correspondence with the latter, either personal or in writing, as occasions may require, on terms of equality and reciprocal respect. If disrespectfully treated or aggrieved in any way by the local authorities, said officers on the one hand shall have the right to make representation of the same to the superior officers of the Chinese Government, who will see that full inquiry and strict justice be had in the premises; and on the other hand, the said Consuls will carefully avoid all acts of unnecessary offence to, or collision with, the officers and people of China.

ARTICLE V.

At each of the said five ports, citizens of the United States lawfully engaged in commerce, shall be permitted to import from their own or any other ports into China, and sell there, and purchase therein, and export to their own or any other ports, all manner of merchandize, of which the importation or exportation is not prohibited by this Treaty, paying the duties which are prescribed by the Tariff herein before established, and no other charges whatsoever.

ARTICLE VI.

Whenever any merchant-vessel belonging to the United States shall enter either of the said five ports for trade, her papers shall be lodged with the Consul, or person charged with affairs, who will report the same to the commissioner of customs; and tonnage duty shall be paid on said vessel at the rate of five mace per ton, if she be over one hundred and fifty tons burden; and one mace per ton if she be of the burden of one hundred and fifty tons or under, according to the amount of her tonnage as specified in the register; said payment to be in full of the former charges of measurement and other fees, which are wholly abolished. And if any vessel, which having anchored at one of the said ports, and there paid tonnage duty, shall have occasion to go to any others of the said ports to complete the disposal of her cargo, the Consul, or person charged with affairs, will report the same to the commissioner of customs, who, on the departure of the said vessel will note in the port-clearance that the tonnage duties have been paid, and report the same to the other custom-houses; in which case on entering another port the said vessel will only pay duty there on her cargo, but shall not be subject to the payment of tonnage duty a second time.

ARTICLE VII.

No Tonnage duty shall be required on boats belonging to citizens of the United States, employed in the conveyance of passengers, baggage, letters, and articles of provision, or others not subject to duty to or from any of the five ports. All cargo-boats, however, conveying merchandize subject to duty shall pay the regular tonnage duty of one mace per ton, provided they belong to citizens of the United States, but not if hired by them from subjects of China.

ARTICLE VIII.

Citizens of the United States for their vessels bound in shall be allowed to engage pilots, who will report said vessels at the passes and take them into port; and when the lawful duties have all been paid they may engage pilots to leave port. It shall also be lawful for them to hire at pleasure, servants, compradors, linguists, and writers, and passage or cargo boats, and to employ laborers, seamen, and persons for whatever necessary service for a reasonable compensation to be agreed on by the parties, or settled by application to the consular officer of their government, without interference on the part of the local officers of the Chinese government.

. . .

ARTICLE XVI.

The Chinese Government will not hold itself responsible for any debts which may happen to be due from subjects of China to citizens of the United States, or for frauds committed by them: but citizens of the United States may seek redress in law; and on suitable representation being made to the Chinese local authorities through the Consul, they will cause due examination in the premises, and take all proper steps to compel satisfaction. But in case the debtor be dead, or without property, or have absconded, the creditor cannot be indemnified according to the old system of the co-hong so called. And if citizens of the United States be indebted to subjects of China, the latter may seek redress in the same way through the Consul, but without any responsibility for the debt on the part of the United States.

ARTICLE XVII.

Citizens of the United States residing or sojourning at any of the ports open to foreign commerce, shall enjoy all proper accommodation in obtaining houses and places of business, or in hiring sites from the inhabitants on which to construct houses and places of business, and also hospitals, churches and cemeteries. The local authorities of the two Governments shall select in concert the sites for the foregoing objects, having due regard to the feelings of the people in the location thereof: and the parties interested will fix the rent by mutual agreement, the proprietors on the one hand not demanding any exorbitant price, nor the merchants on the other unreasonably insisting on particular spots, but each conducting with justice and moderation. And any desecration of said cemeteries by subjects of China shall be severely punished according to law.

At the places of anchorage of the vessels of the United States, the citizens of the United States, merchants, seamen, or others sojourning there, may pass and repass in the immediate neighborhood; but they shall not at their pleasure make excursions into the country among the villages at large, nor shall they repair to public marts for the purpose of disposing of goods unlawfully and in fraud of the revenue.

And, in order to the preservation of the public pence, the local officers of government at each of the five ports, shall, in concert with the Consuls, define the limits beyond which it shall not be lawful for citizens of the United States to go.

ARTICLE XVIII.

It shall be lawful for the officers or citizens of the United States to employ scholars and people of any part of China without distinction of persons, to teach any of the languages of the Empire, and to assist in literary labors; and the persons so employed shall not, for that cause, be subject to any injury on the part either of the government or of individuals: and it shall in like manner be lawful for citizens of the United States to purchase all manner of books in China.

ARTICLE XIX.

All citizens of the United States in China, peaceably attending to their affairs, being placed on a common footing of amity and goodwill with subjects of China, shall receive and enjoy, for themselves and everything appertaining to them, the special protection of the local authorities of Government, who shall defend them from all insult or injury of any sort on the part of the Chinese. If their dwellings or property be threatened or attacked by mobs, incendiaries, or other violent or lawless persons, the local officers, on requisition of the Consul, will immediately dispatch a military force to disperse the rioters, and will apprehend the guilty individuals, and punish them with the utmost rigor of the law.

ARTICLE XX.

Citizens of the United States who may have imported merchandize into any of the free ports of China, and paid the duty thereof, if they desire to re-export the same, in part or in whole, to any other of the said ports, shall be entitled to make application, through their Consul, to the Superintendant of Customs, who, in order to prevent frauds on the revenue, shall cause examination to be made by suitable officers to see that the duties paid on such goods, as entered on the custom-house books, correspond with the representation made, and that the goods remain with their original marks unchanged, and shall then make a memorandum in the port-clearance, of the goods, and the amount of duties paid on the same, and deliver the same to the merchant; and shall also certify the facts to the officers of customs of the other ports. All which being done, on the arrival in port of the vessel in which the goods are laden, and everything being found on examination there to correspond, she shall be permitted to break bulk and land the said goods, without being subject to the payment of any additional duty thereon. But if, on such examination, the superintendent of customs shall detect any fraud on the revenue in the case, then the goods shall be subject to forfeiture and confiscation to the Chinese Government.

ARTICLE XXI.

Subjects of China who may be guilty of any criminal act towards citizens of the United States, shall be arrested and punished by the Chinese authorities according to the laws of China: and citizens of the United States, who may commit any crime in China, shall be subject to be tried and punished only by the Consul, or other public functionary of the United States, thereto authorized according to the laws of the United States. And in order to the prevention of all controversy and disaffection, justice shall be equitably and impartially administered on both sides.

ARTICLE XXII.

Relations of peace and amity between the United States and China being established by this Treaty, and the vessels of the United States being admitted to trade freely to and from the five ports of China open to foreign commerce, it is further agreed that in case at any time hereafter, China should be at war with any foreign nation whatever, and for that cause should exclude such nation from entering her ports, still the vessels of the United States shall not the less continue to pursue their commerce in freedom and security, and to transport goods to and from the ports of the belligerent parties, full respect being paid to the neutrality of the flag of the United States: Provided that the said flag shall not protect vessels engaged in the transportation of officers or soldiers in the enemy's service; nor shall said flag be fraudulently used to enable the enemy's ships with their cargoes to enter the ports of China; but all such vessels so offending shall be subject to forfeiture and confiscation to the Chinese Government.

ARTICLE XXIII.

The Consuls of the United States at each of the five ports open to foreign trade, shall make annually to the respective Governors-general thereof, a detailed report of the number of vessels belonging to the United States which have entered and left said ports during the year, and of the amount and value of goods imported or exported in said vessels, for transmission to and inspection of the Board of Revenue.

ARTICLE XXIV.

If citizens of the United States have special occasion to address any communication to the Chinese local officers of government, they shall submit the same to their consul, or other officer, to determine if the language be proper find respectful, find the matter just and right; in which event he shall transmit the same to the appropriate authorities for their consideration and action in the premises. In like manner, if subjects of China have special occasion to address the consul of the United States, they shall submit the communication to the local authorities of their own Government, to determine if the language be respectful and proper and the matter just and right; in which ease the said authorities will transmit the same to the Consul or other officer for his consideration and action in the premises. And if controversies arise between citizens of the United States and subjects of China, which cannot be amicably settled otherwise, the same shall be examined and decided conformably to justice and equitably by the public officers of the two nations acting in conjunction.

ARTICLE XXV.

All questions in regard to rights, whether of property or person, arising between citizens of the United States in China shall be subject to the jurisdiction, and regulated by the authorities of their own Government. And all controversies occurring in China between citizens of the United Slates and the subjects of any other government, shall be regulated by the treaties existing between the United States and such governments respectively, without interference on the part of China.

ARTICLE XXVI.

Merchant vessels of the United States lying in the waters of the five ports of China open to foreign commerce, will be under the jurisdiction of the officers of their own government, who, with the masters and owners thereof, will manage the same without control on the part of China. For injuries done to the citizens or the commerce of the United States by any foreign power, the Chinese Government will not hold itself bound to make reparation. But if the merchant-vessels of the United States, while within the waters over which the Chinese government exercises jurisdiction, be plundered by robbers or pirates, then the Chinese local authorities, civil and military, on receiving information thereof, will arrest the said robbers or pirates, and punish them according to law, and will cause all the property which can be recovered, to be placed in the hands of the nearest consul, or other officer of the United States, to be by him restored to the true owner. But if, by reason of the extent of territory and numerous population of China, it should, in any ease, happen that the robbers cannot be apprehended, or the property only in part recovered, then the law will take its course in regard to the local authorities, but the Chinese government will not make indemnity for the goods lost.

ARTICLE XXVII.

If any vessel of the United States shall be wrecked or stranded on the coast of China, and be subjected to plunder or other damage, the proper officers of government on receiving information of the fact, will immediately adopt measures for their relief and security; and the persons on board shall receive friendly treatment, and be enabled at once to repair to the most convenient of the free ports, and shall enjoy all facilities for obtaining supplies of provisions and water. And if a vessel shall be forced in whatever way to take refuge in any port other than one of the free ports, then in like manner the persons on board shall receive friendly treatment, and the means of safety and security.

ARTICLE XXVIII.

Citizens of the United States, their vessels and property, shall not be subject to any embargo; nor shall they be seized or forcibly detained for any pretense of the public service; but they shall be suffered to prosecute their commerce in quiet, and without molestation or embarrassment.

. . .

In Faith Whereof, We, the respective Plenipotentiaries of the United States of America, and of the Ta Tsing Empire, as aforesaid, have signed and sealed these Presents. Done at Wang Shia, this third day of July, in the Year of our Lord Jesus Christ, one thousand eight hundred and forty-four; and of Taoukwung, the twenty-fourth year, fifth month, and eighteenth day.

C. CUSHING [Seal] [Signature and seal of TSIYENG]

Commodore Perry and his fleet arrive in Japan as part of a U.S. naval expedition on July 8, 1853. This historic event shapes Japanese-U.S. relations well into the twentieth century. (Library of Congress)

- **Document: Treaty of Amity and Commerce (otherwise known as the Harris Treaty)**
- **Date:** July 29, 1858
- **Significance:** Similar to the opening of China, the opening of Japan through gunboat diplomacy took place in 1853, when Commodore Perry sailed into Edo harbor and concluded a short treaty, mainly about provisions, with the Tokugawa shogunate. The Harris Treaty is the trade equivalent and opened up Japan to American goods.
- **Source:** United States Statutes at Large, Volume 12: 36th–37th Congresses, 1859–1863, p. 1052. Boston: Little, Brown and Company, 1863.

TREATY OF AMITY AND COMMERCE BETWEEN THE UNITED STATES AND JAPAN

ARTICLE I.

There shall henceforth be perpetual peace and friendship between the United States of America and His Majesty the [shogun] of Japan and his successors.

ARTICLE 111.

In addition to the ports of Shimoda and Hakodate, the following ports and towns shall be opened on the dates respectively appended to them, that is to say: Kanagawa, on the 4th of July, 1859, Nagasaki, on the 4th of July, 1859; Niigata, on the 1st of January, 1860; Hyogo, on the 1st of January, 1863.

... Six months after the opening of Kanagawa, the port of Shimoda shall be closed as a place of residence and trade for American citizens. In all the foregoing ports and towns American citizens may permanently reside; they shall have the right to lease ground, and purchase the buildings thereon, and may erect dwellings and warehouses....

No wall, fence, or gate shall be erected by the Japanese around the place of residence of the Americans, or anything done which may prevent a free egress and ingress to the same.

From the 1st of January, 1862, Americans shall be allowed to reside in the City of Edo; and from the 1st of January, 1863, in the City of Osaka, for the purposes of trade only. In each of these two cities a suitable place within which they may hire houses, and the distance they may go, shall be arranged by the American Diplomatic Agent and the Government of Japan....

The Japanese Government will cause this clause to be made public in every part of the Empire as soon as the ratifications of this Treaty shall be exchanged. Munitions of war shall only be sold to the Japanese Government and foreigners....

Did You Know?

Commodore Matthew C. Perry

Commodore Matthew C. Perry (1794–1858) commanded the expedition that established U.S. relations with Japan. Perry began his naval career at the age of 15, became captain of the first naval steamship, the *Fulton*, in 1837, and was promoted to Commodore in 1842. In 1846–1847 he commanded the Gulf squadron during the Mexican War. In 1852, Perry was authorized by President Millard Fillmore to sail to Japan, a country that had been closed to outsiders since the seventeenth century. The goal of opening up Japan to U.S. commerce became increasingly popular after the British opened up China to Western commerce after defeating it in the First Opium War (1839–1843). On July 8, 1853, Perry sailed into Edo Bay with four ships and presented representatives of the Japanese Emperor with the text of a proposed commercial and friendship treaty. Perry then sailed for China but returned to Japan in February 1854 with an even more powerful fleet. With such firepower on display, on March 31, 1854, Japan agreed to the treaty, ensuring that humane treatment would be extended to sailors shipwrecked in Japanese territory, that U.S. ships were permitted to purchase coal in Japan, and that the ports of Shimoda and Hakodate would be opened to American commerce. With this mission, Commodore Perry is credited with opening Japan to the outside world, not only ending Japan's isolation but also setting in motion domestic forces that led to the Meiji Restoration.

ARTICLE IV.

Duties shall be paid to the Government of Japan on all goods landed in the country, and on all articles of Japanese production that are exported as cargo, according to the tariff hereunto appended....

The importation of opium is prohibited; and, any American vessel coming to Japan for the purposes of trade having more than four pounds weight of opium on board, such surplus quantity shall be seized and destroyed by the Japanese authorities. All goods imported into Japan and which have paid the duty fixed by this Treaty, may be transported by the Japanese into any part of the empire without the payment of any tax, excise, or transit duty whatever.

No higher duties shall be paid by Americans on goods imported into Japan than are fixed by this Treaty, nor shall any higher duties be paid by Americans than are levied on the same description of goods if imported in Japanese vessels, or the vessels of any other nation.

ARTICLE VI.

Americans committing offenses against Japanese shall be tried in American Consular courts, and, when guilty, shall be punished according to American law. Japanese committing offenses against Americans shall be tried by the Japanese authorities and punished according to Japanese law. The Consular courts shall be open to Japanese creditors, to enable them to recover their just claims against American citizens; and the Japanese courts shall in like manner be open to American citizens for the recovery of their just claims against Japanese.…

ARTICLE VIII.

Americans in Japan shall be allowed the free exercise of their religion, and for this purpose shall have the right to erect suitable places of worship. No injury shall be done to such buildings, nor any insult be offered to the religious worship of the Americans. American citizens shall not injure any Japanese temple or shrine, or offer any insult or injury to Japanese religious ceremonies, or to the objects of their worship.

The Americans and Japanese shall not do anything that may be calculated to excite religious animosity. The Government of Japan has already abolished the practice of trampling on religious emblems.

ARTICLE X.

The Japanese Government may purchase or construct in the United States ships-of-war, steamers, merchant ships, whale ships, cannon, munitions of war, and arms of all kinds, and any other things it may require. It shall have the right to engage in the United States scientific, naval and military men, artisans of all kind, and mariners to enter into its service.…

ARTICLE XIII.

After the 4th of July, 1872, upon the desire of either the American or Japanese Governments, and on one year's notice given by either party, this Treaty, and such portions of the Treaty of Kanagawa as remain unrevoked by this Treaty, together with the regulations of trade hereunto annexed, or those that may be hereafter introduced, shall be subject to revision by Commissioners appointed on both sides for this purpose, who will be empowered to decide and insert therein, such amendments as experience shall prove to be desirable.

ARTICLE XIV.

This Treaty shall go into effect on the 4th of July, 1859.… This Treaty is executed in quadruplicate, each copy being written in English, Japanese, and Dutch languages, all the versions having the same meaning and intention, but the Dutch version shall be considered as being the original.…

- **Document: John O'Sullivan, "Annexation,"** *United States Magazine and Democratic Review*
- **Date:** July–August 1845
- **Significance:** John O'Sullivan was an influential political writer for the Democratic Party. In this essay he called for the annexation of Texas to the United States, which for a long time had been a controversial issue. The significance of this essay also lies with the use of the term *Manifest Destiny*, which clearly describes U.S. foreign policy at that time.
- **Source:** John O'Sullivan, "Annexation," *United States Magazine and Democratic Review 17*, no. 1 (July–August 1845): 5–10

It is now time for the opposition to the Annexation of Texas to cease, all further agitation of the waters of bitterness and strife, at least in connexion with this question, —even though it may perhaps be required of us as a necessary condition of the freedom of our institutions, that we must live on for ever in a state of unpausing struggle and excitement upon some subject of party division or other. But, in regard

In *American Progress,* painted by John Gast in 1872, an allegorical female figure of America leads pioneers and railroads westward as Native Americans and buffalo flee. The concept of manifest destiny represented in the painting related to the belief that the United States had a moral and divine mandate to colonize the lands west of the Mississippi. (Library of Congress)

to Texas, enough has now been given to party. It is time for the common duty of Patriotism to the Country to succeed;—or if this claim will not be recognized, it is at least time for common sense to acquiesce with decent grace in the inevitable and the irrevocable.

Texas is now ours. Already, before these words are written, her Convention has undoubtedly ratified the acceptance, by her Congress, of our proffered invitation into the Union; and made the requisite changes in her already republican form of constitution to adapt it to its future federal relations. Her star and her stripe may already be said to have taken their place in the glorious blazon of our common nationality; and the sweep of our eagle's wing already includes within its circuit the wide extent of her fair and fertile land. She is no longer to us a mere geographical space—a certain combination of coast, plain, mountain, valley, forest and stream. She is no longer to us a mere country on the map. She comes within the dear and sacred designation of Our Country; no longer a *"pays,"* she is a part of *"la patrie;"* and that which is at once a sentiment and a virtue, Patriotism, already begins to thrill for her too within the national heart. It is time then that all should cease to treat her as alien, and even adverse—cease to denounce and vilify all and everything connected with her accession—cease to thwart and oppose the remaining steps for its consummation; or where such efforts are felt to be unavailing, at least to embitter the hour of reception by all the most ungracious frowns of aversion and words of unwelcome. There has been enough of all this. It has had its fitting day during the period when, in common with every other possible question of practical policy that can arise, it unfortunately became one of the leading topics of party division, of presidential electioneering. But that period has passed, and with it let its prejudices and its passions, its discords and its denunciations, pass away too. The next session of Congress will see the representatives of the new young State in their places in both our halls of national legislation, side by side with those of the old Thirteen. Let their reception into "the family" be frank, kindly, and cheerful, as befits such an occasion, as comports not less with our own self-respect than patriotic duty towards them. Ill betide those foul birds that delight to file their own nest, and disgust the ear with perpetual discord of ill-omened croak.

Why, were other reasoning wanting, in favor of now elevating this question of the reception of Texas into the Union, out of the lower region of our past party dissensions, up to its proper level of a high and broad nationality, it surely is to be found, found abundantly, in the manner in which other nations have undertaken to intrude themselves into it, between us and the proper parties to the case, in a spirit of hostile interference against us, for the avowed object of thwarting our policy and hampering our power, limiting our greatness and checking the fulfillment of our manifest destiny to overspread the continent allotted by Providence for the free development of our yearly multiplying millions. This we have seen done by England, our old rival and enemy; and by France, strangely coupled with her against us, under the influence of the Anglicism strongly tinging the policy of her present prime minister, Guizot. The zealous activity with which this effort to defeat us was pushed by the representatives of those governments, together with the character of intrigue accompanying it, fully constituted that case of foreign interference, which Mr. Clay himself declared should, and would unite us all in maintaining the common cause of our country against foreigner and the foe. We are only astonished that this effect has not been more fully and strongly produced, and that the burst of indignation against this unauthorized, insolent and hostile interference against us, has not been more general even among the party before opposed to Annexation, and has not rallied the national spirit and national pride unanimously upon that policy. We are very sure that if Mr. Clay himself were now to add another letter to his former Texas correspondence, he would express this sentiment, and carry out the idea already strongly stated in one of them, in a manner which would tax all the powers of blushing belonging to some of his party adherents.

It is wholly untrue, and unjust to ourselves, the pretence that the Annexation has been a measure of spoliation, unrightful and unrighteous—of military conquest under forms of peace and law—of territorial aggrandizement at the expense of justice, and justice due by a double sanctity to the weak. This view of the question is wholly unfounded, and has been before so amply refuted in these pages, as well as in a thousand other modes, that we shall not again dwell upon it. The independence of Texas was complete and absolute. It was an independence, not only in fact, but of right. No obligation of duty towards Mexico tended in the least degree to restrain our right to effect the desired recovery of the fair province once our own—whatever motives of policy might have prompted a more deferential consideration of her feelings and her pride, as involved in the question. If Texas became peopled with an American population; it was by no contrivance of our government, but on the express invitation of that of Mexico herself; accompanied with such guaranties of State independence, and the maintenance of a federal system analogous to our own, as constituted a compact fully justifying the strongest measures of redress on the part of those afterwards deceived in this guaranty, and sought to be enslaved under the yoke imposed by its violation. She was released, rightfully and absolutely released, from all Mexican allegiance, or duty of cohesion to the Mexican political body, by the acts and fault of Mexico herself, and Mexico alone. There never was a clearer case. It was not revolution; it was resistance to revolution: and resistance under such circumstances as left independence the necessary resulting state, caused by the abandonment of those with whom her former federal association had existed. What then can be more preposterous than all this clamor by Mexico and the Mexican interest, against Annexation, as a violation of any rights of hers, any duties of ours?

We would not be understood as approving in all its features the expediency or propriety of the mode in which the measure, rightful and wise as it is in itself, has been carried into effect. Its history has been a sad tissue of diplomatic blundering. How much better it might have been managed—how much more smoothly, satisfactorily, and successfully! Instead of our present relations with Mexico—instead of the serious risks which have been run, and those plausibilities of opprobrium which we have had to combat, not without great difficulty, nor with entire success—instead of the difficulties which now throng the path to a satisfactory settlement of all our unsettled questions with Mexico—Texas might, by a more judicious and conciliatory diplomacy, have been as securely in the Union as she is now—her boundaries defined—California probably ours—and Mexico and ourselves united by closer ties than ever; of mutual friendship and mutual support in resistance to the intrusion of European interference in the affairs of the American republics. All this might have been, we little doubt, already secured, had counsels less violent, less rude, less one-sided, less eager in precipitation from motives widely foreign to the national question, presided over the earlier stages of its history. We cannot too deeply regret the mismanagement which has disfigured the history of this question; and especially the neglect of the means which would have been so easy of satisfying even the unreasonable pretensions and the excited pride and passion of Mexico. The singular result has been produced, that while our neighbor has, in truth, no real right to blame or complain—when all the wrong is on her side, and there has been on ours a degree of delay and forbearance, in deference to her pretensions, which is to be paralleled by few precedents in the history of other nations—we have yet laid ourselves open to a great deal of denunciation hard to repel, and impossible to silence; and all history will carry it down as a certain fact, that Mexico would have declared war against us, and would have waged it seriously, if she had not been prevented by that very weakness which should have constituted her best defence.

We plead guilty to a degree of sensitive annoyance—for the sake of the honor of our country, and its estimation in the public opinion of the world—which does not find even in satisfied conscience full consolation for the very necessity of seeking consolation there. And it is for this state of things that we hold responsible that gratuitous mismanagement—wholly apart from the main substantial rights and merits of the question, to which alone it is to be ascribed; and which had its origin in its earlier stages, before the accession of Mr. Calhoun to the department of State.

California probably, next fall away from the loose adhesion which, in such a country as Mexico, holds a remote province in a slight equivocal kind of dependence on the metropolis. Imbecile and distracted, Mexico never can exert any real governmental authority over such a country. The impotence of the one and the distance of the other, must make the relation one of virtual independence; unless, by stunting the province of all natural growth, and forbidding that immigration which can alone develop its capabilities and fulfil the purposes of its creation, tyranny may retain a military dominion, which is no government in the, legitimate sense of the term. In the case of California this is now impossible. The Anglo-Saxon foot is already on its borders. Already the advance guard of the irresistible army of Anglo-Saxon emigration has begun to pour down upon it, armed with the plough and the rifle, and marking its trail with schools and colleges, courts and representative halls, mills and meeting-houses. A population will soon be in actual occupation of California, over which it will be idle for Mexico to dream of dominion. They will necessarily become independent. All this without agency of our government, without responsibility of our people—in the natural flow of events, the spontaneous working of principles, and the adaptation of the tendencies and wants of the human race to the elemental circumstances in the midst of which they find themselves placed. And they will have a right to independence—to self-government—to the possession of the homes conquered from the wilderness by their own labors and dangers, sufferings and sacrifices—a better and a truer right than the artificial tide of sovereignty in Mexico, a thousand miles distant, inheriting from Spain a title good only against those who have none better. Their right to independence will be the natural right of self-government belonging to any community

Did You Know?

Manifest Destiny and Westward Expansionism

The term "Manifest Destiny" emerged in the 1830s–1840s and expressed the belief that Anglo-Saxon Americans were divinely ordained to expand their civilization and institutions across the North American continent and beyond. It justified westward expansionism not just as territorial aggrandizement but as the further spread of liberty and economic opportunity. Native Americans, even those such as the Cherokee Nation that had adopted the English language in order to assimilate and be considered "civilized," were pushed off their land by force or by fraudulent treaties. To justify war with Mexico, one senator argued that liberty required progress and the "almost unlimited power of expansion." By the late nineteenth century, Manifest Destiny fused with Social Darwinism to justify the American expansion beyond the continental boundaries of the United States into the Caribbean and Pacific regions. In 1899, President William McKinley defended control of the Philippines, Cuba, and Puerto Rico as a "great trust" that the United States carried "under the providence of God and in the name of human progress and civilization." Westward expansionism was not without its critics. For example, newspaper editor Horace Greeley opposed war with Mexico, arguing that "only idiots or demons" sought territorial conquest that would ruin their own nation.

strong enough to maintain it—distinct in position, origin and character, and free from any mutual obligations of membership of a common political body, binding it to others by the duty of loyalty and compact of public faith. This will be their title to independence; and by this title, there can be no doubt that the population now fast streaming down upon California will both assert and maintain that independence. Whether they will then attach themselves to our Union or not, is not to be predicted with any certainty. Unless the projected railroad across the continent to the Pacific be carried into effect, perhaps they may not; though even in that case, the day is not distant when the Empires of the Atlantic and Pacific would again flow together into one, as soon as their inland border should approach each other. But that great work, colossal as appears the plan on its first suggestion, cannot remain long unbuilt. Its necessity for this very purpose of binding and holding together in its iron clasp our fast-settling Pacific region with that of the Mississippi valley—the natural facility of the route— the ease with which any amount of labor for the construction can be drawn in from the overcrowded populations of Europe, to be paid in the lands made valuable by the progress of the work itself—and its immense utility to the commerce of the world with the whole eastern Asia, alone almost sufficient for the support of such a road— these host of considerations give assurance that the day cannot be distant which shall witness the conveyance of the representatives from Oregon and California to Washington within less time than a few years ago was devoted to a similar journey by those from Ohio; while the magnetic telegraph will enable the editors of the "San Francisco Union," the "Astoria Evening Post," or the "Nootka Morning News," to set up in type the first half of the President's Inaugural before the echoes of the latter half shall have died away beneath the lofty porch of the Capitol, as spoken from his lips.

Away, then, with all idle French talk of *balances of power* on the American Continent. There is no growth in Spanish America! Whatever progress of population there may be in the British Canadas, is only for their own early severance of their present colonial relation to the little island three thousand miles across the Atlantic; soon to be followed by Annexation, and destined to swell the still accumulating momentum of our progress. And whosoever may hold the balance, though they should cast into the opposite scale all the bayonets and cannon, not only of France and England, but of Europe entire, how would it kick the beam against the simple, solid weight of the two hundred and fifty, or three hundred millions—and American millions—destined to gather beneath the flutter of the stripes and stars, in the fast hastening year of the Lord 1845!

FURTHER READING

Brown, C. H. (1980) *Agents of Manifest Destiny: The Lives and Times of the Filibusters*. Chapel Hill: University of North Carolina Press.

Greenberg, A. (2005) *Manifest Manhood and the Antebellum American Empire*. Cambridge: Cambridge University Press.

Herring, G. (2008) *From Colony to Superpower: U.S. Foreign Relations since 1776*. Oxford: Oxford University Press.

Hietala, T. (1985) *Manifest Destiny: Anxious Aggrandizement in Late Jacksonian America*. Ithaca, NY: Cornell University Press.

Hunt, M. (1987) *Ideology and U.S. Foreign Policy*. New Haven, CT: Yale University Press.

3

WILLIAM McKINLEY
TO
WOODROW WILSON:
BEYOND REGIONALISM AND
ISOLATIONISM

INTRODUCTION

This era starts with President McKinley's policy summarized by the motto "Duty, Dollars, Destiny," which characterized the early American flirtation with traditional imperialism. This period of American foreign policy is full of jingoism, bellicosity, self- assurance, paternalism, and an obviously Eurocentric imperialist ethos. The United States, spurred on by Alfred Mahan's Social Darwinist theory that naval powers can control the world, attempted to build an empire similar to those of Europe, first by going to war in Cuba and the Philippines and then by annexing many island nations in the Pacific, including Hawaii in 1898. It is a time of unstable bank institutions and the yellow press, highlighted by the Randolph Hearst–Joseph Pulitzer rivalry. In 1898, egged on by an unforgiving press demanding that the nation not forget the sinking of the battleship *Maine* in the harbor of Havana, the United States went to war with Spain and won so overwhelmingly that the Spanish would forever remember this war as the "the great catastrophe."

The United States defeated Spain in four months without so much as a major battle in what was titled "a splendid little war," a war that also initiated U.S. involvement in the Philippines, a former Spanish colony now freed by the U.S. forces. As the United States prepared to defeat the Spanish in the Philippines, they promised Filipinos independence, only to break that promise once they had secured the islands. This sparked a long-running guerrilla war undertaken by Filipinos led by Emilio Aguinaldo, ironically the same person sent to the islands to promote American interests. Extending the doctrine of Manifest Destiny and fusing it with the ideas of Social Darwinism, U.S. leaders could not understand why the "little brown people" in the Philippines were putting up so much resistance when the American policymakers' only interest was to civilize them. Rudyard Kipling wrote his famous poem "The White Man's Burden" to extol the imperial design of the United States.

Arguably the most important figure to arise as these events unfolded was Theodore Roosevelt, who became president of the United States in 1901 after an assassin's bullet killed President McKinley in Buffalo, New York. Roosevelt embodied a more bellicose approach to exporting U.S. rule, and became famous for riding up San Juan Hill in Cuba with his "Rough Riders." Under Roosevelt, the United States proceeded to annex Puerto Rico, Wake Island, part of Samoa, and Guam to go along with its previous conquests and complete its dominance of the Pacific Ocean, bringing its reach closer to China and Japan. President Roosevelt is generally considered less interventionist as president than as a member of the

Did You Know?

Yellow Journalism

Yellow journalism is a term describing news media that appear to pander to the public's inexhaustible hunger for the trivial, often aggrandizing minor issues, using scaremongering to attract new readers, using pseudo-scientific misinformation, outright fake reporting, and unabashed self-promotion. The term originated in the United States during the Gilded Age (1865–1901), although examples exist today in many countries, most notably in the United Kingdom with its tabloid press. In the United States, the term was coined specifically for two competing newspapers: William Randolph Hearst's *New York Journal* and Joseph Pulitzer's *New York World*. The color yellow comes from the first comic strip to be included in the papers of the day, the "Yellow Kid." (Comic strips, of course, are now a standard feature in most newspapers.) The foreign policy heyday of yellow journalism occurred during the Spanish-American War, when Hearst's newspaper produced sensational headlines calling for war after the sinking of the battleship *Maine* in Havana's harbor. Hearst himself was involved in sending an artist, Fredric Remington, to Cuba to report on the war of Cuban independence. When Remington telegraphed Hearst that all was quiet and that it looked like no war was about to take place, Hearst famously replied "Please remain. You furnish the pictures, I'll furnish the war" (Knightly 2001). As if that were not bad enough, many people accused yellow journalism in general, but also Pulitzer in particular, of providing the moral impetus for the assassination of President McKinley, who was shot in Buffalo, N.Y., on September 6, 1901, after two separate articles had run in the papers calling for his murder.

McKinley cabinet, but that point is highly debatable considering the end results of the Roosevelt presidency in foreign affairs.

The main reason Roosevelt is considered less bellicose as president is that he was actively involved in mediating the disputes between Russia and Japan and between France and Germany, for which he received the Nobel Peace Prize, one of several American presidents to win this prestigious award. In fact, he was very active on the diplomatic scene internationally, completing 24 bilateral agreements after arbitration (Herring 2008). He agreed to participate in a peace conference, originally called by the Russian czar at The Hague in 1899, and actively mediated the dispute between Germany and France over the colony of Morocco. However, as president Roosevelt basically created the state of Panama, after a revolt in the Colombian territory, so that he could bring the Panama Canal under U.S. control, a control that did not end until the year 2000. Most importantly, his legacy in international relations is in part the famous Roosevelt Corollary, by which the United States asserts its claim over its smaller Central American neighbors whether they liked it or not. Porfirio Diaz, president and strongman of Mexico, witnessing the consequences of Roosevelt's policies, once lamented, "Poor Mexico, so far from God, so close to the United States."

Roosevelt was the first president to create "Banana republics," a term referring to small Central American countries ruled by dictators or small elite cliques, usually kleptocracies, basically by relying on the wealth generated by the agricultural production of bananas. His attempt to control these countries only increased the paternalistic trend in the United States and fully supported "crony capitalism" regarding foreign nations. He used the military as a means of settling disputes, starting interventions in many Central American and Caribbean nations, which continued, on and off, through the twentieth century.

Roosevelt was succeeded by his protégé, William Howard Taft, and dollar diplomacy was continued, resulting in a dynamic known as neoimperialism. The presidency of William Howard Taft unraveled his close relationship with his mentor and friend Roosevelt, and led to a split in the Republican Party, with the majority of Republicans supporting Taft and a large section defecting to a new party formed by Theodore Roosevelt, called the Progressive or Bull Moose Party (a title derived from Roosevelt's claim that he was as strong as a Bull Moose). This quarrel split the Republican Party votes, leading to their defeat by the Democrat Woodrow Wilson, an avowed Christian, former professor and president of Princeton University, and former governor of New Jersey.

Woodrow Wilson became the 28th president of the United States of America at a very turbulent time. Inaugurated in 1912, Wilson spent most of his first term keeping the United States out of World War I. In his first years in office, the Balkan wars broke out. The First Balkan War took place between Serbia, Bulgaria, Greece, and the collapsing Ottoman Empire. The Christian states in the Balkans were attempting to redraw the map of the peninsula at the expense of a slow, corrupt, and collapsing regime in Istanbul. In 1913 the Treaty of London ended the First Balkan War, in which the main change was the division of the territory of ancient Macedonia among three neighboring countries, with the lion's share going to Greece. The Russians were the prime diplomatic state advocating for their Slavic cousins in the Balkans, while the British advocated for the Greeks. Austria-Hungary, the other major empire in the region, was completely opposed to the change in the status quo. Germany switched sides, and instead of backing its ally the Ottoman Turks, it decided to support Bulgarian claims in order to win favor with Bulgaria, which would later be its ally in World War I.

The Second Balkan War was started by the Bulgarians, who were unsatisfied with the territorial gains made during after the First Balkan War and the general settlement of disputes. The Bulgarians attacked their former allies Serbia and Greece in 1913. The Bulgarians did not fare well during this war, and the Serb-Greek coalition pushed far into Bulgarian territory, forcing the Bulgarian government to call for an armistice, during which the Treaty of Bucharest was negotiated. As a result of this treaty, Bulgaria lost the majority of its gains from the First Balkan War. With the region completely destabilized and different nationalities making all sorts of irredentist territorial claims, the Serbs of Bosnia-Herzegovina demanded to be unified with Serbia.

On June 28, 1914, a Serbian nationalist group known as the Black Hand, led by a student named Gavrilo Princip, assassinated the heir to the throne of Austria-Hungary in Sarajevo, with the assistance of the Serbian secret service. The Austrians were predictably upset, but also coldly calculating. They made unacceptable demands on Serbia while aiming to erase Russia's influence in the region, something the Russians naturally were unwilling to accept. On August 1, 1914, the entire European continent was engulfed in World War I, otherwise known as the War to End All Wars.

Having spent his entire first term trying unsuccessfully to mediate among the European powers and keeping the United States out of war, President Wilson won reelection in 1916 by explicitly arguing that he had kept the United States out of the war. However, events eventually occurred that made Wilson's policy of neutrality untenable: the start of unrestricted submarine warfare, which claimed many American cargo ships and lives; the sinking of the passenger ship *Lusitania* off the coast of Ireland; and, finally, an attempt by the Germans to enlist the Mexicans in an attack on the United States, in what is known as the Zimmerman Telegram. These events convinced President Wilson to abandon his neutral stance and enter the war on the side of the forces of the Triple Entente against the forces of the Central Powers. The U.S. Congress declared war on April 4, 1917. World War I ended the following year with a clear victory for the Triple Entente, culminating in the Treaty of Versailles.

President Wilson's claim to fame as a world leader comes at the end of World War I. First, he was involved in negotiating the Treaty of Versailles. And second, he promoted the creation of an international organization known as the League of Nations, an organization that would be dedicated to preventing the resumption of hostilities and promoting the peaceful resolution of disputes between nations. Wilson proposed 14 points by which states would behave internationally, which, if adopted, would severely restrict their ability and need to fight wars. In his presentation to the U.S. Congress (included in the documents of this chapter), he proposed the abolition of secret treaties, freedom of the seas, free trade, disarmament, adjustment of colonial claims, and several adjustments to borders in Europe and around the world that could potentially reignite warfare among European rivals. He proposed the peaceful dissolution of the Ottoman Empire and self-determination for ethnic groups within it, so as to prevent further wars of independence in the Balkans and elsewhere. His proposals for the creation of the League of Nations were included in the first section of the Treaty of Versailles (also included among the documents of this chapter).

Ever since the end of World War I, Wilsonian foreign policy has become synonymous with idealism, and sometimes even with pacifism. But the truth is that apart from the European theater, the United States did not change its behavior regarding its southern sphere of influence, nor did the United States stop meddling in the domestic affairs of other states. During the Wilson administration, the United States intervened in Latin America with greater frequency, invading Mexico, Cuba, Nicaragua, Haiti, and Panama. In the case of Haiti, the United States forces intervened to establish a president that Wilson himself had chosen for the Caribbean country. Wilson also set the early tone of the rivalry between the United States and what would become the Soviet Union when, in 1917, after the Bolshevik Revolution (also known as the October Revolution), he sent troops to fight on the side of the czarist forces and then for the Kerensky government in order to prevent the Bolsheviks from seizing and consolidating power. Over 1,000 troops died fighting the Soviet Communists, and the U.S. forces remained in Russia until 1920.

- **Document: President Theodore Roosevelt's Address to Congress, December 6, 1904: The Roosevelt Corollary**
- **Date:** December 6, 1904
- **Significance:** The Roosevelt Corollary is the culmination of American expansionism in Central America and the Caribbean. It is the start of a long history of interventions and imperial relations between the United States and its southern neighbors.
- **Source:** John T. Woolley and Gerhard Peters, *The American Presidency Project* [online]. Santa Barbara, CA. Available from World Wide Web: http://www.presidency.ucsb.edu/ws/?pid=29545.

In treating of our foreign policy and of the attitude that this great Nation should assume in the world at large, it is absolutely necessary to consider the Army and the Navy, and the Congress, through which the thought of the Nation finds its expression, should keep ever vividly in mind the fundamental fact that it is impossible to treat our foreign policy, whether this policy takes shape in the effort to secure justice for others or justice for ourselves, save as conditioned upon the attitude we are willing to take toward our Army, and especially toward our Navy. It is not merely unwise, it is contemptible, for a nation, as for an individual, to use high-sounding language to proclaim its purposes, or to take positions which are ridiculous if unsupported by potential force, and then to refuse to provide this force. If there is no intention of providing and keeping the force necessary to back up a strong attitude, then it is far better not to assume such an attitude.

The steady aim of this Nation, as of all enlightened nations, should be to strive to bring ever nearer the day when there shall prevail throughout the world the peace of justice. There are kinds of peace which are highly undesirable, which are in the long run as destructive as any war. Tyrants and oppressors have many times made a

President Theodore Roosevelt poses next to a globe, 1903. (Library of Congress)

wilderness and called it peace. Many times peoples who were slothful or timid or shortsighted, who had been enervated by ease or by luxury, or misled by false teachings, have shrunk in unmanly fashion from doing duty that was stern and that needed self-sacrifice, and have sought to hide from their own minds their shortcomings, their ignoble motives, by calling them love of peace. The peace of tyrannous terror, the peace of craven weakness, the peace of injustice, all these should be shunned as we shun unrighteous war. The goal to set before us as a nation, the goal which should be set before all mankind, is the attainment of the peace of justice, of the peace which comes when each nation is not merely safe-guarded in its own rights, but scrupulously recognizes and performs its duty toward others. Generally peace tells for righteousness; but if there is conflict between the two, then our fealty is due first to the cause of righteousness. Unrighteous wars are common, and unrighteous peace is rare; but both should be shunned. The right of freedom and the responsibility for the exercise of that right can not be divorced. One of our great poets has well and finely said that freedom is not a gift that tarries long in the hands of cowards. Neither does it tarry long in the hands of those too slothful, too dishonest, or too unintelligent to exercise it. The eternal vigilance which is the price of liberty must be exercised, sometimes to guard against outside foes; although of course far more often to guard against our own selfish or thoughtless shortcomings.

If these self-evident truths are kept before us, and only if they are so kept before us, we shall have a clear idea of what our foreign policy in its larger aspects should be. It is our duty to remember that a nation has no more right to do injustice to another nation, strong or weak, than an individual has to do injustice to another individual; that the same moral law applies in one case as in the other. But we must also remember that it is as much the duty of the Nation to guard its own rights and its own interests as it is the duty of the individual so to do. Within the Nation the individual has now delegated this right to the State, that is, to the representative of all the individuals, and it is a maxim of the law that for every wrong there is a remedy. But in international law we have not advanced by any means as far as we have advanced in municipal law. There is as yet no judicial way of enforcing a right in international law. When one nation wrongs another or wrongs many others, there is no tribunal before which the wrongdoer can be brought. Either it is necessary supinely to acquiesce in the wrong, and thus put a premium upon brutality and aggression, or else it is necessary for the aggrieved nation valiantly to stand up for its rights. Until some method is devised by which there shall be a degree of international control over offending nations, it would be a wicked thing for the most civilized powers, for those with most sense of international obligations and with keenest and most generous appreciation of the difference between right and wrong, to disarm. If the great civilized nations of the present day should completely disarm, the result would mean an immediate recrudescence of barbarism in one form or another. Under any circumstances a sufficient armament would have to be kept up to serve the purposes of international police; and until international cohesion and the sense of international duties and rights are far more advanced than at present, a nation desirous both of securing respect for itself and of doing good to others must have a force adequate for the work which it feels is allotted to it as its part of the general world duty. Therefore it follows that a self-respecting, just, and far-seeing nation should on the one hand endeavor by every means to aid in the development of the various movements which tend to provide substitutes for war, which tend to render nations in their actions toward one another, and indeed toward their own peoples, more responsive to the general sentiment of humane and civilized mankind; and on the other hand that it should keep prepared, while scrupulously avoiding wrongdoing itself, to repel any wrong, and in exceptional cases to take action which in a more advanced stage of international relations would come under the head of the exercise of the international police. A great free people owes it to itself and to all mankind not to sink into helplessness before the powers of evil.

We are in every way endeavoring to help on, with cordial good will, every movement which will tend to bring us into more friendly relations with the rest of mankind. In pursuance of this policy I shall shortly lay before the Senate treaties of arbitration with all powers which are willing to enter into these treaties with us. It is not possible at this period of the world's development to agree to arbitrate all matters, but there are many matters of possible difference between us and other nations which can be thus arbitrated. Furthermore, at the request of the Interparliamentary Union, an eminent body composed of practical statesmen from all countries, I have asked the Powers to join with this Government in a second Hague conference, at which it is hoped that the work already so happily begun at The Hague may be carried some steps further toward completion. This carries out the desire expressed by the first Hague conference itself.

It is not true that the United States feels any land hunger or entertains any projects as regards the other nations of the Western Hemisphere save such as are for their welfare. All that this country desires is to see the neighboring countries stable, orderly, and prosperous. Any country whose people conduct themselves well can count upon our hearty friendship. If a nation shows that it knows how to act with reasonable efficiency and decency in social and political matters, if it keeps order and pays its obligations, it need fear no interference from the United States. Chronic wrongdoing, or an impotence which results in a general loosening of the ties of civilized society, may in America, as elsewhere, ultimately require intervention by some civilized nation, and in the Western Hemisphere the adherence of the United States to the Monroe Doctrine may force the United States, however reluctantly, in flagrant cases of such wrongdoing or impotence, to the exercise of an international police power. If every country washed by the Caribbean Sea would show the progress in stable and just civilization which with the aid of the Platt Amendment Cuba has shown since our troops left the island, and which so many of the republics in both Americas are constantly and brilliantly showing, all question of interference by this Nation with their affairs would be at an end. Our interests and those of our southern neighbors are in reality identical. They have great natural riches, and if within their borders the reign of law and justice obtains, prosperity is sure to come to them. While they thus obey the primary laws of civilized society they may rest assured that they will be treated by us in a spirit of cordial and helpful sympathy. We would interfere with them only in the last resort, and then only if it became evident that their inability or unwillingness to do justice at home and abroad had violated the rights of the United States or had invited foreign aggression to the detriment of the entire body of American nations. It is a mere truism to say that every nation, whether in America or anywhere else, which desires to maintain its freedom, its independence, must ultimately realize that the right of such independence can not be separated from the responsibility of making good use of it.

In asserting the Monroe Doctrine, in taking such steps as we have taken in regard to Cuba, Venezuela, and Panama, and in endeavoring to circumscribe the theater of war in the Far East, and to secure the open door in China, we have acted in our own interest as well as in the interest of humanity at large. There are, however, cases in which, while our own interests are not greatly involved, strong appeal is made to our sympathies. Ordinarily it is very much wiser and more useful for us to concern ourselves with striving for our own moral and material betterment here at home than to concern ourselves with trying to better the condition of things in other nations. We have plenty of sins of our own to war against, and under ordinary circumstances we can do more for the general uplifting of humanity by striving with heart and soul to put a stop to civic corruption, to brutal lawlessness and violent race prejudices here at home than by passing resolutions and wrongdoing elsewhere. Nevertheless there are occasional crimes committed on so vast a scale and of such peculiar horror as to make us doubt whether it is not our manifest duty to endeavor at least to show our disapproval of the deed and our sympathy with those who have suffered by it. The cases must be extreme in which such a course is justifiable. There must be no effort made to remove the mote from our brother's eye if we refuse to remove the beam from our own. But in extreme cases action may be justifiable and proper. What form the action shall take must depend upon the circumstances of the case; that is, upon the degree of the atrocity and upon our power to remedy it. The cases in which we could interfere by force of arms as we interfered to put a stop to intolerable conditions in Cuba are necessarily very few. Yet it is not to be expected that a people like ours, which in spite of certain very obvious shortcomings, nevertheless as a whole shows by its consistent practice its belief in the principles of civil and religious liberty and of orderly freedom, a people among whom even the worst crime, like the crime of lynching, is never more than sporadic, so that individuals and not classes are molested in their fundamental rights—it is inevitable that such a nation should desire eagerly to give expression to its horror on an occasion like that of the massacre of the Jews in Kishenef, or when it witnesses such systematic and long-extended cruelty and oppression as the cruelty and oppression of which the Armenians have been the victims, and which have won for them the indignant pity of the civilized world.

Did You Know?

The Roosevelt Corollary

In 1904 the Dominican Republic was bankrupt, and President Teddy Roosevelt worried that countries such as Germany would intervene to collect their debts. Roosevelt issued his "corollary" when in 1904 he told Congress that "Chronic wrongdoing . . . may in America, as elsewhere, ultimately require intervention by some civilized nation, and in the Western Hemisphere the adherence of the United States to the Monroe Doctrine may force the United States, however reluctantly, in flagrant cases of such wrongdoing or impotence, to the exercise of an international police power." With that, the United States intervened in the Dominican Republic and took over its customs collections to pay its foreign debts. The Roosevelt Corollary was also used to justify U.S. intervention in Cuba, Nicaragua, Mexico, and Haiti.

- **Document: President Theodore Roosevelt's Nobel Peace Prize Acceptance Speech**
- **Date:** December 10, 1906
- **Significance:** This Nobel Peace Prize was awarded because of Roosevelt's involvement in bringing about the end to the Russo-Japanese War, but it was controversial because the Nobel Prize was awarded to a president with a direct involvement in the suppression of the Philippine insurrection, which some claim included the crime of genocide.
- **Source:** The Nobel Peace Prize, 1906. Theodore Roosevelt. Acceptance Speech. Available at http://nobelprize.org/nobel_prizes/peace/laureates/1906/roosevelt-acceptance.html. © The Nobel Foundation 1906.

Acceptance by Herbert H. D. Peirce, American Envoy.

Since President Roosevelt was not present at the award ceremony on December 10, 1906, Mr. Herbert H. D. Peirce read the president's telegram.

I deeply regret that my residence in your capital has been as yet too brief to enable me to address you in your own vigorous language. But "had I a thousand several tongues", they would be inadequate to express to you the deep emotion with which I appear before you to receive, on behalf of the President of the United States, this distinguished testimonial of your recognition of those acts which stamp him as pre-eminent in devotion to the cause of peace and goodwill on earth.

I will not vainly attempt, by any words of mine, to add to the lustre of the name of Theodore Roosevelt. His acts proclaim him, and you, Gentlemen of the Norwegian Storting, by this award of the Nobel Peace Prize, a foundation conceived in God-like love of mankind, have blazoned to the world your recognition of his wise use of his great office in the best interests of humanity.

I quote President Roosevelt's words in a telegram from him, recently received by me, when I say that he regards the award of this prize as one of the greatest honors which any man, in any position, throughout the world, can receive.

Speaking for my countrymen, I may say that this award will deeply appeal to the hearts of our people and knit closer those bonds of sympathy which unite us in the brotherhood of nations.

To me, who have enjoyed the inestimable privilege of witnessing in the course of current affairs the earnest desire with which the chief magistrate of my country is imbued to promote the cause of peace, in the interest of all mankind, when peace comports with that honorable self-respect which nations as well as individuals owe to themselves, this award seems most markedly felicitous, and I rejoice greatly in the good fortune which permits me to be the medium of transmission of this token of your appreciation of the profound love for, and lofty sense of duty to his fellowmen which is the guiding principle of his official life.

The President has directed me to read to you, Mr. President, the following message which he has telegraphed to me for that purpose:

"I am profoundly moved and touched by the signal honor shown me through your body in conferring upon me the Nobel Peace Prize. There is no gift I could appreciate more and I wish it were in my power fully to express my gratitude. I thank you for it, and I thank you on behalf of the United States; for what I did, I was able to accomplish only as the representative of the nation of which, for the time being, I am president. After much thought, I have concluded that the best and most fitting way to apply the amount of the prize is by using it as a foundation to establish at Washington a permanent industrial peace committee. The object will be to strive for better and more equitable relations among my countrymen who are engaged, whether as capitalists or as wage workers, in industrial and agricultural pursuits. This will carry out the purpose of the founder of the prize, for in modern life it is as important to work for the cause of just and righteous peace in the industrial world as in the world of nations.

I again express to you the assurance of my deep and lasting gratitude and appreciation.

Theodore Roosevelt"

- **Document: Hay–Bunau-Varilla Treaty**
- **Date:** November 18, 1903
- **Significance:** The treaty of Hay and Bunau-Varilla is another example of American imperialism in regard to Latin America. Two weeks after Panama gained independence from Colombia, this treaty secured the rights of building the canal in Panama, giving the United States absolute authority over it.
- **Source:** *American Historical Documents, 1000–1904.* Volume XLIII. The Harvard Classics. New York: P. F. Collier & Son, 1909–1914.

CONVENTION FOR THE CONSTRUCTION OF A SHIP CANAL

The President of the United States of America, John Hay, Secretary of State, and the Government of the Republic of Panama, Philippe Bunau-Varilla, Envoy Extraordinary and Minister Plenipotentiary of the Republic of Panama, thereunto specially empowered by said government, who after communicating with each other their respective full powers, found to be in good and due form, have agreed upon and concluded the following articles:

ARTICLE I

The United States guarantees and will maintain the independence of the Republic of Panama.

ARTICLE II

The Republic of Panama grants to the United States in perpetuity the use, occupation and control of a zone of land and land under water for the construction maintenance, operation, sanitation and protection of said Canal of the width of ten miles extending to the distance of five miles on each side of the center line of the route of the Canal to be constructed; the said zone beginning in the Caribbean Sea three marine miles from mean low water mark and extending to and across the Isthmus of Panama into the Pacific ocean to a distance of three marine miles from mean low water mark with the proviso that the cities of Panama and Colon and the harbors adjacent to said cities, which are included within the boundaries of the zone above described, shall not be included within this grant. The Republic of Panama further grants to the United States in perpetuity the use, occupation and control of any other lands and waters outside of the zone above described which may be necessary and convenient for the construction, maintenance, operation, sanitation and protection of the said Canal or of any auxiliary canals or other works necessary and convenient for the construction, maintenance, operation, sanitation and protection of the said enterprise.

The Republic of Panama further grants in like manner to the United States in perpetuity all islands within the limits of the zone above described and in addition thereto the group of small islands in the Bay of Panama, named, Perico, Naos, Culebra and Flamenco.

After 10 years of construction, the Panama Canal opens on August 15, 1914. The 40-mile canal created a shortcut that lessened the voyage between the east and west coasts of North America by 7,000 miles. (U.S. Army Corps of Engineers)

ARTICLE III

The Republic of Panama grants to the United States all the rights, power and authority within the zone mentioned and described in Article II of this agreement and within the limits of all auxiliary lands and waters mentioned and described in said Article II which the United States would possess and exercise if it were the sovereign of the territory within which said lands and waters are located to the entire exclusion of the exercise by the Republic of Panama of any such sovereign rights, power or authority.

ARTICLE IV

As rights subsidiary to the above grants the Republic of Panama grants in perpetuity to the United States the right to use the rivers, streams, lakes and other bodies of water within its limits for navigation, the supply of water or water-power or other purposes, so far as the use of said rivers, streams, lakes and bodies of water and the waters thereof may be necessary and convenient for the construction, maintenance, operation, sanitation and protection of the said Canal.

ARTICLE V

The Republic of Panama grants to the United States in perpetuity a monopoly for the construction, maintenance and operation of any system of communication by means of canal or railroad across its territory between the Caribbean Sea and the Pacific ocean.

ARTICLE VI

The grants herein contained shall in no manner invalidate the titles or rights of private land holders or owners of private property in the said zone or in or to any of the lands or waters granted to the United States by the provisions of any Article of this treaty, nor shall they interfere with the rights of way over the public roads passing through the said zone or over any of the said lands or waters unless said rights of way or private rights shall conflict with rights herein granted to the United States in which case, the rights of the United States shall be superior. All damages caused to the owners of private lands or private property of any kind by reason of the grants contained in this treaty or by reason of the operations of the United States, its agents or employees, or by reason of the construction, maintenance, operation, sanitation and protection of the said Canal or of the works of sanitation and protection herein provided for, shall be appraised and settled by a joint Commission appointed by the Governments of the United States and the Republic of Panama, whose decisions as to such damages shall be final and whose awards as to such damages shall be paid solely by the United States. No part of the work on said Canal or the Panama railroad or on any auxiliary works relating thereto and authorized by the terms of this treaty shall be prevented, delayed or impeded by or pending such proceedings to ascertain such damages. The appraisal of said private lands and private property and the assessment of damages to them shall be based upon their value before the date of this convention.

ARTICLE VII

The Republic of Panama grants to the United States within the limits of the cities of Panama and Colon and their adjacent harbors and within the territory adjacent thereto the right to acquire by purchase or by the exercise of the right of eminent domain, any lands, buildings, water rights or other properties necessary and convenient for the construction, maintenance, operation and protection of the Canal and of any works of sanitation, such as the collection and disposition of sewage and the distribution of water in the said cities of Panama and Colon, which in the discretion of the United States may be necessary and convenient for the construction, maintenance, operation, sanitation and protection of the said Canal and railroad. All such works of sanitation, collection and disposition of sewage and distribution of water in the cities of Panama and Colon shall be made at the expense of the United States, and the Government of the United States, its agents or nominees shall be authorized to impose and collect water rates and sewerage rates which shall be sufficient to provide for the payment of interest and the amortization of the principal of the cost of said works within a period of fifty years and upon the expiration of said term of fifty years the system of sewers and water works shall revert to and become the properties of the cities of Panama and Colon respectively, and the use of the water shall be free to the inhabitants of Panama and Colon, except to the extent that water rates may be necessary for the operation and maintenance of said system of sewers and water.

The Republic of Panama agrees that the cities of Panama and Colon shall comply in perpetuity with the sanitary ordinances whether of a preventive or curative character prescribed by the United States and in case the Government of Panama is unable or fails in its duty to enforce this compliance by the cities of Panama and Colon with the sanitary ordinances of the United States the Republic of Panama grants to the United States the right and authority to enforce the same.

The same right and authority are granted to the United States for the maintenance of public order in the cities of Panama and Colon and the territories and harbors adjacent thereto in case the Republic of Panama should not be, in the judgment of the United States, able to maintain such order.

ARTICLE VIII

The Republic of Panama grants to the United States all rights which it now has or hereafter may acquire to be property of the New Panama Canal Company and the Panama Railroad Company as a result of the transfer of sovereignty from the Republic of Colombia to the Republic of Panama over the Isthmus of Panama and authorizes the New Panama Canal Company to sell and transfer to the United States its rights, privileges, properties and concessions as well as the Panama Railroad and all the shares or part of the shares of that company; but the public lands situated outside of the zone described in Article II of this treaty now included in the concessions to both said enterprises and not required in the construction or operation of the Canal shall revert to the Republic of Panama except any property now owned by or in the possession of said companies within Panama or Colon or the ports or terminals thereof.

ARTICLE IX

The United States agrees that the ports at either entrance of the Canal and the waters thereof, and the Republic of Panama agrees that the towns of Panama and Colon shall be free for all time so that there shall not be imposed or collected custom house tolls, tonnage, anchorage, lighthouse, wharf, pilot, or quarantine dues or any other charges or taxes of any kind upon any vessel using or passing through the Canal or belonging to or employed by the United States, directly or indirectly, in connection with the construction, maintenance, operation, sanitation and protection of the main Canal, or auxiliary works, or upon the cargo, officers, crew, or passengers of any such vessels, except such tolls and charges as may be imposed by the United States for the use of the Canal and other works, and except tolls and charges imposed by the Republic of Panama upon merchandise destined to be introduced for the consumption of the rest of the Republic of Panama, and upon vessels touching at the ports of Colon and Panama and which do not cross the Canal.

The Government of the Republic of Panama shall have the right to establish in such ports and in the towns of Panama and Colon such houses and guards as it may deem necessary to collect duties on importations destined to other portions of Panama and to prevent contraband trade. The United States shall have the right to make use of the towns and harbors of Panama and Colon as places of anchorage, and for making repairs, for loading, unloading, depositing, or transshipping cargoes either in transit or destined for the service of the Canal and for other works pertaining to the Canal.

ARTICLE X

The Republic of Panama agrees that there shall not be imposed any taxes, national, municipal, departmental, or of any other class, upon the Canal, the railways and auxiliary works, tugs and other vessels employed in the service of the Canal, store houses, work shops, offices, quarters for laborers, factories of all kinds, warehouses, wharves, machinery and other works, property, and effects appertaining to the Canal or railroad and auxiliary works, or their officers or employees, situated within the cities of Panama and Colon, and that there shall not be imposed contributions or charges of a personal character of any kind upon officers, employees, laborers, and other individuals in the service of the Canal and railroad and auxiliary works.

ARTICLE XI

The United States agrees that the official dispatches of the Government of the Republic of Panama shall be transmitted over any telegraph and telephone lines established for canal purposes and used for public and private business at rates not higher than those required from officials in the service of the United States.

ARTICLE XII

The Government of the Republic of Panama shall permit the immigration and free access to the lands and workshops of the Canal and its auxiliary works of all employees and workmen of Whatever nationality under contract to work upon or seeking employment upon or in any wise connected with the said Canal and its auxiliary works, with their respective families, and all such persons shall be free and exempt from the military service of the Republic of Panama.

ARTICLE XIII

The United States may import at any time into the said zone and auxiliary lands, free of custom duties, imposts, taxes, or other charges, and without any restrictions, any and all vessels, dredges, engines, cars, machinery, tools, explosives, materials, supplies, and other articles necessary and convenient in the construction, maintenance, operation, sanitation and protection of the Canal and auxiliary works, and all provisions, medicines, clothing, supplies and other things necessary and convenient for the officers, employees, workmen and laborers in the service and employ of the United States and for their families. If any such articles are disposed of for use outside of the zone and auxiliary lands granted to the United States and within the territory of the Republic, they shall be subject to the same import or other duties as like articles imported under the laws of the Republic of Panama.

ARTICLE XIV

As the price or compensation for the rights, powers and privileges granted in this convention by the Republic of Panama to the United States, the Government of the United States agrees to pay to the Republic of Panama the sum of ten million dollars ($10,000,000) in gold coin of the United States on the exchange of the ratification of this convention and also an annual payment during the life of this convention of two hundred and fifty thousand dollars ($250,000) in like gold coin, beginning nine years after the date aforesaid.

The provisions of this Article shall be in addition to all other benefits assured to the Republic of Panama under this convention.

But no delay or difference opinion under this Article or any other provisions of this treaty shall affect or interrupt the full operation and effect of this convention in all other respects.

ARTICLE XV

The joint commission referred to in Article VI shall be established as follows:

Did You Know?

Social Darwinism

Social Darwinism is the application of Charles Darwin's theory of evolution and natural selection to social and economic life. English philosopher Herbert Spencer was the first to argue that society operated as a "jungle" in which the "survival of the fittest" was the law, meaning the strongest survive while the weak and feeble are weeded out. Social Darwinism rejects any attempts to intervene in this "natural" process, and sees any attempt to protect the weak and the poor or restrain the powerful as ineffective and counterproductive. Critics argued that Social Darwinism advocated a "dog-eat-dog" world. In the United States, Social Darwinism became popular in the 1870s–1880s and was promoted by prominent men such as Andrew Carnegie and William Graham Sumner, each of whom used it to defend the status quo, promote the unrestrained competition of free market capitalism, and oppose social legislation for the poor. In the 1890s, naval strategist Alfred Thayer Mahan used Social Darwinism to justify overseas expansion and imperialism by the United States, updating the notion of Manifest Destiny, which saw "inferior" nations giving way to superior nations such as the United States. Extreme forms of Social Darwinism lent support to the eugenics movement in the early twentieth century, which defined intelligence and strength in genetic terms, positing Anglo-Saxons as the top of a racial hierarchy. Social Darwinism lost popularity after 1914, first because anthropologists such as Franz Boas rejected purely genetic and biological understandings of intelligence and second because it was blamed for German militarism and the emergence of Nazism. Nevertheless, the underlying ideas of Social Darwinism remain influential because they reinforce the American ideals of "rugged individualism" and laissez-faire capitalism.

The President of the United States shall nominate two persons and the President of the Republic of Panama shall nominate two persons and they shall proceed to a decision; but in case of disagreement of the Commission (by reason of their being equally divided in conclusion) an umpire shall be appointed by the two Governments who shall render the decision. In the event of the death, absence, or incapacity of a Commissioner or Umpire, or of his omitting, declining or ceasing to act, his place shall be filled by the appointment of another person in the manner above indicated. All decisions by a majority of the Commission or by the Umpire shall be final.

ARTICLE XVI

The two Governments shall make adequate provision by future agreement for the pursuit, capture, imprisonment, detention and delivery within said zone and auxiliary lands to the authorities of the Republic of Panama of persons charged with the commitment of crimes, felonies or misdemeanors without said zone and for the pursuit, capture, imprisonment, detention and delivery without said zone to the authorities of the United States of persons charged with the commitment of crimes, felonies and misdemeanors within said zone and auxiliary lands.

ARTICLE XVII

The Republic of Panama grants to the United States the use of all the ports of the Republic open to commerce as places of refuge for any vessels employed in the Canal enterprise, and for all vessels passing or bound to pass through the Canal which may be in distress and be driven to seek refuge in said ports. Such vessels shall be exempt from anchorage and tonnage dues on the part of the Republic of Panama.

. . .

Done at the City of Washington the 18th day of November in the year of our Lord nineteen hundred and three.

- **Document: President Wilson's Address to the U.S. Congress** (Wilson's Fourteen Points)
- **Date:** January 8, 1918
- **Significance:** The culmination of Wilsonian thinking about a new world order in the aftermath of World War I, this speech is the articulation of Wilson's Fourteen Points to the U.S. Congress.
- **Source:** President Wilson's Message to Congress, January 8, 1918; Records of the United States Senate: Record Group 4. Records of the United States Senate, National Archives.

PRESIDENT WILSON'S ADDRESS TO CONGRESS (DELIVERED IN JOINT SESSION)

Gentlemen of the Congress:

Once more, as repeatedly before, the spokesmen of the Central Empires have indicated their desire to discuss the objects of the war and the possible basis of a general peace. Parleys have been in progress at Brest-Litovsk between Russian representatives and representatives of the Central Powers to which the attention of all the belligerents have been invited for the purpose of ascertaining whether it may be possible to extend these parleys into a general conference with regard to terms of peace and settlement.

The Russian representatives presented not only a perfectly definite statement of the principles upon which they would be willing to conclude peace but also an equally definite program of the concrete application of those principles. The representatives of the Central Powers, on their part, presented an outline of settlement which, if much less definite, seemed susceptible of liberal interpretation until their specific program of practical terms was added. That program proposed no concessions at all either to the sovereignty of Russia or to the preferences of the populations with whose fortunes it dealt, but meant, in a word, that the Central Empires were to keep every foot of territory their armed forces had occupied—every province, every city, every point of vantage—as a permanent addition to their territories and their power.

It is a reasonable conjecture that the general principles of settlement which they at first suggested originated with the more liberal statesmen of Germany and Austria, the men who have begun to feel the force of their own people's thought and purpose, while the concrete terms of actual settlement came from the military leaders who have no thought but to keep what they have got. The negotiations have been broken off. The Russian representatives were sincere and in earnest. They cannot entertain such proposals of conquest and domination.

The whole incident is full of significances. It is also full of perplexity. With whom are the Russian representatives dealing? For whom are the representatives of the Central Empires speaking? Are they speaking for the majorities of their respective parliaments or for the minority parties, that military and imperialistic minority which has so far dominated their whole policy and controlled the affairs of Turkey and of the Balkan states which have felt obliged to become their associates in this war?

The Russian representatives have insisted, very justly, very wisely, and in the true spirit of modern democracy, that the conferences they have been holding with the Teutonic and Turkish statesmen should be held within open, not closed, doors, and all the world has been audience, as was desired. To whom have we been listening, then? To those who speak the spirit and intention of the resolutions of the German Reichstag of the 9th of July last, the spirit and intention of the Liberal leaders and parties of Germany, or to those who resist and defy that spirit and intention and insist upon conquest and subjugation? Or are we listening, in fact, to both, unreconciled and in open and hopeless contradiction? These are very serious and pregnant questions. Upon the answer to them depends the peace of the world.

But, whatever the results of the parleys at Brest-Litovsk, whatever the confusions of counsel and of purpose in the utterances of the spokesmen of the Central Empires, they have again attempted to acquaint the world with their objects in the war and have again challenged their adversaries to say what their objects are and what sort of settlement they would deem just and satisfactory. There is no good reason why that challenge should not be responded to, and responded to with the utmost candor. We did not wait for it. Not once, but again and again, we have laid our whole thought and purpose before the world, not in general terms only, but each time with sufficient definition to make it clear what sort of definite terms of settlement must necessarily spring out of them. Within the last week Mr. Lloyd George has spoken with admirable candor and in admirable spirit for the people and Government of Great Britain.

There is no confusion of counsel among the adversaries of the Central Powers, no uncertainty of principle, no vagueness of detail. The only secrecy of counsel, the only lack of fearless frankness, the only failure to make definite statement of the objects of the war, lies with Germany and her allies. The issues of life and death hang upon these definitions. No statesman who has the least conception of his responsibility ought for a moment to permit himself to continue this tragical and appalling outpouring of blood and treasure unless he is sure beyond a peradventure that the objects of the vital sacrifice are part and parcel of the very life of Society and that the people for whom he speaks think them right and imperative as he does.

There is, moreover, a voice calling for these definitions of principle and of purpose which is, it seems to me, more thrilling and more compelling than any of the many moving voices with which the troubled air of the world is filled. It is the voice of the Russian people. They are prostrate and all but hopeless, it would seem, before the grim power of Germany, which has hitherto known no relenting and no pity. Their power, apparently, is shattered. And yet their soul is not subservient. They will not yield either in principle or in action. Their conception of what is right, of what is humane and honorable for them to accept, has been stated with a frankness, a largeness of view, a generosity of spirit, and a universal human sympathy which must challenge the admiration of every friend of mankind; and they have refused to compound their ideals or desert others that they themselves may be safe.

They call to us to say what it is that we desire, in what, if in anything, our purpose and our spirit differ from theirs; and I believe that the people of the United States would wish me to respond, with utter simplicity and frankness. Whether their present leaders believe it or not, it is our heartfelt desire and hope that some way may be opened whereby we may be privileged to assist the people of Russia to attain their utmost hope of liberty and ordered peace.

It will be our wish and purpose that the processes of peace, when they are begun, shall be absolutely open and that they shall involve and permit henceforth no secret understandings of any kind. The day of conquest and aggrandizement is gone by; so is also the day of secret covenants entered into in the interest of particular governments and likely at some unlooked-for moment to upset the peace of the world. It is this happy fact, now clear to the view of every public man whose thoughts do not still linger in an age that is dead and gone, which makes it possible for every nation whose purposes are consistent with justice and the peace of the world to avow nor or at any other time the objects it has in view.

We entered this war because violations of right had occurred which touched us to the quick and made the life of our own people impossible unless they were corrected and the world secure once for all against their recurrence. What we demand in this war, therefore, is nothing peculiar to ourselves. It is that the world be made fit and safe to live in; and particularly that it be made safe for every peace-loving nation which, like our own, wishes to live its own life, determine its own institutions, be assured of justice and fair dealing by the other peoples of the world as against force and selfish aggression. All the peoples of the world are in effect partners in this interest, and for our own part we see very clearly that unless justice be done to others it will not be done to us. The program of the world's peace, therefore, is our program; and that program, the only possible program, as we see it, is this:

I. Open covenants of peace, openly arrived at, after which there shall be no private international understandings of any kind but diplomacy shall proceed always frankly and in the public view.

II. Absolute freedom of navigation upon the seas, outside territorial waters, alike in peace and in war, except as the seas may be closed in whole or in part by international action for the enforcement of international covenants.

III. The removal, so far as possible, of all economic barriers and the establishment of an equality of trade conditions among all the nations consenting to the peace and associating themselves for its maintenance.

IV. Adequate guarantees given and taken that national armaments will be reduced to the lowest point consistent with domestic safety.

V. A free, open-minded, and absolutely impartial adjustment of all colonial claims, based upon a strict observance of the principle that in determining all such questions of sovereignty the interests of the populations concerned must have equal weight with the equitable claims of the government whose title is to be determined.

VI. The evacuation of all Russian territory and such a settlement of all questions affecting Russia as will secure the best and freest cooperation of the other nations of the world in obtaining for her an unhampered and unembarrassed opportunity for the independent determination of her own political development and national policy and assure her of a sincere welcome into the society of free nations under institutions of her own choosing; and, more than a welcome, assistance also of every kind that she may need and may herself desire. The treatment accorded Russia by her sister nations in the months to come will be the acid test of their good will, of their comprehension of her needs as distinguished from their own interests, and of their intelligent and unselfish sympathy.

VII. Belgium, the whole world will agree, must be evacuated and restored, without any attempt to limit the sovereignty which she enjoys in common with all other free nations. No other single act will serve as this will serve to restore confidence among the nations in the laws which they have themselves set and determined for the government of their relations with one another. Without this healing act the whole structure and validity of international law is forever impaired.

VIII. All French territory should be freed and the invaded portions restored, and the wrong done to France by Prussia in 1871 in the matter of Alsace-Lorraine, which has unsettled the peace of the world for nearly fifty years, should be righted, in order that peace may once more be made secure in the interest of all.

IX. A readjustment of the frontiers of Italy should be effected along clearly recognizable lines of nationality.

X. The peoples of Austria-Hungary, whose place among the nations we wish to see safeguarded and assured, should be accorded the freest opportunity to autonomous development.

XI. Rumania, Serbia, and Montenegro should be evacuated; occupied territories restored; Serbia accorded free and secure access to the sea; and the relations of the several Balkan states to one another determined by friendly counsel along historically established lines of allegiance and nationality; and international guarantees of the political and economic independence and territorial integrity of the several Balkan states should be entered into.

XII. The Turkish portion of the present Ottoman Empire should be assured a secure sovereignty, but the other nationalities which are now under Turkish rule should be assured an undoubted security of life and an absolutely unmolested opportunity of autonomous development, and the Dardanelles should be permanently opened as a free passage to the ships and commerce of all nations under international guarantees.

XIII. An independent Polish state should be erected which should include the territories inhabited by indisputably Polish populations, which should be assured a free and secure access to the sea, and whose political and economic independence and territorial integrity should be guaranteed by international covenant.

XIV. A general association of nations must be formed under specific covenants for the purpose of affording mutual guarantees of political independence and territorial integrity to great and small states alike.

In regard to these essential rectifications of wrong and assertions of right we feel ourselves to be intimate partners of all the governments and peoples associated together against the Imperialists. We cannot be separated in interest or divided in purpose. We stand together until the end. For such arrangements and covenants we are willing to fight and to continue to fight until they are achieved; but only because we wish the right to prevail and desire a just and stable peace such as can be secured only by removing the chief provocations to war, which this program does remove. We have no jealousy of German greatness, and there is nothing in this program that impairs it. We grudge her no achievement or distinction of learning or of pacific enterprise such as have made her record very bright and very enviable. We do not wish to injure her or to block in any way her legitimate influence or power. We do not wish to fight her either with arms or with hostile arrangements of trade if she is willing to associate herself with us and the other peace-loving nations of the world in covenants of justice and law and fair dealing. We wish her only to accept a place of equality among the peoples of the world,—the new world in which we now live, —instead of a place of mastery.

Neither do we presume to suggest to her any alteration or modification of her institutions. But it is necessary, we must frankly say, and necessary as a preliminary to any intelligent dealings with her on our part, that we should know whom her spokesmen speak for when they speak to us, whether for the Reichstag majority or for the military party and the men whose creed is imperial domination.

We have spoken now, surely, in terms too concrete to admit of any further doubt or question. An evident principle runs through the whole program I have outlined. It is the principle of justice to all peoples and nationalities, and their right to live on equal terms of liberty and safety with one another, whether they be strong or weak.

Unless this principle be made its foundation no part of the structure of international justice can stand. The people of the United States could act upon no other principle; and to the vindication of this principle they are ready to devote their lives, their honor, and everything they possess. The moral climax of this the culminating and final war for human liberty has come, and they are ready to put their own strength, their own highest purpose, their own integrity and devotion to the test.

- **Document:** Treaty of Versailles
- **Date:** June 28, 1919
- **Significance:** This treaty is culmination of the Paris Peace conference and the official end to World War I. It is also the basis of the German objections that would bring instability to Germany and eventually lead to World War II.
- **Source:** The Versailles Treaty June 28, 1919. The Avalon Project, http://avalon.law.yale.edu/subject_menus/versailles_menu.asp.

Did You Know?

Wilson and the Zimmerman Telegram

When a German submarine sank the British ship the *Lusitania* in 1915, killing more than 1,000 people, including 128 Americans, President Wilson condemned the attack but elected not to enter World War I. Indeed, campaigning for reelection in 1916, Wilson's slogan was, "He Kept Us Out of War." Even when Germany declared a policy of unrestricted submarine warfare in January 1917, Wilson severed diplomatic ties with Germany but still did not declare war. But the United States soon found out about a secret message, the "Zimmerman telegram," in which the German government proposed an alliance with Mexico and discussed the possibility of Mexico regaining territory it had lost to the United States in the Mexican-American War. Germany's submarine warfare and its overtures to Mexico in direct violation of the Monroe Doctrine finally led the United States to declare war on Germany, on April 6, 1917. To build support for the war, Wilson undertook a public information campaign that successfully steered anger at German aggression away from neutrality and isolationism toward engagement. Despite the isolationist sentiment that the war in Europe was a distant conflict that reflected tangled European rivalries, Wilson helped pass the Selective Service Act in May 1917, which gradually increased the size of the U.S. armed forces from 200,000 to almost four million by the end of the war.

TREATY OF PEACE BETWEEN THE ALLIED AND ASSOCIATED POWERS AND GERMANY

THE UNITED STATES OF AMERICA, THE BRITISH EMPIRE, FRANCE, ITALY AND JAPAN, these Powers being described in the present Treaty as the Principal Allied and Associated Powers,

BELGIUM, BOLIVIA, BRAZIL, CHINA, CUBA, ECUADOR, GREECE, GUATEMALA, HAITI, THE HEDJAZ, HONDURAS, LIBERIA, NICARAGUA, PANAMA, PERU, POLAND, PORTUGAL, ROUMANIA, THE SERB-CROAT-SLOVENE STATE, SIAM, CZECHOSLOVAKIA AND URUGUAY, these Powers constituting with the Principal Powers mentioned above the Allied and Associated Powers, of the one part;

And GERMANY of the other part;

BEARING IN MIND that on the request of the Imperial German Government an armistice was granted on 11 November 1918 to Germany by the Principal Allied and Associated Powers in order that a Treaty of Peace might be concluded with her, and

THE ALLIED AND ASSOCIATED POWERS being equally desirous that the war in which they were successively involved directly or indirectly and which originated in the declaration of war by Austria-Hungary on 28 July 1914 against Serbia, the declaration of war by Germany against Russia on 1 August 1914, and against France on 3 August 1914, and in the invasion of Belgium, should be replaced by a firm and durable peace,

. . .

Acting in the name of the German Empire and of each and every component State,

Who having communicated their full powers found in good and due form have agreed as follows: From the coming into force of the present Treaty the state of war will terminate.

From that moment and subject to the provisions of this Treaty official relations with Germany, and with any of the German States, will be resumed by the Allied and Associated Powers.

Part I—The Covenant of the League of Nations

THE HIGH CONTRACTING PARTIES,

IN ORDER TO PROMOTE international co-operation and to achieve international peace and security
by the acceptance of obligations not to resort to war
by the prescription of open, just and honourable relations between nations
by the firm establishment of the understandings of international law as the actual rule of conduct among Governments, and
by the maintenance of justice and a scrupulous respect for all treaty obligations in the dealings of organised peoples with one another
AGREE to this Covenant of the League of Nations.

Article 1

The original Members of the League of Nations shall be those of the Signatories which are named in the Annex to this Covenant and also such of those other States named in the Annex as shall accede without reservation to this Covenant. Such accession shall be effected by a Declaration deposited with the Secretariat within two months of the coming into force of the Covenant. Notice thereof shall be sent to all other Members of the League.

Any fully self-governing State, Dominion, or Colony not named in the Annex may become a Member of the League if its admission is agreed to by two-thirds of the Assembly provided that it shall give effective guarantees of its sincere intention to observe its international obligations, and shall accept such regulations as may be prescribed by the League in regard to its military, naval, and air forces and armaments.

Any Member of the League may, after two years' notice of its intention so to do, withdraw from the League, provided that all its international obligations and all its obligations under this Covenant shall have been fulfilled at the time of its withdrawal.

Article 2

The action of the League under this Covenant shall be effected through the instrumentality of an Assembly and of a Council, with a permanent Secretariat.

Article 3

The Assembly shall consist of Representatives of the Members of the League.

The Assembly shall meet at stated intervals and from time to time as occasion may require at the Seat of the League or at such other place as may be decided upon.

The Assembly may deal at its meetings with any matter within the sphere of action of the League or affecting the peace of the world.

At meetings of the Assembly each Member of the League shall have one vote, and may not have more than three Representatives.

Article 4

The Council shall consist of Representatives of the Principal Allied and Associated Powers, together with Representatives of four other Members of the League. These four Members of the League shall be selected by the Assembly from time to time in its discretion. Until the appointment of the Representatives of the four Members of the League first selected by the Assembly, Representatives of Belgium, Brazil, Spain, and Greece shall be members of the Council.

With the approval of the majority of the Assembly, the Council may name additional Members of the League whose Representatives shall always be members of the Council; the Council with like approval may increase the number of Members of the League to be selected by the Assembly for representation on the Council.

The Council shall meet from time to time as occasion may require, and at least once a year, at the Seat of the League, or at such other place as may be decided upon.

The Council may deal at its meetings with any matter within the sphere of action of the League or affecting the peace of the world.

Any Member of the League not represented on the Council shall be invited to send a Representative to sit as a member at any meeting of the Council during the consideration of matters specially affecting the interests of that Member of the League.

At meetings of the Council, each Member of the League represented on the Council shall have one vote, and may have not more than one Representative.

Article 5

Except where otherwise expressly provided in this Covenant or by the terms of the present Treaty, decisions at any meeting of the Assembly or of the Council shall require the agreement of all the Members of the League represented at the meeting.

All matters of procedure at meetings of the Assembly or of the Council, including the appointment of Committees to investigate particular matters, shall be regulated by the Assembly or by the Council and may be decided by a majority of the Members of the League represented at the meeting.

The first meeting of the Assembly and the first meeting of the Council shall be summoned by the President of the United States of America.

Article 6

The permanent Secretariat shall be established at the Seat of the League. The Secretariat shall comprise a Secretary General and such secretaries and staff as may be required.

The first Secretary General shall be the person named in the Annex; thereafter the Secretary General shall be appointed by the Council with the approval of the majority of the Assembly.

The secretaries and staff of the Secretariat shall be appointed by the Secretary General with the approval of the Council.

The Secretary General shall act in that capacity at all meetings of the Assembly and of the Council.

The expenses of the Secretariat shall be borne by the Members of the League in accordance with the apportionment of the expenses of the International Bureau of the Universal Postal Union.

Article 7

The Seat of the League is established at Geneva.

The Council may at any time decide that the Seat of the League shall be established elsewhere.

All positions under or in connection with the League, including the Secretariat, shall be open equally to men and women.

Representatives of the Members of the League and officials of the League when engaged on the business of the League shall enjoy diplomatic privileges and immunities.

The buildings and other property occupied by the League or its officials or by Representatives attending its meetings shall be inviolable.

Article 8

The Members of the League recognise that the maintenance of peace requires the reduction of national armaments to the lowest point consistent with national safety and the enforcement by common action of international obligations.

The Council, taking account of the geographical situation and circumstances of each State, shall formulate plans for such reduction for the consideration and action of the several Governments.

Such plans shall be subject to reconsideration and revision at least every ten years.

After these plans shall have been adopted by the several Governments, the limits of armaments therein fixed shall not be exceeded without the concurrence of the Council.

The Members of the League agree that the manufacture by private enterprise of munitions and implements of war is open to grave objections. The Council shall advise how the evil effects attendant upon such manufacture can be prevented, due regard being had to the necessities of those Members of the League which are not able to manufacture the munitions and implements of war necessary for their safety.

The Members of the League undertake to interchange full and frank information as to the scale of their armaments, their military, naval, and air programmes and the condition of such of their industries as are adaptable to war-like purposes.

Article 9

A permanent Commission shall be constituted to advise the Council on the execution of the provisions of Articles 1 and 8 and on military, naval and air questions generally.

Article 10

The Members of the League undertake to respect and preserve as against external aggression the territorial integrity and existing political independence of all Members of the League. In case of any such aggression or in case of any threat or danger of such aggression the Council shall advise upon the means by which this obligation shall be fulfilled.

Article 11

Any war or threat of war, whether immediately affecting any of the Members of the League or not, is hereby declared a matter of concern to the whole League, and the League shall take any action that may be deemed wise and effectual to safeguard the peace of nations. In case any such emergency should arise the Secretary General shall on the request of any Member of the League forthwith summon a meeting of the Council.

It is also declared to be the friendly right of each Member of the League to bring to the attention of the Assembly or of the Council any circumstance whatever affecting international relations which threatens to disturb international peace or the good understanding between nations upon which peace depends.

Article 12

The Members of the League agree that if there should arise between them any dispute likely to lead to a rupture, they will submit the matter either to arbitration or to inquiry by the Council, and they agree in no case to resort to war until three months after the award by the arbitrators or the report by the Council.

In any case under this Article the award of the arbitrators shall be made within a reasonable time, and the report of the Council shall be made within six months after the submission of the dispute.

Article 13

The Members of the League agree that whenever any dispute shall arise between them which they recognise to be suitable for submission to arbitration and which cannot be satisfactorily settled by diplomacy, they will submit the whole subject-matter to arbitration.

Disputes as to the interpretation of a treaty, as to any question of international law, as to the existence of any fact which if established would constitute a breach of any international obligation, or as to the extent and nature of the reparation to be made or any such breach, are declared to be among those which are generally suitable for submission to arbitration.

For the consideration of any such dispute the court of arbitration to which the case is referred shall be the Court agreed on by the parties to the dispute or stipulated in any convention existing between them.

The Members of the League agree that they will carry out in full good faith any award that may be rendered, and that they will not resort to war against a Member of the League which complies therewith. In the event of any failure to carry out such an award, the Council shall propose what steps should be taken to give effect thereto.

Article 14

The Council shall formulate and submit to the Members of the League for adoption plans for the establishment of a Permanent Court of International Justice. The Court shall be competent to hear and determine any dispute of an international character which the parties thereto submit to it. The Court may also give an advisory opinion upon any dispute or question referred to it by the Council or by the Assembly.

Article 15

If there should arise between Members of the League any dispute likely to lead to a rupture, which is not submitted to arbitration in accordance with Article 13, the Members of the League agree that they will submit the matter to the Council. Any party to the dispute may effect such submission by giving notice of the existence of the dispute to the Secretary General, who will make all necessary arrangements for a full investigation and consideration thereof.

The League of Nations at its opening session in Geneva in 1920. (Corel)

For this purpose the parties to the dispute will communicate to the Secretary General, as promptly as possible, statements of their case with all the relevant facts and papers, and the Council may forthwith direct the publication thereof.

The Council shall endeavour to effect a settlement of the dispute, and if such efforts are successful, a statement shall be made public giving such facts and explanations regarding the dispute and the terms of settlement thereof as the Council may deem appropriate.

If the dispute is not thus settled, the Council either unanimously or by a majority vote shall make and publish a report containing a statement of the facts of the dispute and the recommendations which are deemed just and proper in regard thereto.

Any Member of the League represented on the Council may make public a statement of the facts of the dispute and of its conclusions regarding the same.

If a report by the Council is unanimously agreed to by the members thereof other than the Representatives of one or more of the parties to the dispute, the Members of the League agree that they will not go to war with any party to the dispute which complies with the recommendations of the report.

If the Council fails to reach a report which is unanimously agreed to by the members thereof, other than the Representatives of one or more of the parties to the dispute, the Members of the League reserve to themselves the right to take such action as they shall consider necessary for the maintenance of right and justice.

If the dispute between the parties is claimed by one of them, and is found by the Council, to arise out of a matter which by international law is solely within the domestic jurisdiction of that party, the Council shall so report, and shall make no recommendation as to its settlement.

The Council may in any case under this Article refer the dispute to the Assembly. The dispute shall be so referred at the request of either party to the dispute, provided that such request be made within fourteen days after the submission of the dispute to the Council.

In any case referred to the Assembly, all the provisions of this Article and of Article 12 relating to the action and powers of the Council shall apply to the action and powers of the Assembly, provided that a report made by the Assembly, if concurred in by the Representatives of those Members of the League represented on the Council and of a majority of the other Members of the League, exclusive in each case of the Representatives of the parties to the dispute shall have the same force as a report by the Council concurred in by all the members thereof other than the Representatives of one or more of the parties to the dispute.

Article 16

Should any Member of the League resort to war in disregard of its covenants under Articles 12, 13, or 15, it shall *ipso facto* be deemed to have committed an act of war against all other Members of the League, which hereby undertake immediately to subject it to the severance of all trade or financial relations, the prohibition of all intercourse between their nationals and the nationals of the covenant-breaking State, and the prevention of all financial, commercial, or personal intercourse between the nationals of the covenant-breaking State and the nationals of any other State, whether a Member of the League or not.

It shall be the duty of the Council in such case to recommend to the several Governments concerned what effective military, naval, or air force the Members of the League shall severally contribute to the armed forces to be used to protect the covenants of the League.

The Members of the League agree, further, that they will mutually support one another in the financial and economic measures which are taken under this Article, in order to minimise the loss and inconvenience resulting from the above measures, and that they will mutually support one another in resisting any special measures aimed at one of their number by the covenant-breaking State, and that they will take the necessary steps to afford passage through their territory to the forces of any of the Members of the League which are co-operating to protect the covenants of the League.

Any Member of the League which has violated any covenant of the League may be declared to be no longer a Member of the League by a vote of the Council concurred in by the Representatives of all the other Members of the League represented thereon.

Article 17

In the event of a dispute between a Member of the League and a State which is not a Member of the League, or between States not Members of the League, the State or States, not Members of the League shall be invited to accept the obligations of membership in the League for the purposes of such dispute, upon such conditions as the Council may deem just. If such invitation is accepted, the provisions of

Articles 12 to 16 inclusive shall be applied with such modifications as may be deemed necessary by the Council.

Upon such invitation being given the Council shall immediately institute an inquiry into the circumstances of the dispute and recommend such action as may seem best and most effectual in the circumstances.

If a State so invited shall refuse to accept the obligations of membership in the League for the purposes of such dispute, and shall resort to war against a Member of the League, the provisions of Article 16 shall be applicable as against the State taking such action.

If both parties to the dispute when so invited refuse to accept the obligations of membership in the League for the purpose of such dispute, the Council may take such measures and make such recommendations as will prevent hostilities and will result in the settlement of the dispute.

Article 18

Every treaty or international engagement entered into hereafter by any Member of the League shall be forthwith registered with the Secretariat and shall as soon as possible be published by it. No such treaty or international engagement shall be binding until so registered.

Article 19

The Assembly may from time to time advise the reconsideration by Members of the League of treaties which have become inapplicable and the consideration of international conditions whose continuance might endanger the peace of the world.

Article 20

The Members of the League severally agree that this Covenant is accepted as abrogating all obligations or understandings *inter se* which are inconsistent with the terms thereof, and solemnly undertake that they will not hereafter enter into any engagements inconsistent with the terms thereof.

In case any Member of the League shall, before becoming a Member of the League, have undertaken any obligations inconsistent with the terms of this Covenant, it shall be the duty of such Member to take immediate steps to procure its release from such obligations.

Article 21

Nothing in this Covenant shall be deemed to affect the validity of international engagements, such as treaties of arbitration or regional understandings like the Monroe doctrine, for securing the maintenance of peace.

Article 22

To those colonies and territories which as a consequence of the late war have ceased to be under the sovereignty of the States which formerly governed them and which are inhabited by peoples not yet able to stand by themselves under the strenuous conditions of the modern world, there should be applied the principle that the well-being and development of such peoples form a sacred trust of civilisation and that securities for the performance of this trust should be embodied in this Covenant.

The best method of giving practical effect to this principle is that the tutelage of such peoples should be entrusted to advanced nations who by reason of their resources, their experience or their geographical position can best undertake this responsibility, and who are willing to accept it, and that this tutelage should be exercised by them as Mandatories on behalf of the League.

The character of the mandate must differ according to the stage of the development of the people, the geographical situation of the territory, its economic conditions, and other similar circumstances.

Certain communities formerly belonging to the Turkish Empire have reached a stage of development where their existence as independent nations can be provisionally recognised subject to the rendering of administrative advice and assistance by a Mandatory until such time as they are able to stand alone. The wishes of these communities must be a principal consideration in the selection of the Mandatory.

Other peoples, especially those of Central Africa, are at such a stage that the Mandatory must be responsible for the administration of the territory under conditions which will guarantee freedom of conscience and religion, subject only to the maintenance of public order and morals, the prohibition of abuses such as the slave trade, the arms traffic, and the liquor traffic, and the prevention of the establishment of fortifications or military and naval bases and of military training of the natives for other than police purposes and the defence of territory, and will also secure equal opportunities for the trade and commerce of other Members of the League.

There are territories, such as South-West Africa and certain of the South Pacific Islands, which, owing to the sparseness of their population, or their small size, or their remoteness from the centres of civilisation, or their geographical contiguity to the territory of the Mandatory, and other circumstances, can be best administered under the laws of the Mandatory as integral portions of its territory, subject to the safeguards above mentioned in the interests of the indigenous population.

In every case of mandate, the Mandatory shall render to the Council an annual report in reference to the territory committed to its charge.

The degree of authority, control, or administration to be exercised by the Mandatory shall, if not previously agreed upon by the Members of the League, be explicitly defined in each case by the Council.

A permanent Commission shall be constituted to receive and examine the annual reports of the Mandatories and to advise the Council on all matters relating to the observance of the mandates.

Article 23

Subject to and in accordance with the provisions of international conventions existing or hereafter to be agreed upon, the Members of the League:

(a) will endeavour to secure and maintain fair and humane conditions of labour for men, women, and children, both in their own countries and in all countries to which their commercial and industrial relations extend, and for that purpose will establish and maintain the necessary international organisations;

(b) undertake to secure just treatment of the native inhabitants of territories under their control;

(c) will entrust the League with the general supervision over the execution of agreements with regard to the traffic in women and children, and the traffic in opium and other dangerous drugs;

(d) will entrust the League with the general supervision of the trade in arms and ammunition with the countries in which the control of this traffic is necessary in the common interest;

(e) will make provision to secure and maintain freedom of communications and of transit and equitable treatment for the commerce of all Members of the League. In this connection, the special necessities of the regions devastated during the war of 1914–1918 shall be borne in mind;

(f) will endeavour to take steps in matters of international concern for the prevention and control of disease.

. . .

Section III. Left Bank of the Rhine

Article 42

Germany is forbidden to maintain or construct any fortifications either on the left bank of the Rhine or on the right bank to the west of a line drawn 50 kilometres to the East of the Rhine.

Article 43

In the area defined above the maintenance and the assembly of armed forces, either permanently or temporarily, and military maneuvers of any kind, as well as the upkeep of all permanent works for mobilization, are in the same way forbidden.

. . .

Section IV. Saar Basin

Article 45

As compensation for the destruction of the coal-mines in the north of France and as part payment towards the total reparation due from Germany for the damage resulting from the war, Germany cedes to France in full and absolute possession, with exclusive rights of exploitation, unencumbered and free from all debts and charges of any kind, the coal-mines situated in the Saar Basin as defined in Article 48.

Article 46

In order to assure the rights and welfare of the population and to guarantee to France complete freedom in working the mines, Germany agrees to the provisions of Chapters I and II of the Annex hereto.

Article 47

In order to make in due time permanent provision for the government of the Saar Basin in accordance with the wishes of the populations, France and Germany agree to the provisions of Chapter III of the Annex hereto.

Article 48

The boundaries of the territory of the Saar Basin, as dealt with in the present stipulations, will be fixed as follows:

On the south and south-west: by the frontier of France as fixed by the present Treaty.

. . .

A Commission composed of five members, one appointed by France, one by Germany, and three by the Council of the League of Nations, which will select nationals of other Powers, will be constituted within fifteen days from the coming into force of the present Treaty, to trace on the spot the frontier line described above. In those parts of the preceding line which do not coincide with administrative boundaries, the Commission will endeavour to keep to the line indicated, while taking into consideration, so far as is possible, local economic interests and existing communal boundaries. The decisions of this Commission will be taken by a majority, and will be binding on the parties concerned.

Article 49

Germany renounces in favour of the League of Nations, in the capacity of trustee, the government of the territory defined above. At the end of fifteen years from the coming into force of the present Treaty the inhabitants of the said territory shall be called upon to indicate the sovereignty under which they desire to be placed.

Article 50

The stipulations under which the cession of the mines in the Saar Basin shall be carried out, together with the measures intended to guarantee the rights and the well-being of the inhabitants and the government of the territory, as well as the conditions in accordance with which the plebiscite herein before provided for is to be made, are laid down in the Annex hereto. This Annex shall be considered as an integral part of the present Treaty, and Germany declares her adherence to it.

. . .

Chapter I. Cession and Exploitation of Mining Property

1. From the date of the coming into force of the present Treaty, all the deposits of coal situated within the Saar Basin as defined in Article 48 of the said Treaty, become the complete and absolute property of the French State. The French State will have the right of working or not working the said mines, or of transferring to a third party the right of working them, without having to obtain any previous authorisation or to fulfil any formalities.

The French State may always require that the German mining laws and regulations referred to below shall be applied in order to ensure the determination of its rights.

2. The right of ownership of the French State will apply not only to the deposits which are free and for which concessions have not yet been granted, but also to the deposits for which concessions have already been granted, whoever may be the present proprietors, irrespective of whether they belong to the Prussian State, to the Bavarian State, to other States or bodies, to companies or to individuals, whether they have been worked or not, or whether a right of exploitation distinct from the right of the owners of the surface of the soil has or has not been recognised.

3. As far as concerns the mines which are being worked, the transfer of the ownership to the French State will apply to all the accessories and subsidiaries of the said mines, in particular to their plant and equipment both on and below the surface to their extracting machinery, their plants for transforming coal into electric power, coke and by-products, their workshops means of communication, electric lines, plant for catching and distributing water, land, buildings such as offices, managers, employees, and workmen's dwellings, schools, hospitals and dispensaries, their stocks and supplies of every description, their archives and plans, and in general everything which those who own or exploit the mines possess or enjoy for the purpose of exploiting the mines and their accessories and subsidiaries.

The transfer will apply also to the debts owing for products delivered before the entry into possession by the French State and after the signature of the present Treaty, and to deposits of money made by customers, whose rights will be guaranteed by the French State.

4. The French State will acquire the property free and clear of all debts and charges. Nevertheless, the rights acquired, or in course of being acquired, by the employees of the mines and their accessories and subsidiaries at the date of the coming into force of the present Treaty, in connection with pensions for old age or disability, will not be affected. In return, Germany must pay over to the French State a sum representing the actuarial amounts to which the said employees are entitled.

5. The value of the property thus ceded to the French State will be determined by the Reparation Commission referred to in Article 233 of Part VIII (Reparation) of the present Treaty.

This value shall be credited to Germany in part payment of the amount due for reparation.

It will be for Germany to indemnify the proprietors or parties concerned, whoever they may be.

6. No tariff shall be established on the German railways and canals which may directly or indirectly discriminate to the prejudice of the transport of the personnel or products of the mines and their accessories or subsidiaries, or of the material necessary to their exploitation. Such transport shall enjoy all the rights and privileges which any international railway conventions may guarantee to similar products of French origin.

...

Section V. Alsace-Lorraine

The HIGH CONTRACTING PARTIES, recognising the moral obligation to redress the wrong done by Germany in 1871 both to the rights of France and to the wishes of the population of Alsace and Lorraine, which were separated from their country in spite of the solemn protest of their representatives at the Assembly of Bordeaux,

AGREE upon the following Articles:

Article 51

The territories which were ceded to Germany in accordance with the Preliminaries of Peace signed at Versailles on 26 February 1871, and the Treaty of Frankfort of 10 May 1871, are restored to French sovereignty as from the date of the Armistice of 11 November 1918. The provisions of the Treaties establishing the delimitation of the frontiers before 1871 shall be restored.

Article 52

The German Government shall hand over without delay to the French Government all archives, registers, plans, titles and documents of every kind concerning the civil, military, financial, judicial or other administrations of the territories restored to French sovereignty. If any of these documents, archives, registers, titles or plans nave been misplaced, they will be restored by the German Government on the demand of the French Government.

...

Section VII. Czecho-Slovak State

Article 81

Germany, in conformity with the action already taken by the Allied and Associated Powers, recognises the complete independence of the Czecho-Slovak State which will include the autonomous territory of the Ruthenians to the south of the Carpathians. Germany hereby recognises the frontiers of this State as determined by the Principal Allied and Associated Powers and the other interested States.

Article 82

The old frontier as it existed on 3 August 1914, between Austria-Hungary and the German Empire will constitute the frontier between Germany and the Czecho-Slovak State.

. . .

Section VIII. Poland

Article 87

Germany, in conformity with the action already taken by the Allied and Associated Powers, recognises the complete independence of Poland, and renounces in her favour all rights and title over the territory bounded by the Baltic Sea, the eastern frontier of Germany as laid down in Article 27 of Part II (Boundaries of Germany) of the present Treaty up to a point situated about 2 kilometres to the east of Lorzendorf, then a line to the acute angle which the northern boundary of Upper Silesia makes about 3 kilometres north-west of Simmenau, then the boundary of Upper Silesia to its meeting point with the old frontier between Germany and Russia, then this frontier to the point where it crosses the course of the Niemen, and then the northern frontier of East Prussia as laid down in Article 28 of Part II aforesaid.

The provisions of this Article do not, however, apply to the territories of East Prussia and the Free City of Danzig, as defined in Article 28 of Part II (Boundaries of Germany) and in Article 100 of Section XI (Danzig) of this Part.

The boundaries of Poland not laid down in the present Treaty will be subsequently determined by the Principal Allied and Associated Powers.

A Commission consisting of seven members, five of whom shall be nominated by the Principal Allied and Associated Powers, one by Germany and one by Poland, shall be constituted fifteen days after the coming into force of the present Treaty to delimit on the spot the frontier line between Poland and Germany.

The decisions of the Commission will be taken by a majority of votes and shall be binding upon the parties concerned.

. . .

Section XIV. Russia and Russian States

Article 116

Germany acknowledges and agrees to respect as permanent and inalienable the independence of all the territories which were part of the former Russian Empire on 1 August 1914. In accordance with the provisions of Article 259 of Part IX (Financial Clauses) and Article 292 of Part X (Economic Clauses) Germany accepts definitely the abrogation of the Brest-Litovsk Treaties and of all other treaties, conventions, and agreements entered into by her with the Maximalist Government in Russia.

The Allied and Associated Powers formally reserve the rights of Russia to obtain from Germany restitution and reparation based on the principles of the present Treaty.

Article 117

Germany undertakes to recognise the full force of all treaties or agreements which may be entered into by the Allied and Associated Powers with States now existing or coming into existence in future in the whole or part of the former Empire of Russia as it existed on 1 August 1914, and to recognise the frontiers of any such States as determined therein.

Article 118

In territory outside her European frontiers as fixed by the present Treaty, Germany renounces all rights, titles and privileges whatever in or over territory which belonged to her or to her allies, and all rights, titles and privileges whatever their origin which she held as against the Allied and Associated Powers. Germany hereby undertakes to recognise and to conform to the measures which may be taken now or in the future by the Principal Allied and Associated Powers, in agreement where necessary with third Powers, in order to carry the above stipulation into effect. In particular Germany declares her acceptance of the following Articles relating to certain special subjects.

Section I. German Colonies

Article 119

Germany renounces in favour of the Principal Allied and Associated Powers all her rights and titles over her oversea possessions.

. . .

Section II. China

Article 128

Germany renounces in favour of China all benefits and privileges resulting from the provisions of the final Protocol signed at Peking on 7 September 1901, and from all annexes, notes and documents supplementary thereto. She likewise renounces in favour of China any claim to indemnities accruing thereunder subsequent to 14 March 1917.

. . .

Section V. General Articles

Article 211

After the expiration of a period of three months from the coming into force of the present Treaty, the German laws must have been modified and shall be maintained by the German Government in conformity with this Part of the present Treaty.

Within the same period all the administrative or other measures relating to the execution of this Part of the Treaty must have been taken.

. . .

Section I. Prisoners of War

Article 214

The repatriation of prisoners of war and interned civilians shall take place as soon as possible after the coming into force of the present Treaty and shall be carried out with the greatest rapidity.

Article 215

The repatriation of German prisoners of war and interned civilians shall, in accordance with Article 214, be carried out by a Commission composed of representatives of the Allied and Associated Powers on the one part and of the German Government on the other part.

For each of the Allied and Associated Powers a Sub-Commission, composed exclusively of Representatives of the interested Power and of Delegates of the German Government, shall regulate the details of carrying into effect the repatriation of the prisoners of war.

. . .

Part VIII—Reparation

Section I. General Provisions

Article 231

The Allied and Associated Governments affirm and Germany accepts the responsibility of Germany and her allies for causing all the loss and damage to which the Allied and Associated Governments and their nationals have been subjected as a consequence of the war imposed upon them by the aggression of Germany and her allies.

Article 232

The Allied and Associated Governments recognise that the resources of Germany are not adequate, after taking into account permanent diminutions of such resources which will result from other provisions of the present Treaty, to make complete reparation for all such loss and damage.

The Allied and Associated Governments, however, require, and Germany undertakes, that she will make compensation for all damage done to the civilian population of the Allied and Associated Powers and to their property during the period of the belligerency of each as an Allied or Associated Power against Germany by such aggression by land, by sea and from the air, and in general all damage as defined in Annex I hereto.

In accordance with Germany's pledges, already given, as to complete restoration for Belgium, Germany undertakes, in addition to the compensation for damage elsewhere in this Part provided for, as a consequence of the violation of the Treaty of 1839, to make reimbursement of all sums which Belgium has borrowed from the Allied and Associated Governments up to 11 November 1918, together with interest at the rate of five percent (5%) per annum on such sums. This amount shall be determined by the Reparation Commission, and the German Government undertakes thereupon forthwith to make a special issue of bearer bonds to an equivalent amount payable in marks gold, on 1 May 1926, or, at the option of the German Government, on the 1 May in any year up to 1926. Subject to the foregoing, the form of such bonds shall be determined by the Reparation Commission. Such bonds shall be handed over to the Reparation Commission, which has authority to take and acknowledge receipt thereof on behalf of Belgium.

Article 233

The amount of the above damage for which compensation is to be made by Germany shall be determined by an Inter-Allied Commission, to be called the Reparation Commission and constituted in the form and with the powers set forth hereunder and in Annexes II to VII inclusive hereto.

This Commission shall consider the claims and give to the German Government a just opportunity to be heard.

The findings of the Commission as to the amount of damage defined as above shall be concluded and notified to the German Government on or before 1 May 1921, as representing the extent of that Government's obligations.

The Commission shall concurrently draw up a schedule of payments prescribing the time and manner for securing and discharging the entire obligation within a period of thirty years from 1 May 1921. If, however, within the period mentioned, Germany fails to discharge her obligations, any balance remaining unpaid may, within the discretion of the Commission, be postponed for settlement in subsequent years, or may be handled otherwise in such manner as the Allied and Associated Governments, acting in accordance with the procedure laid down in this Part of the present Treaty, shall determine.

. . .

Part IX—Financial Clauses

Article 248

Subject to such exceptions as the Reparation Commission may approve, a first charge upon all the assets and revenues of the German Empire and its constituent States shall be the cost of reparation and all other costs arising under the present Treaty or any treaties or agreements supplementary thereto or under arrangements concluded between Germany and the Allied and Associated Powers during the Armistice or its extensions.

Up to 1 May 1921, the German Government shall not export or dispose of, and shall forbid the export or disposal of, gold without the previous approval of the Allied and Associated Powers acting through the Reparation Commission.

Article 249

There shall be paid by the German Government the total cost of all armies of the Allied and Associated Governments in occupied German territory from the date of the signature of the Armistice of 11 November 1918, including the keep of men and beasts, lodging and billeting, pay and allowances, salaries and wages, bedding, heating, lighting, clothing, equipment, harness and saddlery, armament and rolling-stock, air services, treatment of sick and wounded, veterinary and remount services, transport service of all sorts (such as by rail, sea or river, motor lorries), communications and correspondence, and in general the cost of all administrative or technical services the working of which is necessary for the training of troops and for keeping their numbers up to strength and preserving their military efficiency.

The cost of such liabilities under the above heads so far as they relate to purchases or requisitions by the Allied and Associated Governments in the occupied territories shall be paid by the German Government to the Allied and Associated Governments in marks at the current or agreed rate of exchange. All other of the above costs shall be paid in gold marks.

. . .

Part X—Economic Clauses

Section I. Commercial Relations

Chapter I. Customs Regulations, Duties and Restrictions

Article 264

Germany undertakes that goods the produce or manufacture of any one of the Allied or Associated States imported into Germany territory, from whatsoever place arriving, shall not be subjected to other or higher duties or charges (including internal charges) than those to which the like goods the produce or manufacture of any other such State or of any other foreign country are subject.

Germany will not maintain or impose any prohibition or restriction on the importation into German territory of any goods the produce or manufacture of the territories of any one of the Allied or Associated States, from whatsoever place arriving, which shall not equally extend to the importation of the like goods the produce or manufacture of any other such State or of any other foreign country.

Article 265

Germany further undertakes that, in the matter of the regime applicable on importation, no discrimination against the commerce of any of the Allied and

Associated States as compared with any other of the said States or any other foreign country shall be made, even by indirect means, such as customs regulations or procedure, methods of verification or analysis conditions of payment of duties, tariff classification or interpretation, or the operation of monopolies.

. . .

Chapter V. General Articles

Article 280

The obligations imposed on Germany by Chapter I and by Articles 271 and 272 of Chapter II above shall cease to have effect five years from the date of the coming into force of the present Treaty, unless otherwise provided in the text, or unless the Council of the League of Nations shall, at least twelve months before the expiration of that period, decide that these obligations shall be maintained for a further period with or without amendment.

Article 276 of Chapter IV shall remain in operation, with or without amendment, after the period of five years for such further period, if any, not exceeding five years, as may be determined by a majority of the Council of the League of Nations.

Article 281

If the German Government engages in international trade, it shall not in respect thereof have or be deemed to have any rights, privileges or immunities of sovereignty.

. . .

Section IV. Property, Rights and Interests

Article 297

The question of private property, rights and interests in an enemy country shall be settled according to the principles laid down in this Section and to the provisions of the Annex hereto.

(a) The exceptional war measures and measures of transfer (defined in paragraph 3 of the Annex hereto) taken by Germany with respect to the property, rights and interests of nationals of Allied or Associated Powers, including companies and associations in which they are interested, when liquidation has not been completed, shall be immediately discontinued or stayed and the property, rights and interests concerned restored to their owners, who shall enjoy full rights therein in accordance with the provisions of Article 298.

(b) Subject to any contrary stipulations which may be provided for in the present Treaty, the Allied and Associated Powers reserve the right to retain and liquidate all property, rights and interests belonging at the date of the coming into force of the present Treaty to German nationals, or companies controlled by them, within their territories, colonies, possessions and protectorates including territories ceded to them by the present Treaty.

The liquidation shall be carried out in accordance with the laws of the Allied or Associated State concerned, and the German manowners shall not be able to dispose of such property, rights or interests nor to subject them to any charge without the consent of that State.

German nationals who acquire *ipso facto* the nationality of an Allied or Associated Power in accordance with the provisions of the present Treaty will not be considered as German nationals within the meaning of this paragraph.

. . .

PROTOCOL

With a view to indicating precisely the conditions in which certain provisions of the Treaty of even date are to be carried out, it is agreed by the High Contracting Parties that:

(1) A Commission will be appointed by the Principal Allied and Associated Powers to supervise the destruction of the fortifications of Heligoland in accordance with the Treaty. This Commission will be authorized to decide what portion of the works protecting the coast from sea erosion are to be maintained and what proportion must be destroyed;

(2) Sums reimbursed by Germany to German nationals to indemnify them in respect of the interests which they may be found to possess in the railways and mines referred to in the second paragraph of Article 156 shall be credited to Germany against the sums due by way of reparation;

(3) The list of persons to be handed over to the Allied and Associated Governments by Germany under the second paragraph of Article 228 shall be communicated to the German Government within a month from the coming into force of the Treaty;

(4) The Reparation Commission referred to in Article 240 and paragraphs 2, 3 and 4 of Annex IV cannot require trade secrets or other confidential information to be divulged;

(5) From the signature of the Treaty and within the ensuing four months Germany will be entitled to submit for examination by the Allied and Associated Powers documents and proposals in order to expedite the work connected with reparation, and thus to shorten the investigation and to accelerate the decisions;

(6) Proceedings will be taken against persons who have committed punishable offences in the liquidation of German property, and the Allied and Associated Powers will welcome any information or evidence which the German Government can furnish on this subject.

DONE at Versailles, the twenty-eighth day of June, one thousand nine hundred and nineteen.

FURTHER READING

Beisner, R. (1986) *From the Old Diplomacy to the New, 1865–1900*. Arlington Heights, IL: Harlan Davidson.

Healy, D. (1970) *U.S. Expansionism: The Imperialist Age in the 1890s*. Madison, WI: University of Wisconsin Press.

Herring, G. (2008) *From Colony to Superpower: U.S. Foreign Relations since 1776*. Oxford: Oxford University Press.

Kendrick, C. (1992) *The Presidency of Woodrow Wilson*. Lawrence, KS: The University Press of Kansas.

Kennedy, P. (1987) *The Rise and the Fall of the Great Powers*. New York: Random House.

Knightly, P. (2001) *The First Casualty: The War Correspondent as a Hero and Myth-Maker from Crimea to Kosovo*. 2nd ed. London: Prion Books.

Knock, T. (1992) *To End All Wars: Woodrow Wilson and the Quest for a New World Order*. New York: Oxford University Press.

Link, A. (1954) *Woodrow Wilson and the Progressive Era, 1910–1917*. New York: Harper.

Ninkovich, F. (1986) "Theodore Roosevelt: Civilization as Ideology," *Diplomatic History*, 10 (Summer), 221–245.

4

FRANKLIN D. ROOSEVELT: FROM THE ARSENAL OF DEMOCRACY TO SUPERPOWER STATUS

INTRODUCTION

The post-Wilsonian world saw the United States withdraw from the international stage, turn inward, and enter what is generally considered the most isolationist time in American history. There are serious questions, however, about whether the United States was actually isolationist during this time or whether it simply changed its mode of international involvement by using economics and trade as its primary foreign policy tools (Herring 2008). Primarily concerned with controlling Latin America and the expansion of trade globally, the United States rejected becoming a member of the League of Nations President Wilson worked so hard to set up in the Treaty of Versailles.

After a decade of enormous gains, the U.S. stock market collapsed on Tuesday, October 29, 1929, known as "Black Tuesday," an event that marked the beginning of the Great Depression. Panicked investors dumped their stocks, and by 1932–1933 the stock market had fallen 80% from its high in the late 1920s. Motivated by protectionism, Congress passed the infamous Smoot-Hawley Act of 1930, raising tariffs on imported goods—an act that was seen as a trade war by European governments, which retaliated in kind, thus bringing world trade to a near standstill. The British and French left the gold standard, and eventually the United States did, too. By 1930 U.S. factories began closing, and between 1929 and 1932, U.S. exports fell by 70 percent. U.S. investment in Europe dried up, causing financial panics in European countries that depended on U.S. investment to manage their debt and reparation payments from World War I. Banks began failing by the hundreds in 1932–1933, and by 1933 depositors saw $140 billion disappear. President Roosevelt eventually closed all U.S. banks in March of 1933 for a three-day "bank holiday," allowing them to reopen slowly and with new regulations under the Federal Deposit Insurance Corporation in order to rebuild trust in banks and to protect deposits.

For the United States and the global economy, the impact of the Great Depression was immense. In the United States unemployment reached 25 percent in 1933, while in other countries unemployment reached as high as 33 percent. Farming and construction both declined by 60 percent, and world trade was reduced by two-thirds. The United States saw the construction of shanty towns, popularly called "Hoovervilles," after President Herbert Hoover. Hoover became increasingly unpopular due to his unwillingness to take bold government action to ameliorate economic problems. The political consequences of the Great Depression would be catastrophic for the world, leading to another World War that changed the face of the earth.

In the United States, the immediate political consequences of the Great Depression included a

Did You Know?

John Maynard Keynes

John Maynard Keynes (1883–1946) was a British economist who is nowadays considered the father of modern economic thought. Most famously, Keynes revolutionized economic thought by arguing that neoclassical economics was faulty because the free market includes no self-correcting mechanism. Obviously aided by the Great Depression, in which the free market seemed unable to correct its downward spiral, Keynes argued that the way to correct the market in times of depression is by deficit spending, that is, government spending to artificially stimulate demand. During the Great Depression the U.S. government did exactly that through a series of public works programs under the National Industrial Recovery Act (NIRA). Keynes most famously participated in the conference that ended World War I at Versailles, at which he disagreed with the principal players' position that Germany must pay high war reparations. In fact, in his most famous work, *The Economic Consequences of the Peace*, Keynes argued that high reparations would bring about a catastrophe. By 1928 Germany was hit by hyperinflation, and with its economy in shambles, it saw the rise of the National Socialist Party (Nazi party) and Adolf Hitler, which led to World War II. Keynes's contemporary rival in economic thought was Friedrich Hayek, an Austrian economist and defender of classical liberalism, whose famous work *The Road to Serfdom* argued that even regulated capitalism would introduce socialism and paternalistically implement central planning of the economy.

realignment of political fortunes. The Democrats emerged in 1932 as the majority party for at least two decades; the political economy was transformed by the use of Keynesian policies, by which Roosevelt's "New Deal" policies stimulated the economy by creating artificial demand; the labor movement demanded more from their government; and—most important in the area of U.S. foreign policy—there was a complete indifference toward a world that was becoming increasingly dangerous. Isolationism was the order of the day in Congress, fueled by the popular belief that if the United States could not solve its domestic problems, it had no business attempting to solve problems beyond its borders. Even with newly elected President Roosevelt and a Democratic Congress, the prevailing mood was to deal with the economy while ignoring foreign policy.

Franklin Delano Roosevelt, a distant cousin of Theodore Roosevelt, attempted to change course in U.S. foreign policy and involve the United States in world affairs, but in the first part of what would be an unprecedented four-term presidency, he failed to achieve his aims. FDR failed to involve the United States in the World Court and became a timid and rather weak international presence. Yet he was able to change policies regarding Latin America. In what today is known as the "Good Neighbor" policy, which started with Hoover's withdrawal of forces from the Caribbean and Central America, FDR promised to not invade these nations again and explicitly renounced military interventions, even while stopping short of repudiating Theodore Roosevelt's "Roosevelt Corollary" (see Chapter 3). FDR was arguably successful at accomplishing this change in policy partly because the nation was in no mood for military adventures, something that would be the dominant theme in the 1930s, and partly because the United States had previously helped install several well-known pro–United States dictators who ensured stability through political repression, thus allowing the United States to reduce its presence in the region. Among the pro–United States dictators in Latin America were Trujillo of the Dominican Republic, Batista of Cuba, and Somoza of Nicaragua, to name a few. In fact, the policy of the United States was so explicit that when describing one of these leaders, FDR famously exclaimed "He is a son of a bitch, but he is ours!" The Good Neighbor policy did have a positive side, however; it led to the permanent reduction of tariffs on trade with most Latin American countries. For his efforts, FDR received the nickname "El Gran Democrata" (the Grand Democrat) from the leaders of the Central and South American countries (Herring 2008: 501).

Meanwhile, however, the entire world was on the path toward World War II, starting with the inability of the League of Nations to keep its charter relevant in world politics because of the absence of major powers and the unwillingness of these powers to act when necessary. The first major test for U.S. foreign policy came in the area of American-Japanese relations. The Chinese region known as Manchuria was the spark of a war between Russia and Japan. With an eye on Manchuria's rich mineral deposits, the government of Japan wanted to break its dependency on the United States. It staged an incident in the city of Mukden (now Shenyang, China) that served as the pretext for a full-scale invasion, leading to the establishment of a Japanese-controlled state in 1931. The Japanese, installing the last of the Chinese emperors, Henry Pu Yi, established the State of Manchukuo. Predictably, at the time, this was not seen as a major war but as a minor skirmish, despite the potential effects for Russo-Japanese relations, not to mention for China. Japanese actions provoked the world, but since the League of Nations was not willing to act, these actions went unanswered.

A couple of years after the incident at Mukden, Germany, which was suffering from hyperinflation, economic stagnation, and a political crisis, gave Adolf Hitler's National Socialist Party (Nazi party) a near-majority in the election of 1933. Feeling that he had no other options, the president of Germany, Paul von Hindenburg, appointed Adolf Hitler chancellor of Germany. Hitler's meteoric rise to power allowed him to pursue fascist policies borrowed from Benito Mussolini's Italian Fascist party, including dress code and salute, in order to solidify his power.

Germany's most important issue was its dissatisfaction with the Treaty of Versailles, and Hitler made it his mission to completely dismantle it. Throughout the 1930s the German leadership of the Nazi party worked to transform the state into a machine in which the party and the state were indistinguishable. In 1934 the Nazi leaders, using elite forces and the secret services, killed more than 700 officers of the German army, beginning on what is known today as the "night of the long knives" (June 29–30), in order to finalize their complete control over the state apparatus. The Nazis then followed Hitler and attacked what they saw as unwanted elements in their society, most importantly communists and Jews. Hitler's hatred of Jewish people was legendary, eventually leading him to strip Jews of their civil and political rights, force them into overcrowded and unsanitary ghettoes, attack all Jewish-owned businesses in an incident known as Kristallnacht (1938), and finally to attempt to kill all European Jews in his "final solution" otherwise known as the Holocaust (or Shoah, in Hebrew).

While the internal transformation of the German state was of great interest to world leaders, they would not intervene, not even when Austria became part of the German Third Reich in 1938. A stolen referendum won with 97.25 percent of the vote allowed Hitler to triumphantly seize control of his native land.

Meanwhile, the Italian leader, Benito Mussolini, the father of Fascism, invaded Abyssinia in 1935 on behalf of the Italian crown and conquered the poor African empire in eight months (approximately twice as much time as Hitler's army would take to conquer nearly all of Western Europe). The League of Nations responded by imposing sanctions on Italy, a policy that failed because Italy could still trade with the United States and Russia as well as purchase much-needed oil for its army and its industry. The United States, hiding behind the Neutrality Acts, remained neutral all this time, and the Europeans validated their own inaction by following the example set by the United States. Hitler and Mussolini signed a friendship agreement in 1936, creating what would become known as the Axis (which later would include Japan).

Under the auspices of the Axis, German and Italian military forces, the air force in particular, would fight

Did You Know?

Origins of Fascism

Fascist movements in Europe are shaped by two historical trends of the late nineteenth century. First, mass political movements and parties developed as a challenge to the control of government and politics by small groups of social elites or ruling classes. Second, many intellectuals, artists, and political thinkers began to reject the philosophical emphasis on rationality and progress made famous by the Enlightenment of the eighteenth century. More immediate causes can be found in the aftermath of World War I, when conditions in Italy and Germany allowed fascist leaders to prey on social anxieties, identify scapegoats, and mobilize the masses behind a great leader who promised to revive national glory. The first European fascist movement emerged in post–World War I Italy, led by Benito Mussolini. Mussolini formed the Italian Combat Veterans League, which eventually grew into the National Fascist party. Despite limited electoral success in 1921, Mussolini's party was invited into a ruling coalition, which positioned the Fascists to seize power in 1925. Similarly, in Germany, Adolf Hitler also rose to power by intimidation and the manipulation of democratic elections. After his Nazi party won the elections of 1932, in 1933 Hitler suspended the constitution and declared himself "Führer." While German fascism was more racist and totalitarian than its Italian counterpart, there are shared elements. Once established, fascism as a system of government relies on close coordination of political and industrial elites to establish national economic policy. Socially, fascism portrays the "nation" as an organic whole whose members are culturally and/or racially superior. Because fascism also glorifies war, struggle, and national renewal, fascist governments use martial tactics to suppress dissidents and expand the nation's influence through territorial expansionism.

on behalf of the third fascist government of Europe, that of Francisco Franco, who overthrew the democratically elected government of Spain and immersed his country in a vicious civil war (1936–1939). The United States, still neutral, was fascinated by this war, as was the rest of the world. Democratically minded volunteers from across the globe came to fight on behalf of the leftist government besieged by the Spanish military. The American volunteers in this war, called the "Lincoln Brigade," suffered heavy losses in battle. The Spanish Civil War—a war that drew some of the world's greatest literary minds, such as George Orwell, Ernest Hemingway, and André Malraux, to take part—was the dress rehearsal for World War II, but the European powers were still unable to counteract the Axis intervention and Franco took power.

By the late 1930s, the Axis, having solidified its defensive pact, moved beyond aggressive rhetoric to aggressive actions. The Japanese moved on China's capital city, Nanking (now Nanjing, Jiangsu province); their many atrocities perpetrated there are known as the "rape of Nanking." The German government demanded that the Germans living in the Czechoslovakian region known as the Sudetenland be granted autonomy and, later, that they be reunited with Germany; both demands were rejected by Czechoslovakia. In what became known as the "Munich Crisis"—nowadays considered the prime example of appeasement—British Prime Minister Neville Chamberlain flew to Munich and gave Adolf Hitler what he wanted in exchange for "peace in our time." Avoiding war was the primary motivation of both France and Britain in Munich, and when they appeased Hitler, the British Prime Minister received a telegram from President Roosevelt that read: "Good Man."

Besieged by interest groups wanting to avoid war and ethnic groups calling for neutrality, including German Americans, Italian Americans, Irish Americans, and Catholics generally across the United States, FDR was relieved to have avoided war at that time (Herring 2008). Yet the lesson from Munich is that if international aggressors are given what they want, they will eventually ask for more. Hitler got his war in 1939. After securing his eastern flank in a secret agreement with Soviet leader Joseph Stalin, Hitler attacked Western Europe with a vengeance, and he conquered most of it in a matter of months. The speed and abilities of the German army, coupled with the collapse of France, shook the U.S. political establishment to its core and allowed the U.S. president to move away from neutrality toward helping the Allies against the Axis.

President Roosevelt was an astute politician, and he used his powers to evade the Neutrality Acts in order to gently mobilize his country toward eventual entry into the war, in 1941. He used his persuasive powers in a series of "fireside chats" broadcast by radio to argue that the United States, even though neutral, could not avoid seeing the moral imperatives in the war being waged in Europe. He called for America to be the "arsenal of democracy" against fascism and, even though bound by law, he found ways to help Britain in its battle against Germany. He gave Britain destroyers from the U.S. Navy in exchange for military bases, he expanded the U.S. Navy's control of the western Atlantic all the way to Iceland, and he invented a further way of helping the financially devastated British government through a "lend/lease" program. He argued that the executive branch should be uninhibited in its duties as the primary foreign policymaker in the United States and used his powers to punish Japanese aggression in China by imposing trade sanctions on Japan. This last move, however, backfired when the military-dominated government of Japan responded not by pursuing a negotiated settlement with the United States but by initiating a war with the United States when it attacked the U.S. naval base in Pearl

Harbor, Hawaii, on December 7, 1941, an attack that killed thousands of U.S. sailors and destroyed several ships. American neutrality was no more, and within days, the United States entered World War II on two fronts.

During FDR's presidency, the United States improved its domestic economy by establishing new regulatory agencies and laws governing the workplace, emerged victorious from World War II, firmly established itself in Latin America, and, finally, acquired new interests in the Middle East, Southeast Asia, and elsewhere around the globe. FDR's foreign policy achievements cannot be overstated; he was not only an effective manager of the war and its contingencies but a great leader with the foresight to set a long-term agenda for the United States. He also helped create the United Nations, carrying forward the Wilsonian notion that an international body could potentially prevent future conflicts from blossoming into full-scale wars. At the end of World War II, the future for the United States was bright: It emerged as a global superpower, taking over from the British, who had to adjust to their new status as a second-class global power. World War II saw the beginning of the dismantling of the British and French empires and the emergence of the United States as a preeminent economic, military, and political power on the world stage.

On the other hand, FDR's policies in regions such as Latin America and the Middle East sowed the seeds of future wars and conflicts that would challenge future U.S. presidents. FDR's negotiations with Middle Eastern powers such as Iran and Saudi Arabia were the cornerstone of a Middle East policy that remains problematic, and his involvement in Southeast Asia would lead to U.S. involvement in a war in Vietnam that could not be won. His commitments to wartime allies would create a great deal of resentment after the war was over, in the Soviet Union and China, for example, and would plunge the United States into a "Cold War" that would completely transform the United States and the world once again.

- **Document: First Neutrality Act**
- **Date:** August 31, 1935
- **Importance:** The Neutrality Acts were a congressional way of tying the hands of President Roosevelt and keeping the United States out of World War II. The first neutrality act rejected the executive's demands that it be allowed to impose sanctions selectively and it imposed a universal embargo on arms and war materiel for war parties.
- **Source:** Neutrality Act of August 31, 1935, 49 Stat. 1081; 22 U.S.C. 441. U.S. Department of State, Publication 1983, *Peace and War: United States Foreign Policy, 1931–1941* (Washington, D.C.: U.S., Government Printing Office, 1943, pp. 265–271).

"Neutrality Act" of August 31, 1935, JOINT RESOLUTION

Providing for the prohibition of the export of arms, ammunition, and implements of war to belligerent countries; the prohibition of the transportation of arms, ammunition, and implements of war by vessels of the United States for the use of belligerent states; for the registration and licensing of persons engaged in the business of manufacturing, exporting, or importing arms, ammunition, or implements of war; and restricting travel by American citizens on belligerent ships during war.

Resolved by the Senate and House of Representatives of the United States of America in Congress assembled, That upon the outbreak or during the progress of war between, or among, two or more foreign states, the President shall proclaim such fact, and it shall thereafter be unlawful to export arms, ammunition, or implements of war from any place in the United States, or possessions of the United States, to any port of such belligerent states, or to any neutral port for transshipment to, or for the use of, a belligerent country.

The President, by proclamation, shall definitely enumerate the arms, ammunition, or implements of war, the export of which is prohibited by this Act.

The President may, from time to time, by proclamation, extend such embargo upon the export of arms, ammunition, or implements of war to other states as and when they may become involved in such war.

Whoever, in violation of any of the provisions of this section, shall export, or attempt to export, or cause to be exported, arms, ammunition, or implements of war from the United States, or any of its possessions, shall be fined not more than $10,000 or imprisoned not more than five years, or both, and the property, vessel, or vehicle containing the same shall be subject to the provisions of sections 1 to 8, inclusive, title 6, chapter 30, of the Act approved June 15, 1917 (40 Stat. 223–225; U.S.C., title 22, secs. 238–245).

In the case of the forfeiture of any arms, ammunition, or implements of war by reason of a violation of this Act, no public or private sale shall be required; but such arms, ammunition, or implements of war shall be delivered to the Secretary of War for such use or disposal thereof as shall be approved by the President.

When in the judgment of the President the conditions which have caused him to issue his proclamation have ceased to exist he shall revoke the same and the provisions hereof shall thereupon cease to apply.

Except with respect to prosecutions committed or forfeitures incurred prior to March 1, 1936, this section and all proclamations issued thereunder shall not be effective after February 29, 1936.

SEC. 2. That for the purpose of this Act—(a) The term "Board" means the National Munitions Control Board which is hereby established to carry out the provisions of this Act. The Board shall consist of the Secretary of State, who shall be chairman and executive officer of the Board; the Secretary of the Treasury; the Secretary of War; the Secretary of the Navy; and the Secretary of Commerce. Except as otherwise provided in this Act, or by other law, the administration of this Act is vested in the Department of State; (b) The term "United States" when used in a geographical sense, includes the several States and Territories, the insular possessions of the United States (including the Philippine Islands), the Canal Zone, and the District of Columbia; (c) The term "person" includes a partnership, company, association, or corporation, as well as a natural person.

Within ninety days after the effective date of this Act, or upon first engaging in business, every person who engages in the business of manufacturing, exporting, or importing any of the arms, ammunition, and implements of war referred to in this Act, whether as an exporter, importer, manufacturer, or dealer, shall register with the Secretary of State his name, or business name, principal place of business, and places of business in the United States, and a list of the arms, ammunition, and implements of war which he manufactures, imports, or exports.

Every person required to register under this section shall notify the Secretary of State of any change in the arms, ammunition, and implements of war which he exports, imports, or manufactures; and upon such notification the Secretary of State shall issue to such person an amended certificate of registration, free of charge, which shall remain valid until the date of expiration of the original certificate. Every person required to register under the provisions of this section shall pay a registration fee of $500, and upon receipt of such fee the Secretary of State shall issue a registration certificate valid for five years, which shall be renewable for further periods of five years upon the payment of each renewal of a fee of $500.

It shall be unlawful for any person to export, or attempt to export, from the United States any of the arms, ammunition, or implements of war referred to in this Act to any other country or to import, or attempt to import, to the United States from any other country any of the arms, ammunition, or implements of war referred to in this Act without first having obtained a license there for.

All persons required to register under this section shall maintain, subject to the inspection of the Board, such permanent records of manufacture for export, importation, and exportation of arms, ammunition, and implements of war as the Board shall prescribe.

Licenses shall be issued to persons who have registered as provided for, except in cases of export or import licenses where exportation of arms, ammunition, or implements of war would be in violation of this Act or any other law of the United States, or of a treaty to which the United States is a party, in which cases such licenses shall not be issued.

The Board shall be called by the Chairman and shall hold at least one meeting a year.

No purchase of arms, ammunition, and implements of war shall be made on behalf of the United States by any officer, executive department, or independent establishment of the Government from any person who shall have failed to register under the provisions of this Act.

The Board shall make an annual report to Congress, copies of which shall be distributed as are other reports transmitted to Congress. Such report shall contain such information and data collected by the Board as may be considered of value in the determination of questions connected with the control of trade in arms, ammunition, and implements of war. It shall include a list of all persons required to register under the provisions of this Act, and full information concerning the licenses issued hereunder.

The Secretary of State shall promulgate such rules and regulations with regard to the enforcement of this section as he may deem necessary to carry out its provisions.

The President is hereby authorized to proclaim upon recommendation of the Board from time to time a list of articles which shall be considered arms, ammunition, and implements of war for the purposes of this section.

This section shall take effect on the ninetieth day after the date of its enactment.

SEC. 3. Whenever the President shall issue the proclamation provided for in section 1 of this Act, thereafter it shall be unlawful for any American vessel to carry any arms, ammunition, or implements of war to any port of the belligerent countries named in such proclamation as being at war, or to any neutral port for transshipment to, or for the use of, a belligerent country.

Whoever, in violation of the provisions of this section, shall take, attempt to take, or shall authorize, hire, or solicit another to take any such vessel carrying such cargo out of port or from the jurisdiction of the United States shall be fined not more than $10,000 or imprisoned not more than five years, or both; and, in addition, such vessel, her tackle, apparel, furniture, equipment, and the arms, ammunition, and implements of war on board shall be forfeited to the United States.

When the President finds the conditions which have caused him to issue his proclamation have ceased to exist, he shall revoke his proclamation, and the provisions of this section shall thereupon cease to apply.

SEC. 4. Whenever, during any war in which the United States is neutral, the President, or any person hereunto authorized by him, shall have cause to believe that any vessel, domestic or foreign, whether requiring clearance or not, is about to carry out of a port of the United States, or its possession, men or fuel, arms, ammunition, implements of war, or other supplies to any warship, tender, or supply ship of a foreign belligerent nation, but the evidence is not deemed sufficient to justify forbidding the departure of the vessel as provided for by section 1, title V, chapter 30, of the Act approved June 15, 1917 (40 Stat. [221[22]]; U.S.C. title 18, sec. 31), and if, in the President's judgment, such action will serve to maintain peace between the United States and foreign nations, or to protect the commercial interests of the United States and its citizens, or to promote the security of the United States, he shall have the power and it shall be his duty to require the owner, master, or person in command thereof, before departing from a port of the United States, or any of its possessions, for a foreign port, to give a bond to the United States, with sufficient sureties, in such amount as he shall deem proper, conditioned that the vessel will not deliver the men, or the cargo, or any part thereof, to any warship, tender, or supply ship of a belligerent nation; and, if the President, or any person thereunto authorized by him, shall find that a vessel, domestic or foreign, in a port of the United States, or one of its possessions, has previously cleared from such port during such war and delivered its cargo or any part thereof to a warship, tender, or supply ship of a belligerent nation, he may prohibit the departure of such vessel during the duration of the war.

SEC. 5. Whenever, during any war in which the United States is neutral, the President shall find that special restrictions placed on the use of the ports and territorial waters of the United States, or of its possessions, by the submarines of a foreign nation will serve to maintain peace between the United States and foreign nations, or to protect the commercial interests of the United States and its citizens, or to promote the security of the United States, and shall make proclamation thereof, it shall thereafter be unlawful for any such submarine to enter a port or the territorial waters of the United States or any of its possessions, or to depart there from, except under such conditions and subject to such limitations as the President may prescribe. When, in his judgment, the conditions which have caused him to issue his proclamation have ceased to exist, he shall revoke his proclamation and the provisions of this section shall thereupon cease to apply.

SEC. 6. Whenever, during any war in which the United States is neutral, the President shall find that the maintenance of peace between the United States and foreign nations, or the protection of the lives of citizens of the United States, or the

Did You Know?

Isolationism

The United States has a long tradition of avoiding entanglements with European powers and pursuing a policy of non-interference in European conflicts. Both George Washington and Thomas Jefferson promoted friendly relations with European nations but without "permanent" and "entangling" alliances. The flip side was the Monroe Doctrine's assertion that the United States expected European powers to reciprocate and refrain from interfering in the Western Hemisphere. Isolationism and expansionism coexisted in nineteenth-century American politics. The U.S. entrance into World War I, however, was the first major break from isolationism, even though political leaders such as Robert La Follette of Wisconsin opposed entrance into what many saw as a European conflict. After World War I, isolationism returned, and is one reason why the United States did not join the League of Nations. Isolationism was strongest in rural and small-town America in the Midwest and Great Plains, and was supported by many Irish Americans and German Americans. Isolationist leaders denounced Eastern urban business, financial, and political elites who they accused of profiting from the entanglement of the United States in European affairs. In 1940, German military triumphs in Europe forced many political elites to realize that the United States could not survive as "Fortress America." Emerging from World War II as an undisputed economic and political superpower, the United States found that isolationism had become impractical, even if Americans periodically express a desire to disengage from the entanglements of international obligations.

protection of the commercial interests of the United States and its citizens, or the security of the United States requires that the American citizens should refrain from traveling as passengers on the vessels of any belligerent nation, he shall so proclaim, and thereafter no citizen of the United States shall travel on any vessel of any belligerent nation except at his own risk, unless in accordance with such rules and regulations as the President shall prescribe: Provided, however, That the provisions of this section shall not apply to a citizen travelling on the vessel of a belligerent whose voyage was begun in advance of the date of the President's proclamation, and who had no opportunity to discontinue his voyage after that date: And provided further, That they shall not apply under ninety days after the date of the President's proclamation to a citizen returning from a foreign country to the United States or to any of its possessions. When, in the President's judgment, the conditions which have caused him to issue his proclamation have ceased to exist, he shall revoke his proclamation and the provisions of this section shall thereupon cease to apply.

SEC. 7. In every case of the violation of any of the provisions of this Act where a specific penalty is not herein provided, such violator or violators, upon conviction, shall be fined not more than $10,000 or imprisoned not more than five years, or both.

SEC. 8. If any of the provisions of this Act, or the application thereof to any person or circumstance, is held invalid, the remainder of the Act, and the application of such provision to other persons or circumstances, shall not be affected thereby.

SEC. 9. The sum of $25,000 is hereby authorized to be appropriated, out of any money in the Treasury not otherwise appropriated, to be expended by the Secretary of State in administering this Act.

Approved, August 31, 1935.

- **Document:** "Arsenal of Democracy" Fireside Chat
- **Date:** December 29, 1940
- **Importance:** Over a period of nine years, President Roosevelt broadcast a series of "fireside chats" to the U.S. public. In one of the most important of these radio addresses, Roosevelt urged the people to think about the situation in Europe. He called for the United States

to be the "arsenal of democracy," thus preparing the United States for entrance into World War II.

- **Source:** Fireside Chats of Franklin D. Roosevelt, "On National Security," December 29, 1940. Franklin D. Roosevelt Library, Hyde Park, New York.

President Franklin D. Roosevelt's Radio Address Delivered on December 29, 1940.

My friends:

This is not a fireside chat on war. It is a talk on national security; because the nub of the whole purpose of your President is to keep you now, and your children later, and your grandchildren much later, out of a last-ditch war for the preservation of

President Franklin D. Roosevelt delivers one of his popular fireside chats, a series of evening radio talks to the American public. Roosevelt used these chats to explain New Deal programs during the Great Depression and war policies during World War II. (Library of Congress)

American independence, and all of the things that American independence means to you and to me and to ours.

Tonight, in the presence of a world crisis, my mind goes back eight years to a night in the midst of a domestic crisis. It was a time when the wheels of American industry were grinding to a full stop, when the whole banking system of our country had ceased to function. I well remember that while I sat in my study in the White House, preparing to talk with the people of the United States, I had before my eyes the picture of all those Americans with whom I was talking. I saw the workmen in the mills, the mines, the factories, the girl behind the counter, the small shopkeeper, the farmer doing his spring plowing, the widows and the old men wondering about their life's savings. I tried to convey to the great mass of American people what the banking crisis meant to them in their daily lives.

Tonight, I want to do the same thing, with the same people, in this new crisis which faces America. We met the issue of 1933 with courage and realism. We face this new crisis, this new threat to the security of our nation, with the same courage and realism. Never before since Jamestown and Plymouth Rock has our American civilization been in such danger as now. For on September 27th, 1940—this year—by an agreement signed in Berlin, three powerful nations, two in Europe and one in Asia, joined themselves together in the threat that if the United States of America interfered with or blocked the expansion program of these three nations—a program aimed at world control—they would unite in ultimate action against the United States.

The Nazi masters of Germany have made it clear that they intend not only to dominate all life and thought in their own country, but also to enslave the whole of Europe, and then to use the resources of Europe to dominate the rest of the world. It was only three weeks ago that their leader stated this: "There are two worlds that stand opposed to each other." And then in defiant reply to his opponents he said this: "Others are correct when they say: 'With this world we cannot ever reconcile ourselves.' I can beat any other power in the world." So said the leader of the Nazis.

In other words, the Axis not merely admits but the Axis proclaims that there can be no ultimate peace between their philosophy—their philosophy of government— and our philosophy of government. In view of the nature of this undeniable threat, it can be asserted, properly and categorically, that the United States has no right or reason to encourage talk of peace until the day shall come when there is a clear intention on the part of the aggressor nations to abandon all thought of dominating or conquering the world.

At this moment the forces of the States that are leagued against all peoples who live in freedom are being held away from our shores. The Germans and the Italians are being blocked on the other side of the Atlantic by the British and by the Greeks, and by thousands of soldiers and sailors who were able to escape from subjugated countries. In Asia the Japanese are being engaged by the Chinese nation in another great defense. In the Pacific Ocean is our fleet.

Some of our people like to believe that wars in Europe and in Asia are of no concern to us. But it is a matter of most vital concern to us that European and Asiatic war-makers should not gain control of the oceans which lead to this hemisphere. One hundred and seventeen years ago the Monroe Doctrine was conceived by our government as a measure of defense in the face of a threat against this hemisphere by an alliance in Continental Europe. Thereafter, we stood guard in the Atlantic, with the British as neighbors. There was no treaty. There was no "unwritten agreement." And yet there was the feeling, proven correct by history, that we as neighbors could settle any disputes in peaceful fashion. And the fact is that during the whole of this time the Western Hemisphere has remained free from aggression from Europe or from Asia.

Does anyone seriously believe that we need to fear attack anywhere in the Americas while a free Britain remains our most powerful naval neighbor in the Atlantic? And does anyone seriously believe, on the other hand, that we could rest easy if the Axis powers were our neighbors there? If Great Britain goes down, the Axis powers will control the Continents of Europe, Asia, Africa, Austral-Asia, and the high seas. And they will be in a position to bring enormous military and naval resources against this hemisphere. It is no exaggeration to say that all of us in all the Americas would be living at the point of a gun—a gun loaded with explosive bullets, economic as well as military. We should enter upon a new and terrible era in which the whole world, our hemisphere included, would be run by threats of brute force. And to survive in such a world, we would have to convert ourselves permanently into a militaristic power on the basis of war economy.

Some of us like to believe that even if Britain falls, we are still safe, because of the broad expanse of the Atlantic and of the Pacific. But the width of those oceans is not what it was in the days of clipper ships. At one point between Africa and Brazil the distance is less than it is from Washington to Denver, Colorado, five hours for the latest type of bomber. And at the north end of the Pacific Ocean, America and Asia almost touch each other. Why, even today we have planes that could fly from the British Isles to New England and back again without refueling. And remember that the range of the modern bomber is ever being increased.

During the past week many people in all parts of the nation have told me what they wanted me to say tonight. Almost all of them expressed a courageous desire to hear the plain truth about the gravity of the situation. One telegram, however, expressed the attitude of the small minority who want to see no evil and hear no evil, even though they know in their hearts that evil exists. That telegram begged me not to tell again of the ease with which our American cities could be bombed by any hostile power which had gained bases in this Western Hemisphere. The gist of that telegram was: "Please, Mr. President, don't frighten us by telling us the facts." Frankly and definitely there is danger ahead—danger against which we must prepare. But we well know that we cannot escape danger, or the fear of danger, by crawling into bed and pulling the covers over our heads.

Some nations of Europe were bound by solemn nonintervention pacts with Germany. Other nations were assured by Germany that they need never fear invasion. Nonintervention pact or not, the fact remains that they were attacked, overrun, thrown into modern slavery at an hour's notice—or even without any notice at all. As an exiled leader of one of these nations said to me the other day, "The notice was a minus quantity. It was given to my government two hours after German troops had poured into my country in a hundred places." The fate of these nations tells us what it means to live at the point of a Nazi gun.

The Nazis have justified such actions by various pious frauds. One of these frauds is the claim that they are occupying a nation for the purpose of "restoring order." Another is that they are occupying or controlling a nation on the excuse that they are "protecting it" against the aggression of somebody else. For example, Germany has said that she was occupying Belgium to save the Belgians from the British. Would she then hesitate to say to any South American country: "We are occupying you to protect you from aggression by the United States"? Belgium today is being used as an invasion base against Britain, now fighting for its life. And any South

American country, in Nazi hands, would always constitute a jumping off place for German attack on any one of the other republics of this hemisphere.

Analyze for yourselves the future of two other places even nearer to Germany if the Nazis won. Could Ireland hold out? Would Irish freedom be permitted as an amazing pet exception in an unfree world? Or the islands of the Azores, which still fly the flag of Portugal after five centuries? You and I think of Hawaii as an outpost of defense in the Pacific. And yet the Azores are closer to our shores in the Atlantic than Hawaii is on the other side.

There are those who say that the Axis powers would never have any desire to attack the Western Hemisphere. That is the same dangerous form of wishful thinking which has destroyed the powers of resistance of so many conquered peoples. The plain facts are that the Nazis have proclaimed, time and again, that all other races are their inferiors and therefore subject to their orders. And most important of all, the vast resources and wealth of this American hemisphere constitute the most tempting loot in all of the round world.

Let us no longer blind ourselves to the undeniable fact that the evil forces which have crushed and undermined and corrupted so many others are already within our own gates. Your government knows much about them and every day is ferreting them out. Their secret emissaries are active in our own and in neighboring countries. They seek to stir up suspicion and dissension, to cause internal strife. They try to turn capital against labor, and vice versa. They try to reawaken long slumbering racial and religious enmities which should have no place in this country. They are active in every group that promotes intolerance. They exploit for their own ends our own natural abhorrence of war. These trouble-breeders have but one purpose. It is to divide our people, to divide them into hostile groups and to destroy our unity and shatter our will to defend ourselves.

There are also American citizens, many of them in high places, who, unwittingly in most cases, are aiding and abetting the work of these agents. I do not charge these American citizens with being foreign agents. But I do charge them with doing exactly the kind of work that the dictators want done in the United States. These people not only believe that we can save our own skins by shutting our eyes to the fate of other nations. Some of them go much further than that. They say that we can and should become the friends and even the partners of the Axis powers. Some of them even suggest that we should imitate the methods of the dictatorships. But Americans never can and never will do that.

The experience of the past two years has proven beyond doubt that no nation can appease the Nazis. No man can tame a tiger into a kitten by stroking it. There can be no appeasement with ruthlessness. There can be no reasoning with an incendiary bomb. We know now that a nation can have peace with the Nazis only at the price of total surrender. Even the people of Italy have been forced to become accomplices of the Nazis; but at this moment they do not know how soon they will be embraced to death by their allies.

The American appeasers ignore the warning to be found in the fate of Austria, Czechoslovakia, Poland, Norway, Belgium, the Netherlands, Denmark, and France. They tell you that the Axis powers are going to win anyway; that all of this bloodshed in the world could be saved, that the United States might just as well throw its influence into the scale of a dictated peace and get the best out of it that we can. They call it a "negotiated peace." Nonsense! Is it a negotiated peace if a gang of outlaws surrounds your community and on threat of extermination makes you pay tribute to save your own skins? For such a dictated peace would be no peace at all. It would be only another armistice, leading to the most gigantic armament race and the most devastating trade wars in all history. And in these contests the Americas would offer the only real resistance to the Axis power. With all their vaunted efficiency, with all their parade of pious purpose in this war, there are still in their background the concentration camp and the servants of God in chains.

The history of recent years proves that the shootings and the chains and the concentration camps are not simply the transient tools but the very altars of modern dictatorships. They may talk of a "new order" in the world, but what they have in mind is only a revival of the oldest and the worst tyranny. In that there is no liberty, no religion, no hope. The proposed "new order" is the very opposite of a United States of Europe or a United States of Asia. It is not a government based upon the consent of the governed. It is not a union of ordinary, self-respecting men and women to protect themselves and their freedom and their dignity from oppression. It is an unholy alliance of power and pelf to dominate and to enslave the human race.

The British people and their allies today are conducting an active war against this unholy alliance. Our own future security is greatly dependent on the outcome of that fight. Our ability to "keep out of war" is going to be affected by that outcome. Thinking in terms of today and tomorrow, I make the direct statement to the American people that there is far less chance of the United States getting into war if we do all we can now to support the nations defending themselves against attack by the Axis than if we acquiesce in their defeat, submit tamely to an Axis victory, and wait our turn to be the object of attack in another war later on.

If we are to be completely honest with ourselves, we must admit that there is risk in any course we may take. But I deeply believe that the great majority of our people agree that the course that I advocate involves the least risk now and the greatest hope for world peace in the future.

The people of Europe who are defending themselves do not ask us to do their fighting. They ask us for the implements of war, the planes, the tanks, the guns, the freighters which will enable them to fight for their liberty and for our security. Emphatically, we must get these weapons to them, get them to them in sufficient volume and quickly enough so that we and our children will be saved the agony and suffering of war which others have had to endure.

Let not the defeatists tell us that it is too late. It will never be earlier. Tomorrow will be later than today.

Certain facts are self-evident.

In a military sense Great Britain and the British Empire are today the spearhead of resistance to world conquest. And they are putting up a fight which will live forever in the story of human gallantry. There is no demand for sending an American expeditionary force outside our own borders. There is no intention by any member of your government to send such a force. You can therefore, nail, nail any talk about sending armies to Europe as deliberate untruth. Our national policy is not directed toward war. Its sole purpose is to keep war away from our country and away from our people.

Democracy's fight against world conquest is being greatly aided, and must be more greatly aided, by the rearmament of the United States and by sending every ounce and every ton of munitions and supplies that we can possibly spare to help the defenders who are in the front lines. And it is no more un-neutral for us to do that than it is for Sweden, Russia, and other nations near Germany to send steel and ore and oil and other war materials into Germany every day in the week.

We are planning our own defense with the utmost urgency, and in its vast scale we must integrate the war needs of Britain and the other free nations which are resisting aggression. This is not a matter of sentiment or of controversial personal opinion. It is a matter of realistic, practical military policy, based on the advice of our military experts who are in close touch with existing warfare. These military and naval experts and the members of the Congress and the Administration have a single-minded purpose: the defense of the United States.

This nation is making a great effort to produce everything that is necessary in this emergency, and with all possible speed. And this great effort requires great sacrifice. I would ask no one to defend a democracy which in turn would not defend every one in the nation against want and privation. The strength of this nation shall not be diluted by the failure of the government to protect the economic well-being of its citizens. If our capacity to produce is limited by machines, it must ever be remembered that these machines are operated by the skill and the stamina of the workers.

As the government is determined to protect the rights of the workers, so the nation has a right to expect that the men who man the machines will discharge their full responsibilities to the urgent needs of defense. The worker possesses the same human dignity and is entitled to the same security of position as the engineer or the manager or the owner. For the workers provide the human power that turns out the destroyers, and the planes, and the tanks. The nation expects our defense industries to continue operation without interruption by strikes or lockouts. It expects and insists that management and workers will reconcile their differences by voluntary or legal means, to continue to produce the supplies that are so sorely needed. And on the economic side of our great defense program, we are, as you know, bending every effort to maintain stability of prices and with that the stability of the cost of living.

Nine days ago I announced the setting up of a more effective organization to direct our gigantic efforts to increase the production of munitions. The appropriation of vast sums of money and a well-coordinated executive direction of our defense efforts are not in themselves enough. Guns, planes, ships and many other things have to be built in the factories and the arsenals of America. They have to be produced by workers and managers and engineers with the aid of machines which in turn have to be built by hundreds of thousands of workers throughout the land. In this great work there has been splendid cooperation between the government and industry and labor. And I am very thankful.

American industrial genius, unmatched throughout all the world in the solution of production problems, has been called upon to bring its resources and its talents into action. Manufacturers of watches, of farm implements, of Linotypes and cash registers and automobiles, and sewing machines and lawn mowers and locomotives, are now making fuses and bomb packing crates and telescope mounts and shells and pistols and tanks.

But all of our present efforts are not enough. We must have more ships, more guns, more planes—more of everything. And this can be accomplished only if we discard the notion of "business as usual." This job cannot be done merely by superimposing on the existing productive facilities the added requirements of the nation for defense. Our defense efforts must not be blocked by those who fear the future consequences of surplus plant capacity. The possible consequences of failure of our defense efforts now are much more to be feared. And after the present needs of our defense are past, a proper handling of the country's peacetime needs will require all of the new productive capacity, if not still more. No pessimistic policy about the future of America shall delay the immediate expansion of those industries essential to defense. We need them.

I want to make it clear that it is the purpose of the nation to build now with all possible speed every machine, every arsenal, every factory that we need to manufacture our defense material. We have the men, the skill, the wealth, and above all, the will. I am confident that if and when production of consumer or luxury goods in certain industries requires the use of machines and raw materials that are essential for defense purposes, then such production must yield, and will gladly yield, to our primary and compelling purpose.

So I appeal to the owners of plants, to the managers, to the workers, to our own government employees to put every ounce of effort into producing these munitions swiftly and without stint. With this appeal I give you the pledge that all of us who are officers of your government will devote ourselves to the same whole-hearted extent to the great task that lies ahead.

As planes and ships and guns and shells are produced, your government, with its defense experts, can then determine how best to use them to defend this hemisphere. The decision as to how much shall be sent abroad and how much shall remain at home must be made on the basis of our overall military necessities.

We must be the great arsenal of democracy.

For us this is an emergency as serious as war itself. We must apply ourselves to our task with the same resolution, the same sense of urgency, the same spirit of patriotism and sacrifice as we would show were we at war.

We have furnished the British great material support and we will furnish far more in the future. There will be no "bottlenecks" in our determination to aid Great Britain. No dictator, no combination of dictators, will weaken that determination by threats of how they will construe that determination. The British have received invaluable military support from the heroic Greek Army and from the forces of all the governments in exile. Their strength is growing. It is the strength of men and women who value their freedom more highly than they value their lives.

I believe that the Axis powers are not going to win this war. I base that belief on the latest and best of information.

We have no excuse for defeatism. We have every good reason for hope—hope for peace, yes, and hope for the defense of our civilization and for the building

Did You Know?

Allied Conferences During World War II

Although there were more than 20 conferences between the Allies during World War II, the most important and recognized conferences are those including principal players such as presidents and prime ministers. Of these, there are four.

The **Teheran Conference** occurred from November 28 to December 1, 1943, in Teheran, the capital of Iran, between U.S. President Roosevelt, British Prime Minister Churchill, and Soviet Secretary General Stalin. The primary declarations were to support the Yugoslav partisans against the Nazi forces, to call on Turkey to join the allies, to start a conference on the United Nations, and for the Soviet Union to declare war on Japan once Germany was defeated.

The **Bretton Woods Conference**, held at the Mount Washington Hotel in Bretton Woods, New Hampshire, brought together representatives of 44 nations from July 1 to July 15, 1944, to discuss the shape of the international economy at the end of the war. This famous conference produced three separate but linked institutions that still regulate the global economy: the International Bank for Reconstruction and Development (IBRD), which later became the World Bank, the International Monetary Fund (IMF), and the General Agreement on Tariffs and Trade (GATT), which later became the World Trade Organization (WTO).

The **Yalta Conference** took place in the resort town of Yalta in the Crimea from February 4 to February 11, 1945. The conference was attended by Roosevelt, Churchill, and Stalin, where they agreed to concentrate on the unconditional defeat of Germany, its denazification and demilitarization, and its administrative partitioning between the United States, the Soviet Union, Britain, and France. The status of Poland was agreed and free elections were promised, while Joseph Stalin agreed to declare war on Japan, to join the conference on the United Nations, and to help hunt the Nazi leadership.

The **Potsdam Conference** took place in occupied territory in Potsdam, Germany, from July 17 to August 2, 1945. The main participants were Joseph Stalin, Harry S. Truman, and Winston Churchill, who was replaced on July 28 by his successor in office, Clement Attlee. The main issues addressed included agreements on the future of Germany, which included denazification, demilitarization, democratization, and de-cartelization. Also decided were issues such as the elements of Nazi war crimes prosecutions, war reparations, the expulsion of all German nationals from places in Eastern Europe, and the reversal of all German territorial gains including the Alsace-Loraine region, the Sudetenland, and western Poland. It was at Potsdam that Truman was informed of a successful atom bomb test; he told Churchill but mentioned "a new weapon" only casually to Stalin.

Nothing contained in the present Charter shall authorize the United Nations to intervene in matters which are essentially within the domestic jurisdiction of any state or shall require the Members to submit such matters to settlement under the present Charter; but this principle shall not prejudice the application of enforcement measures under Chapter VII.

CHAPTER II: MEMBERSHIP

Article 3

The original Members of the United Nations shall be the states which, having participated in the United Nations Conference on International Organization at San Francisco, or having previously signed the Declaration by United Nations of 1 January 1942, sign the present Charter and ratify it in accordance with Article 110.

Article 4

Membership in the United Nations is open to all other peace-loving states which accept the obligations contained in the present Charter and, in the judgment of the Organization, are able and willing to carry out these obligations.

The admission of any such state to membership in the United Nations will be effected by a decision of the General Assembly upon the recommendation of the Security Council.

Article 5

A Member of the United Nations against which preventive or enforcement action has been taken by the Security Council may be suspended from the exercise of the rights and privileges of membership by the General Assembly upon the recommendation of the Security Council. The exercise of these rights and privileges may be restored by the Security Council.

Article 6

A Member of the United Nations which has persistently violated the Principles contained in the present Charter may be expelled from the Organization by the General Assembly upon the recommendation of the Security Council.

CHAPTER III: ORGANS

Article 7

There are established as principal organs of the United Nations: a General Assembly, a Security Council, an Economic and Social Council, a Trusteeship Council, an International Court of Justice and a Secretariat.

Such subsidiary organs as may be found necessary may be established in accordance with the present Charter.

Article 8

The United Nations shall place no restrictions on the eligibility of men and women to participate in any capacity and under conditions of equality in its principal and subsidiary organs.

CHAPTER IV: THE GENERAL ASSEMBLY

Composition

Article 9

The General Assembly shall consist of all the Members of the United Nations.
Each Member shall have not more than five representatives in the General Assembly.

Functions and Powers

Article 10

The General Assembly may discuss any questions or any matters within the scope of the present Charter or relating to the powers and functions of any organs provided for in the present Charter, and, except as provided in Article 12, may make recommendations to the Members of the United Nations or to the Security Council or to both on any such questions or matters.

Article 11

The General Assembly may consider the general principles of co-operation in the maintenance of international peace and security, including the principles governing disarmament and the regulation of armaments, and may make recommendations with regard to such principles to the Members or to the Security Council or to both.
The General Assembly may discuss any questions relating to the maintenance of international peace and security brought before it by any Member of the United Nations, or by the Security Council, or by a state which is not a Member of the United Nations in accordance with Article 35, paragraph 2, and, except as provided in Article 12, may make recommendations with regard to any such questions to the state or states concerned or to the Security Council or to both. Any such question on which action is necessary shall be referred to the Security Council by the General Assembly either before or after discussion.
The General Assembly may call the attention of the Security Council to situations which are likely to endanger international peace and security.

The powers of the General Assembly set forth in this Article shall not limit the general scope of Article 10.

Article 12

While the Security Council is exercising in respect of any dispute or situation the functions assigned to it in the present Charter, the General Assembly shall not make any recommendation with regard to that dispute or situation unless the Security Council so requests.

The Secretary-General, with the consent of the Security Council, shall notify the General Assembly at each session of any matters relative to the maintenance of international peace and security which are being dealt with by the Security Council and shall similarly notify the General Assembly, or the Members of the United Nations if the General Assembly is not in session, immediately the Security Council ceases to deal with such matters.

Article 13

The General Assembly shall initiate studies and make recommendations for the purpose of: a. promoting international co-operation in the political field and encouraging the progressive development of international law and its codification; b. promoting international co-operation in the economic, social, cultural, educational, and health fields, and assisting in the realization of human rights and fundamental freedoms for all without distinction as to race, sex, language, or religion.

The further responsibilities, functions and powers of the General Assembly with respect to matters mentioned in paragraph 1 (b) above are set forth in Chapters IX and X.

. . .

Voting

Article 18

Each member of the General Assembly shall have one vote.

Decisions of the General Assembly on important questions shall be made by a two-thirds majority of the members present and voting. These questions shall include: recommendations with respect to the maintenance of international peace and security, the election of the non-permanent members of the Security Council, the election of the members of the Economic and Social Council, the election of members of the Trusteeship Council in accordance with paragraph 1 (c) of Article 86, the admission of new Members to the United Nations, the suspension of the rights and privileges of membership, the expulsion of Members, questions relating to the operation of the trusteeship system, and budgetary questions.

Decisions on other questions, including the determination of additional categories of questions to be decided by a two-thirds majority, shall be made by a majority of the members present and voting.

Article 19

A Member of the United Nations which is in arrears in the payment of its financial contributions to the Organization shall have no vote in the General Assembly if the amount of its arrears equals or exceeds the amount of the contributions due from it for the preceding two full years. The General Assembly may, nevertheless, permit such a Member to vote if it is satisfied that the failure to pay is due to conditions beyond the control of the Member.

Procedure

Article 20

The General Assembly shall meet in regular annual sessions and in such special sessions as occasion may require. Special sessions shall be convoked by the Secretary-General at the request of the Security Council or of a majority of the Members of the United Nations.

Article 21

The General Assembly shall adopt its own rules of procedure. It shall elect its President for each session.

Article 22

The General Assembly may establish such subsidiary organs as it deems necessary for the performance of its functions.

CHAPTER V: THE SECURITY COUNCIL

Composition

Article 23

The Security Council shall consist of fifteen Members of the United Nations. The Republic of China, France, the Union of Soviet Socialist Republics, the United Kingdom of Great Britain and Northern Ireland, and the United States of America shall be permanent members of the Security Council. The General Assembly shall elect ten other Members of the United Nations to be non-permanent members of the Security Council, due regard being specially paid, in the first instance to the contribution of Members of the United Nations to the maintenance of international peace and security and to the other purposes of the Organization, and also to equitable geographical distribution.

The non-permanent members of the Security Council shall be elected for a term of two years. In the first election of the non-permanent members after the increase of the membership of the Security Council from eleven to fifteen, two of the four additional members shall be chosen for a term of one year. A retiring member shall not be eligible for immediate re-election.

Each member of the Security Council shall have one representative.

Functions and Powers

Article 24

In order to ensure prompt and effective action by the United Nations, its Members confer on the Security Council primary responsibility for the maintenance of international peace and security, and agree that in carrying out its duties under this responsibility the Security Council acts on their behalf.

In discharging these duties the Security Council shall act in accordance with the Purposes and Principles of the United Nations. The specific powers granted to the Security Council for the discharge of these duties are laid down in Chapters VI, VII, VIII, and XII.

The Security Council shall submit annual and, when necessary, special reports to the General Assembly for its consideration.

Article 25

The Members of the United Nations agree to accept and carry out the decisions of the Security Council in accordance with the present Charter.

Article 26

In order to promote the establishment and maintenance of international peace and security with the least diversion for armaments of the world's human and economic resources, the Security Council shall be responsible for formulating, with the assistance of the Military Staff Committee referred to in Article 47, plans to be submitted to the Members of the United Nations for the establishment of a system for the regulation of armaments.

Voting

Article 27

Each member of the Security Council shall have one vote.

Decisions of the Security Council on procedural matters shall be made by an affirmative vote of nine members.

Decisions of the Security Council on all other matters shall be made by an affirmative vote of nine members including the concurring votes of the permanent members; provided that, in decisions under Chapter VI, and under paragraph 3 of Article 52, a party to a dispute shall abstain from voting.

Procedure

Article 28

The Security Council shall be so organized as to be able to function continuously. Each member of the Security Council shall for this purpose be represented at all times at the seat of the Organization.

The Security Council shall hold periodic meetings at which each of its members may, if it so desires, be represented by a member of the government or by some other specially designated representative.

The Security Council may hold meetings at such places other than the seat of the Organization as in its judgment will best facilitate its work.

Article 29

The Security Council may establish such subsidiary organs as it deems necessary for the performance of its functions.

Article 30

The Security Council shall adopt its own rules of procedure, including the method of selecting its President.

Article 31

Any Member of the United Nations which is not a member of the Security Council may participate, without vote, in the discussion of any question brought before the Security Council whenever the latter considers that the interests of that Member are specially affected.

Article 32

Any Member of the United Nations which is not a member of the Security Council or any state which is not a Member of the United Nations, if it is a party to a dispute under consideration by the Security Council, shall be invited to participate, without vote, in the discussion relating to the dispute. The Security Council shall lay down such conditions as it deems just for the participation of a state which is not a Member of the United Nations.

Chapter VI: Pacific Settlement of Disputes

Article 33

The parties to any dispute, the continuance of which is likely to endanger the maintenance of international peace and security, shall, first of all, seek a solution by negotiation, enquiry, mediation, conciliation, arbitration, judicial settlement, resort to regional agencies or arrangements, or other peaceful means of their own choice.

President Harry S. Truman looks on as Secretary of State Edward R. Stettinius, seated, signs the United Nations Security Charter for the United States in San Francisco, June 26, 1945. (AP Photo)

The Security Council shall, when it deems necessary, call upon the parties to settle their dispute by such means.

Article 34

The Security Council may investigate any dispute, or any situation which might lead to international friction or give rise to a dispute, in order to determine whether the continuance of the dispute or situation is likely to endanger the maintenance of international peace and security.

Article 35

Any Member of the United Nations may bring any dispute, or any situation of the nature referred to in Article 34, to the attention of the Security Council or of the General Assembly.

A state which is not a Member of the United Nations may bring to the attention of the Security Council or of the General Assembly any dispute to which it is a party if it accepts in advance, for the purposes of the dispute, the obligations of pacific settlement provided in the present Charter.

The proceedings of the General Assembly in respect of matters brought to its attention under this Article will be subject to the provisions of Articles 11 and 12.

Article 36

The Security Council may, at any stage of a dispute of the nature referred to in Article 33 or of a situation of like nature, recommend appropriate procedures or methods of adjustment.

The Security Council should take into consideration any procedures for the settlement of the dispute which have already been adopted by the parties.

In making recommendations under this Article the Security Council should also take into consideration that legal disputes should as a general rule be referred by the parties to the International Court of Justice in accordance with the provisions of the Statute of the Court.

Article 37

Should the parties to a dispute of the nature referred to in Article 33 fail to settle it by the means indicated in that Article, they shall refer it to the Security Council.

If the Security Council deems that the continuance of the dispute is in fact likely to endanger the maintenance of international peace and security, it shall decide whether to take action under Article 36 or to recommend such terms of settlement as it may consider appropriate.

Article 38

Without prejudice to the provisions of Articles 33 to 37, the Security Council may, if all the parties to any dispute so request, make recommendations to the parties with a view to a pacific settlement of the dispute.

CHAPTER VII: ACTION WITH RESPECT TO THREATS TO THE PEACE, BREACHES OF THE PEACE, AND ACTS OF AGGRESSION

Article 39

The Security Council shall determine the existence of any threat to the peace, breach of the peace, or act of aggression and shall make recommendations, or decide what measures shall be taken in accordance with Articles 41 and 42, to maintain or restore international peace and security.

Article 40

In order to prevent an aggravation of the situation, the Security Council may, before making the recommendations or deciding upon the measures provided for in Article 39, call upon the parties concerned to comply with such provisional measures as it deems necessary or desirable. Such provisional measures shall be without prejudice to the rights, claims, or position of the parties concerned. The Security Council shall duly take account of failure to comply with such provisional measures.

Article 41

The Security Council may decide what measures not involving the use of armed force are to be employed to give effect to its decisions, and it may call upon the Members of the United Nations to apply such measures. These may include complete or partial interruption of economic relations and of rail, sea, air, postal, telegraphic, radio, and other means of communication, and the severance of diplomatic relations.

Article 42

Should the Security Council consider that measures provided for in Article 41 would be inadequate or have proved to be inadequate, it may take such action by air, sea, or land forces as may be necessary to maintain or restore international peace and security. Such action may include demonstrations, blockade, and other operations by air, sea, or land forces of Members of the United Nations.

Article 43

All Members of the United Nations, in order to contribute to the maintenance of international peace and security, undertake to make available to the Security Council, on its call and in accordance with a special agreement or agreements, armed forces, assistance, and facilities, including rights of passage, necessary for the purpose of maintaining international peace and security.

Such agreement or agreements shall govern the numbers and types of forces, their degree of readiness and general location, and the nature of the facilities and assistance to be provided.

The agreement or agreements shall be negotiated as soon as possible on the initiative of the Security Council. They shall be concluded between the Security Council and Members or between the Security Council and groups of Members and shall be subject to ratification by the signatory states in accordance with their respective constitutional processes.

Article 44

When the Security Council has decided to use force it shall, before calling upon a Member not represented on it to provide armed forces in fulfilment of the obligations assumed under Article 43, invite that Member, if the Member so desires, to participate in the decisions of the Security Council concerning the employment of contingents of that Member's armed forces.

Article 45

In order to enable the United Nations to take urgent military measures, Members shall hold immediately available national air-force contingents for combined international enforcement action. The strength and degree of readiness of these contingents and plans for their combined action shall be determined within the limits laid down in the special agreement or agreements referred to in Article 43, by the Security Council with the assistance of the Military Staff Committee.

Article 46

Plans for the application of armed force shall be made by the Security Council with the assistance of the Military Staff Committee.

Article 47

There shall be established a Military Staff Committee to advise and assist the Security Council on all questions relating to the Security Council's military requirements for the maintenance of international peace and security, the employment and command of forces placed at its disposal, the regulation of armaments, and possible disarmament.

The Military Staff Committee shall consist of the Chiefs of Staff of the permanent members of the Security Council or their representatives. Any Member of the United Nations not permanently represented on the Committee shall be invited by the Committee to be associated with it when the efficient discharge of the Committee's responsibilities requires the participation of that Member in its work.

The Military Staff Committee shall be responsible under the Security Council for the strategic direction of any armed forces placed at the disposal of the Security Council. Questions relating to the command of such forces shall be worked out subsequently.

The Military Staff Committee, with the authorization of the Security Council and after consultation with appropriate regional agencies, may establish regional sub-committees.

Article 48

The action required to carry out the decisions of the Security Council for the maintenance of international peace and security shall be taken by all the Members of the United Nations or by some of them, as the Security Council may determine.

Such decisions shall be carried out by the Members of the United Nations directly and through their action in the appropriate international agencies of which they are members.

Article 49

The Members of the United Nations shall join in affording mutual assistance in carrying out the measures decided upon by the Security Council.

Article 50

If preventive or enforcement measures against any state are taken by the Security Council, any other state, whether a Member of the United Nations or not, which finds itself confronted with special economic problems arising from the carrying out of those measures shall have the right to consult the Security Council with regard to a solution of those problems.

Article 51

Nothing in the present Charter shall impair the inherent right of individual or collective self-defence if an armed attack occurs against a Member of the United Nations, until the Security Council has taken measures necessary to maintain international peace and security. Measures taken by Members in the exercise of this right of self-defence shall be immediately reported to the Security Council and shall not in any way affect the authority and responsibility of the Security Council under the present Charter to take at any time such action as it deems necessary in order to maintain or restore international peace and security.

. . .

CHAPTER X: THE ECONOMIC AND SOCIAL COUNCIL

Composition

Article 61

The Economic and Social Council shall consist of fifty-four Members of the United Nations elected by the General Assembly.

Subject to the provisions of paragraph 3, eighteen members of the Economic and Social Council shall be elected each year for a term of three years. A retiring member shall be eligible for immediate re-election.

At the first election after the increase in the membership of the Economic and Social Council from twenty-seven to fifty-four members, in addition to the members elected in place of the nine members whose term of office expires at the end of that year, twenty-seven additional members shall be elected. Of these twenty-seven additional members, the term of office of nine members so elected shall expire at the end of one year, and of nine other members at the end of two years, in accordance with arrangements made by the General Assembly.

Each member of the Economic and Social Council shall have one representative.

Functions and Powers

Article 62

The Economic and Social Council may make or initiate studies and reports with respect to international economic, social, cultural, educational, health, and related matters and may make recommendations with respect to any such matters to the General Assembly to the Members of the United Nations, and to the specialized agencies concerned.

It may make recommendations for the purpose of promoting respect for, and observance of, human rights and fundamental freedoms for all.

It may prepare draft conventions for submission to the General Assembly, with respect to matters falling within its competence.

It may call, in accordance with the rules prescribed by the United Nations, international conferences on matters falling within its competence.

Article 63

The Economic and Social Council may enter into agreements with any of the agencies referred to in Article 57, defining the terms on which the agency concerned shall be brought into relationship with the United Nations. Such agreements shall be subject to approval by the General Assembly.

It may co-ordinate the activities of the specialized agencies through consultation with and recommendations to such agencies and through recommendations to the General Assembly and to the Members of the United Nations.

Article 64

The Economic and Social Council may take appropriate steps to obtain regular reports from the specialized agencies. It may make arrangements with the Members of the United Nations and with the specialized agencies to obtain reports on the steps taken to give effect to its own recommendations and to recommendations on matters falling within its competence made by the General Assembly.

It may communicate its observations on these reports to the General Assembly.

Article 65

The Economic and Social Council may furnish information to the Security Council and shall assist the Security Council upon its request.

Article 66

The Economic and Social Council shall perform such functions as fall within its competence in connection with the carrying out of the recommendations of the General Assembly.

It may, with the approval of the General Assembly, perform services at the request of Members of the United Nations and at the request of specialized agencies.

It shall perform such other functions as are specified elsewhere in the present Charter or as may be assigned to it by the General Assembly.

Voting

Article 67

Each member of the Economic and Social Council shall have one vote.

Decisions of the Economic and Social Council shall be made by a majority of the members present and voting.

Procedure

Article 68

The Economic and Social Council shall set up commissions in economic and social fields and for the promotion of human rights, and such other commissions as may be required for the performance of its functions.

Article 69

The Economic and Social Council shall invite any Member of the United Nations to participate, without vote, in its deliberations on any matter of particular concern to that Member.

Article 70

The Economic and Social Council may make arrangements for representatives of the specialized agencies to participate, without vote, in its deliberations and in those of the commissions established by it, and for its representatives to participate in the deliberations of the specialized agencies.

Article 71

The Economic and Social Council may make suitable arrangements for consultation with non-governmental organizations which are concerned with matters within its competence. Such arrangements may be made with international organizations and, where appropriate, with national organizations after consultation with the Member of the United Nations concerned.

Article 72

The Economic and Social Council shall adopt its own rules of procedure, including the method of selecting its President.

The Economic and Social Council shall meet as required in accordance with its rules, which shall include provision for the convening of meetings on the request of a majority of its members.

. . .

CHAPTER XIV: THE INTERNATIONAL COURT OF JUSTICE

Article 92

The International Court of Justice shall be the principal judicial organ of the United Nations. It shall function in accordance with the annexed Statute, which is based upon the Statute of the Permanent Court of International Justice and forms an integral part of the present Charter.

Article 93

All Members of the United Nations are *ipso facto* parties to the Statute of the International Court of Justice.

A state which is not a Member of the United Nations may become a party to the Statute of the International Court of Justice on conditions to be determined in each case by the General Assembly upon the recommendation of the Security Council.

Article 94

Each Member of the United Nations undertakes to comply with the decision of the International Court of Justice in any case to which it is a party.

If any party to a case fails to perform the obligations incumbent upon it under a judgment rendered by the Court, the other party may have recourse to the Security Council, which may, if it deems necessary, make recommendations or decide upon measures to be taken to give effect to the judgment.

Article 95

Nothing in the present Charter shall prevent Members of the United Nations from entrusting the solution of their differences to other tribunals by virtue of agreements already in existence or which may be concluded in the future.

Article 96

The General Assembly or the Security Council may request the International Court of Justice to give an advisory opinion on any legal question.

Other organs of the United Nations and specialized agencies, which may at any time be so authorized by the General Assembly, may also request advisory opinions of the Court on legal questions arising within the scope of their activities.

CHAPTER XV: THE SECRETARIAT

Article 97

The Secretariat shall comprise a Secretary-General and such staff as the Organization may require. The Secretary-General shall be appointed by the General Assembly upon the recommendation of the Security Council. He shall be the chief administrative officer of the Organization.

Article 98

The Secretary-General shall act in that capacity in all meetings of the General Assembly, of the Security Council, of the Economic and Social Council, and of the Trusteeship Council, and shall perform such other functions as are entrusted to him by these organs. The Secretary-General shall make an annual report to the General Assembly on the work of the Organization.

Article 99

The Secretary-General may bring to the attention of the Security Council any matter which in his opinion may threaten the maintenance of international peace and security.

Article 100

In the performance of their duties the Secretary-General and the staff shall not seek or receive instructions from any government or from any other authority external to the Organization. They shall refrain from any action which might reflect on their position as international officials responsible only to the Organization.

Each Member of the United Nations undertakes to respect the exclusively international character of the responsibilities of the Secretary-General and the staff and not to seek to influence them in the discharge of their responsibilities.

Article 101

The staff shall be appointed by the Secretary-General under regulations established by the General Assembly.

Appropriate staffs shall be permanently assigned to the Economic and Social Council, the Trusteeship Council, and, as required, to other organs of the United Nations. These staffs shall form a part of the Secretariat.

The paramount consideration in the employment of the staff and in the determination of the conditions of service shall be the necessity of securing the highest standards of efficiency, competence, and integrity. Due regard shall be paid to the importance of recruiting the staff on as wide a geographical basis as possible.

. . .

FURTHER READING

Beschloss, M. (2002) *The Conquerors: Roosevelt, Truman and the Destruction of Hitler's Germany, 1941–1945*. New York: Simon & Schuster.

Hayek, F. A. (1944). *The Road to Serfdom*. Chicago: Chicago University Press.

Herring, G. (2008) *From Colony to Superpower: U.S. Foreign Relations since 1776*. Oxford: Oxford University Press.

Kennedy, P. (1987) *The Rise and the Fall of the Great Powers*. New York: Random House.

Keynes, J. M. (1920) *The Economic Consequences of the Peace*. New York: Harcourt Brace.

Kindleberger, C. (1986) *The World in Depression: 1929–1939*. Berkeley: University of California Press.

Leuchtenburg, W. (1997) *The FDR Years*. New York: Columbia University Press.

Miscamble, W. (2007) *From Roosevelt to Truman: Potsdam, Hiroshima, and the Cold War*. Cambridge: Cambridge University Press.

Range, W. (1959) *FDR's World Order*. Athens: University of Georgia Press.

Schoultz, L. (1998) *Beneath the United States: A History of U.S. Policy Toward Latin America*. Cambridge, MA: Harvard University Press.

5

HARRY TRUMAN
TO
LYNDON B. JOHNSON:
CONTAINMENT

INTRODUCTION

By the end of President Roosevelt's years in the White House, many things had changed in the United States, including the outlook regarding foreign policy. Having discarded its previous timidity with respect to foreign entanglements, the United States succeeded the British Empire as a global superpower and presided over the dismantling of European (primarily the British and French) empires while introducing its own principles of governance to the world. President Roosevelt led the way by helping to create the United Nations as a successor to the impotent League of Nations and to establish a new world financial structure, decided at Bretton Woods in July 1944. The formation of the International Monetary Fund (IMF) and World Bank at the United Nations Monetary and Financial Conference held at Bretton Woods were designed to revive the global economy but also revolved around the industrial and technological might of the United States. While some U.S. allies bristled at the aggressiveness of these plans, they had little power after the destruction brought about by World War II. Besides, they sorely needed the United States to help rebuild their infrastructure and revamp their failing economies.

Two months after the Yalta Conference, at which Roosevelt, Churchill, and Stalin negotiated the future of post–World War II Europe, President Roosevelt died, on April 12, 1945, elevating Vice President Harry S. Truman of Independence, Missouri, to the U.S. presidency. Previously seen as a parochial politician with little knowledge of world politics (FDR had not even told him about the Manhattan Project), Truman faced the daunting challenge of filling the huge shoes left behind by the giant that was FDR, and his decisions would dramatically impact post–World War II U.S. foreign policy. In July 1945, Truman participated in the Potsdam Conference, at which the future of Germany was debated, the borders of Poland were set, and demands for Japanese surrender were issued. Truman made it clear that the United States wanted to dominate the occupation of postwar Japan, and when Emperor Hirohito refused to surrender, Truman made the ultimate choice to drop atomic bombs on the Japanese cities of Hiroshima and Nagasaki in August 1945. Within days Japan ceased hostilities, and by September 2, it formally surrendered.

While Truman was deeply distrustful of Soviet intentions in Europe, the Soviets were similarly mistrustful of U.S. intentions, and by the spring of 1945, it was clear that the two sides had conflicting views about the future of Europe. The United States assumed the Yalta Conference guaranteed free elections for Poland, but Stalin argued that the Yalta Conference ensured that Poland would be within the Soviet sphere of influence. The Soviets also wanted to extract industrial equipment and raw materials from Western- controlled zones in Germany. The United States, along with Britain, viewed Soviet intransigence over Eastern Europe as a harbinger of Soviet expansionism. Public opinion in the United States turned against the Soviets, and U.S. foreign policy reflected and reinforced this anticommunist mood. Although the debate between orthodox and revisionist historians of the Cold War is by no means over, the mistrust and misunderstanding between the United States and the Soviet Union generated a self-fulfilling prophecy: The United States and the Soviet Union quickly adopted aggressive stances toward each other, and the Cold War was under way.

Initially, the dominant U.S. assessment of the Soviet Union came from George F. Kennan, the *charge d'affairs* at the U.S. Embassy in Moscow, who in February 1946 sent what came to be known as the "long telegram." Kennan saw the Soviet Union as a threat to the United States, driven by an autocratic Joseph Stalin and an expansionistic communist ideology. Seeing no possibility for peaceful coexistence between the two superpowers, Kennan advocated the use of U.S. force to confront and contain the Soviets. These views were shared by military leaders such as Generals George Patton and Douglas MacArthur as well as the British; in March 1946, Winston Churchill warned that the Soviets were dropping an "iron curtain" across the middle of Europe. The Soviet Union, meanwhile, justified these fears when it ruthlessly established Soviet-controlled regimes in Romania, Bulgaria, and Poland. The Soviets were motivated by mistrust of the United States as well as a desire to establish a buffer zone between itself and Western Europe, but these actions were taken by the United States as proof of the inherent expansionism of the Soviet Union.

The first Cold War test of Truman's foreign policy came in Greece, which in the aftermath of World War II was engulfed in a bloody civil war between the communist organizations that had served as the resistance against the Axis during the war and the government of Greece, which had spent the war in British-controlled Cairo. Initially, as part of the agreement between Churchill and Stalin at the Moscow conference in 1944, Greece was to be part of the Western sphere of influence. When the Greek communists who dominated much of the countryside objected, the British sent military forces to help the Greek government fight the communists. Soon after, however, it became clear that the British could not continue helping the Greek government, and Britain informed the United States that it would be withdrawing. This event marked the end of British dominance in the world and the ascent of U.S. supremacy.

In early 1947, President Truman responded by articulating the "Truman Doctrine" in a speech to the U.S. Congress, in which he exalted the efforts of the Greek government and pledged to "support free peoples who are resisting attempted subjugation by armed minorities or by outside pressures.... I believe that our help should be primarily through economic and financial aid, which is essential to economic stability and orderly political processes." In short, for Truman, the defense of Greece against communism was also the defense of the United States against the Soviet Union, regardless of what the Greeks wanted or the fact that the Greek monarchy was as repressive as some purely autocratic regimes. By 1947, writing under the pseudonym "X" in *Foreign Affairs* magazine, George Kennan argued that the proper foreign policy of the United States should be a "firm and vigilant containment of Russian expansive tendencies."

In 1947, as part of the effort to help Europe revive and to establish Western Europe as a U.S. ally against communism, the United States created the European Recovery Plan, dubbed the Marshall Plan after Secretary of State George Marshall. After rejecting an invitation to join in the plan, the Soviets responded by organizing their Eastern European satellites in their own Association for Mutual Economic Assistance, or Comecon, in 1949. Between 1948 and 1952, the Marshal Plan provided $13 billion to Western European countries, a dazzling amount by the standards of the day (Herring 2008: 620). Although U.S. priorities had been made clear to the world, the plan still had to be approved by Congress and was defended along three main lines: (1) Defense against communism requires a strong European opposition to Stalinist plans; (2) an economically devastated Europe was a breeding ground for radical ideologies within which communist movements may emerge; and (3) financially insecure European nations could only be future trading partners if the United States provided enormous amounts of aid to get their economies up and running.

When the commanding general in Berlin announced plans for currency reform in West Germany, the Soviets responded by sealing off Berlin. Faced with another Cold War crisis, Truman responded to the Berlin blockade with an airlift of supplies to Berliners, and after 11 months the Soviets abandoned the blockade, making the airlift a triumph of U.S. determination and ingenuity. The Berlin crisis also led to the creation in April 1949 of the North Atlantic Treaty Organization (NATO), a defense organization specifically designed to defend Western Europe against Soviet aggression. The Soviets responded in 1955 by forming the Warsaw Pact for mutual defense among the USSR and its Eastern European satellites.

Under Truman, the United States and other countries, notably Great Britain, assisted the Zionists in establishing the state of Israel. Truman's decision to grant diplomatic recognition to Israel went against some of his own advisers' view that doing so would harm United States-Arab relations in the Middle East and jeopardize much-needed oil supplies for the U.S. economy. Truman's decision would create ripple effects that all future presidents would face.

With the Soviet Union and the United States already deadlocked in a battle of wills and strategic tit-for-tat exchanges, the next major crisis was not far away. First, in 1949, communists emerged victorious in mainland China's civil war, leading to domestic squabbles in the United States over whether it had "lost" China by focusing solely on Europe. The communist victory in China led to a reformulation of U.S. foreign policy and a truly global Cold War. In April 1950 the State Department issued a report known as National Security Council Paper (NSC-68) that divided the world into forces of "slavery" and "freedom." Further, it argued that the United States should use force as needed to resist communism anywhere and everywhere, and recommended an immense military buildup that would enable the United States to become a world policeman. This report found a receptive President Truman, who acted on its recommendations when a crisis emerged in Korea.

World War II ended with Korea divided along the 38th parallel, with a Soviet-backed North Korea facing off against a United States-backed South Korea. On June 25, 1950, North Korea, with Soviet equipment and Chinese training, invaded South Korea and pushed the American and South Korean forces all the way to Pusan in what is known as the Pusan perimeter. The United States, taking advantage of a Soviet boycott of the UN, pushed for action by the UN Security Council, and while coming to the defense of South Korea was officially a UN action it was in reality led by U.S. Generals Douglas MacArthur, Mathew Ridgway, and Mark Clark. General MacArthur undertook a counteroffensive in 1950 when he landed forces at Inchon, 150 miles behind North Korean lines, and proceeded to push the overextended communist forces deep into northern territory. An immensely popular general in the United States, MacArthur advocated a full-scale attack on Chinese Manchuria, eliciting a Chinese counteroffensive that drove the UN forces into retreat. The legendary warrior MacArthur and President Truman almost came to blows over U.S. foreign policy, resulting in MacArthur's dismissal by Truman.

The Korean War eventually ended in a stalemate with the boundary between North and South Korea straddling the 38th parallel. The Truman presidency ended with a larger and reorganized U.S. military that had a more permanent presence as an arm of U.S. Cold War foreign policy.

After winning the 1952 election, Republican Dwight Eisenhower, a retired general and World War II hero, entered the White House in 1953 and largely continued Truman's foreign policy of containment. Eisenhower brought the Korean War to a close, pledging to personally visit Korea if necessary. And when Joseph Stalin was succeeded by a more pragmatic Nikita Khrushchev, United States–Soviet relations entered a new competitive phase. Keenly aware that the United States would be financially strained to match the Soviet and Chinese land armies, Eisenhower shifted U.S. policy toward the buildup of nuclear weapons to back up the doctrine that the threat of massive retaliation would deter communist expansion in Europe. This doctrine, however, spurred the Soviets to build up their own nuclear stockpile. In 1956, reformers emerged in Eastern European countries such as Hungary, and the Soviets responded by ruthlessly crushing the reformists and installing hardline rulers. The United States and NATO elected not to respond to pleas for aid by Hungarian freedom fighters because doing so risked opening up full-scale war in Europe.

Outside of Europe, the 1950s was a decade of conflict by proxy in which the two superpowers indirectly fought each other around the world by supporting leaders and movements positively predisposed to them, a policy that in some cases exacerbated their tense relations. By 1953, Eisenhower's foreign policy also looked to contain communism in the "third world." The United States helped install a pro–United States regime in Iran in 1953 by helping to overthrow the democratically elected Mossadeq regime and installing the autocratic Shah of Iran, who would rule until the Iranian Revolution in 1979. In Central America, the United States removed what it saw as a potentially socialist regime in Honduras in 1954 but could not prevent the Cuban dictator Batista's overthrow by Fidel Castro's revolutionaries in 1959. In Southeast Asia, the United States helped pay three-quarters of the costs for France to maintain its colonial rule against communist rebels in Vietnam, but the French military was defeated in 1954, resulting in a divided Vietnam. The United States entered into the breach to back the anti-communists in South Vietnam. And in the Middle East, the United States supported Israeli policies in the region, a move that antagonized Arab nations and produced a Pan-Arabist movement led by Gamal Abdel Nasser of Egypt. Increasingly, U.S. policymakers viewed the world in Manichean terms, and the nationalist Nasser did not fit the model of a leader who should be supported by U.S. taxpayer dollars. A subsequent fallout in United States–Egypt relations produced what is known as the Suez Canal Crisis in 1956, in which three staunch U.S. allies, Britain, France, and Israel, attacked Egypt over the nationalization of the Suez Canal. The crisis ended when the United States pressed for a quick cease-fire in order to maintain its standing with oil-producing Arab nations.

After Eisenhower's two terms, he was succeeded by a charismatic young Democratic senator, John Fitzgerald Kennedy. Kennedy's foreign policy maintained the policy of containment, but Kennedy himself was seen as vulnerable by the Soviets. And despite overwhelming military power, Kennedy soon found out the limits of military might alone for winning the "hearts and minds" of people in third-world nations. In 1961, in an effort to counteract Castroism in Latin America, Kennedy launched the Alliance for Progress, an economic development program that linked aid to social reform.

Unhappy with a potential Soviet satellite only 90 miles from Florida, Kennedy clearly thought the best way to block Castroism was to remove him from power. In April 1961 a group of Cuban exiles, with the help of the Central Intelligence Agency, attempted to overthrow the Cuban regime and failed, a fiasco known as the "Bay of Pigs." Next, the Soviet Union began establishing missile bases in Cuba in 1962. In the "thirteen days" of September 1962, also known as the Cuban Missile Crisis, the standoff between the United States and the USSR brought the world to the brink of thermonuclear warfare. Then the Soviets "blinked," and Kennedy was credited with containing its expansion. In the meantime, the crisis in Vietnam was becoming acute, and President Kennedy changed U.S. policy from financial aid to South Vietnam to military support when he sent about 16,000 military "advisers" to South Vietnam. In 1963 the United States, Britain, and the USSR signed the Limited Test Ban Treaty, which banned nuclear testing in outer space and underwater.

President Kennedy's assassination in 1963 brought yet another cold warrior into the White House, Lyndon B. Johnson. Elected for his first full term as the peace candidate in 1964, Johnson continued Kennedy's commitment to South Vietnam by sending 5,000 more troops. In August 1964 Johnson announced that U.S. Navy ships were attacked in international waters in the Gulf of Tonkin. Congress responded with the Gulf of Tonkin resolution, giving Johnson the power to "take all necessary measures" to protect U.S. forces. Originally seeking to limit U.S. troop involvement, Johnson ordered bombings of North Vietnamese targets. When this proved ineffective, Johnson gave in to the wishes of General William Westmoreland and Secretary of Defense Robert McNamara and authorized an increase in the strength of U.S. combat troops, to 275,000 in 1966 and 485,000 by the end of 1967.

Johnson's troop buildup turned a South Vietnamese war into an American war. While the United States claimed it was winning in Vietnam, North Vietnam's "Tet Offensive" on January 30, 1968, despite being a military failure for North Vietnam, convinced the American public that the war was an endless quagmire. When General Westmoreland requested 200,000 additional troops, Johnson reevaluated his approach and decided to disengage. The war was not only domestically unpopular but had hampered U.S. relations globally. Johnson's focus on the unpopular war in Vietnam led him to not seek reelection in 1968.

In the Middle East, President Johnson oversaw the territorial expansion of Israel in the "Six Day War" in 1967 after providing arms to the Israelis, who proceeded to defeat Egypt and occupy the West Bank of the Jordan River, creating another ripple effect in United States–Arab relations and handing a resounding defeat to President Nasser of Egypt.

In summary, between the end of World War II and the 1968 election, and through the administrations of Democratic and Republican presidents, the United States established itself as the leader of the Western Hemisphere and the "free world," strengthened its status as one of two superpowers, engaged in covert and overt military actions to counteract and contain the spread of communism, and maintained a policy of containment regarding the Soviet Union.

- **Document: The Long Telegram**
- **Date:** February 22, 1946
- **Significance:** This was the first of two significant interventions by George Kennan into U.S. foreign policy that swayed the Truman administration toward an aggressive stance against the Soviet Union.
- **Source:** Telegram, George Kennan to George Marshall ["Long Telegram"], February 22, 1946. Harry S. Truman Administration File, Elsey Papers.

861.00/2 - 2246: Telegram
The Charge in the Soviet Union (Kennan) to the Secretary of State
SECRET
Moscow, February 22, 1946—9 p.m. [Received February 22—3:52 p.m.]
511. Answer to Dept's 284, Feb 3 [13] involves questions so intricate, so delicate, so
strange to our form of thought, and so important to analysis of our international
environment that I cannot compress answers into single brief message without yield-
ing to what I feel would be dangerous degree of over-simplification. I hope, therefore, Dept will bear with me if I submit in answer to this question five parts,
subjects of which will be roughly as follows:

(1) Basic features of post-war Soviet outlook.
(2) Background of this outlook.
(3) Its projection in practical policy on official level.
(4) Its projection on unofficial level.
(5) Practical deductions from standpoint of US policy.

I apologize in advance for this burdening of telegraphic channel; but questions
involved are of such urgent importance, particularly in view of recent events, that
our answers to them, if they deserve attention at all, seem to me to deserve it at
once. There follows:

President Truman meets with his foreign policy advisors on November 13, 1947. Shown (l-r): President Truman; Undersecretary
of State Robert Lovett; George F. Kennan, Director of the Policy Planning Staff of the State Department; Charles E. Bohlen, special
assistant to Secretary Marshall. (Bettmann/Corbis)

Part 1: Basic Features of Post War Soviet Outlook, as Put Forward by Official Propaganda Machine

Are as Follows:

(a) USSR still lives in antagonistic "capitalist encirclement" with which in the long run there can be no permanent peaceful coexistence. As stated by Stalin in 1927 to a delegation of American workers:

"In course of further development of international revolution there will emerge two centers of world significance: a socialist center, drawing to itself the countries which tend toward socialism, and a capitalist center, drawing to itself the countries that incline toward capitalism. Battle between these two centers for command of world economy will decide fate of capitalism and of communism in entire world."

(b) Capitalist world is beset with internal conflicts, inherent in nature of capitalist society. These conflicts are insoluble by means of peaceful compromise. Greatest of them is that between England and US.

(c) Internal conflicts of capitalism inevitably generate wars. Wars thus generated may be of two kinds: intra-capitalist wars between two capitalist states, and wars of intervention against socialist world. Smart capitalists, vainly seeking escape from inner conflicts of capitalism, incline toward latter.

(d) Intervention against USSR, while it would be disastrous to those who undertook it, would cause renewed delay in progress of Soviet socialism and must therefore be forestalled at all costs.

(e) Conflicts between capitalist states, though likewise fraught with danger for USSR, nevertheless hold out great possibilities for advancement of socialist cause, particularly if USSR remains militarily powerful, ideologically monolithic and faithful to its present brilliant leadership.

(f) It must be borne in mind that capitalist world is not all bad. In addition to hopelessly reactionary and bourgeois elements, it includes (1) certain wholly enlightened and positive elements united in acceptable communistic parties and (2) certain other elements (now described for tactical reasons as progressive or democratic) whose reactions, aspirations and activities happen to be "objectively" favorable to interests of USSR These last must be encouraged and utilized for Soviet purposes.

(g) Among negative elements of bourgeois-capitalist society, most dangerous of all are those whom Lenin called false friends of the people, namely moderate-socialist or social-democratic leaders (in other words, non-Communist left-wing). These are more dangerous than out-and-out reactionaries, for latter at least march under their true colors, whereas moderate left-wing leaders confuse people by employing devices of socialism to seine interests of reactionary capital.

So much for premises. To what deductions do they lead from standpoint of Soviet policy? To following:

(a) Everything must be done to advance relative strength of USSR as factor in international society. Conversely, no opportunity most be missed to reduce strength and influence, collectively as well as individually, of capitalist powers.

(b) Soviet efforts, and those of Russia's friends abroad, must be directed toward deepening and exploiting of differences and conflicts between capitalist powers. If these eventually deepen into an "imperialist" war, this war must be turned into revolutionary upheavals within the various capitalist countries.

(c) "Democratic-progressive" elements abroad are to be utilized to maximum to bring pressure to bear on capitalist governments along lines agreeable to Soviet interests.

(d) Relentless battle must be waged against socialist and social-democratic leaders abroad.

Part 2: Background of Outlook

Before examining ramifications of this party line in practice there are certain aspects of it to which I wish to draw attention.

First, it does not represent natural outlook of Russian people. Latter are, by and large, friendly to outside world, eager for experience of it, eager to measure against it talents they are conscious of possessing, eager above all to live in peace and enjoy fruits of their own labor. Party line only represents thesis which official propaganda machine puts forward with great skill and persistence to a public often remarkably resistant in the stronghold of its innermost thoughts. But party line is binding for outlook and conduct of people who make up apparatus of power—party, secret police and Government—and it is exclusively with these that we have to deal.

Second, please note that premises on which this party line is based are for most part simply not true. Experience has shown that peaceful and mutually profitable coexistence of capitalist and socialist states is entirely possible. Basic internal conflicts in advanced countries are no longer primarily those arising out of capitalist ownership of means of production, but are ones arising from advanced urbanism and industrialism as such, which Russia has thus far been spared not by socialism but only by her own backwardness. Internal rivalries of capitalism do not always generate wars; and not all wars are attributable to this cause. To speak of possibility of intervention against USSR today, after elimination of Germany and Japan and after example of recent war, is sheerest nonsense. If not provoked by forces of intolerance and subversion "capitalist" world of today is quite capable of living at peace with itself and with Russia. Finally, no sane person has reason to doubt sincerity of moderate socialist leaders in Western countries. Nor is it fair to deny success of their efforts to improve conditions for working population whenever, as in Scandinavia, they have been given chance to show what they could do.

Falseness of those premises, every one of which predates recent war, was amply demonstrated by that conflict itself Anglo-American differences did not turn out to be major differences of Western World. Capitalist countries, other than those of Axis, showed no disposition to solve their differences by joining in crusade against USSR. Instead of imperialist war turning into civil wars and revolution, USSR found itself obliged to fight side by side with capitalist powers for an avowed community of aim.

Nevertheless, all these theses, however baseless and disproven, are being boldly put forward again today. What does this indicate? It indicates that Soviet party line is not based on any objective analysis of situation beyond Russia's borders; that it has, indeed, little to do with conditions outside of Russia; that it arises mainly from basic inner-Russian necessities which existed before recent war and exist today.

At bottom of Kremlin's neurotic view of world affairs is traditional and instinctive Russian sense of insecurity. Originally, this was insecurity of a peaceful agricultural people trying to live on vast exposed plain in neighborhood of fierce nomadic peoples. To this was added, as Russia came into contact with economically advanced West, fear of more competent, more powerful, more highly organized societies in that area. But this latter type of insecurity was one which afflicted rather Russian rulers than Russian people; for Russian rulers have invariably sensed that their rule was relatively archaic in form fragile and artificial in its psychological foundation, unable to stand comparison or contact with political systems of Western countries. For this reason they have always feared foreign penetration, feared direct contact between Western world and their own, feared what would happen if Russians learned truth about world without or if foreigners learned truth about world within. And they have learned to seek security only in patient but deadly struggle for total destruction of rival power, never in compacts and compromises with it.

It was no coincidence that Marxism, which had smoldered ineffectively for half a century in Western Europe, caught hold and blazed for first time in Russia. Only in this land which had never known a friendly neighbor or indeed any tolerant equilibrium of separate powers, either internal or international, could a doctrine thrive which viewed economic conflicts of society as insoluble by peaceful means. After establishment of Bolshevist regime, Marxist dogma, rendered even more truculent and intolerant by Lenin's interpretation, became a perfect vehicle for sense of insecurity with which Bolsheviks, even more than previous Russian rulers, were afflicted. In this dogma, with its basic altruism of purpose, they found justification for their instinctive fear of outside world, for the dictatorship without which they did not know how to rule, for cruelties they did not dare not to inflict, for sacrifice they felt bound to demand. In the name of Marxism they sacrificed every single ethical value in their methods and tactics. Today they cannot dispense with it. It is fig leaf of their moral and intellectual respectability. Without it they would stand before history, at best, as only the last of that long succession of cruel and wasteful Russian rulers who have relentlessly forced country on to ever new heights of military power in order to guarantee external security of their internally weak regimes. This is why Soviet purposes most always be solemnly clothed in trappings of Marxism, and why no one should underrate importance of dogma in Soviet affairs. Thus Soviet leaders are driven [by?] necessities of their own past and present position to put forward which [apparent omission] outside world as evil, hostile and menacing, but as bearing within itself germs of creeping disease and destined to be wracked with growing internal convulsions until it is given final Coup de grace by rising power of socialism and yields to new and better world. This thesis provides justification for that increase of military and police power of Russian state, for that isolation of Russian population from outside world, and for that fluid and constant pressure to extend limits of Russian police power which are together the natural and instinctive urges of Russian rulers. Basically this is only the steady advance of uneasy Russian nationalism, a centuries old movement in which conceptions of offense and defense are inextricably confused. But in new guise of international Marxism, with its honeyed promises to a desperate and war torn outside world, it is more dangerous and insidious than ever before.

It should not be thought from above that Soviet party line is necessarily disingenuous and insincere on part of all those who put it forward. Many of them are too ignorant of outside world and mentally too dependent to question [apparent omission] self-hypnotism, and who have no difficulty making themselves believe what they find it comforting and convenient to believe. Finally we have the unsolved mystery as to who, if anyone, in this great land actually receives accurate and unbiased information about outside world. In atmosphere of oriental secretiveness and conspiracy which pervades this Government, possibilities for distorting or poisoning sources and currents of information are infinite. The very disrespect of Russians for objective truth—indeed, their disbelief in its existence—leads them to view all stated facts as instruments for furtherance of one ulterior purpose or another. There is good reason to suspect that this Government is actually a conspiracy within a conspiracy; and I for one am reluctant to believe that Stalin himself receives anything like an objective picture of outside world. Here there is ample scope for the type of subtle intrigue at which Russians are past masters. Inability of foreign governments to place their case squarely before Russian policy makers—extent to which they are delivered up in their relations with Russia to good graces of obscure and unknown advisors whom they never see and cannot influence—this to my mind is most disquieting feature of diplomacy in Moscow, and one which Western statesmen would do well to keep in mind if they would understand nature of difficulties encountered here.

Part 3: Projection of Soviet Outlook in Practical Policy on Official Level

We have now seen nature and background of Soviet program. What may we expect by way of its practical implementation?

Soviet policy, as Department implies in its query under reference, is conducted on two planes: (1) official plane represented by actions undertaken officially in name of Soviet Government; and (2) subterranean plane of actions undertaken by agencies for which Soviet Government does not admit responsibility.

Policy promulgated on both planes will be calculated to serve basic policies (a) to (d) outlined in part 1. Actions taken on different planes will differ considerably, but will dovetail into each other in purpose, timing and effect.

On official plane we must look for following:

(a) Internal policy devoted to increasing in every way strength and prestige of Soviet state: intensive military-industrialization; maximum development of armed forces; great displays to impress outsiders; continued secretiveness about internal matters, designed to conceal weaknesses and to keep opponents in dark.

(b) Wherever it is considered timely and promising, efforts will be made to advance official limits of Soviet power. For the moment, these efforts are restricted to certain neighboring points conceived of here as being of immediate strategic necessity, such as Northern Iran, Turkey, possibly Bornholm. However, other points may at any time come into question, if and as concealed Soviet political power is extended to new areas. Thus a "friendly" Persian Government might be asked to grant Russia a port on Persian Gulf. Should Spain fall under Communist control, question of Soviet base at Gibraltar Strait might be activated. But such claims will appear on official level only when unofficial preparation is complete.

(c) Russians will participate officially in international organizations where they see opportunity of extending Soviet power or of inhibiting or diluting power of others. Moscow sees in UNO not the mechanism for a permanent and stable world society founded on mutual interest and aims of all nations, but an arena in which aims just mentioned can be favorably pursued. As long as UNO is considered here to serve this purpose, Soviets will remain with it. But if at any time they come to conclusion that it is serving to embarrass or frustrate their aims for power expansion and if they see better prospects for pursuit of these aims along other lines, they will not hesitate to abandon UNO. This would imply, however, that they felt themselves strong enough to split unity of other nations by their withdrawal to render UNO ineffective as a threat to their aims or security, replace it with an international weapon more effective from their viewpoint. Thus Soviet attitude toward UNO will depend largely on loyalty of other nations to it, and on degree of vigor, decisiveness and cohesion with which those nations defend in UNO the peaceful and hopeful concept of international life, which that organization represents to our way of thinking. I reiterate, Moscow has no abstract devotion to UNO ideals. Its attitude to that organization will remain essentially pragmatic and tactical.

(d) Toward colonial areas and backward or dependent peoples, Soviet policy, even on official plane, will be directed toward weakening of power and influence and contacts of advanced Western nations, on theory that in so far as this policy is successful, there will be created a vacuum which will favor Communist-Soviet penetration. Soviet pressure for participation in trusteeship arrangements thus represents, in my opinion, a desire to be in a position to complicate and inhibit exertion of Western influence at such points rather than to provide major channel for exerting of Soviet power. Latter motive is not lacking, but for this Soviets prefer to rely on other channels than official trusteeship arrangements. Thus we may expect to find Soviets asking for admission everywhere to trusteeship or similar arrangements and using levers thus acquired to weaken Western influence among such peoples.

(e) Russians will strive energetically to develop Soviet representation in, and official ties with, countries in which they sense Strong possibilities of opposition to Western centers of power. This applies to such widely separated points as Germany, Argentina, Middle Eastern countries, etc.

(f) In international economic matters, Soviet policy will really be dominated by pursuit of autarchy for Soviet Union and Soviet-dominated adjacent areas taken together. That, however, will be underlying policy. As far as official line is concerned, position is not yet clear. Soviet Government has shown strange reticence since termination hostilities on subject foreign trade. If large scale long term credits should be forthcoming, I believe Soviet Government may eventually again do lip service, as it did in 1930's to desirability of building up international economic exchanges in general. Otherwise I think it possible Soviet foreign trade may be restricted largely to Soviet's own security sphere, including occupied areas in Germany, and that a cold official shoulder may be turned to principle of general economic collaboration among nations.

(g) With respect to cultural collaboration, lip service will likewise be rendered to desirability of deepening cultural contacts between peoples, but this will not in practice be interpreted in any way which could weaken security position of Soviet peoples. Actual manifestations of Soviet policy in this respect will be restricted to arid channels of closely shepherded official visits and functions, with superabundance of vodka and speeches and dearth of permanent effects.

(h) Beyond this, Soviet official relations will take what might be called "correct" course with individual foreign governments, with great stress being laid on prestige of Soviet Union and its representatives and with punctilious attention to protocol as distinct from good manners.

Part 4: Following May Be Said as to What We May Expect by Way of Implementation of Basic Soviet Policies on Unofficial, or Subterranean Plane, i.e. on Plane for Which Soviet Government Accepts No Responsibility

Agencies utilized for promulgation of policies on this plane are following:

1. Inner central core of Communist Parties in other countries. While many of persons who compose this category may also appear and act in unrelated public capacities, they are in reality working closely together as an underground operating directorate of world communism, a concealed Comintern tightly coordinated and directed by Moscow. It is important to remember that this inner core is actually working on underground lines, despite legality of parties with which it is associated.
2. Rank and file of Communist Parties. Note distinction is drawn between those and persons defined in paragraph 1. This distinction has become much sharper in recent years. Whereas formerly foreign Communist Parties represented a curious (and from Moscow's standpoint often inconvenient) mixture of conspiracy and legitimate activity, now the conspiratorial element has been neatly concentrated in inner circle and ordered underground, while rank and file—no longer even taken into confidence about realities of movement—are thrust forward as bona fide internal partisans of certain political tendencies within their respective countries, genuinely innocent of conspiratorial connection with foreign states. Only in certain countries where communists are numerically strong do they now regularly appear and act as a body. As a rule they are used to penetrate, and to influence or dominate, as case may be, other organizations less likely to be suspected of being tools of Soviet Government, with a view to accomplishing their purposes through [apparent omission] organizations, rather than by direct action as a separate political party.
3. A wide variety of national associations or bodies which can be dominated or influenced by such penetration. These include: labor unions, youth leagues, women's organizations, racial societies, religious societies, social organizations, cultural groups, liberal magazines, publishing houses, etc.
4. International organizations which can be similarly penetrated through influence over various national components. Labor, youth and women's organizations are prominent among them. Particular, almost vital importance is attached in this connection to international labor movement. In this, Moscow sees possibility of sidetracking western governments in world affairs and building up international lobby capable of compelling governments to take actions favorable to Soviet interests in various countries and of paralyzing actions disagreeable to USSR.
5. Russian Orthodox Church, with its foreign branches, and through it the Eastern Orthodox Church in general.
6. Pan-Slav movement and other movements (Azerbaijan, Armenian, Turcoman, etc.) based on racial groups within Soviet Union.
7. Governments or governing groups willing to lend themselves to Soviet purposes in one degree or another, such as present Bulgarian and Yugoslav

Governments, North Persian regime, Chinese Communists, etc. Not only propaganda machines but actual policies of these regimes can be placed extensively at disposal of USSR.

It may be expected that component parts of this far-flung apparatus will be utilized in accordance with their individual suitability, as follows:

(a) To undermine general political and strategic potential of major western powers. Efforts will be made in such countries to disrupt national self confidence, to hamstring measures of national defense, to increase social and industrial unrest, to stimulate all forms of disunity. All persons with grievances, whether economic or racial, will be urged to seek redress not in mediation and compromise, but in defiant violent struggle for destruction of other elements of society. Here poor will be set against rich, black against white, young against old, newcomers against established residents, etc.

(b) On unofficial plane particularly violent efforts will be made to weaken power and influence of Western Powers of [on] colonial backward, or dependent peoples. On this level, no holds will be barred. Mistakes and weaknesses of western colonial administration will be mercilessly exposed and exploited. Liberal opinion in Western countries will be mobilized to weaken colonial policies. Resentment among dependent peoples will be stimulated. And while latter are being encouraged to seek independence of Western Powers, Soviet dominated puppet political machines will be undergoing preparation to take over domestic power in respective colonial areas when independence is achieved.

(c) Where individual governments stand in path of Soviet purposes pressure will be brought for their removal from office. This can happen where governments directly oppose Soviet foreign policy aims (Turkey, Iran), where they seal their territories off against Communist penetration (Switzerland, Portugal), or where they compete too strongly, like Labor Government in England, for moral domination among elements which it is important for Communists to dominate. (Sometimes, two of these elements are present in a single case. Then Communist opposition becomes particularly shrill and savage.[)]

(d) In foreign countries Communists will, as a rule, work toward destruction of all forms of personal independence, economic, political or moral. Their system can handle only individuals who have been brought into complete dependence on higher power. Thus, persons who are financially independent—such as individual businessmen, estate owners, successful farmers, artisans and all those who exercise local leadership or have local prestige, such as popular local clergymen or political figures, are anathema. It is not by chance that even in USSR local officials are kept constantly on move from one job to another, to prevent their taking root.

(e) Everything possible will be done to set major Western Powers against each other. Anti-British talk will be plugged among Americans, anti-American talk among British. Continentals, including Germans, will be taught to abhor both Anglo-Saxon powers. Where suspicions exist, they will be fanned; where not, ignited. No effort will be spared to discredit and combat all efforts which threaten to lead to any sort of unity or cohesion among other [apparent omission] from which Russia might be excluded. Thus, all forms of international organization not amenable to Communist penetration and control, whether it be the Catholic [apparent omission] international economic concerns, or the international fraternity of royalty and aristocracy, must expect to find themselves under fire from many, and often [apparent omission].

(f) In general, all Soviet efforts on unofficial international plane will be negative and destructive in character, designed to tear down sources of strength beyond reach of Soviet control. This is only in line with basic Soviet instinct that there can be no compromise with rival power and that constructive work can start only when Communist power is doming. But behind all this will be applied insistent, unceasing pressure for penetration and command of key positions in administration and especially in police apparatus of foreign countries. The Soviet regime is a police regime par excellence, reared in the dim half world of Tsarist police intrigue, accustomed to think primarily in terms of police power. This should never be lost sight of in ganging Soviet motives.

Part 5: [Practical Deductions from Standpoint of US Policy]

In summary, we have here a political force committed fanatically to the belief that with US there can be no permanent modus vivendi that it is desirable and necessary that the internal harmony of our society be disrupted, our traditional way of life be destroyed, the international authority of our state be broken, if Soviet power is to be secure. This political force has complete power of disposition over energies of one of world's greatest peoples and resources of world's richest national territory, and is borne along by deep and powerful currents of Russian nationalism. In addition, it has an elaborate and far flung apparatus for exertion of its influence in other countries, an apparatus of amazing flexibility and versatility, managed by people whose experience and skill in underground methods are presumably without parallel in history. Finally, it is seemingly inaccessible to considerations of reality in its basic reactions. For it, the vast fund of objective fact about human society is not, as with us, the measure against which outlook is constantly being tested and re-formed, but a grab bag from which individual items are selected arbitrarily and tendenciously to bolster an outlook already preconceived. This is admittedly not a pleasant picture. Problem of how to cope with this force in [is] undoubtedly greatest task our diplomacy has ever faced and probably greatest it will ever have to face. It should be point of departure from which our political general staff work at present juncture should proceed. It should be approached with same thoroughness and care as solution of major strategic problem in war, and if necessary, with no smaller outlay in planning effort. I cannot attempt to suggest all answers here. But I would like to record my conviction that problem is within our power to solve—and that without recourse to any general military conflict. And in support of this conviction there are certain observations of a more encouraging nature I should like to make:

(1) Soviet power, unlike that of Hitlerite Germany, is neither schematic nor adventuristic. It does not work by fixed plans. It does not take unnecessary risks. Impervious to logic of reason, and it is highly sensitive to logic of force. For this reason it can easily withdraw—and usually does when strong resistance is encountered at any point. Thus, if the adversary has sufficient force

and makes clear his readiness to use it, he rarely has to do so. If situations are properly handled there need be no prestige-engaging showdowns.

(2) Gauged against Western World as a whole, Soviets are still by far the weaker force. Thus, their success will really depend on degree of cohesion, firmness and vigor which Western World can muster. And this is factor which it is within our power to influence.

(3) Success of Soviet system, as form of internal power, is not yet finally proven. It has yet to be demonstrated that it can survive supreme test of successive transfer of power from one individual or group to another. Lenin's death was first such transfer, and its effects wracked Soviet state for 15 years. After Stalin's death or retirement will be second. But even this will not be final test. Soviet internal system will now be subjected, by virtue of recent territorial expansions, to series of additional strains which once proved severe tax on Tsardom. We here are convinced that never since termination of civil war have mass of Russian people been emotionally farther removed from doctrines of Communist Party than they are today. In Russia, party has now become a great and—for the moment—highly successful apparatus of dictatorial administration, but it has ceased to be a source of emotional inspiration. Thus, internal soundness and permanence of movement need not yet be regarded as assured.

(4) All Soviet propaganda beyond Soviet security sphere is basically negative and destructive. It should therefore be relatively easy to combat it by any intelligent and really constructive program.

For those reasons I think we may approach calmly and with good heart problem of how to deal with Russia. As to how this approach should be made, I only wish to advance, by way of conclusion, following comments:

(1) Our first step must be to apprehend, and recognize for what it is, the nature of the movement with which we are dealing. We must study it with same courage, detachment, objectivity, and same determination not to be emotionally provoked or unseated by it, with which doctor studies unruly and unreasonable individual.

(2) We must see that our public is educated to realities of Russian situation. I cannot over-emphasize importance of this. Press cannot do this alone. It must be done mainly by Government, which is necessarily more experienced and better informed on practical problems involved. In this we need not be deterred by [ugliness?] of picture. I am convinced that there would be far less hysterical anti-Sovietism in our country today if realities of this situation were better understood by our people. There is nothing as dangerous or as terrifying as the unknown. It may also be argued that to reveal more information on our difficulties with Russia would reflect unfavorably on Russian-American relations. I feel that if there is any real risk here involved, it is one which we should have courage to face, and sooner the better. But I cannot see what we would be risking. Our stake in this country, even coming on heels of tremendous demonstrations of our friendship for Russian people, is remarkably small. We have here no investments to guard, no actual trade to lose, virtually no citizens to protect, few cultural contacts to preserve. Our only stake lies in what we hope rather than what we have;

and I am convinced we have better chance of realizing those hopes if our public is enlightened and if our dealings with Russians are placed entirely on realistic and matter-of-fact basis.

(3) Much depends on health and vigor of our own society. World communism is like malignant parasite which feeds only on diseased tissue. This is point at which domestic and foreign policies meets. Every courageous and incisive measure to solve internal problems of our own society, to improve self-confidence, discipline, morale and community spirit of our own people, is a diplomatic victory over Moscow worth a thousand diplomatic notes and joint communiqués. If we cannot abandon fatalism and indifference in face of deficiencies of our own society, Moscow will profit—Moscow cannot help profiting by them in its foreign policies.

(4) We must formulate and put forward for other nations a much more positive and constructive picture of sort of world we would like to see than we have put forward in past. It is not enough to urge people to develop political processes similar to our own. Many foreign peoples, in Europe at least, are tired and frightened by experiences of past, and are less interested in abstract freedom than in security. They are seeking guidance rather than responsibilities. We should be better able than Russians to give them this. And unless we do, Russians certainly will.

(5) Finally we must have courage and self-confidence to cling to our own methods and conceptions of human society. After all, the greatest danger that can befall us in coping with this problem of Soviet communism, is that we shall allow ourselves to become like those with whom we are coping.

KENNAN

800.00B International Red Day/2 -2546: Airgram

- **Document: President Truman's Speech to Congress: The Truman Doctrine**
- **Date:** March 12, 1947
- **Significance:** In this address, President Truman outlines what came to be known as the "Truman Doctrine."
- **Source:** *Congressional Record*, 80 Cong., 1 Sess., pp. 1980–1981.

PRESIDENT HARRY S. TRUMAN'S ADDRESS BEFORE A JOINT SESSION OF CONGRESS, MARCH 12, 1947

Mr. President, Mr. Speaker, Members of the Congress of the United States:

The gravity of the situation which confronts the world today necessitates my appearance before a joint session of the Congress. The foreign policy and the national security of this country are involved.

One aspect of the present situation, which I wish to present to you at this time for your consideration and decision, concerns Greece and Turkey.

President Harry Truman addresses Congress on March 12, 1947. Truman spelled out what became known as the Truman Doctrine, a program whereby the United States would provide assistance to those countries resisting pressures from communism. It became the cornerstone of the Containment policy. (Harry S. Truman Presidential Library)

The United States has received from the Greek Government an urgent appeal for financial and economic assistance. Preliminary reports from the American Economic Mission now in Greece and reports from the American Ambassador in Greece corroborate the statement of the Greek Government that assistance is imperative if Greece is to survive as a free nation.

I do not believe that the American people and the Congress wish to turn a deaf ear to the appeal of the Greek Government.

Greece is not a rich country. Lack of sufficient natural resources has always forced the Greek people to work hard to make both ends meet. Since 1940, this industrious and peace loving country has suffered invasion, four years of cruel enemy occupation, and bitter internal strife.

When forces of liberation entered Greece they found that the retreating Germans had destroyed virtually all the railways, roads, port facilities, communications, and merchant marine. More than a thousand villages had been burned. Eighty-five per cent of the children were tubercular. Livestock, poultry, and draft animals had almost disappeared. Inflation had wiped out practically all savings.

As a result of these tragic conditions, a militant minority, exploiting human want and misery, was able to create political chaos which, until now, has made economic recovery impossible.

Greece is today without funds to finance the importation of those goods which are essential to bare subsistence. Under these circumstances the people of Greece cannot make progress in solving their problems of reconstruction. Greece is in desperate need of financial and economic assistance to enable it to resume purchases of food, clothing, fuel and seeds. These are indispensable for the subsistence of its people and are obtainable only from abroad. Greece must have help to import the goods necessary to restore internal order and security, so essential for economic and political recovery.

The Greek Government has also asked for the assistance of experienced American administrators, economists and technicians to insure that the financial and other aid given to Greece shall be used effectively in creating a stable and self-sustaining economy and in improving its public administration.

The very existence of the Greek state is today threatened by the terrorist activities of several thousand armed men, led by Communists, who defy the government's authority at a number of points, particularly along the northern boundaries. A Commission appointed by the United Nations Security Council is at present investigating disturbed conditions in northern Greece and alleged border violations along the frontier between Greece on the one hand and Albania, Bulgaria, and Yugoslavia on the other.

Meanwhile, the Greek Government is unable to cope with the situation. The Greek army is small and poorly equipped. It needs supplies and equipment if it is to restore the authority of the government throughout Greek territory. Greece must have assistance if it is to become a self-supporting and self-respecting democracy.

The United States must supply that assistance. We have already extended to Greece certain types of relief and economic aid but these are inadequate.

There is no other country to which democratic Greece can turn.

No other nation is willing and able to provide the necessary support for a democratic Greek government.

The British Government, which has been helping Greece, can give no further financial or economic aid after March 31. Great Britain finds itself under the necessity of reducing or liquidating its commitments in several parts of the world, including Greece.

We have considered how the United Nations might assist in this crisis. But the situation is an urgent one requiring immediate action and the United Nations and its related organizations are not in a position to extend help of the kind that is required.

It is important to note that the Greek Government has asked for our aid in utilizing effectively the financial and other assistance we may give to Greece, and in improving its public administration. It is of the utmost importance that we supervise the use of any funds made available to Greece, in such a manner that each dollar spent will count toward making Greece self-supporting, and will help to build an economy in which a healthy democracy can flourish.

No government is perfect. One of the chief virtues of a democracy, however, is that its defects are always visible and under democratic processes can be pointed out and corrected. The Government of Greece is not perfect. Nevertheless it represents eighty-five per cent of the members of the Greek Parliament who were chosen in an election last year. Foreign observers, including 692 Americans, considered this election to be a fair expression of the views of the Greek people.

The Greek Government has been operating in an atmosphere of chaos and extremism. It has made mistakes. The extension of aid by this country does not mean that the United States condones everything that the Greek Government has done or will do. We have condemned in the past, and we condemn now, extremist measures of the right or the left. We have in the past advised tolerance, and we advise tolerance now.

Greece's neighbor, Turkey, also deserves our attention.

The future of Turkey as an independent and economically sound state is clearly no less important to the freedom-loving peoples of the world than the future of Greece. The circumstances in which Turkey finds itself today are considerably different from those of Greece. Turkey has been spared the disasters that have beset Greece. And during the war, the United States and Great Britain furnished Turkey with material aid.

Nevertheless, Turkey now needs our support.

Since the war Turkey has sought financial assistance from Great Britain and the United States for the purpose of effecting that modernization necessary for the maintenance of its national integrity.

That integrity is essential to the preservation of order in the Middle East.

The British government has informed us that, owing to its own difficulties can no longer extend financial or economic aid to Turkey.

As in the case of Greece, if Turkey is to have the assistance it needs, the United States must supply it. We are the only country able to provide that help.

I am fully aware of the broad implications involved if the United States extends assistance to Greece and Turkey, and I shall discuss these implications with you at this time.

One of the primary objectives of the foreign policy of the United States is the creation of conditions in which we and other nations will be able to work out a way of life free from coercion. This was a fundamental issue in the war with Germany and Japan. Our victory was won over countries which sought to impose their will, and their way of life, upon other nations.

To ensure the peaceful development of nations, free from coercion, the United States has taken a leading part in establishing the United Nations. The United Nations is designed to make possible lasting freedom and independence for all its members. We shall not realize our objectives, however, unless we are willing to help free peoples to maintain their free institutions and their national integrity against aggressive movements that seek to impose upon them totalitarian regimes. This is no more than a frank recognition that totalitarian regimes imposed on free peoples, by direct or indirect aggression, undermine the foundations of international peace and hence the security of the United States.

The peoples of a number of countries of the world have recently had totalitarian regimes forced upon them against their will. The Government of the United States has made frequent protests against coercion and intimidation, in violation of the Yalta agreement, in Poland, Rumania, and Bulgaria. I must also state that in a number of other countries there have been similar developments.

At the present moment in world history nearly every nation must choose between alternative ways of life. The choice is too often not a free one.

One way of life is based upon the will of the majority, and is distinguished by free institutions, representative government, free elections, guarantees of individual liberty, freedom of speech and religion, and freedom from political oppression.

The second way of life is based upon the will of a minority forcibly imposed upon the majority. It relies upon terror and oppression, a controlled press and radio; fixed elections, and the suppression of personal freedoms.

I believe that it must be the policy of the United States to support free peoples who are resisting attempted subjugation by armed minorities or by outside pressures.

I believe that we must assist free peoples to work out their own destinies in their own way.

I believe that our help should be primarily through economic and financial aid which is essential to economic stability and orderly political processes.

The world is not static, and the status quo is not sacred. But we cannot allow changes in the status quo in violation of the Charter of the United Nations by such methods as coercion, or by such subterfuges as political infiltration. In helping free and independent nations to maintain their freedom, the United States will be giving effect to the principles of the Charter of the United Nations.

It is necessary only to glance at a map to realize that the survival and integrity of the Greek nation are of grave importance in a much wider situation. If Greece should fall under the control of an armed minority, the effect upon its neighbor, Turkey, would be immediate and serious. Confusion and disorder might well spread throughout the entire Middle East.

Moreover, the disappearance of Greece as an independent state would have a profound effect upon those countries in Europe whose peoples are struggling against great difficulties to maintain their freedoms and their independence while they repair the damages of war.

It would be an unspeakable tragedy if these countries, which have struggled so long against overwhelming odds, should lose that victory for which they sacrificed so much. Collapse of free institutions and loss of independence would be disastrous not only for them but for the world. Discouragement and possibly failure would quickly be the lot of neighboring peoples striving to maintain their freedom and independence.

Should we fail to aid Greece and Turkey in this fateful hour, the effect will be far reaching to the West as well as to the East.

We must take immediate and resolute action.

I therefore ask the Congress to provide authority for assistance to Greece and Turkey in the amount of $400,000,000 for the period ending June 30, 1948. In requesting these funds, I have taken into consideration the maximum amount of relief assistance which would be furnished to Greece out of the $350,000,000 which I recently requested that the Congress authorize for the prevention of starvation and suffering in countries devastated by the war.

In addition to funds, I ask the Congress to authorize the detail of American civilian and military personnel to Greece and Turkey, at the request of those countries, to assist in the tasks of reconstruction, and for the purpose of supervising the use of such financial and material assistance as may be furnished. I recommend that authority also be provided for the instruction and training of selected Greek and Turkish personnel.

Finally, I ask that the Congress provide authority which will permit the speediest and most effective use, in terms of needed commodities, supplies, and equipment, of such funds as may be authorized.

If further funds, or further authority, should be needed for purposes indicated in this message, I shall not hesitate to bring the situation before the Congress. On this subject the Executive and Legislative branches of the Government must work together.

This is a serious course upon which we embark.

I would not recommend it except that the alternative is much more serious. The United States contributed $341,000,000,000 toward winning World War II. This is an investment in world freedom and world peace.

The assistance that I am recommending for Greece and Turkey amounts to little more than 1 tenth of 1 per cent of this investment. It is only common sense that we should safeguard this investment and make sure that it was not in vain.

The seeds of totalitarian regimes are nurtured by misery and want. They spread and grow in the evil soil of poverty and strife. They reach their full growth when the hope of a people for a better life has died. We must keep that hope alive.

The free peoples of the world look to us for support in maintaining their freedoms.

If we falter in our leadership, we may endanger the peace of the world—and we shall surely endanger the welfare of our own nation.

Did You Know?

The Universal Declaration of Human Rights

The Universal Declaration of Human Rights is a legal document that declares "all human beings are born free and equal" without regard to race, sex, language, religion, political affiliation, or the status of the territory on which they were born. It was drafted primarily by John Peters Humphrey, a Canadian human rights lawyer who was appointed by the UN Secretary General to write it. The declaration divides human rights into four separate categories: (1) individual freedoms, such as the right to life and freedom; (2) rights of individuals in political society, such the right to a nationality; (3) rights of individuals in the spiritual and ideological realms, such as freedom of religion; and (4) rights in the social and economic realm, such as the right to education. The declaration was adopted by the UN General Assembly on December 10, 1948, and was championed by the First Lady of the United States, Eleanor Roosevelt, in the hopes that the declaration would have the same effect on the world that the Declaration of Independence had had for the United States. The Universal Declaration of Human Rights has been adopted almost universally and remains important despite the fact that it is not a binding treaty. Nongovernmental organizations such as Amnesty International monitor governments and issue reports critical of regimes that violate the human rights embodied in the universal declaration.

Great responsibilities have been placed upon us by the swift movement of events. I am confident that the Congress will face these responsibilities squarely.

- **Document: George C. Marshall's Commencement Speech at Harvard University**
- **Date:** June 5, 1947
- **Significance:** This speech was the presentation of the so-called Marshall Plan by George C. Marshall, the Secretary of State of the United States.
- **Source:** George C. Marshall, "European Initiative Essential to Economic Recovery," *Department of State Bulletin*, 16(415) (1947), 1159–1160.

The Marshall Plan Speech

I need not tell you gentlemen that the world situation is very serious. That must be apparent to all intelligent people. I think one difficulty is that the problem is one of such enormous complexity that the very mass of facts presented to the public by press and radio make it exceedingly difficult for the man in the street to reach a clear appraisement of the situation. Furthermore, the people of this country are distant from the troubled areas of the earth and it is hard for them to comprehend the plight and consequent reactions of the long-suffering peoples, and the effect of those reactions on their governments in connection with our efforts to promote peace in the world.

In considering the requirements for the rehabilitation of Europe the physical loss of life, the visible destruction of cities, factories, mines and railroads was correctly estimated, but it has become obvious during recent months that this visible destruction was probably less serious than the dislocation of the entire fabric of European economy. For the past ten years conditions have been highly abnormal. The feverish preparation for war and the more feverish maintenance of the war effort engulfed all aspects of national economies. Machinery has fallen into disrepair or is entirely obsolete. Under the arbitrary and destructive Nazi rule, virtually every possible enterprise was geared into the German war machine. Long-standing commercial ties, private institutions, banks, insurance companies and shipping companies disappeared, through loss of capital, absorption through nationalization or by simple destruction. In many countries, confidence in the local currency has been severely shaken. The breakdown of the business structure of Europe during the war was complete. Recovery has been seriously retarded by the fact that two years after the close of hostilities a peace settlement with Germany and Austria has not been agreed upon. But even given a more prompt solution of these difficult problems, the rehabilitation of the economic structure of Europe quite evidently will require a much longer time and greater effort than had been foreseen.

There is a phase of this matter which is both interesting and serious. The farmer has always produced the foodstuffs to exchange with the city dweller for the other necessities of life. This division of labor is the basis of modern civilization. At the present time it is threatened with breakdown. The town and city industries are not producing adequate goods to exchange with the food-producing farmer. Raw materials and fuel are in short supply. Machinery is lacking or worn out. The farmer of the peasant cannot find the goods for sale which he desires to purchase. So the sale of his farm produce for money which he cannot use seems to him an unprofitable transaction. He, therefore, has withdrawn many fields from crop cultivation and is using them for grazing. He feeds more grain to stock and finds for himself and his family an ample supply of food, however short he may be on clothing and the other ordinary gadgets of civilization. Meanwhile people in the cities are short of food and fuel. So the governments are forced to use their foreign money and credits to procure these necessities abroad. This process exhausts funds which are urgently needed for reconstruction. This is a very serious situation is rapidly developing which bodes no good for the world. The modern system of the division of labor upon which the exchange of products is based is in danger of breaking down.

The truth of the matter is that Europe's requirements for the next three or four years of foreign food and other essential products—principally from America—are so much greater than her present ability to pay that she must have substantial additional help, or face economic, social and political deterioration of a very grave character.

The remedy lies in breaking the vicious circle and restoring the confidence of the European people in the economic future of their own countries and of Europe as a whole. The manufacturer and the farmer throughout wide areas must be able and willing to exchange their products for currencies the continuing value of which is not open to question.

Aside from the demoralizing effect on the world at large and the possibilities of disturbances arising as a result of the desperation of the people concerned, the consequences to the economy of the United States should be apparent to all. It is logical that the United States should do whatever it is able to do to assist in the return of normal economic health in the world, without which there can be no political stability and no assured peace. Our policy is directed not against any country or doctrine but against hunger, poverty, desperation and chaos. Its purpose should be the revival of a working economy in the world so as to permit the emergence of political and social conditions in which free institutions can exist. Such assistance, I am convinced, must not be on a peace-meal basis as various crises develop. Any assistance that this Government may render in the future should provide a cure rather than a mere palliative. Any government that is willing to assist in the task of recovery will find full cooperation, I am sure, on the part of the United States Government. Any government which maneuvers to block the recovery of other countries cannot expect help from us. Furthermore, governments, political parties or groups which seek to perpetuate human misery in order to profit therefrom politically or otherwise will encounter the opposition of the United States.

It is already evident that, before the United States Government can proceed much further in its efforts to alleviate the situation and help start the European world on its way to recovery, there must be some agreement among the countries of Europe as to the requirements of the situation and the part those countries themselves will take in order to give proper effect to whatever action might be undertaken by this Government. It would be neither fitting nor efficacious for this Government to undertake to draw up unilaterally a program designed to place Europe on its feet economically. This is the business of the Europeans. The initiative, I think, must come from Europe. The role of this country should consist of friendly aid in the drafting of a European program and of later support of such a program so far as it may be practical for us to do so. The program should be a joint one, agreed to by a number, if not all European nations.

An essential part of any successful action on the part of the United States is an understanding on the part of the people of America of the character of the problem and the remedies to be applied. Political passion and prejudice should have no part. With foresight, and a willingness on the part of our people to face up to the vast responsibility which history has clearly placed upon our country, the difficulties I have outlined can and will be overcome.

- **Document: NSC-68**
- **Date:** April 14, 1950
- **Significance:** This document is quite possibly the most important expression of the Cold War foreign policy that the United States would follow for nearly five decades. Written by Paul Nitze, one of the architects of U.S. anti-Soviet policies, it proposes ways to check Soviet expansion worldwide.
- **Source:** U.S. National Security Council, "A Report to the National Security Council by the Executive Secretary on United States Objectives and Programs for National Security." April 14, 1950. http://www.trumanlibrary.org/hst/l.htm.

UNITED STATES OBJECTIVES AND PROGRAMS FOR NATIONAL SECURITY

A Report to the President Pursuant to the President's Directive of January 31, 1950

Contents

Terms of Reference
Analysis
I. Background of the Present World Crisis
II. The Fundamental Purpose of the United States
III. The Fundamental Design of the Kremlin
IV. The Underlying Conflict in the Realm of Ideas and Values Between the U.S. Purpose and the Kremlin Design

Nature of the Conflict
Objectives
Means

V. Soviet Intentions and Capabilities—Actual and Potential
VI. U.S. Intentions and Capabilities—Actual and Potential

VII. Present Risks

VIII. Atomic Armaments

A. Military Evaluation of U.S. and U.S.S.R. Atomic Capabilities

B. Stockpiling and Use of Atomic Weapons

C. International Control of Atomic Energy

IX. Possible Courses of Action

Introduction

The Role of Negotiation

A. The First Course—Continuation of Current Policies, with Current and Currently Projected Programs for Carrying Out These Projects

B. The Second Course—Isolation

C. The Third Course—War

D. The Remaining Course of Action—A Rapid Build-up of Political, Economic, and Military Strength in the Free World

Conclusions

Recommendations

. . .

ANALYSIS
I. Background of the Present Crisis

Within the past thirty-five years the world has experienced two global wars of tremendous violence. It has witnessed two revolutions—the Russian and the Chinese—of extreme scope and intensity. It has also seen the collapse of five empires—the Ottoman, the Austro-Hungarian, German, Italian, and Japanese—and the drastic decline of two major imperial systems, the British and the French. During the span of one generation, the international distribution of power has been fundamentally altered. For several centuries it had proved impossible for any one nation to gain such preponderant strength that a coalition of other nations could not in time face it with greater strength. The international scene was marked by recurring periods of violence and war, but a system of sovereign and independent states was maintained, over which no state was able to achieve hegemony.

Two complex sets of factors have now basically altered this historic distribution of power. First, the defeat of Germany and Japan and the decline of the British and French Empires have interacted with the development of the United States and the Soviet Union in such a way that power increasingly gravitated to these two centers. Second, the Soviet Union, unlike previous aspirants to hegemony, is animated by a new fanatic faith, antithetical to our own, and seeks to impose its absolute authority over the rest of the world. Conflict has, therefore, become endemic and is waged, on the part of the Soviet Union, by violent or non-violent methods in accordance with the dictates of expediency. With the development of increasingly terrifying weapons of mass destruction, every individual faces the ever-present possibility of annihilation should the conflict enter the phase of total war.

On the one hand, the people of the world yearn for relief from the anxiety arising from the risk of atomic war. On the other hand, any substantial further extension of the area under the domination of the Kremlin would raise the possibility that no coalition adequate to confront the Kremlin with greater strength could be assembled.

It is in this context that this Republic and its citizens in the ascendancy of their strength stand in their deepest peril.

The issues that face us are momentous, involving the fulfillment or destruction not only of this Republic but of civilization itself. They are issues which will not await our deliberations. With conscience and resolution this Government and the people it represents must now take new and fateful decisions.

II. Fundamental Purpose of the United States

The fundamental purpose of the United States is laid down in the Preamble to the Constitution: " . . . to form a more perfect Union, establish justice, insure domestic Tranquility, provide for the common defence, promote the general Welfare, and secure the Blessings of Liberty to ourselves and our Posterity." In essence, the fundamental purpose is to assure the integrity and vitality of our free society, which is founded upon the dignity and worth of the individual.

Three realities emerge as a consequence of this purpose: Our determination to maintain the essential elements of individual freedom, as set forth in the Constitution and Bill of Rights; our determination to create conditions under which our free and democratic system can live and prosper; and our determination to fight if necessary to defend our way of life, for which as in the Declaration of Independence, "with a firm reliance on the protection of Divine Providence, we mutually pledge to each other our lives, our Fortunes, and our sacred Honor."

III. Fundamental Design of the Kremlin

The fundamental design of those who control the Soviet Union and the international communist movement is to retain and solidify their absolute power, first in the Soviet Union and second in the areas now under their control. In the minds of the Soviet leaders, however, achievement of this design requires the dynamic extension of their authority and the ultimate elimination of any effective opposition to their authority.

The design, therefore, calls for the complete subversion or forcible destruction of the machinery of government and structure of society in the countries of the non-Soviet world and their replacement by an apparatus and structure subservient to and controlled from the Kremlin. To that end Soviet efforts are now directed toward the domination of the Eurasian land mass. The United States, as the principal center of power in the non-Soviet world and the bulwark of opposition to Soviet expansion, is the principal enemy whose integrity and vitality must be subverted or destroyed by one means or another if the Kremlin is to achieve its fundamental design.

IV. The Underlying Conflict in the Realm of ideas and Values between the U.S. Purpose and the Kremlin Design

A. NATURE OF CONFLICT

The Kremlin regards the United States as the only major threat to the conflict between idea of slavery under the grim oligarchy of the Kremlin, which has come to a crisis with the polarization of power described in Section I, and the exclusive possession of atomic weapons by the two protagonists. The idea of freedom, moreover, is peculiarly and intolerably subversive of the idea of slavery. But the converse is not true. The implacable purpose of the slave state to eliminate the challenge of freedom has placed the two great powers at opposite poles. It is this fact which gives the present polarization of power the quality of crisis.

The free society values the individual as an end in himself, requiring of him only that measure of self-discipline and self-restraint which make the rights of each individual compatible with the rights of every other individual. The freedom of the individual has as its counterpart, therefore, the negative responsibility of the individual not to exercise his freedom in ways inconsistent with the freedom of other individuals and the positive responsibility to make constructive use of his freedom in the building of a just society.

From this idea of freedom with responsibility derives the marvelous diversity, the deep tolerance, the lawfulness of the free society. This is the explanation of the strength of free men. It constitutes the integrity and the vitality of a free and democratic system. The free society attempts to create and maintain an environment in which every individual has the opportunity to realize his creative powers. It also explains why the free society tolerates those within it who would use their freedom to destroy it. By the same token, in relations between nations, the prime reliance of the free society is on the strength and appeal of its idea, and it feels no compulsion sooner or later to bring all societies into conformity with it.

For the free society does not fear, it welcomes, diversity. It derives its strength from its hospitality even to antipathetic ideas. It is a market for free trade in ideas, secure in its faith that free men will take the best wares, and grow to a fuller and better realization of their powers in exercising their choice.

The idea of freedom is the most contagious idea in history, more contagious than the idea of submission to authority. For the breadth of freedom cannot be tolerated in a society which has come under the domination of an individual or group of individuals with a will to absolute power. Where the despot holds absolute power—the absolute power of the absolutely powerful will—all other wills must be subjugated in an act of willing submission, a degradation willed by the individual upon himself under the compulsion of a perverted faith. It is the first article of this faith that he finds and can only find the meaning of his existence in serving the ends of the system. The system becomes God, and submission to the will of God becomes submission to the will of the system. It is not enough to yield outwardly to the system—even Gandhian non-violence is not acceptable—for the spirit of resistance and the devotion to a higher authority might then remain, and the individual would not be wholly submissive.

The same compulsion which demands total power over all men within the Soviet state without a single exception, demands total power over all Communist Parties and all states under Soviet domination. Thus Stalin has said that the theory and tactics of Leninism as expounded by the Bolshevik party are mandatory for the proletarian parties of all countries. A true internationalist is defined as one who unhesitatingly upholds the position of the Soviet Union and in the satellite states true patriotism is love of the Soviet Union. By the same token the "peace policy" of the Soviet Union, described at a Party Congress as "a more advantageous form of fighting capitalism," is a device to divide and immobilize the non-Communist world, and the peace the Soviet Union seeks is the peace of total conformity to Soviet policy.

The antipathy of slavery to freedom explains the iron curtain, the isolation, the autarchy of the society whose end is absolute power. The existence and persistence of the idea of freedom is a permanent and continuous threat to the foundation of the slave society; and it therefore regards as intolerable the long continued existence of freedom in the world. What is new, what makes the continuing crisis, is the polarization of power which now inescapably confronts the slave society with the free.

The assault on free institutions is world-wide now, and in the context of the present polarization of power a defeat of free institutions anywhere is a defeat everywhere. The shock we sustained in the destruction of Czechoslovakia was not in the measure of Czechoslovakia's material importance to us. In a material sense, her capabilities were already at Soviet disposal. But when the integrity of Czechoslovak institutions was destroyed, it was in the intangible scale of values that we registered a loss more damaging than the material loss we had already suffered.

Thus unwillingly our free society finds itself mortally challenged by the Soviet system. No other value system is so wholly irreconcilable with ours, so implacable in its purpose to destroy ours, so capable of turning to its own uses the most dangerous and divisive trends in our own society, no other so skillfully and powerfully evokes the elements of irrationality in human nature everywhere, and no other has the support of a great and growing center of military power.

B. OBJECTIVES

The objectives of a free society are determined by its fundamental values and by the necessity for maintaining the material environment in which they flourish. Logically and in fact, therefore, the Kremlin's challenge to the United States is directed not only to our values but to our physical capacity to protect their environment. It is a challenge which encompasses both peace and war and our objectives in peace and war must take account of it.

> Thus we must make ourselves strong, both in the way in which we affirm our values in the conduct of our national life, and in the development of our military and economic strength.
> We must lead in building a successfully functioning political and economic system in the free world. It is only by practical affirmation, abroad as well as at home, of our essential values, that we can preserve our own integrity, in which lies the real frustration of the Kremlin design.
> But beyond thus affirming our values our policy and actions must be such as to foster a fundamental change in the nature of the Soviet system, a change toward which the frustration of the design is the first and perhaps the most important step. Clearly it will not only be less costly but more effective if this change occurs to a maximum extent as a result of internal forces in Soviet society.

In a shrinking world, which now faces the threat of atomic warfare, it is not an adequate objective merely to seek to check the Kremlin design, for the absence of order among nations is becoming less and less tolerable. This fact imposes on us, in our own interests, the responsibility of world leadership. It demands that we make the attempt, and accept the risks inherent in it, to bring about order and justice by means consistent with the principles of freedom and democracy. We should limit our requirement of the Soviet Union to its participation with other nations on the basis of equality and respect for the rights of others. Subject to this requirement, we must with our allies and the former subject peoples seek to create a world society based on the principle of consent. Its framework cannot be inflexible. It will consist of many national communities of great and varying abilities and resources, and hence of war potential. The seeds of conflicts will inevitably exist or will come into being. To acknowledge this is only to acknowledge the impossibility of a final solution. Not to acknowledge it can be fatally dangerous in a world in which there are no final solutions.

All these objectives of a free society are equally valid and necessary in peace and war. But every consideration of devotion to our fundamental values and to our national security demands that we seek to achieve them by the strategy of the cold war. It is only by developing the moral and material strength of the free world that the Soviet regime will become convinced of the falsity of its assumptions and that the pre-conditions for workable agreements can be created. By practically demonstrating the integrity and vitality of our system the free world widens the area of possible agreement and thus can hope gradually to bring about a Soviet acknowledgement of realities which in sum will eventually constitute a frustration of the Soviet design. Short of this, however, it might be possible to create a situation which will induce the Soviet Union to accommodate itself, with or without the conscious abandonment of its design, to coexistence on tolerable terms with the non-Soviet world. Such a development would be a triumph for the idea of freedom and democracy. It must be an immediate objective of United States policy.

There is no reason, in the event of war, for us to alter our overall objectives. They do not include unconditional surrender, the subjugation of the Russian peoples or a Russia shorn of its economic potential. Such a course would irrevocably unite the Russian people behind the regime which enslaves them. Rather these objectives contemplate Soviet acceptance of the specific and limited conditions requisite to an international environment in which free institutions can flourish, and in which the Russian peoples will have a new chance to work out their own destiny. If we can make the Russian people our allies in the enterprise we will obviously have made our task easier and victory more certain.

The objectives outlined in NSC 20/4 (November 23, 1948) . . . are fully consistent with the objectives stated in this paper, and they remain valid. The growing intensity of the conflict which has been imposed upon us, however, requires the changes of emphasis and the additions that are apparent. Coupled with the probable fission bomb capability and possible thermonuclear bomb capability of the Soviet Union, the intensifying struggle requires us to face the fact that we can expect no lasting abatement of the crisis unless and until a change occurs in the nature of the Soviet system.

C. MEANS

The free society is limited in its choice of means to achieve its ends.

Compulsion is the negation of freedom, except when it is used to enforce the rights common to all. The resort to force, internally or externally, is therefore a last resort for a free society. The act is permissible only when one individual or groups of individuals within it threaten the basic rights of other individuals or when another society seeks to impose its will upon it. The free society cherishes and protects as fundamental the rights of the minority against the will of a majority, because these rights are the inalienable rights of each and every individual.

The resort to force, to compulsion, to the imposition of its will is therefore a difficult and dangerous act for a free society, which is warranted only in the face of even greater dangers. The necessity of the act must be clear and compelling; the act must commend itself to the overwhelming majority as an inescapable exception to the basic idea of freedom; or the regenerative capacity of free men after the act has been performed will be endangered.

The Kremlin is able to select whatever means are expedient in seeking to carry out its fundamental design. Thus it can make the best of several possible worlds, conducting the struggle on those levels where it considers it profitable and enjoying the benefits of a pseudo-peace on those levels where it is not ready for a contest. At the ideological or psychological level, in the struggle for men's minds, the conflict is worldwide. At the political and economic level, within states and in the relations between states, the struggle for power is being intensified. And at the military level, the Kremlin has thus far been careful not to commit a technical breach of the peace, although using its vast forces to intimidate its neighbors, and to support an aggressive foreign policy, and not hesitating through its agents to resort to arms in favorable circumstances. The attempt to carry out its fundamental design is being pressed, therefore, with all means which are believed expedient in the present situation, and the Kremlin has inextricably engaged us in the conflict between its design and our purpose.

We have no such freedom of choice, and least of all in the use of force. Resort to war is not only a last resort for a free society, but it is also an act which cannot definitively end the fundamental conflict in the realm of ideas. The idea of slavery can only be overcome by the timely and persistent demonstration of the superiority of the idea of freedom. Military victory alone would only partially and perhaps only temporarily affect the fundamental conflict, for although the ability of the Kremlin to threaten our security might be for a time destroyed, the resurgence of totalitarian forces and the re-establishment of the Soviet system or its equivalent would not be long delayed unless great progress were made in the fundamental conflict.

Practical and ideological considerations therefore both impel us to the conclusion that we have no choice but to demonstrate the superiority of the idea of freedom by its constructive application, and to attempt to change the world situation by means short of war in such a way as to frustrate the Kremlin design and hasten the decay of the Soviet system.

For us the role of military power is to serve the national purpose by deterring an attack upon us while we seek by other means to create an environment in which our free society can flourish, and by fighting, if necessary, to defend the integrity and vitality of our free society and to defeat any aggressor. The Kremlin uses Soviet military power to back up and serve the Kremlin design. It does not hesitate to use military force aggressively if that course is expedient in the achievement of its design. The differences between our fundamental purpose and the Kremlin design, therefore, are reflected in our respective attitudes toward and use of military force.

Our free society, confronted by a threat to its basic values, naturally will take such action, including the use of military force, as may be required to protect those values. The integrity of our system will not be jeopardized by any measures, covert or overt, violent or non-violent, which serve the purposes of frustrating the Kremlin design, nor does the necessity for conducting ourselves so as to affirm our values in actions as well as words forbid such measures, provided only they are appropriately calculated to that end and are not so excessive or misdirected as to make us enemies of the people instead of the evil men who have enslaved them.

But if war comes, what is the role of force? Unless we so use it that the Russian people can perceive that our effort is directed against the regime and its power for aggression, and not against their own interests, we will unite the regime and the people in the kind of last ditch fight in which no underlying problems are solved, new ones are created, and where our basic principles are obscured and compromised. If we do not in the application of force demonstrate the nature of our objectives we will, in fact, have compromised from the outset our fundamental purpose. In the words of the *Federalist* (No. 28) "The means to be employed must be proportioned to the extent of the mischief." The mischief may be a global war or it may be a Soviet campaign for limited objectives. In either case we should take no avoidable initiative which would cause it to become a war of annihilation, and if we have the forces to defeat a Soviet drive for limited objectives it may well be to our interest not to let it become a global war. Our aim in applying force must be to compel the acceptance of terms consistent with our objectives, and our capabilities for the application of force should, therefore, within the limits of what we can sustain over the long pull, be congruent to the range of tasks which we may encounter.

V. Soviet Intentions and Capabilities

A. POLITICAL AND PSYCHOLOGICAL

The Kremlin's design for world domination begins at home. The first concern of a despotic oligarchy is that the local base of its power and authority be secure. The massive fact of the iron curtain isolating the Soviet peoples from the outside world, the repeated political purges within the USSR and the institutionalized crimes of the MVD [the Soviet Ministry of Internal Affairs] are evidence that the Kremlin does not feel secure at home and that "the entire coercive force of the socialist state" is more than ever one of seeking to impose its absolute authority over "the economy, manner of life, and consciousness of people" (Vyshinski, *The Law of the Soviet State*, p. 74). Similar evidence in the satellite states of Eastern Europe leads to the conclusion that this same policy, in less advanced phases, is being applied to the Kremlin's colonial areas.

Being a totalitarian dictatorship, the Kremlin's objectives in these policies is the total subjective submission of the peoples now under its control. The concentration camp is the prototype of the society which these policies are designed to achieve, a society in which the personality of the individual is so broken and perverted that he participates affirmatively in his own degradation.

The Kremlin's policy toward areas not under its control is the elimination of resistance to its will and the extension of its influence and control. It is driven to follow this policy because it cannot, for the reasons set forth in Chapter IV, tolerate the existence of free societies; to the Kremlin the most mild and inoffensive free society is an affront, a challenge and a subversive influence. Given the nature of the Kremlin, and the evidence at hand, it seems clear that the ends toward which this policy is directed are the same as those where its control has already been established.

The means employed by the Kremlin in pursuit of this policy are limited only by considerations of expediency. Doctrine is not a limiting factor; rather it dictates the employment of violence, subversion, and deceit, and rejects moral considerations. In any event, the Kremlin's conviction of its own infallibility has made its devotion to theory so subjective that past or present pronouncements as to doctrine offer no reliable guide to future actions. The only apparent restraints on resort to war are, therefore, calculations of practicality.

With particular reference to the United States, the Kremlin's strategic and tactical policy is affected by its estimate that we are not only the greatest immediate obstacle which stands between it and world domination, we are also the only power which could release forces in the free and Soviet worlds which could destroy it. The Kremlin's policy toward us is consequently animated by a peculiarly virulent blend of hatred and fear. Its strategy has been one of attempting to undermine the complex of forces, in this country and in the rest of the free world, on which our power is based. In this it has both adhered to doctrine and followed the sound principle of seeking maximum results with minimum risks and commitments. The present application of this strategy is a new form of expression for traditional Russian caution. However, there is no justification in Soviet theory or practice for predicting that, should the Kremlin become convinced that it could cause our downfall by one conclusive blow, it would not seek that solution.

In considering the capabilities of the Soviet world, it is of prime importance to remember that, in contrast to ours, they are being drawn upon close to the maximum possible extent. Also in contrast to us, the Soviet world can do more with less—it has a lower standard of living, its economy requires less to keep it functioning, and its military machine operates effectively with less elaborate equipment and organization.

The capabilities of the Soviet world are being exploited to the full because the Kremlin is inescapably militant. It is inescapably militant because it possesses and is possessed by a world-wide revolutionary movement, because it is the inheritor of Russian imperialism, and because it is a totalitarian dictatorship. Persistent crisis, conflict, and expansion are the essence of the Kremlin's militancy. This dynamism serves to intensify all Soviet capabilities.

Two enormous organizations, the Communist Party and the secret police, are an outstanding source of strength to the Kremlin. In the Party, it has an apparatus designed to impose at home an ideological uniformity among its people and to act abroad as an instrument of propaganda, subversion and espionage. In its police apparatus, it has a domestic repressive instrument guaranteeing under present circumstances the continued security of the Kremlin. The demonstrated capabilities of these two basic organizations, operating openly or in disguise, in mass or through single agents, is unparalleled in history. The party, the police and the conspicuous might of the Soviet military machine together tend to create an overall impression of irresistible Soviet power among many peoples of the free world.

The ideological pretensions of the Kremlin are another great source of strength. Its identification of the Soviet system with communism, its peace campaigns and its championing of colonial peoples may be viewed with apathy, if not cynicism, by the oppressed totalitariat of the Soviet world, but in the free world these ideas find favorable responses in vulnerable segments of society. They have found a particularly receptive audience in Asia, especially as the Asiatics have been impressed by what has been plausibly portrayed to them as the rapid advance of the USSR from a backward society to a position of great world power. Thus, in its pretensions to being (a) the source of a new universal faith and (b) the model "scientific" society, the Kremlin cynically identifies itself with the genuine aspirations of large numbers of people, and places itself at the head of an international crusade with all of the benefits which derive therefrom.

Finally, there is a category of capabilities, strictly speaking neither institutional nor ideological, which should be taken into consideration. The extraordinary flexibility of Soviet tactics is certainly a strength. It derives from the utterly amoral and opportunistic conduct of Soviet policy. Combining this quality with the elements of secrecy, the Kremlin possesses a formidable capacity to act with the widest tactical latitude, with stealth, and with speed.

The greatest vulnerability of the Kremlin lies in the basic nature of its relations with the Soviet people.

That relationship is characterized by universal suspicion, fear, and denunciation. It is a relationship in which the Kremlin relies, not only for its power but its very survival, on intricately devised mechanisms of coercion. The Soviet monolith is held together by the iron curtain around it and the iron bars within it, not by any force of natural cohesion. These artificial mechanisms of unity have never been intelligently challenged by a strong outside force. The full measure of their vulnerability is therefore not yet evident.

The Kremlin's relations with its satellites and their peoples is likewise a vulnerability. Nationalism still remains the most potent emotional-political force. The well-known ills of colonialism are compounded, however, by the excessive demands of the Kremlin that its satellites accept not only the imperial authority of Moscow but that they believe in and proclaim the ideological primacy and infallibility of the Kremlin. These excessive requirements can be made good only through extreme coercion. The result is that if a satellite feels able to effect its independence of the Kremlin, as Tito was able to do, it is likely to break away.

In short, Soviet ideas and practices run counter to the best and potentially the strongest instincts of men, and deny their most fundamental aspirations. Against an adversary which effectively affirmed the constructive and hopeful instincts of men and was capable of fulfilling their fundamental aspirations, the Soviet system might prove to be fatally weak.

The problem of succession to Stalin is also a Kremlin vulnerability. In a system where supreme power is acquired and held through violence and intimidation, the transfer of that power may well produce a period of instability.

In a very real sense, the Kremlin is a victim of, its own dynamism. This dynamism can become a weakness if it is frustrated, if in its forward thrusts it encounters a superior force which halts the expansion and exerts a superior counterpressure. Yet the Kremlin cannot relax the condition of crisis and mobilization, for to do so would be to lose its dynamism, whereas the seeds of decay within the Soviet system would begin to flourish and fructify.

The Kremlin is, of course, aware of these weaknesses. It must know that in the present world situation they are of secondary significance. So long as the Kremlin retains the initiative, so long as it can keep on the offensive unchallenged by clearly superior counter-force—spiritual as well as material—its vulnerabilities are largely inoperative and even concealed by its successes. The Kremlin has not yet been given real reason to fear and be diverted by the rot within its system.

B. ECONOMIC

The Kremlin has no economic intentions unrelated to its overall policies. Economics in the Soviet world is not an end in itself. The Kremlin's policy, in so far as it has to do with economics, is to utilize economic processes to contribute to the overall strength, particularly the war-making capacity of the Soviet system. The material welfare of the totalitariat is severely subordinated to the interest of the system.

As for capabilities, even granting optimistic Soviet reports of production, the total economic strength of the U.S.S.R. compares with that of the U.S. as roughly one to four. This is reflected not only in gross national product (1949: USSR $65 billion; U.S. $250 billion), but in production of key commodities in 1949:

. . .

C. MILITARY

The Soviet Union is developing the military capacity to support its design for world domination. The Soviet Union actually possesses armed forces far in excess of those necessary to defend its national territory. These armed forces are probably not yet considered by the Soviet Union to be sufficient to initiate a war which would involve the United States. This excessive strength, coupled now with an atomic capability, provides the Soviet Union with great coercive power for use in time of peace in furtherance of its objectives and serves as a deterrent to the victims of its aggression from taking any action in opposition to its tactics which would risk war.

Should a major war occur in 1950 the Soviet Union and its satellites are considered by the Joint Chiefs of Staff to be in a sufficiently advanced state of preparation immediately to undertake and carry out the following campaigns.

   a. To overrun Western Europe, with the possible exception of the Iberian and Scandinavian Peninsulas; to drive toward the oil-bearing areas of the Near and Middle East; and to consolidate Communist gains in the Far East;
   b. To launch air attacks against the British Isles and air and sea attacks against the lines of communications of the Western Powers in the Atlantic and the Pacific;
   c. To attack selected targets with atomic weapons, now including the likelihood of such attacks against targets in Alaska, Canada, and the United States. Alternatively, this capability, coupled with other actions open to the Soviet Union, might deny the United Kingdom as an effective base of operations for allied forces. It also should be possible for the Soviet Union to prevent any allied "Normandy" type amphibious operations intended to force a reentry into the continent of Europe.

After the Soviet Union completed its initial campaigns and consolidated its positions in the Western European area, it could simultaneously conduct:

   a. Full-scale air and limited sea operations against the British Isles;
   b. Invasions of the Iberian and Scandinavian Peninsulas;
   c. Further operations in the Near and Middle East, continued air operations against the North American continent, and air and sea operations against Atlantic and Pacific lines of communication; and
   d. Diversionary attacks in other areas.

During the course of the offensive operations listed in the second and third paragraphs above, the Soviet Union will have an air defense capability with respect to the vital areas of its own and its satellites' territories which can oppose but cannot prevent allied air operations against these areas.

It is not known whether the Soviet Union possesses war reserves and arsenal capabilities sufficient to supply its satellite armies or even its own forces throughout a long war. It might not be in the interest of the Soviet Union to equip fully its satellite armies, since the possibility of defections would exist.

It is not possible at this time to assess accurately the finite disadvantages to the Soviet Union which may accrue through the implementation of the Economic Co-operation Act of 1948, as amended, and the Mutual Defense Assistance Act of 1949. It should be expected that, as this implementation progresses, the internal security situation of the recipient nations should improve concurrently. In addition, a strong United States military position, plus increases in the armaments of the nations of Western Europe, should strengthen the determination of the recipient nations to counter Soviet moves and in event of war could be considered as likely to delay operations and increase the time required for the Soviet Union to overrun Western Europe. In all probability, although United States backing will stiffen their determination, the armaments increase under the present aid programs will not be of any major consequence prior to 1952. Unless the military strength of the Western European nations is increased on a much larger scale than under current programs and at an accelerated rate, it is more than likely that those nations will not be able to oppose even by 1960 the Soviet armed forces in war with any degree of effectiveness. Considering the Soviet Union military capability, the long-range allied military objective in Western Europe must envisage an increased military strength in that area sufficient possibly to deter the Soviet Union from a major war or, in any event, to delay materially the overrunning of Western Europe and, if feasible, to hold a bridgehead on the continent against Soviet Union offensives.

. . .

The Soviet Union now has aircraft able to deliver the atomic bomb. Our Intelligence estimates assign to the Soviet Union an atomic bomber capability already in excess of that needed to deliver available bombs. We have at present no evaluated estimate regarding the Soviet accuracy of delivery on target. It is believed that the Soviets cannot deliver their bombs on target with a degree of accuracy comparable to ours, but a planning estimate might well place it at 40–60 percent of bombs sorted. For planning purposes, therefore, the date the Soviets possess an atomic stockpile of 200 bombs would be a critical date for

Did You Know?

Arab Nationalism to Fundamentalism

Arab nationalism is based on the concept of an Arab nation that has Arabic as its language and is Muslim in religion. Generally, the origins of Arab nationalism trace back to the Arab resistance to Ottoman Turk rule in the nineteenth century. The post–World War II Arab nationalist movement starts with a humiliating defeat in 1948 at the hands of the Israelis, which created the impetus for pan-Arab unity. The first attempt to integrate was between Syria and Jordan in the 1940s. A second attempt came in 1958 following the Suez crisis, with Syria and Egypt forming the United Arabic Republic and attempting to integrate Iraq and Yemen, but this ended with the death of the charismatic leader Gamal Abdel Nasser. Another integration attempt came between Syria and Iraq through the intra-party links that existed, since both countries were ruled by the Baath party, but this failed, largely due to leadership issues, as did another attempt to integrate undertaken by Libyan leader Muammar Kaddafi in 1972. With the decline of Arab nationalism, which the United States and European powers viewed antagonistically because of its potential ties with the Soviet Union, came the rise of Islamic fundamentalism, now the United States' foremost concern in the region. Islamic fundamentalism bases its conception of unity on the belief in the religion of Islam and includes more than the pan-Arab nation. As Arab nationalism declined, a particularly conservative sect of Islam, Wahhabism, originated in Saudi Arabia, has flourished as a driving force behind Islamic fundamentalism.

the United States, for the delivery of 100 atomic bombs on targets in the United States would seriously damage this country.

At the time the Soviet Union has a substantial atomic stockpile and if it is assumed that it will strike a strong surprise blow and if it is assumed further that its atomic attacks will be met with no more effective defense opposition than the United States and its allies have programmed, results of those attacks could include:

a. Laying waste to the British Isles and thus depriving the Western Powers of their use as a base;
b. Destruction of the vital centers and of the communications of Western Europe, thus precluding effective defense by the Western Powers; and
c. Delivering devastating attacks on certain vital centers of the United States and Canada.

The possession by the Soviet Union of a thermonuclear capability in addition to this substantial atomic stockpile would result in tremendously increased damage.

During this decade, the defensive capabilities of the Soviet Union will probably be strengthened, particularly by the development and use of modern aircraft, aircraft warning and communications devices, and defensive guided missiles.

- **Document: President Dwight D. Eisenhower's Speech to Congress**
- **Date:** January 5, 1957
- **Significance:** In his message to the U.S. Congress, President Eisenhower outlines what came to be known as the Eisenhower Doctrine, which aimed to support regimes in order to keep them free from Soviet influence, especially after the disastrous attack on Egypt from Britain, France, and Israel.
- **Source:** Dwight D. Eisenhower, *Public Papers of the Presidents of the United States: Dwight D. Eisenhower, 1957*. Washington, D.C.: GPO, 1958.

Special Message to the Congress on the Situation in the Middle East, January 1957.

To the Congress of the United States:

First may I express to you my deep appreciation of your courtesy in giving me, at some inconvenience to yourselves, this early opportunity of addressing you on a matter I deem to be of grave importance to our country.

In my forthcoming State of the Union Message, I shall review the international situation generally. There are worldwide hopes which we can reasonably entertain, and there are worldwide responsibilities which we must carry to make certain that freedom—including our own—may be secure.

There is, however, a special situation in the Middle East which I feel I should, even now, lay before you.

Before doing so it is well to remind ourselves that our basic national objective in international affairs remains peace—a world peace based on justice. Such a peace must include all areas, all peoples of the world if it is to be enduring. There is no nation, great or small, with which we would refuse to negotiate, in mutual good faith, with patience and in the determination to secure a better understanding between us. Out of such understandings must, and eventually will, grow confidence and trust, indispensable ingredients to a program of peace and to plans for lifting from us all the burdens of expensive armaments. To promote these objectives, our government works tirelessly, day by day, month by month, year by year. But until a degree of success crowns our efforts that will assure to all nations peaceful existence, we must, in the interests of peace itself, remain vigilant, alert and strong.

I.

The Middle East has abruptly reached a new and critical stage in its long and important history. In past decades many of the countries in that area were not fully self-governing. Other nations exercised considerable authority in the area and the security of the region was largely built around their power. But since the First World War there has been a steady evolution toward self-government and independence. This development the United States has

General of the Armies Dwight D. Eisenhower, proved to be an excellent coalition leader as supreme commander of the Allied Expeditionary Forces, European Theater of Operations. He was subsequently the first commander of North Atlantic Treaty Alliance (NATO) forces, then president of the United States (1953–1961). (National Archives)

welcomed and has encouraged. Our country supports without reservation the full sovereignty and independence of each and every nation of the Middle East.

The evolution to independence has in the main been a peaceful process. But the area has been often troubled. Persistent crosscurrents of distrust and fear with raids back and forth across national boundaries have brought about a high degree of instability in much of the Mid East. Just recently there have been hostilities involving Western European nations that once exercised much influence in the area. Also the relatively large attack by Israel in October has intensified the basic differences between that nation and its Arab neighbors. All this instability has been heightened and, at times, manipulated by International Communism.

II.

Russia's rulers have long sought to dominate the Middle East. That was true of the Czars and it is true of the Bolsheviks. The reasons are not hard to find. They do not affect Russia's security, for no one plans to use the Middle East as a base for aggression against Russia. Never for a moment has the United States entertained such a thought.

The Soviet Union has nothing whatsoever to fear from the United States in the Middle East, or anywhere else in the world, so long as its rulers do not themselves first resort to aggression.

That statement I make solemnly and emphatically.

Neither does Russia's desire to dominate the Middle East spring from its own economic interest in the area. Russia does not appreciably use or depend upon the Suez Canal. In 1955 Soviet traffic through the Canal represented only about three fourths of 1% of the total. The Soviets have no need for, and could provide no market for, the petroleum resources which constitute the principal natural wealth of the area. Indeed, the Soviet Union is a substantial exporter of petroleum products.

The reason for Russia's interest in the Middle East is solely that of power politics. Considering her announced purpose of Communizing the world, it is easy to understand her hope of dominating the Middle East.

This region has always been the crossroads of the continents of the Eastern Hemisphere. The Suez Canal enables the nations of Asia and Europe to carry on the commerce that is essential if these countries are to maintain well-rounded and prosperous economies. The Middle East provides a gateway between Eurasia and Africa.

It contains about two thirds of the presently known oil deposits of the world and it normally supplies the petroleum needs of many nations of Europe, Asia and Africa. The nations of Europe are peculiarly dependent upon this supply, and this dependency relates to transportation as well as to production! This has been vividly demonstrated since the closing of the Suez Canal and some of the pipelines. Alternate ways of transportation and, indeed, alternate sources of power can, if necessary, be developed. But these cannot be considered as early prospects.

These things stress the immense importance of the Middle East. If the nations of that area should lose their independence, if they were dominated by alien forces hostile to freedom, that would be both a tragedy for the area and for many other free nations whose economic life would be subject to near strangulation. Western Europe would be endangered just as though there had been no Marshall Plan, no North Atlantic Treaty Organization. The free nations of Asia and Africa, too, would be placed in serious jeopardy. And the countries of the Middle East would lose the markets upon which their economies depend. All this would have the most adverse, if not disastrous, effect upon our own nation's economic life and political prospects.

Then there are other factors which transcend the material. The Middle East is the birthplace of three great religions—Moslem, Christian and Hebrew. Mecca and Jerusalem are more than places on the map. They symbolize religions which teach that the spirit has supremacy over matter and that the individual has a dignity and rights of which no despotic government can rightfully deprive him. It would be intolerable if the holy places of the Middle East should be subjected to a rule that glorifies atheistic materialism.

International Communism, of course, seeks to mask its purposes of domination by expressions of good will and by superficially attractive offers of political, economic and military aid. But any free nation, which is the subject of Soviet enticement, ought, in elementary wisdom, to look behind the mask.

Remember Estonia, Latvia and Lithuania! In 1939 the Soviet Union entered into mutual assistance pacts with these then dependent countries; and the Soviet Foreign Minister, addressing the Extraordinary Fifth Session of the Supreme Soviet in October 1939, solemnly and publicly declared that "we stand for the scrupulous and punctilious observance of the pacts on the basis of complete reciprocity, and we declare that all the nonsensical talk about the Sovietization of the Baltic countries is only to the interest of our common enemies and of all anti-Soviet provocateurs." Yet in 1940, Estonia, Latvia and Lithuania were forcibly incorporated into the Soviet Union.

Soviet control of the satellite nations of Eastern Europe has been forcibly maintained in spite of solemn promises of a contrary intent, made during World War II.

Stalin's death brought hope that this pattern would change. And we read the pledge of the Warsaw Treaty of 1955 that the Soviet Union would follow in satellite countries "the principles of mutual respect for their independence and sovereignty and noninterference in domestic affairs." But we have just seen the subjugation of Hungary by naked armed force. In the aftermath of this Hungarian tragedy, world respect for and belief in Soviet promises have sunk to a new low. International Communism needs and seeks a recognizable success.

Thus, we have these simple and indisputable facts:

1. The Middle East, which has always been coveted by Russia, would today be prized more than ever by International Communism.
2. The Soviet rulers continue to show that they do not scruple to use any means to gain their ends.
3. The free nations of the Mid East need, and for the most part want, added strength to assure their continued independence.

III.

Our thoughts naturally turn to the United Nations as a protector of small nations. Its charter gives it primary responsibility for the maintenance of international peace and security. Our country has given the United Nations its full support in relation to the hostilities in Hungary and in Egypt. The United Nations was able to bring about a cease-fire and withdrawal of hostile forces from Egypt because it was dealing with governments and peoples who had a decent respect for the opinions of mankind as reflected in the United Nations General Assembly. But in the case of Hungary, the situation was different. The Soviet Union vetoed action by the Security Council to require the withdrawal of Soviet armed forces from Hungary. And it has shown callous indifference to the recommendations, even the censure, of the General Assembly. The United Nations can always be helpful, but it cannot be a wholly dependable protector of freedom when the ambitions of the Soviet Union are involved.

IV.

Under all the circumstances I have laid before you, a greater responsibility now devolves upon the United States. We have shown, so that none can doubt, our dedication to the principle that force shall not be used internationally for any aggressive purpose and that the integrity and independence of the nations of the Middle East should be inviolate. Seldom in history has a nation's dedication to principle been tested as severely as ours during recent weeks.

There is general recognition in the Middle East, as elsewhere, that the United States does not seek either political or economic domination over any other people. Our desire is a world environment of freedom, not servitude. On the other hand many, if not all, of the nations of the Middle East are aware of the danger that stems from International Communism and welcome closer cooperation with the United States to realize for themselves the United Nations goals of independence, economic well-being and spiritual growth.

If the Middle East is to continue its geographic role of uniting rather than separating East and West; if its vast economic resources are to serve the well-being of the peoples there, as well as that of others; and if its cultures and religions and their shrines are to be preserved for the uplifting of the spirits of the peoples, then the United States must make more evident its willingness to support the independence of the freedom-loving nations of the area.

V.

Under these circumstances I deem it necessary to seek the cooperation of the Congress. Only with that cooperation can we give the reassurance needed to deter aggression, to give courage and confidence to those who are dedicated to freedom and thus prevent a chain of events which would gravely endanger all of the free world.

There have been several Executive declarations made by the United States in relation to the Middle East. There is the Tripartite Declaration of May 25, 1950, followed by the Presidential assurance of October 31, 1950, to the King of Saudi Arabia. There is the Presidential declaration of April 9, 1956, that the United States will within constitutional means oppose any aggression in the area. There is our Declaration of November 29, 1956, that a threat to the territorial integrity or political independence of Iran, Iraq, Pakistan, or Turkey would be viewed by the United States with the utmost gravity.

Nevertheless, weaknesses in the present situation and the increased danger from International Communism, convince me that basic United States policy should now find expression in joint action by the Congress and the Executive. Furthermore, our joint resolve should be so couched as to make it apparent that if need be our words will be backed by action.

VI.

It is nothing new for the President and the Congress to join to recognize that the national integrity of other free nations is directly related to our own security.

We have joined to create and support the security system of the United Nations. We have reinforced the collective security system of the United Nations by a series of collective defense arrangements. Today we have security treaties with 42 other nations which recognize that our peace and security are intertwined. We have joined to take decisive action in relation to Greece and Turkey and in relation to Taiwan.

Thus, the United States through the joint action of the President and the Congress, or, in the case of treaties, the Senate, has manifested in many endangered areas its purpose to support free and independent governments—and peace—against external menace, notably the menace of International Communism. Thereby we have helped to maintain peace and security during a period of great danger. It is now essential that the United States should manifest through joint action of the President and the Congress our determination to assist those nations of the Mid East area, which desire that assistance.

The action which I propose would have the following features.

It would, first of all, authorize the United States to cooperate with and assist any nation or group of nations in the general area of the Middle East in the development of economic strength dedicated to the maintenance of national independence.

It would, in the second place, authorize the Executive to undertake in the same region programs of military assistance and cooperation with any nation or group of nations which desires such aid.

It would, in the third place, authorize such assistance and cooperation to include the employment of the armed forces of the United States to secure and protect the territorial integrity and political independence of such nations, requesting such aid, against overt armed aggression from any nation controlled by International Communism.

These measures would have to be consonant with the treaty obligations of the United States, including the Charter of the United Nations and with any action or recommendations of the United Nations. They would also, if armed attack occurs, be subject to the overriding authority of the United Nations Security Council in accordance with the Charter.

The present proposal would, in the fourth place, authorize the President to employ, for economic and defensive military purposes, sums available under the Mutual Security Act of 1954, as amended, without regard to existing limitations.

The legislation now requested should not include the authorization or appropriation of funds because I believe that, under the conditions I suggest, presently appropriated funds will be adequate for the balance of the present fiscal year ending June 30. I shall, however, seek in subsequent legislation the authorization of $200,000,000 to be available during each of the fiscal years 1958 and 1959 for discretionary use in the area, in addition to the other mutual security programs for the area hereafter provided for by the Congress.

VII.

This program will not solve all the problems of the Middle East. Neither does it represent the totality of our policies for the area. There are the problems of Palestine and relations between Israel and the Arab States, and the future of the Arab refugees. There is the problem of the future status of the Suez Canal. These difficulties are aggravated by International Communism, but they would exist quite apart from that threat. It is not the purpose of the legislation I propose to deal directly with these problems. The United Nations is actively concerning itself with all these matters, and we are supporting the United Nations. The United States has made clear, notably by Secretary Dulles' address of August 26, 1955, that we are willing to do much to assist the United Nations in solving the basic problems of Palestine.

The proposed legislation is primarily designed to deal with the possibility of Communist aggression, direct and indirect. There is imperative need that any lack of power in the area should be made good, not by external or alien force, but by the increased vigor and security of the independent nations of the area.

Experience shows that indirect aggression rarely if ever succeeds where there is reasonable security against direct aggression; where the government disposes of loyal security forces, and where economic conditions are such as not to make Communism seem an attractive alternative. The program I suggest deals with all three aspects of this matter and thus with the problem of indirect aggression.

It is my hope and belief that if our purpose be proclaimed, as proposed by the requested legislation, that very fact will serve to halt any contemplated aggression. We shall have heartened the patriots who are dedicated to the independence of their nations. They will not feel that they stand alone, under the menace of great power. And I should add that patriotism is, throughout this area, a powerful sentiment. It is true that fear sometimes perverts true patriotism into fanaticism and to the acceptance of dangerous enticements from without. But if that fear can be allayed, then the climate will be more favorable to the attainment of worthy national ambitions.

And as I have indicated, it will also be necessary for us to contribute economically to strengthen those countries, or groups of countries, which have governments manifestly dedicated to the preservation of independence and resistance to subversion. Such measures will provide the greatest insurance against Communist inroads. Words alone are not enough.

VII.

Let me refer again to the requested authority to employ the armed forces of the United States to assist to defend the territorial integrity and the political independence of any nation in the area against Communist armed aggression. Such authority would not be exercised except at the desire of the nation attacked. Beyond this it is my profound hope that this authority would never have to be exercised at all.

Nothing is more necessary to assure this than that our policy with respect to the defense of the area be promptly and clearly determined and declared. Thus the United Nations and all friendly governments, and indeed governments which are not friendly, will know where we stand.

If, contrary to my hope and expectation, a situation arose which called for the military application of the policy which I ask the Congress to join me in proclaiming, I would of course maintain hour-by-hour contact with the Congress if it were in session. And if the Congress were not in session, and if the situation had grave implications, I would, of course, at once call the Congress into special session.

In the situation now existing, the greatest risk, as is often the case, is that ambitious despots may miscalculate. If power-hungry Communists should either falsely or correctly estimate that the Middle East is inadequately defended, they might be tempted to use open measures of armed attack. If so, that would start a chain of circumstances which would almost surely involve the United States in military action. I am convinced that the best insurance against this dangerous contingency is to make clear now our readiness to cooperate fully and freely with our friends of the Middle East in ways consonant with the purposes and principles of the United Nations. I intend promptly to send a special mission to the Middle East to explain the cooperation we are prepared to give.

IX.

The policy which I outline involves certain burdens and indeed risks for the United States. Those who covet the area will not like what is proposed. Already, they are grossly distorting our purpose. However, before this Americans have seen our nation's vital interests and human freedom in jeopardy, and their fortitude and resolution have been equal to the crisis, regardless of hostile distortion of our words, motives and actions.

Indeed, the sacrifices of the American people in the cause of freedom have, even since the close of World War II, been measured in many billions of dollars and in thousands of the precious lives of our youth. These sacrifices, by which great areas of the world have been preserved to freedom, must not be thrown away.

In those momentous periods of the past, the President and the Congress have united, without partisanship, to serve the vital interests of the United States and of the free world.

The occasion has come for us to manifest again our national unity in support of freedom and to show our deep respect for the rights and independence of every nation—however great, however small. We seek not violence, but peace. To this purpose we must now devote our energies, our determination, ourselves.

DWIGHT D. EISENHOWER

- **Document: President John F. Kennedy's Inaugural Address to the Nation**
- **Date:** January 20, 1961
- **Significance:** In what came to be known as the "Freedom Doctrine" speech, President Kennedy commits the country to supporting freedom around the globe. Most famously, he urges Americans to "Ask not what your country can do for you—ask what you can do for your country."
- **Source:** John F. Kennedy, *Public Papers of the Presidents of the United States: John F. Kennedy, 1961*. Washington, D.C.: GPO, 1962, pp. 1–3.

Inaugural Address of John F. Kennedy
FRIDAY, JANUARY 20, 1961

Vice President Johnson, Mr. Speaker, Mr. Chief Justice, President Eisenhower, Vice President Nixon, President Truman, reverend clergy, fellow citizens, we observe today not a victory of party, but a celebration of freedom—symbolizing an end, as well as a beginning—signifying renewal, as well as change. For I have sworn before you and Almighty God the same solemn oath our forebears prescribed nearly a century and three quarters ago.

The world is very different now. For man holds in his mortal hands the power to abolish all forms of human poverty and all forms of human life. And yet the same revolutionary beliefs for which our forebears fought are still at issue around the globe—the belief that the rights of man come not from the generosity of the state, but from the hand of God.

We dare not forget today that we are the heirs of that first revolution. Let the word go forth from this time and place, to friend and foe alike, that the torch has been passed to a new generation of Americans born in this century, tempered by war, disciplined by a hard and bitter peace, proud of our ancient heritage—and unwilling to witness or permit the slow undoing of those human rights to which this Nation has always been committed, and to which we are committed today at home and around the world.

Let every nation know, whether it wishes us well or ill, that we shall pay any price, bear any burden, meet any hardship, support any friend, oppose any foe, in order to assure the survival and the success of liberty.

This much we pledge—and more.

To those old allies whose cultural and spiritual origins we share, we pledge the loyalty of faithful friends. United, there is little we cannot do in a host of cooperative ventures. Divided, there is little we can do—for we dare not meet a powerful challenge at odds and split asunder.

To those new States whom we welcome to the ranks of the free, we pledge our word that one form of colonial control shall not have passed away merely to be replaced by a far more iron tyranny. We shall not always expect to find them supporting our view. But we shall always hope to find them strongly supporting their own freedom—and to remember that, in the past, those who foolishly sought power by riding the back of the tiger ended up inside.

To those peoples in the huts and villages across the globe struggling to break the bonds of mass misery, we pledge our best efforts to help them help themselves, for whatever period is required—not because the Communists may be doing it, not because we seek their votes, but because it is right. If a free society cannot help the many who are poor, it cannot save the few who are rich.

To our sister republics south of our border, we offer a special pledge—to convert our good words into good deeds—in a new alliance for progress—to assist free men and free governments in casting off the chains of poverty. But this peaceful revolution of hope cannot become the prey of hostile powers. Let all our neighbors know that we shall join with them to oppose aggression or subversion anywhere in the Americas. And let every other power know that this Hemisphere intends to remain the master of its own house.

To that world assembly of sovereign states, the United Nations, our last best hope in an age where the instruments of war have far outpaced the instruments of peace, we renew our pledge of support—to prevent it from becoming merely a forum for invective—to strengthen its shield of the new and the weak—and to enlarge the area in which its writ may run.

Finally, to those nations who would make themselves our adversary, we offer not a pledge but a request: that both sides begin anew the quest for peace, before the dark powers of destruction unleashed by science engulf all humanity in planned or accidental self-destruction.

We dare not tempt them with weakness. For only when our arms are sufficient beyond doubt can we be certain beyond doubt that they will never be employed.

But neither can two great and powerful groups of nations take comfort from our present course—both sides overburdened by the cost of modern weapons, both rightly alarmed by the steady spread of the deadly atom, yet both racing to alter that uncertain balance of terror that stays the hand of mankind's final war.

So let us begin anew—remembering on both sides that civility is not a sign of weakness, and sincerity is always subject to proof. Let us never negotiate out of fear. But let us never fear to negotiate.

Let both sides explore what problems unite us instead of belaboring those problems which divide us.

Let both sides, for the first time, formulate serious and precise proposals for the inspection and control of arms—and bring the absolute power to destroy other nations under the absolute control of all nations.

Let both sides seek to invoke the wonders of science instead of its terrors. Together let us explore the stars, conquer the deserts, eradicate disease, tap the ocean depths, and encourage the arts and commerce.

Let both sides unite to heed in all corners of the earth the command of Isaiah—to "undo the heavy burdens . . . and to let the oppressed go free."

And if a beachhead of cooperation may push back the jungle of suspicion, let both sides join in creating a new endeavor, not a new balance of power, but a new world of law, where the strong are just and the weak secure and the peace preserved.

All this will not be finished in the first 100 days. Nor will it be finished in the first 1,000 days, nor in the life of this Administration, nor even perhaps in our lifetime on this planet. But let us begin.

In your hands, my fellow citizens, more than in mine, will rest the final success or failure of our course. Since this country was founded, each generation of Americans has been summoned to give testimony to its national loyalty. The graves of young Americans who answered the call to service surround the globe.

Now the trumpet summons us again—not as a call to bear arms, though arms we need; not as a call to battle, though embattled we are—but a call to bear the burden of a long twilight struggle, year in and year out, "rejoicing in hope, patient in tribulation"—a struggle against the common enemies of man: tyranny, poverty, disease, and war itself.

Can we forge against these enemies a grand and global alliance, North and South, East and West, that can assure a more fruitful life for all mankind? Will you join in that historic effort?

In the long history of the world, only a few generations have been granted the role of defending freedom in its hour of maximum danger. I do not shrink from this responsibility—I welcome it. I do not believe that any of us would exchange places with any other people or any other generation. The energy, the faith, the devotion which we bring to this endeavor will light our country and all who serve it—and the glow from that fire can truly light the world.

And so, my fellow Americans: ask not what your country can do for you—ask what you can do for your country.

My fellow citizens of the world: ask not what America will do for you, but what together we can do for the freedom of man.

Finally, whether you are citizens of America or citizens of the world, ask of us the same high standards of strength and sacrifice which we ask of you. With a good conscience our only sure reward, with history the final judge of our deeds, let us go forth to lead the land we love, asking His blessing and His help, but knowing that here on earth God's work must truly be our own.

FURTHER READING

Ambrose, S. (1991) *Eisenhower: Soldier and President*. New York: Simon and Schuster.
Gaddis, J. L. (1989) *The Long Peace: Inquiries in the History of the Cold War*. Oxford: Oxford University Press.
Gaddis, J. L. (2005) *The Cold War: A New History*. New York: Penguin.
Hogan, M. (1987) *The Marshall Plan: America, Britain, and the Reconstruction of Europe, 1947–1952*. Cambridge: Cambridge University Press.
McCullough, D. (1993) *Truman*. New York: Simon and Schuster.
Thompson, N. (2009) *The Hawk and the Dove: Paul Nitze, George Kennan, and the History of the Cold War*. New York: Henry Holt & Co.
Westad, O. A. (2007) *The Global Cold War: Third World Interventions and the Making of Our Times*. Cambridge: Cambridge University Press.

6

RICHARD M. NIXON
TO
RONALD REAGAN:
TOWARD THE END OF THE
COLD WAR

INTRODUCTION

When President Richard M. Nixon came to the White House after the 1968 election, he promised he had a plan to end the increasingly unpopular war in Vietnam. During the previous two administrations, approximately 30,000 American soldiers had perished in Vietnam, a number that would double by the time Nixon left office. And while approximately 300 U.S. servicemen were dying per week in Vietnam prior to the Nixon administration, by the time Nixon left office that number had more than tripled. Nonetheless, Nixon came to office fully anticipating a disengagement from Vietnam without losing the war. Yet his personality and the personality of his national security adviser, Henry Kissinger, undermined his vision and eventually brought about his political disgrace when he resigned in shame in August 1974. At the same time, Nixon was able to achieve a major foreign policy victory by opening up U.S. relations with China, an accomplishment that led Nixon's presidency to be judged more favorably in the realm of foreign policy than domestic policy.

Nixon's foreign policy is fascinating for those enamored with "big idea" foreign policy debates and the impact of personalities on diplomacy. It is no accident that Nixon's foreign policy team was dominated by a central figure, Henry Kissinger, a political scientist from Harvard who was an expert on great statesmen such as Lord Castlereagh and Prince von Metternich as well as balance-of-power diplomacy. No duo in U.S. foreign policymaking has ever been analyzed and dissected more than Nixon and Kissinger because they were capable of the best in diplomacy but also capable of the worst in politics and the pettiest in bureaucratic infighting (Herring 2008: 764).

By early 1969 there were roughly 540,000 U.S. combat troops in Vietnam. Nixon worked to counteract protests and to portray his policies as representing a vast "silent majority" of Americans. The Nixon-Kissinger strategy was to break the will of the North Vietnamese by intensified bombing and hinting that Nixon was mad enough to use nuclear weapons to destroy North Vietnam, a gambit that did not pay off. In July 1969 the president announced the Nixon Doctrine, otherwise known as "Vietnamization," through which the United States would help other countries fight their wars with weapons and money but not U.S. soldiers. As part of this strategy, however, Nixon expanded the war by secretly bombing Cambodia and Laos, culminating in the invasion of Cambodia in 1970. This not only led to the collapse of the governments of Laos and Cambodia but also opened the door to the Khmer Rouge takeover of Cambodia. The Khmer Rouge would go on to brutally kill nearly one-third of the Cambodian population in the "killing fields." The expansion of the war into Cambodia also led to protests on college campuses in the United States and a new military draft. By 1972 Vietnamization resulted in a decrease of U.S. troop levels, to 90,000.

After Nixon's reelection in 1972, he once again ordered heavy bombing of Hanoi with the intention of breaking North Vietnamese resolve. On January 27, 1973, the United States and North Vietnam announced a cease-fire agreement, an agreement that critics saw as a "face-saving" move by the United States to allow it to withdraw its troops prior to a communist takeover. Having kept secrets from his own people, and famously shutting out Congress and his own State Department, President Nixon suffered a series of political blows because of his foreign policy conduct in Southeast Asia. Nixon's excesses led Congress to convene the Church and Pike committees;

their findings, along with the War Powers Resolution of 1973, placed constraints on what was increasingly seen as an "imperial presidency" (Schlesinger 2004).

The greatest achievement of the Nixon era was the opening of China. Taking advantage of a rift between China and the Soviet Union, Henry Kissinger skillfully negotiated, in total secrecy, the first visit by a U.S. president to China, and a subsequent visit to the Soviet Union. There is much historical debate about the gains that Nixon made during these extravagant diplomatic affairs, but the fact remains that China, due to its own considerations but also prompted by the Nixon White House, became more open to the United States and eventually became the United States' largest trading partner. Nixon thus ushered in an era of "détente" in which Cold War tensions were eased, and in this context Nixon signed the Strategic Arms Limitation Treaty in Moscow in May 1972, an agreement that reduced anti-ballistic missiles that lasted until the George W. Bush administration. Nixon always thought he should be respected for these diplomatic accomplishments, and he was envious when Henry Kissinger garnered more praise and attention than he. Shortly after, the Nixon administration was under domestic pressure due to the Watergate scandal, which ultimately forced Nixon to resign in disgrace, ironically leaving Kissinger to run U.S. foreign policy.

Additionally, Nixon faced many regional challenges. With Kissinger, Nixon tried to counteract the emergence of left-leaning governments in Latin America. In Chile, which had just elected the left-leaning Salvador Allende, the United States attempted to economically strangle the country, and when this failed, they resorted to outright unlawful measures by providing right-wing anti-government elements in the Chilean military with weaponry and experts to overthrow the government of Chile. While publicly professing concern over the events unfolding in Chile, the United States supported a coup that resulted in the murder of Chile's President Allende. The new regime installed one of the most notorious Latin American dictators of the twentieth century, General Augusto Pinochet, who is responsible for the killings and disappearances and tens of thousands of his own citizens.

In Asia, Nixon's opening of China infuriated Taiwan and Japan, even contributing to the collapse of the Japanese government of Prime Minster Sato. In the Asian subcontinent, the United States supported Ayub Khan, a dictator who became the leader of Pakistan after the assassination of its prime minister. Disregarding the concerns of India, the landmass of which separated West Pakistan and East Pakistan (now known as Bangladesh), the United States tacitly supported Khan's attack on the Bangladeshis fighting for liberation, resulting in several hundred thousand deaths as well as Khan's invasion of India's Kashmir region, a long-disputed territory between Pakistan and India, threatening to open yet another war on the subcontinent. In Indonesia the United States supported the infamous anti-communist President Suharto, who purged leftists from the Indonesian government and invaded East Timor, resulting in war crimes against the East Timorese.

In Cyprus the United States supported, some say assisted, in the attempted overthrow of the legitimate government of Cyprus under Archbishop Makarios by U.S.-trained Greek colonels, almost producing a regional war between Greece and Turkey when the latter invaded the island, killing thousands and expelling tens of thousands from the occupied northern part of the island. In the Middle East, the United States saved the state of Israel, which was under attack by its Arab neighbors, through the establishment of an airlift campaign, further insinuating the

United States into the Arab-Israeli conflict. And in Africa, in the most prominent war by proxy, the United States supported the anti-communist group UNITA in a civil war in Angola that erupted after the departure of the colonial power, Portugal. This conflict continued into the twenty-first century, until the infamous UNITA leader Jonas Savimbi died in combat in 2002.

After Nixon's resignation, President Gerald Ford's administration had little chance to make an impact in foreign policy. Under Ford, détente continued and the United States, the Soviet Union, and various European nations signed the Helsinki Accords, calling for increased commerce between the Eastern and Western blocs as well as respect for human rights. However, Saigon fell to the North Vietnamese communists in April 1975, and the U.S. domestic economy went into a recession that was exacerbated when Arab oil-producing countries cut off supplies to the United States in an effort to pressure Israel to give back territory it had acquired the 1967 war. In the 1976 presidential election, Ford lost to Democrat Jimmy Carter.

The Carter administration was plagued by problems inherited from previous administrations, such as a shrinking U.S. economy. While continuing arms reduction talks initiated by Nixon, Carter acted on his commitment to decrease United States–Soviet tension by asking the Soviets to agree not only to limitations on missiles but on a reduction of nuclear weaponry. Carter's insistence that human rights be part of U.S. foreign policy, however, did not win him any favors from the Soviets, who, challenged by dissidents such as Andrei Sakharov, saw this as a ploy. After the signing of the second Strategic Arms Limitations Treaty (SALT II), United States–Soviet relations quickly soured when the Soviets invaded Afghanistan in 1979.

Despite emphasizing human rights, Carter was unable to stem the genocide in Cambodia and even supported the anti-communist dictator of Zaire, now known as the Congo. Carter's policies in the Arab world reduced the conflict to a land-for-peace arrangement (Herring 2008: 835), and his support for Palestinian statehood actually mobilized opponents of Palestinian statehood to elect Menachem Begin as prime minister of Israel. However, Carter was able to pull one of the most significant feats in the history of U.S. foreign policy: the rapprochement between Israel and its former enemy Egypt at Camp David in 1978, for which, at least in part, Carter won a Nobel Peace Prize in 2002. The negotiations between Egypt's Anwar Sadat and Israel's Menachem Begin not only produced peace between the two countries, with each leader visiting the other's country for the first time, but also brought Egypt's recognition of the state of Israel and the return of the Sinai Peninsula to Egypt. Sadat, however, was assassinated by Egyptian radicals opposed to his recognition of Israel, an event that signaled the emergence of Islamic fundamentalism as a force in the Middle East.

In Central America, Carter negotiated a treaty with Omar Torrijos of Panama that would gradually return the Panama Canal territory to Panama. In 1980 opponents of the treaty coalesced behind candidate Ronald Reagan, who was critical of it. The straw that broke Carter's presidency, however, was Iran. The United States had backed the brutal, corrupt, yet pro-Western Shah of Iran as an ally from the time it helped install him in 1953. The Shah was deeply unpopular in his own country for political and religious reasons, and his secret service (the SAVAK) was notoriously brutal. In 1979 the Iranian Revolution, led by Ayatollah Khomeini, who denounced the United States as the "Great Satan" and its embassy in Teheran as a "den of spies," took control of Iran and ousted the Shah. When the United States allowed the Shah to seek medical treatment in the United States, Iranian revolutionaries invaded the U.S. embassy on November 4, 1979, eventually holding 52 Americans as hostages. Under pressure, in April 1980 Carter attempted to rescue the hostages by sending a team of Marine commandos to Iran, a botched mission that resulted in the death of eight Marines. Because of a failing economy and a diminished standing in world affairs, Carter lost to Republican Ronald Reagan in 1980. After 444 days in captivity, the American hostages in Teheran were freed on Carter's last day in office, January 20, 1981.

In his two terms as president, Ronald Reagan intensified the Cold War standoff with the Soviet Union, only to open the door to groundbreaking agreements to reduce nuclear stockpiles. Reagan's strategy, his supporters argue, helped the United States win the Cold War and led to the dissolution of the Soviet Union. Reagan was a strident anti-communist who, ironically, developed a strong working relationship with the reformist Soviet leader Michael Gorbachev. Early on, Reagan's tough rhetoric portrayed the Soviet Union as the "evil empire" that could only be dealt with through force. To respond to the Soviet threat, Reagan pushed through a buildup of military forces and weapons systems, and he promoted the anti-ballistic missile defense shield known as the Strategic Defense Initiative (SDI), which critics dubbed "Star Wars." However, after pushing the world toward nuclear brinksmanship, in his second term Reagan worked with Gorbachev to achieve agreements on intermediate range forces (INF) and other nuclear reductions.

In the Middle East, President Reagan's foreign policy fully supported Israel, even giving assent to the Israeli invasion of Lebanon in 1982, an invasion that saw atrocities committed in Lebanese refugee camps. After a 1983 terrorist attack killed 241 U.S. Marines in their barracks in Beirut, Reagan withdrew U.S. peacekeeping troops from Lebanon. And when Libya was implicated in terrorist attacks such as the bombing of Pan Am flight 103, Reagan retaliated by bombing Libya.

Reagan's foreign policy reversed Carter's emphasis on human rights, and the United States lent support to governments that were anti-communist even if they were authoritarian and repressive. Further, under Reagan the United States supported groups seeking to topple leftist governments in the Caribbean and Central America. To block Soviet and Cuban influence, Reagan invaded the tiny island nation of Grenada and supported right-wing governments in Honduras and Guatemala. And in Nicaragua, Reagan sought to undermine the socialist Sandinista regime by mining the harbor of Managua and funneling weapons to the opposition "Contras," whom Reagan dubbed "freedom

Did You Know?

Nicaragua Versus the United States

Following the overthrow of dictator Anastasio Somoza in Nicaragua, a group called the FSLN (Frente Sandinista de Liberación Nacional), otherwise known as the Sandinistas, took control of the country. Named after Alfredo Sandino, a revolutionary leader who rebelled against the United States in the 1930s, the Sandinistas were leftists and therefore were viewed as a communist expansionist threat by the United States. The United States, mainly through the Central Intelligence Agency (CIA), along with the Argentinian dictatorship at the time, provided financial support and weaponry to the Contras, several groups with little ideological cohesion but who resisted the Sandinistas. The Contras were extremely brutal, and soon their behavior forced the U.S. government to sever ties with them, but not before the United States had taken action against the territorial integrity and had violated the sovereignty of the state of Nicaragua. In 1986, Nicaragua took the United States to the International Court of Justice for supporting the Contras, killing its citizens, and violating its sovereignty by mining the harbor of Managua, Nicaragua's capital, among other things. The United States argued that the International Court of Justice had no jurisdiction over the matter, and when the court rejected its claim, the United States withdrew recognition from the International Court. Consequently, the ICJ concluded on a rather one-sided vote that the United States had indeed violated Nicaragua's sovereignty, among other things, and ordered that restitution be paid to the Sandinista government. The United States refused to abide by this ruling and vetoed action at the United Nations Security Council, making it impossible for Nicaragua to receive restitution. Eventually a new Nicaraguan government withdrew its demands on the United States, and the matter was settled in 1991.

fighters." In 1986, it was revealed that the United States had sold weapons to Iran in an effort to win the release of some U.S. hostages in the Middle East and then siphoned some of the money to support the Contras in Nicaragua. While the "Iran-Contra" scandal led to congressional investigations and the resignation of several lower-level officials, such as Colonel Oliver North, it did not seriously damage the reputation of the "Teflon" President Ronald Reagan or of Vice President George H. W. Bush, both of whom claimed they were "out of the loop."

- **Document: President Nixon's Address to the Nation on "Vietnamization"**
- **Date:** November 3, 1969
- **Significance:** In this speech, Nixon describes his overall goal of containment and Vietnamization as a way to end the war in Vietnam. The speech is also famous for Nixon's appeal to the "silent majority," a term popularized by Nixon to express the idea that the majority of Americans did not participate in antiwar demonstrations and instead supported the war in Vietnam.
- **Source:** Richard M. Nixon, *Public Papers of the Presidents of the United States: Richard Nixon, 1969.* Washington, D.C.: GPO, 1971, pp. 901–909.

Good evening, my fellow Americans:

Tonight I want to talk to you on a subject of deep concern to all Americans and to many people in all parts of the world the war in Vietnam.

I believe that one of the reasons for the deep division about Vietnam is that many Americans have lost confidence in what their Government has told them about our policy. The American people cannot and should not be asked to support a policy which involves the overriding issues of war and peace unless they know the truth about that policy. Tonight, therefore, I would like to answer some of the questions that I know are on the minds of many of you listening to me. How and why did America get involved in Vietnam in the first place? How has this administration changed the policy of the previous administration? What has really happened in the negotiations in Paris and on the battle-front in Vietnam? What choices do we have if we are to end the war? What are the prospects for peace?

Now, let me begin by describing the situation I found when I was inaugurated on January 20.

- The war had been going on for 4 years.
- 31,000 Americans had been killed in action.
- The training program for the South Vietnamese was behind schedule.
- 540,000 Americans were in Vietnam with no plans to reduce the number.
- No progress had been made at the negotiations in Paris and the United States had not put forth a comprehensive peace proposal.
- The war was causing deep division at home and criticism from many of our friends as well as our enemies abroad.

In view of these circumstances there were some who urged that I end the war at once by ordering the immediate withdrawal of all American forces. From a political standpoint this would have been a popular and easy course to follow. After all, we became involved in the war while my predecessor was in office. I could blame the defeat which would be the result of my action on him and come out as the peacemaker. Some put it to me quite bluntly: This was the only way to avoid allowing Johnson's war to become Nixon's war. But I had a greater obligation than to think only of the years of my administration and of the next election. I had to think of the effect of my decision on the next generation and on the future of peace and freedom in America and in the world.

Let us all understand that the question before us is not whether some Americans are for peace and some Americans are against peace. The question at issue is not whether Johnson's war becomes Nixon's war. The great question is: How can we win America's peace? Well, let us turn now to the fundamental issue. Why and how did the United States become involved in Vietnam in the first place? Fifteen years ago North Vietnam, with the logistical support of Communist China and the Soviet Union, launched a campaign to impose a Communist government on South Vietnam by instigating and supporting a revolution. In response to the request of the Government of South Vietnam, President Eisenhower sent economic aid and military equipment to assist the people of South Vietnam in their efforts to prevent a Communist takeover. Seven years ago, President Kennedy sent 16,000 military personnel to Vietnam as combat advisers. Four years ago, President Johnson sent American combat forces to South Vietnam.

President Richard Nixon delivers his national address on "Vietnamization" from the White House, November 3, 1969. (AP Photo)

Now, many believe that President Johnson's decision to send American combat forces to South Vietnam was wrong. And many others, I among them, have been strongly critical of the way the war has been conducted. But the question facing us today is: Now that we are in the war, what is the best way to end it? In January I could only conclude that the precipitate withdrawal of American forces from Vietnam would be a disaster not only for South Vietnam but for the United States and for the cause of peace. For the South Vietnamese, our precipitate withdrawal would inevitably allow the Communists to repeat the massacres which followed their takeover in the North 15 years before.

- They then murdered more than 50,000 people and hundreds of thousands more died in slave labor camps.
- We saw a prelude of what would happen in South Vietnam when the Communists entered the city of Hue last year. During their brief rule there, there was a bloody reign of terror in which 3,000 civilians were clubbed, shot to death, and buried in mass graves.
- With the sudden collapse of our support, these atrocities of Hue would become the nightmare of the entire nation and particularly for the million and a half

Catholic refugees who fled to South Vietnam when the Communists took over in the North.

For the United States, this first defeat in our Nation's history would result in a collapse of confidence in American leadership, not only in Asia but through-out the world. Three American Presidents have recognized the great stakes involved in Vietnam and understood what had to be done. In 1963, President Kennedy, with his characteristic eloquence and clarity, said: "...we want to see a stable government there, carrying on a struggle to maintain its national independence. We believe strongly in that. We are not going to withdraw from that effort. In my opinion, for us to withdraw from that effort would mean a collapse not only of South Vietnam, but Southeast Asia. So we are going to stay there." President Eisenhower and President Johnson expressed the same conclusion during their terms of office. For the future of peace, precipitate withdrawal would thus be a disaster of immense magnitude.

- A nation cannot remain great if it betrays its allies and lets down its friends.
- Our defeat and humiliation in South Vietnam without question would promote recklessness in the councils of those great powers who have not yet abandoned their goals of world conquest.
- This would spark violence wherever our commitments help maintain the peace in the Middle East, in Berlin, eventually even in the Western Hemisphere. Ultimately, this would cost more lives. It would not bring peace; it would bring more war.

For these reasons, I rejected the recommendation that I should end the war by immediately withdrawing all of our forces. I chose instead to change American policy on both the negotiating front and battlefront.... We Americans are a do-it-yourself people. We are an impatient people. Instead of teaching someone else to do a job, we like to do it ourselves. And this trait has been carried over into our foreign policy. In Korea and again in Vietnam, the United States furnished most of the money, most of the arms, and most of the men to help the people of those countries defend their freedom against Communist aggression. Before any American troops were committed to Vietnam, a leader of another Asian country expressed this opinion to me when I was traveling in Asia as a private citizen. He said: "When you are trying to assist another nation defend its freedom, U.S. policy should be to help them fight the war but not to fight the war for them." ...

Well, in accordance with this wise counsel, I laid down in Guam three principles as guidelines for future American policy toward Asia:

First, the United States will keep all of its treaty commitments.

Second, we shall provide a shield if a nuclear power threatens the freedom of a nation allied with us or of a nation whose survival we consider vital to our security.

Third, in cases involving other types of aggression, we shall furnish military and economic assistance when requested in accordance with our treaty commitments. But we shall look to the nation directly threatened to assume the primary responsibility of providing the manpower for its defense.

After I announced this policy, I found that the leaders of the Philippines, Thailand, Vietnam, South Korea, and other nations which might be threatened by Communist aggression, welcomed this new direction in American foreign policy. The defense of freedom is everybody's business, not just America's business. And it is particularly the responsibility of the people whose freedom is threatened. In the previous administration, we Americanized the war in Vietnam. In this administration, we are Vietnamizing the search for peace. The policy of the previous administration not only resulted in our assuming the primary responsibility for fighting the war, but even more significantly did not adequately stress the goal of strengthening the South Vietnamese so that they could defend themselves when we left. The Vietnamization plan was launched following Secretary Laird's visit to Vietnam in March. Under the plan, I ordered first a substantial increase in the training and equipment of South Vietnamese forces.

- After 5 years of Americans going into Vietnam, we are finally bringing men home. By December 15, over 60,000 men will have been withdrawn from South Vietnam including 20 percent of all of our combat forces.
- The South Vietnamese have continued to gain in strength. As a result they have been able to take over combat responsibilities from our American troops.

Two other significant developments have occurred since this administration took office.

- Enemy infiltration, infiltration which is essential if they are to launch a major attack, over the last 3 months is less than 20 percent of what it was over the same period last year.
- Most important United States casualties have declined during the last 2 months to the lowest point in 3 years.

Let me now turn to our program for the future. We have adopted a plan which we have worked out in cooperation with the South Vietnamese for the complete withdrawal of all U.S. combat ground forces, and their replacement by South Vietnamese forces on an orderly scheduled timetable. This withdrawal will be made from strength and not from weakness. As South Vietnamese forces become stronger, the rate of American withdrawal can become greater. I have not and do not intend to announce the timetable for our program. And there are obvious reasons for this decision which I am sure you will understand.

As I have indicated on several occasions, the rate of withdrawal will depend on developments on three fronts. One of these is the progress which can be or might be made in the Paris talks. An announcement of a fixed timetable for our withdrawal would completely remove any incentive for the enemy to negotiate an agreement. They would simply wait until our forces had withdrawn and then move in. The other two factors on which we will base our withdrawal decisions are the level of enemy activity and the progress of the training programs of the South Vietnamese forces. And I am glad to be able to report tonight progress on both of these fronts has been greater than we anticipated when we started the program in June for withdrawal. As a result, our timetable for withdrawal is more optimistic now than when we made our first estimates in June.

Now, this clearly demonstrates why it is not wise to be frozen in on a fixed timetable. We must retain the flexibility to base each withdrawal decision on the situation as it is at the time rather than on estimates that are no longer valid. Along with this optimistic estimate, I must in all candor leave one note of caution. If the level of enemy activity significantly increases we might have to adjust our timetable accordingly. However, I want the record to be completely clear on one point. At the time of the bombing halt just a year ago, there was some confusion as to whether there was an understanding on the part of the enemy that if we stopped the bombing of North Vietnam they would stop the shelling of cities in South Vietnam. I want to be sure that there is no misunderstanding on the part of the enemy with regard to our withdrawal program. We have noted the reduced level of infiltration, the reduction of our casualties, and are basing our withdrawal decisions partially on those factors. If the level of infiltration or our casualties increase while we are trying to scale down the fighting, it will be the result of a conscious decision by the enemy. Hanoi could make no greater mistake than to assume that an increase in violence will be to its advantage. If I conclude that increased enemy action jeopardizes our remaining forces in Vietnam, I shall not hesitate to take strong and effective measures to deal with that situation. This is not a threat. This is a statement of policy, which, as Commander in Chief of our Armed Forces, I am making in meeting my responsibility for the protection of American fighting men wherever they may be.

My fellow Americans, I am sure you can recognize from what I have said that we really only have two choices open to us if we want to end this war.

- I can order an immediate, precipitate withdrawal of all Americans from Vietnam without regard to the effects of that action.
- Or we can persist in our search for a just peace through a negotiated settlement if possible, or through continued implementation of our plan for Vietnamization if necessary, a plan in which we will withdraw all our forces from Vietnam on a schedule in accordance with our program, as the South Vietnamese become strong enough to defend their own freedom.

I have chosen this second course. It is not the easy way. It is the right way. It is a plan which will end the war and serve the cause of peace not just in Vietnam but in the Pacific and in the world. In speaking of the consequences of a precipitate withdrawal, I mentioned that our allies would lose confidence in America. Far more dangerous, we would lose confidence in ourselves. Oh, the immediate reaction would be a sense of relief that our men were coming home. But as we saw the consequences of what we had done, inevitable remorse and divisive recrimination would scar our spirit as a people. We have faced other crises in our history and have become stronger by rejecting the easy way out and taking the right way in meeting our challenges. Our greatness as a nation has been our capacity to do what had to be done when we knew our course was right.

I recognize that some of my fellow citizens disagree with the plan for peace I have chosen. Honest and patriotic Americans have reached different conclusions as to how peace should be achieved. In San Francisco a few weeks ago, I saw demonstrators carrying signs reading: "Lose in Vietnam, bring the boys home." Well, one of the strengths of our free society is that any American has a right to reach that conclusion and to advocate that point of view. But as President of the United States, I would be untrue to my oath of office if I allowed the policy of this Nation to be dictated by the minority who hold that point of view and who try to impose it on the Nation by mounting demonstrations in the street. For almost 200 years, the policy of this Nation has been made under our Constitution by those leaders in the Congress and the White House elected by all of the people. If a vocal minority, however fervent its cause, prevails over reason and the will of the majority, this Nation has no future as a free society.

And now I would like to address a word, if I may, to the young people of this Nation who are particularly concerned, and I understand why they are concerned, about this war. I respect your idealism. I share your concern for peace. I want peace as much as you do. There are powerful personal reasons I want to end this war. This week I will have to sign 83 letters to mothers, fathers, wives, and loved ones of men who have given their lives for America in Vietnam. It is very little satisfaction to me that this is only one-third as many letters as I signed the first week in office. There is nothing I want more than to see the day come when I do not have to write any of those letters.

- I want to end the war to save the lives of those brave young men in Vietnam.
- But I want to end it in a way which will increase the chance that their younger brothers and their sons will not have to fight in some future Vietnam someplace in the world.
- And I want to end the war for another reason. I want to end it so that the energy and dedication of you, our young people, now too often directed into bitter hatred against those responsible for the war, can be turned to the great challenges of peace, a better life for all Americans, a better life for all people on this earth.

I have chosen a plan for peace. I believe it will succeed. If it does succeed, what the critics say now won't matter. If it does not succeed, anything I say then won't matter. I know it may not be fashionable to speak of patriotism or national destiny these days. But I feel it is appropriate to do so on this occasion. Two hundred years ago this Nation was weak and poor. But even then, America was the hope of millions in the world. Today we have become the strongest and richest nation in the world. And the wheel of destiny has turned so that any hope the world has for the survival of peace and freedom will be determined by whether the American people have the moral stamina and the courage to meet the challenge of free world leadership. Let historians not record that when America was the most powerful nation in the world we passed on the other side of the road and allowed the last hopes for peace and freedom of millions of people to be suffocated by the forces of totalitarianism.

And so tonight to you, the great silent majority of my fellow Americans, I ask for your support. I pledged in my campaign for the Presidency to end the war in a way that we could win the peace. I have initiated a plan of action which will enable me to keep that pledge. The more support I can have from the American people, the sooner that pledge can be redeemed; for the more divided we are at home, the less likely the enemy is to negotiate at Paris. Let us be united for peace. Let us also be united against defeat. Because let us understand: North Vietnam cannot defeat or humiliate the United States. Only Americans can do that. Fifty years ago, in this room and at this very desk, President Woodrow Wilson spoke words which caught the imagination of a war-weary world. He said: "This is the war to end war." His dream for peace after World War I was shattered on the hard realities of great power politics and Woodrow Wilson died a broken man. Tonight I do not tell you that the war in Vietnam is the war to end wars. But I do say this: I have initiated a plan which will end this war in a way that will bring us closer to that great goal to which Woodrow Wilson and every American President in our history has been dedicated: the goal of a just and lasting peace. As President I hold the responsibility for choosing the best path to that goal and then leading the Nation along it. I pledge to you tonight that I shall meet this responsibility with all of the strength and wisdom I can command in accordance with your hopes, mindful of your concerns, sustained by your prayers. Thank you and goodnight.

- **Document:** SALT I
- **Date:** May 26, 1972
- **Significance:** The United States and the Soviet Union started bilateral negotiations on the limitation of nuclear weaponry, titled the Strategic Arms Limitation Talks, in 1970. The talks concluded in 1972 with the signing of the first SALT treaty and were followed by a second and a new round of negotiations.
- **Source:** "Interim Agreement Between the United States of America and the Union of Soviet Socialist Republics on Certain Measures with Respect to the Limitation of Strategic Offensive Arms." May 26, 1972. United States Treaties and Other International Agreements, 23, pt. 3435.

TREATY BETWEEN THE UNITED STATES OF AMERICA AND THE UNION OF SOVIET SOCIALIST REPUBLICS ON THE LIMITATION OF ANTI-BALLISTIC MISSILE SYSTEMS

Signed at Moscow May 26, 1972. Ratification advised by U.S. Senate August 3, 1972. Ratified by U.S. President September 30, 1972. Proclaimed by U.S. President October 3, 1972. Instruments of ratification exchanged October 3, 1972. Entered into force October 3, 1972

The United States of America and the Union of Soviet Socialist Republics, hereinafter referred to as the Parties,

Proceeding from the premise that nuclear war would have devastating consequences for all mankind,

Considering that effective measures to limit anti-ballistic missile systems would be a substantial factor in curbing the race in strategic offensive arms and would lead to a decrease in the risk of outbreak of war involving nuclear weapons,

Proceeding from the premise that the limitation of anti-ballistic missile systems, as well as certain agreed measures with respect to the limitation of strategic offensive arms, would contribute to the creation of more favorable conditions for further negotiations on limiting strategic arms,

Mindful of their obligations under Article VI of the Treaty on the Non-Proliferation of Nuclear Weapons,

Declaring their intention to achieve at the earliest possible date the cessation of the nuclear arms race and to take effective measures toward reductions in strategic arms, nuclear disarmament, and general and complete disarmament,

Desiring to contribute to the relaxation of international tension and the strengthening of trust between States,

Have agreed as follows:

Article I

1. Each Party undertakes to limit anti-ballistic missile (ABM) systems and to adopt other measures in accordance with the provisions of this Treaty.
2. Each Party undertakes not to deploy ABM systems for a defense of the territory of its country and not to provide a base for such a defense, and not to deploy ABM systems for defense of an individual region except as provided for in Article III of this Treaty.

Article II

1. For the purpose of this Treaty an ABM system is a system to counter strategic ballistic missiles or their elements in flight trajectory, currently consisting of:

    (a) ABM interceptor missiles, which are interceptor missiles constructed and deployed for an ABM role, or of a type tested in an ABM mode; (b) ABM launchers, which are launchers constructed and deployed for launching ABM interceptor missiles; and (c) ABM radars, which are radars constructed and deployed for an ABM role, or of a type tested in an ABM mode.

2. The ABM system components listed in paragraph 1 of this Article include those which are:

    (a) operational; (b) under construction; (c) undergoing testing; (d) undergoing overhaul, repair or conversion; or (e) mothballed.

Article III

Each Party undertakes not to deploy ABM systems or their components except that:

  (a) within one ABM system deployment area having a radius of one hundred and fifty kilometers and centered on the Party's national capital, a Party may deploy: (1) no more than one hundred ABM launchers and no more

Did You Know?

Détente

Détente, French for "release from tension," describes the period of improved United States–Soviet relations from 1972 to 1980. Détente began when President Nixon visited Soviet leader Leonid Brezhnev in May 1972. Both countries stood to benefit if trade was increased and the danger of nuclear war was reduced. Also, Nixon wanted to deflect attention from criticism of his domestic policies and the Vietnam War and run for reelection by highlighting his foreign policy credentials. Further, by visiting China in a historic trip a few months prior, Nixon had strategically exploited the growing rift between China and the USSR to pressure the Soviets into seeking détente. After all, Nixon knew that Brezhnev did not want his rival China to join with the United States and further antagonize the USSR. In 1972, Nixon became the first U.S. president to visit Moscow, where he and Brezhnev signed seven separate agreements covering issues such as arms control, the prevention of accidental military clashes, expanding commerce, and space exploration. In 1972, Congress approved the SALT treaty and a three-year agreement to sell grain to the USSR. In June 1973 Brezhnev visited the United States, and while few new agreements were signed, there was a joint commitment to continuing a peaceful relationship. By 1974, the Watergate investigation had weakened Nixon, and after he resigned, Presidents Ford and Carter continued détente. Although President Carter promoted SALT II, United States–Soviet relations began to cool due to U.S. criticism of the USSR's human rights record. A military buildup initiated by President Carter, the Soviet invasion of Afghanistan in 1979, and the election of Ronald Reagan, who emphasized building a strong military to deter the Soviets, brought détente to a close in 1980.

than one hundred ABM interceptor missiles at launch sites, and (2) ABM radars within no more than six ABM radar complexes, the area of each complex being circular and having a diameter of no more than three kilometers; and (b) within one ABM system deployment area having a radius of one hundred and fifty kilometers and containing ICBM silo launchers, a Party may deploy: (1) no more than one hundred ABM launchers and no more than one hundred ABM interceptor missiles at launch sites, (2) two large phased-array ABM radars comparable in potential to corresponding ABM radars operational or under construction on the date of signature of the Treaty in an ABM system deployment area containing ICBM silo launchers, and (3) no more than eighteen ABM radars each having a potential less than the potential of the smaller of the above-mentioned two large phased-array ABM radars.

. . .

DONE at Moscow on May 26, 1972, in two copies, each in the English and Russian languages, both texts being equally authentic.

FOR THE UNITED STATES OF AMERICA: RICHARD NIXON *President of the United States of America*

FOR THE UNION OF SOVIET SOCIALIST REPUBLICS: L. I. BREZHNEV *General Secretary of the Central Committee of the CPSU*

- **Document: Carter Doctrine**
- **Date:** January 23, 1980
- **Significance:** In this speech President Carter describes his strategy for peace in the Middle East and Central Asia. He reacts to the Soviet invasion of Afghanistan by announcing the U.S. boycott of the summer Olympic Games slated to be held in Moscow in 1980. Additionally, while highlighting the importance of energy conservation, Carter states that United States will do what is necessary to defend American interests in the Middle East.
- **Source:** Jimmy Carter, *Public Papers of the Presidents of the United States: Jimmy Carter, 1980–1981*, Book 1. Washington, D.C.: GPO, 1981, pp. 194–200.

Jimmy Carter's State of the Union Address, 1980

This last few months has not been an easy time for any of us. As we meet tonight, it has never been more clear that the state of our Union depends on the state of the world. And tonight, as throughout our own generation, freedom and peace in the world depend on the state of our Union.

The 1980's have been born in turmoil, strife, and change. This is a time of challenge to our interests and our values and it's a time that tests our wisdom and our skills.

At this time in Iran, 50 Americans are still held captive, innocent victims of terrorism and anarchy. Also at this moment, massive Soviet troops are attempting to subjugate the fiercely independent and deeply religious people of Afghanistan. These two acts—one of international terrorism and one of military aggression—present a serious challenge to the United States of America and indeed to all the nations of the world. Together, we will meet these threats to peace.

I'm determined that the United States will remain the strongest of all nations, but our power will never be used to initiate a threat to the security of any nation or to the rights of any human being. We seek to be and to remain secure—a nation at peace in a stable world. But to be secure we must face the world as it is.

Three basic developments have helped to shape our challenges: the steady growth and increased projection of Soviet military power beyond its own borders; the overwhelming dependence of the Western democracies on oil supplies from the Middle East; and the press of social and religious and economic and political change in the many nations of the developing world, exemplified by the revolution in Iran.

Each of these factors is important in its own right. Each interacts with the others. All must be faced together, squarely and courageously. We will face these challenges, and we will meet them with the best that is in us. And we will not fail.

In response to the abhorrent act in Iran, our Nation has never been aroused and unified so greatly in peacetime. Our position is clear. The United States will not yield to blackmail.

Did You Know?

President Carter's Human Rights Agenda

President Jimmy Carter's major accomplishments include the Panama Canal Treaty of 1978, signing SALT II in 1979, and the Camp David Accords, which led to a landmark peace treaty between Israel and Egypt in 1979. But failures, both domestic and foreign, often overshadow these accomplishments. Domestically, Carter's call to wage the moral equivalent of war on the energy crisis was unable to inspire an increasingly malaise-ridden public that was reeling under the double-pronged problems of unemployment and inflation ("stagflation"). Internationally, Carter's presidency was overwhelmed by the Iranian revolution and subsequent hostage crisis as well as the Soviet invasion of Afghanistan, both in 1979. Nevertheless, Carter's foreign policy is often upheld as unique because of his emphasis on promoting human rights. While his human rights agenda placed Carter in the "dove" camp, he was criticized by "hawks" who saw his idealism as naïve. For instance, Carter's criticism of the Soviet Union's abuse of human rights backfired and contributed to the end of détente. Others argued that Carter realized the importance of human rights as both a diplomatic goal and a strong military presence. For instance, Carter campaigned on a pledge to reduce military expenditures and foreign arms sales, only to increase both during his administration.

Since leaving office, Carter has continued to champion human rights and to lend support to numerous charitable causes, such as Habitat for Humanity. In 1982 he founded the Carter Center at Emory University in Atlanta, Georgia. He continues to write books and travel extensively throughout various developing countries, helping to monitor elections, establish relief efforts, promote human rights, and conduct peace negotiations. For these efforts Carter was awarded the Nobel Peace Prize in 2002.

We continue to pursue these specific goals: first, to protect the present and long-range interests of the United States; secondly, to preserve the lives of the American hostages and to secure, as quickly as possible, their safe release, if possible, to avoid bloodshed which might further endanger the lives of our fellow citizens; to enlist the help of other nations in condemning this act of violence, which is shocking and violates the moral and the legal standards of a civilized world; and also to convince and to persuade the Iranian leaders that the real danger to their nation lies in the north, in the Soviet Union and from the Soviet troops now in Afghanistan, and that the unwarranted Iranian quarrel with the United States hampers their response to this far greater danger to them.

If the American hostages are harmed, a severe price will be paid. We will never rest until every one of the American hostages are released.

But now we face a broader and more fundamental challenge in this region because of the recent military action of the Soviet Union.

Now, as during the last 3 1/2 decades, the relationship between our country, the United States of America, and the Soviet Union is the most critical factor in determining whether the world will live at peace or be engulfed in global conflict.

Since the end of the Second World War, America has led other nations in meeting the challenge of mounting Soviet power. This has not been a simple or a static relationship. Between us there has been cooperation, there has been competition, and at times there has been confrontation.

In the 1940's we took the lead in creating the Atlantic Alliance in response to the Soviet Union's suppression and then consolidation of its East European empire and the resulting threat of the Warsaw Pact to Western Europe.

In the 1950's we helped to contain further Soviet challenges in Korea and in the Middle East, and we rearmed to assure the continuation of that containment.

In the 1960's we met the Soviet challenges in Berlin, and we faced the Cuban missile crisis. And we sought to engage the Soviet Union in the important task of moving beyond the cold war and away from confrontation.

And in the 1970's three American Presidents negotiated with the Soviet leaders in attempts to halt the growth of the nuclear arms race. We sought to establish rules of behavior that would reduce the risks of conflict, and we searched for areas of cooperation that could make our relations reciprocal and productive, not only for the sake of our two nations but for the security and peace of the entire world.

In all these actions, we have maintained two commitments: to be ready to meet any challenge by Soviet military power, and to develop ways to resolve disputes and to keep the peace.

Preventing nuclear war is the foremost responsibility of the two superpowers. That's why we've negotiated the strategic arms limitation treaties—SALT I and SALT II. Especially now, in a time of great tension, observing the mutual constraints imposed by the terms of these treaties will be in the best interest of both countries and will help to preserve world peace. I will consult very closely with the Congress on this matter as we strive to control nuclear weapons. That effort to control nuclear weapons will not be abandoned.

We superpowers also have the responsibility to exercise restraint in the use of our great military force. The integrity and the independence of weaker nations must not be threatened. They must know that in our presence they are secure.

But now the Soviet Union has taken a radical and an aggressive new step. It's using its great military power against a relatively defenseless nation. The implications of the Soviet invasion of Afghanistan could pose the most serious threat to the peace since the Second World War.

The vast majority of nations on Earth have condemned this latest Soviet attempt to extend its colonial domination of others and have demanded the immediate withdrawal of Soviet troops. The Moslem world is especially and justifiably outraged by this aggression against an Islamic people. No action of a world power has ever been so quickly and so overwhelmingly condemned. But verbal condemnation is not enough. The Soviet Union must pay a concrete price for their aggression.

While this invasion continues, we and the other nations of the world cannot conduct business as usual with the Soviet Union. That's why the United States has

Jimmy Carter and Leonid Brezhnev sign the second Strategic Arms Limitation Treaty (SALT II) treaty on June 18, 1979, in Vienna. The treaty was the culmination of a second round of talks between the U.S. and Soviet Union seeking to curtail further development of nuclear arms. (Carter Library)

imposed stiff economic penalties on the Soviet Union. I will not issue any permits for Soviet ships to fish in the coastal waters of the United States. I've cut Soviet access to high-technology equipment and to agricultural products. I've limited other commerce with the Soviet Union, and I've asked our allies and friends to join with us in restraining their own trade with the Soviets and not to replace our own embargoed items. And I have notified the Olympic Committee that with Soviet invading forces in Afghanistan, neither the American people nor I will support sending an Olympic team to Moscow.

The Soviet Union is going to have to answer some basic questions: Will it help promote a more stable international environment in which its own legitimate, peaceful concerns can be pursued? Or will it continue to expand its military power far beyond its genuine security needs, and use that power for colonial conquest? The Soviet Union must realize that its decision to use military force in Afghanistan will be costly to every political and economic relationship it values.

The region which is now threatened by Soviet troops in Afghanistan is of great strategic importance: It contains more than two-thirds of the world's exportable oil. The Soviet effort to dominate Afghanistan has brought Soviet military forces to within 300 miles of the Indian Ocean and close to the Straits of Hormuz, a waterway through which most of the world's oil must flow. The Soviet Union is now attempting to consolidate a strategic position, therefore, that poses a grave threat to the free movement of Middle East oil.

This situation demands careful thought, steady nerves, and resolute action, not only for this year but for many years to come. It demands collective efforts to meet this new threat to security in the Persian Gulf and in Southwest Asia. It demands the participation of all those who rely on oil from the Middle East and who are concerned with global peace and stability. And it demands consultation and close cooperation with countries in the area which might be threatened.

Meeting this challenge will take national will, diplomatic and political wisdom, economic sacrifice, and, of course, military capability. We must call on the best that is in us to preserve the security of this crucial region.

Let our position be absolutely clear: An attempt by any outside force to gain control of the Persian Gulf region will be regarded as an assault on the vital interests of the United States of America, and such an assault will be repelled by any means necessary, including military force.

During the past 3 years, you have joined with me to improve our own security and the prospects for peace, not only in the vital oil-producing area of the Persian Gulf region but around the world. We've increased annually our real commitment for defense, and we will sustain this increase of effort throughout the Five Year Defense Program. It's imperative that Congress approve this strong defense budget for 1981, encompassing a 5-percent real growth in authorizations, without any reduction.

We are also improving our capability to deploy U.S. military forces rapidly to distant areas. We've helped to strengthen NATO and our other alliances, and recently we and other NATO members have decided to develop and to deploy modernized, intermediate-range nuclear forces to meet an unwarranted and increased threat from the nuclear weapons of the Soviet Union.

We are working with our allies to prevent conflict in the Middle East. The peace treaty between Egypt and Israel is a notable achievement which represents a strategic asset for America and which also enhances prospects for regional and world peace. We are now engaged in further negotiations to provide full autonomy for the people of the West Bank and Gaza, to resolve the Palestinian issue in all its aspects, and to preserve the peace and security of Israel. Let no one doubt our commitment to the security of Israel. In a few days we will observe an historic event when Israel makes another major withdrawal from the Sinai and when Ambassadors will be exchanged between Israel and Egypt.

We've also expanded our own sphere of friendship. Our deep commitment to human rights and to meeting human needs has improved our relationship with much of the Third World. Our decision to normalize relations with the People's Republic of China will help to preserve peace and stability in Asia and in the Western Pacific.

We've increased and strengthened our naval presence in the Indian Ocean, and we are now making arrangements for key naval and air facilities to be used by our forces in the region of northeast Africa and the Persian Gulf.

We've reconfirmed our 1959 agreement to help Pakistan preserve its independence and its integrity. The United States will take action consistent with our own laws to assist Pakistan in resisting any outside aggression. And I'm asking the Congress specifically to reaffirm this agreement. I'm also working, along with the leaders of other nations, to provide additional military and economic aid for Pakistan. That request will come to you in just a few days.

In the weeks ahead, we will further strengthen political and military ties with other nations in the region. We believe that there are no irreconcilable differences between us and any Islamic nation. We respect the faith of Islam, and we are ready to cooperate with all Moslem countries.

Finally, we are prepared to work with other countries in the region to share a cooperative security framework that respects differing values and political beliefs, yet which enhances the independence, security, and prosperity of all.

All these efforts combined emphasize our dedication to defend and preserve the vital interests of the region and of the nation which we represent and those of our allies—in Europe and the Pacific, and also in the parts of the world which have such great strategic importance to us, stretching especially through the Middle East and Southwest Asia. With your help, I will pursue these efforts with vigor and with determination. You and I will act as necessary to protect and to preserve our Nation's security.

The men and women of America's Armed Forces are on duty tonight in many parts of the world. I'm proud of the job they are doing, and I know you share that pride. I believe that our volunteer forces are adequate for current defense needs, and I hope that it will not become necessary to impose a draft. However, we must be prepared for that possibility. For this reason, I have determined that the Selective Service System must now be revitalized. I will send legislation and budget proposals to the Congress next month so that we can begin registration and then meet future mobilization needs rapidly if they arise.

We also need clear and quick passage of a new charter to define the legal authority and accountability of our intelligence agencies. We will guarantee that abuses do not recur, but we must tighten our controls on sensitive intelligence information, and we need to remove unwarranted restraints on America's ability to collect intelligence.

The decade ahead will be a time of rapid change, as nations everywhere seek to deal with new problems and age-old tensions. But America need have no fear. We can thrive in a world of change if we remain true to our values and actively engaged in promoting world peace. We will continue to work as we have for peace in the Middle East and southern Africa. We will continue to build our ties with developing nations, respecting and helping to strengthen their national independence which they have struggled so hard to achieve. And we will continue to support the growth of democracy and the protection of human rights.

In repressive regimes, popular frustrations often have no outlet except through violence. But when peoples and their governments can approach their problems together through open, democratic methods, the basis for stability and peace is far more solid and far more enduring. That is why our support for human rights in other countries is in our own national interest as well as part of our own national character.

Peace—a peace that preserves freedom—remains America's first goal. In the coming years, as a mighty nation we will continue to pursue peace. But to be strong abroad we must be strong at home. And in order to be strong, we must continue to face up to the difficult issues that confront us as a nation today.

The crises in Iran and Afghanistan have dramatized a very important lesson: Our excessive dependence on foreign oil is a clear and present danger to our Nation's security. The need has never been more urgent. At long last, we must have a clear, comprehensive energy policy for the United States.

As you well know, I have been working with the Congress in a concentrated and persistent way over the past 3 years to meet this need. We have made progress together. But Congress must act promptly now to complete final action on this vital energy legislation. Our Nation will then have a major conservation effort, important initiatives to develop solar power, realistic pricing based on the true value of oil, strong incentives for the production of coal and other fossil fuels in the United States, and our Nation's most massive peacetime investment in the development of synthetic fuels.

The American people are making progress in energy conservation. Last year we reduced overall petroleum consumption by 8 percent and gasoline consumption by 5 percent below what it was the year before. Now we must do more.

After consultation with the Governors, we will set gasoline conservation goals for each of the 50 States, and I will make them mandatory if these goals are not met.

I've established an import ceiling for 1980 of 8.2 million barrels a day—well below the level of foreign oil purchases in 1977. I expect our imports to be much lower than this, but the ceiling will be enforced by an oil import fee if necessary. I'm prepared to lower these imports still further if the other oil-consuming countries will join us in a fair and mutual reduction.

. . .

Thank you very much.

- **Document: Speech by Caspar Weinberger: Uses of the U.S. Military**
- **Date:** November 28, 1984
- **Significance:** In this speech to the National Press Club, Ronald Reagan's Secretary of Defense, Casper Weinberger describes what is known as the Weinberger Doctrine, detailing how the U.S. military will be deployed in future wars to avoid being caught in quagmires. Weinberger's speech represents how the Reagan administration interpreted the lessons of Vietnam for the United States.
- **Source:** Caspar W. Weinberger, "The Uses of Military Power." Speech given at the National Press Club, Washington, D.C., November 28, 1984.

Uses of Military Power

Thank you for inviting me to be here today with the members of the National Press Club, a group most important to our national security. I say that because a major point I intend to make in my remarks today is that the single most critical element of a successful democracy is a strong consensus of support and agreement for our basic purposes. Policies formed without a clear understanding of what we hope to achieve will never work. And you help to build that understanding among our citizens.

Of all the many policies our citizens deserve—and need—to understand, none is so important as those related to our topic today—the uses of military power.

Deterrence will work only if the Soviets understand our firm commitment to keeping the peace, . . . and only from a well-informed public can we expect to have that national will and commitment.

So today, I want to discuss with you perhaps the most important question concerning keeping the peace. Under what circumstances, and by what means, does a great democracy such as ours reach the painful decision that the use of military force is necessary to protect our interests or to carry out our national policy?

National power has many components, some tangible, like economic wealth, technical pre-eminence. Other components are intangible—such as moral force, or strong national will. Military forces, when they are strong and ready and modern, are a credible—and tangible—addition to a nation's power. When both the intangible national will and those forces are forged into one instrument, national power becomes effective.

In today's world, the line between peace and war is less clearly drawn than at any time in our history. When George Washington, in his farewell address, warned us, as a new democracy, to avoid foreign entanglements, Europe then lay 2–3 months by sea over the horizon. The United States was protected by the width of the oceans. Now in this nuclear age, we measure time in minutes rather than months.

Aware of the consequences of any misstep, yet convinced of the precious worth of the freedom we enjoy, we seek to avoid conflict, while maintaining strong defenses. Our policy has always been to work hard for peace, but to be prepared if war comes. Yet, so blurred have the lines become between open conflict and half-hidden hostile acts that we cannot confidently predict where, or when, or how, or from what direction aggression may arrive. We must be prepared, at any moment, to meet threats ranging in intensity from isolated terrorist acts, to guerrilla action, to full-scale military confrontation.

. . .

We have now restored high morale and pride in the uniform throughout the services. The all-volunteer system is working spectacularly well. Are we willing to forfeit what we have fought so hard to regain?

In maintaining our progress in strengthening America's military deterrent, we face difficult challenges. For we have entered an era where the dividing lines between peace and war are less clearly drawn, the identity of the foe is much less clear. In World Wars I and II, we not only knew who our enemies were, but we shared a clear sense of why the principles espoused by our enemies were unworthy.

Since these two wars threatened our very survival as a free nation and the survival of our allies, they were total wars, involving every aspect of our society. All our means of production, all our resources were devoted to winning. Our policies had the unqualified support of the great majority of our people. Indeed, World Wars I and II ended with the unconditional surrender of our enemies. . . . The only acceptable ending when the alternative was the loss of our freedom.

But in the aftermath of the Second World War, we encountered a more subtle form of warfare—warfare in which, more often than not, the face of the enemy was masked. Territorial expansionism could be carried out indirectly by proxy powers, using surrogate forces aided and advised from afar. Some conflicts occurred under the name of "national liberation," but far more frequently ideology or religion provided the spark to the tinder.

Our adversaries can also take advantage of our open society, and our freedom of speech and opinion to use alarming rhetoric and misinformation to divide and disrupt our unity of purpose. While they would never dare to allow such freedoms to their own people, they are quick to exploit ours by conducting simultaneous military and propaganda campaigns to achieve their ends.

They realize that if they can divide our national will at home, it will not be necessary to defeat our forces abroad. So by presenting issues in bellicose terms, they aim to intimidate western leaders and citizens, encouraging us to adopt conciliatory positions to their advantage.

Meanwhile they remain sheltered from the force of public opinion in their countries, because public opinion there is simply prohibited and does not exist.

Our freedom presents both a challenge and an opportunity. It is true that until democratic nations have the support of the people, they are inevitably at a disadvantage in a conflict. But when they do have that support they cannot be defeated. For democracies have the power to send a compelling message to friend and foe alike by the vote of their citizens. And the American people have sent such a signal by re-electing a strong Chief Executive. They know that President Reagan is willing to accept the responsibility for his actions and is able to lead us through these complex times by insisting that we regain both our military and our economic strength.

In today's world where minutes count, such decisive leadership is more important than ever before. Regardless of whether conflicts are limited, or threats are ill-defined, we must be capable of quickly determining that the threats and conflicts either do or do not affect the vital interests of the United States and our allies. . . . And then responding appropriately.

Those threats may not entail an immediate, direct attack on our territory, and our response may not necessarily require the immediate or direct defense of our homeland. But when our vital national interests and those of our allies are at stake, we cannot ignore our safety, or forsake our allies.

At the same time, recent history has proven that we cannot assume unilaterally the role of the world's defender. We have learned that there are limits to how much of our spirit and blood and treasure we can afford to forfeit in meeting our responsibility to keep peace and freedom. So while we may and should offer substantial amounts of economic and military assistance to our allies in their time of need, and help them maintain forces to deter attacks against them—usually we cannot substitute our troops or our will for theirs.

We should only engage our troops if we must do so as a matter of our own vital national interest. We cannot assume for other sovereign nations the responsibility to defend their territory—without their strong invitation—when our freedom is not threatened.

On the other hand, there have been recent cases where the United States has seen the need to join forces with other nations to try to preserve the peace by helping with negotiations, and by separating warring parties, and thus enabling those warring nations to withdraw from hostilities safely. In the Middle East, which has been torn by conflict for millennia, we have sent our troops in recent years both to the Sinai and to Lebanon, for just such a peacekeeping mission. But we did not configure or equip those forces for combat—they were armed only for their self-defense. Their mission required them to be—and to be recognized as—peacekeepers. We knew that if conditions deteriorated so they were in danger, or if because of the actions of the warring nations, their peace keeping mission could not be realized, then it would be necessary either to add sufficiently to the number and arms of our troops—in short to equip them for combat, . . . or to withdraw them. And so in Lebanon, when we faced just such a choice, because the warring nations did not enter into withdrawal or peace agreements, the President properly withdrew forces equipped only for peacekeeping.

In those cases where our national interests require us to commit combat force we must never let there be doubt of our resolution. When it is necessary for our troops to be committed to combat, we must commit them, in sufficient numbers and we must support them, as effectively and resolutely as our strength permits. When we commit our troops to combat we must do so with the sole object of winning.

Once it is clear our troops are required, because our vital interests are at stake, then we must have the firm national resolve to commit every ounce of strength necessary to win the fight to achieve our objectives. In Grenada we did just that.

Just as clearly, there are other situations where United States combat forces should not be used. I believe the postwar period has taught us several lessons, and from them I have developed six major tests to be applied when we are weighing the use of U.S. combat forces abroad. Let me now share them with you:

(1) First, the United States should not commit forces to combat overseas unless the particular engagement or occasion is deemed vital to our national interest or that of our allies. That emphatically does not mean that we should declare beforehand, as we did with Korea in 1950, that a particular area is outside our strategic perimeter.

(2) Second, if we decide it is necessary to put combat troops into a given situation, we should do so wholeheartedly, and with the clear intention of winning. If we are unwilling to commit the forces or resources necessary to achieve our objectives, we should not commit them at all. Of course if the particular situation requires only limited force to win our objectives, then we should not hesitate to commit forces sized accordingly. When Hitler broke treaties and remilitarized the Rhineland, small combat forces then could perhaps have prevented the holocaust of World War II.

(3) Third, if we do decide to commit forces to combat overseas, we should have clearly defined political and military objectives. And we should know precisely how our forces can accomplish those clearly defined objectives. And we should have and send the forces needed to do just that. As Clausewitz wrote, "no one starts a war—or rather, no one in his senses ought to do so—without first being clear in his mind what he intends to achieve by that war, and how he intends to conduct it." War may be different today than in Clausewitz's time, but the need for well-defined objectives and a consistent strategy is still essential. If we determine that a combat mission has become necessary for our vital national interests, then we must send forces capable to do the job—and not assign a combat mission to a force configured for peacekeeping.

(4) Fourth, the relationship between our objectives and the forces we have committed—their size, composition and disposition—must be continually reassessed and adjusted if necessary. Conditions and objectives invariably change during the course of a conflict. When they do change, then so must our combat requirements. We must continuously keep as a beacon light

before us the basic questions: "is this conflict in our national interest?" "Does our national interest require us to fight, to use force of arms?" If the answers are "yes," then we must win. If the answers are "no," then we should not be in combat.

(5) Fifth, before the U.S. commits combat forces abroad, there must be some reasonable assurance we will have the support of the American people and their elected representatives in Congress. This support cannot be achieved unless we are candid in making clear the threats we face; the support cannot be sustained without continuing and close consultation. We cannot fight a battle with the Congress at home while asking our troops to win a war over-seas or, as in the case of Vietnam, in effect asking our troops not to win, but just to be there.

(6) Finally, the commitment of U.S. forces to combat should be a last resort.

I believe that these tests can be helpful in deciding whether or not we should commit our troops to combat in the months and years ahead. The point we must all keep uppermost in our minds is that if we ever decide to commit forces to com-bat, we must support those forces to the fullest extent of our national will for as long as it takes to win. So we must have in mind objectives that are clearly defined and understood and supported by the widest possible number of our citizens. And those objectives must be vital to our survival as a free nation and to the fulfillment of our responsibilities as a world power. We must also be farsighted enough to sense when immediate and strong reactions to apparently small events can prevent lion-like responses that may be required later. We must never forget those isolationists in Europe who shrugged that "Danzig is not worth a war," and "why should we fight to keep the Rhineland demilitarized?"

. . .

FURTHER READING

Fisk, R. (2005) *The War for Civilization: The Conquest of the Middle East.* London: Fourth Estate.

Gaddis, J. L. (1987) *The Long Peace: Inquiries into the History of the Cold War.* Oxford: Oxford University Press.

Herring, G. (2008) *From Colony to Superpower: U.S. Foreign Relations since 1776.* Oxford: Oxford University Press.

Hitchens, C. (2001) *The Trial of Henry Kissinger.* New York: Verso.

Kissinger, H. (1994) *Diplomacy.* New York: Simon and Schuster.

Kornbluth, P. (2003) *The Pinochet File: A Declassified Dossier on Atrocity and Accountability.* New York: The New Press.

Pollack, K. (2004) *The Persian Puzzle: The Conflict Between Iran and America.* New York: Random House.

Schlesinger, A. (2004) *The Imperial Presidency.* New York: Houghton Mifflin.

Summers, A. (2000) *The Arrogance of Power: The Secret World of Richard Nixon.* New York: Penguin books.

Young, M. (1991) *The Vietnam Wars, 1945–1990.* New York: Harper Collins.

7

GEORGE H. W. BUSH
TO
BILL CLINTON: THE NEW
WORLD ORDER

INTRODUCTION

After Reagan left office in 1988, his vice president, George H. W. Bush, the scion of a patrician northeastern family with a long record of public service, was elected president. Bush's political resume included wide-ranging foreign policy experience. His governing style, and the fact that he knew many world leaders personally, led many to call him the "Rolodex President" (Herring 2008: 900). His campaign emphasized patriotism, family values, getting tough on crime, and a pledge not to raise taxes. However, Bush was dogged by what *Newsweek* magazine (October 19, 1987) termed the "Wimp Factor," referring to his claim that he was out of the loop during the Iran-Contra scandal. Bush reinforced the perception that he would be a low-key president when he appealed for "a kinder face to the nation and a gentler face to the world" in his inaugural address on January 20, 1989. In his early days, he managed the end of the Cold War, highlighted by the fall of the Berlin Wall and the eventual dissolution of the Soviet Union. However, as presidents before him had discovered, events in other regions such as the Middle East and Central America would occupy much of his foreign policy focus.

With the close of the Cold War, President Bush seemed to be the right man for the times. He was a committed internationalist who developed a good working relationship with the Soviet leader Mikhail Gorbachev, with whom he concluded the Strategic Arms Limitations Treaty I (START I; later, Bush and President Boris Yeltsin signed START II, but this treaty was never ratified by the Russian Duma and it never entered into force). However, Bush seemed to not to have expected what followed Gorbachev's policies of *glasnost* and *perestroika* (opening and restructuring), and had difficulty clearly defining the substance of his vision for a "new world order" as a post–Cold War ideal. He soon had faced various crises stemming from the disintegration of the Soviet bloc in Eastern Europe, starting with the collapse of the Polish dictatorship of General Wojciech Jaruzelski, led by Lech Walesa's Solidarity movement. Eastern European countries took Gorbachev's invitation to emulate perestroika, and by the end of 1989 they had peacefully replaced the pro-Soviet leaders of Czechoslovakia, Bulgaria, Romania, and East Germany. The opening of the Berlin Wall on November 9, 1989, signaled the end of the East-West standoff in Europe.

The United States watched these events with great enthusiasm, but also with some degree of caution. Fearing too much unpredictability and instability, Bush wanted to allow Gorbachev room to maneuver in order to avoid total chaos. There was a high level of uncertainty about what would happen to the Soviet Union itself. The answer came in 1990–1991 when the small Baltic republics of Estonia, Lithuania, and Latvia, which had been annexed by the Soviet Union in 1940, began asserting their independence. When Lithuania declared its independence, Gorbachev denied their claims, leading to outright conflict in 1991, in which civilians were killed. In reaction, Bush withheld criticism of Gorbachev, and even urged Baltic nations not to be blinded by "suicidal nationalism" in a speech delivered in Ukraine, a speech quickly labeled "Chicken Kiev" by critics.

Meanwhile, between May and June of 1989, Chinese students protesting university regulations initiated a revolt at Tiananmen Square. This revolt was eventually crushed by the Chinese government, with estimates that over 3,000 people were killed and twice as many wounded when the Chinese army moved in. While the world watched emotionally powerful pictures of pro-democracy student activists being beaten and killed, the United States refused to openly criticize the Chinese government, noting that Sino-American relations were too important. Again, Bush's foreign policy reflected a desire to avoid too much unpredictability and instability.

One area where Bush was not afraid of change was in Central America. Indeed, it is here that Bush first tried to erase the "wimp factor." Panama was ruled by a strongman, General Manuel Noriega, who had been trained in the United States and was formerly on the CIA payroll. However, he found himself on the wrong side of the U.S. war on drugs when he became part of an international drug smuggling pipeline. When Noriega annulled the results of a 1989 election and took control of Panama, Bush declared that he would not negotiate with a thug and a drug criminal. Citing the need to defend the rights of Panamanians and to protect the integrity of the Torrijos-Carter treaty, on December 20, 1989, Bush ordered the U.S. invasion of Panama in an operation dubbed "Just Cause." This effort restored the winner of the Panamanian election, and captured Noriega, who served a 20-year sentence in a federal prison in Florida and was then extradited to France, where he was sentenced to an additional seven years.

After years of watching Iran and Iraq fight, even selling weapons to Iran and providing logistical aid and weaponry to Iraq, the United States soon had a crisis in the Persian Gulf. Seeking control of disputed territory and accusing Kuwait of illegally drilling oil from under Iraqi soil, Iraq invaded Kuwait on August 2, 1990, in all likelihood assuming that the United States would not respond. This gave Iraq control of roughly 20 percent of the world's oil reserves. In response, President Bush mobilized an international effort to contain Iraq and liberate Kuwait from Iraqi rule. President Bush argued that Iraqi ruler Saddam Hussein represented a threat not just to the region but to the entire world order, even comparing Hussein to a modern-day Hitler. Persuading Saudi Arabia to host U.S. armed forces for its own defense, Bush deployed tens of thousands of U.S. troops in Operation Desert Shield. The United States worked through the UN to secure Security Council Resolution 678, authorizing "all necessary means" to liberate Kuwait. And one day after the UN's January 15, 1991, deadline for Iraqi withdrawal passed, Operation Desert Storm opened with massive air strikes in Iraq and on its troops. Within weeks, coalition forces had crushed the Iraqi army, forcing its hasty retreat from Kuwait. With the liberation of Kuwait complete, the United States, unlike in Panama, chose not to invade Iraq in order to remove the strongman Hussein from power—a move many feared would unleash a civil war within Iraq, creating instability for the region (Herring 2008, 911). The Persian Gulf War was the first war to be

Did You Know?

The North America Free Trade Agreement (NAFTA)

In response to the signing of the Maastricht Treaty and the creation of the European Union, then the largest trading block in the world, the United States, Canada, and Mexico initiated talks to create a rival trading block in 1992. The negotiations resulted in the North American Free Trade Agreement (NAFTA) in 1994. NAFTA created the largest trading bloc at the time and provided for the elimination of all barriers to trade between the three North American nations. The agreement immediately eliminated half of all tariff barriers to trade for Mexican products in the United States and a third of the tariff barriers for U.S. products in Mexico, and aimed to eliminate all tariffs within a decade as well as to eliminate all non-tariff barriers to trade between the three nations. The United States–Canadian relationship was already free of tariffs.

The signing of NAFTA by the Clinton administration created an opposition that spanned the political spectrum, giving credence to the old adage "politics make strange bedfellows." NAFTA was opposed by U.S. labor unions, which feared for the loss of jobs to Mexico, as well economic nationalists on the right, such as Pat Buchanan, who worried about national sovereignty. Also opposed to NAFTA was third-party presidential candidate Ross Perot, a billionaire from Texas who argued that once the United States opened its borders, the cheap labor supply in Mexico would lure major industrial sectors to move to Mexico, taking millions of jobs with them. While critics argue that NAFTA sped up the deindustrialization of the United States, others have credited NAFTA with spurring more efficient trade among the three North American economies as well as with generating new jobs due to increased trade.

covered in real time, live on television, with extensive coverage from a new Cable News Network (CNN).

Because the United States was able to use overwhelming force to quickly defeat Iraq as well as invade Panama with minimal U.S. troop casualties, many argued that the United States had finally kicked the "Vietnam Syndrome" and was now willing to support the projection of U.S. military power as long as few U.S. casualties were sustained and the conflict was not protracted. In his 1991 State of the Union address, President Bush envisioned a new world order in which the United States would "bear a major share of leadership" in keeping the world safe and secure since only the United States had "both the moral standing and the means to do so."

Victory in the Persian Gulf would prove to be President Bush's finest hour. However, when running for reelection, he was hampered by a failing domestic economy, and he was seen as out of touch with the concerns of "middle America." Democrat Bill Clinton, guided by the slogan "It's the economy, stupid," defeated Bush in 1992 with help from independent candidate Ross Perot, who garnered 19 percent of the popular vote in a rare three-way presidential contest.

From the Bush administration, President Clinton inherited not only an economy in recession but also some thorny foreign policy problems. The most complicated was the collapse of Yugoslavia into ethnically defined republics, a disintegration that was not just a humanitarian catastrophe but threatened to destabilize the entire

Serbian president Slobodan Milosevic, left, faces Croatian president Franjo Tudjman, right, as U.S. secretary of state Warren Christopher, second from right, and U.S. assistant secretary of state Richard Holbrooke call the Yugoslavian Peace Talks to order November 1, 1995, at Wright-Patterson Air Force Base in Dayton, Ohio. (AP Photo/David Longstreath)

Balkan Peninsula and perhaps even southeast Europe. With a global news media providing grisly pictures of human suffering, there was increased pressure on the United States, Europe, and NATO to do something to end war among the Serbs, Croats, and Bosnian Muslims. During the late Bush and early Clinton administrations, the United States insisted that this war was a European problem, a view aptly summarized in Secretary of State James Baker's comment that "We have no dog in this fight" (Herring 2008: 924). Yet the United States could not stay out of the Balkans, especially when the Europeans failed to find a solution to what President Clinton called the "problem from hell" (Herring 2008: 929). Under growing domestic and international pressure, while Bosnia was mired in a bloody war complete with ethnic cleansing and attempted genocide, the United States brokered the "Dayton Accords," an agreement among the warring factions negotiated in Dayton, Ohio. With the problem of Bosnia seemingly resolved, the larger problem of Yugoslavia remained. In his second term, President Clinton oversaw U.S. involvement in the NATO bombardment of Serbia in order to punish the Slobodan Milosevic regime for its actions in Kosovo. Milosevic, the president of Serbia, was indicted by an International Criminal Court for crimes against humanity, as were the Bosnian Serb leader Radovan Karadzic and the military commander of the Serbian forces in Kosovo, Ratko Mladic. The first died during trial at The Hague, the second is now in custody and awaiting trial, and the third was finally captured in the Spring of 2011.

President Clinton also inherited a crisis in Somalia, where humanitarian suffering led President Bush to send U.S. troops to keep peace and to help distribute humanitarian aid. The peacekeeping troops suffered losses, forcing the United States to rethink its policy. Failing to adhere to standard rules of engagement in peacekeeping operations, the U.S. military got involved in a short conflict with the warlord Mohamed Farah Aidid, who controlled Somalia's capital city, Mogadishu. In their effort to capture Aidid, the United States lost 18 soldiers and had 75 wounded. The domestic reaction was one of bewilderment as critics wondered why the United States committed forces when it had nothing to gain. A stung Clinton administration withdrew U.S. forces from Somalia. Then, when the president of Rwanda was murdered in an attack on his plane as it approached the airport in Kigali, a massive ethnic conflict broke out in Rwanda. Genocide broke out, and approximately one million Tutsis perished at the hands of Hutu militias within three months. The world watched in horror, yet world leaders had no intention of intervening to stop the slaughter. Hutu militia leaders executed 12 Belgian peacekeepers in order to make the UN think twice about deploying a major peacekeeping effort. Smarting from its retreat from

Did You Know?

International Criminal Court

The International Criminal Court (ICC) is the latest of the international courts to be created in order to enforce international law. The ICC is charged with the prosecution of the crimes of genocide, crimes against humanity, war crimes, and crimes of aggression. It came into being in July of 2002 and has a permanent seat at The Hague in the Netherlands, even though several major powers are not party to it, such as Russia, India, China, and the United States. So far, the ICC has 110 members and can only prosecute crimes that were committed after its creation. The original idea behind the creation of the ICC can be traced back to the post–World War II trials at Nuremberg and Tokyo, but the expediencies of the Cold War postponed its creation.

The ICC has indicted several people from four countries: Uganda, Central African Republic, Democratic Republic of the Congo, and Sudan. In the case of Uganda, the court has indicted Josh Kony and others in his Lord's Resistance Army, the most notorious and deadly of children's armies on the African continent. In Congo, the court indicted people in connection with mass killings during the Congolese civil war, while regarding the Central African Republic, the ICC indicted another Congolese official accused of rape and killing in the same war. Most notoriously, the ICC has indicted the president of Sudan, Omar Al-Bashir, and several of his followers and leaders in the state-sponsored militias that have committed genocide in the region known as Darfur. The Sudanese president, however, refuses to acknowledge the jurisdiction of the court and has not surrendered himself or his people to the international community.

Somalia, and perhaps because the United States decided it had no strategic interests in Rwanda, President Clinton's administration chose not to intervene on humanitarian grounds.

In other regions, Clinton dispatched U.S. troops to restore the democratically elected president of Haiti, despite critics who worried about "nation-building." In 1996 the United States helped broker a nuclear test ban treaty. And in 1997 the United States and its European allies worked with a reluctant Russia to add several former Soviet satellite states to NATO, thereby extending NATO's reach deep into Eastern Europe. Throughout his administration, Clinton actively sought to broker an Israeli-Palestinian deal for peace, only to see agreements undermined by extremists on both sides. As Clinton's second term came to a close, he made a strong push to secure a grand bargain for peace in the Middle East.

- **Document: President George H. W. Bush's "New World Order" Speech**
- **Date:** September 11, 1990
- **Significance:** In this speech, President George H. W. Bush argues that the Gulf War presents the world with an opportunity to create a new world order, and details the role the United States will play in shaping it.
- **Source:** George H. W. Bush, *Public Papers of the Presidents of the United States: George Bush, 1991*, Book 1. Washington, D.C.: GPO, pp. 218–222.

George H. W. Bush, President of the U.S.A. Given to a Joint Session of the United States Congress, Washington D.C.

Mr. President, Mr. Speaker, members of the Congress, distinguished guests, fellow Americans, thank very much for that warm welcome. We gather tonight, witness to events in the Persian Gulf as significant as they are tragic. In the early morning hours of August 2, following negotiations and promises by Iraq's dictator Saddam Hussein not to use force, a powerful Iraqi Army invaded its trusting and much weaker neighbor, Kuwait. Within three days, 120,000 Iraqi troops with 850 tanks had poured into Kuwait and moved south to threaten Saudi Arabia. It was then that I decided to act to check that aggression.

At this moment, our brave servicemen and women stand watch in that distant desert and on distant seas, side by side with the forces of more than 20 other distant nations.

They are some of the finest men and women of the United States of America. And they're doing one terrific job.

These valiant Americans were ready at a moment's notice to leave their spouses and their children, to serve on the front line halfway around the world. They remind us who keeps America strong. They do.

In the trying circumstances of the gulf, the morale of our servicemen and women is excellent. In the face of danger, they are brave, they're well-trained and dedicated.

A soldier, Pfc. Wade Merritt of Knoxville, Tennessee, now stationed in Saudi Arabia, wrote his parents of his worries, his love of family, and his hope for peace. But Wade also wrote: "I am proud of my country and its firm stance against inhumane aggression. I am proud of my Army and its men. . . . I am proud to serve my country."

Let me just say, Wade, America is proud of you and is grateful to every soldier, sailor, Marine and airman serving the cause of peace in the Persian Gulf.

I also want to thank the chairman of the Joint Chiefs of Staff, General [Colin L.] Powell, the Chiefs, here tonight, our commander in the Persian Gulf, General H. Norman Schwarzkopf, and the men and women of the Department of Defense. What a magnificent job you all are doing and thank you very very much.

I wish I could say their work is done. But we all know it's not.

So if ever there was a time to put country before self and patriotism before party, the time is now. And let me thank all Americans, especially those in this chamber tonight, for your support for our armed forces and for their mission.

That support will be even more important in the days to come.

So tonight, I want to talk to you about what's at stake—what we must do together to defend civilized values around the world and maintain our economic strength at home.

U.S. Objectives in Persian Gulf

Our objectives in the Persian Gulf are clear, our goals defined and familiar:

> Iraq must withdraw from Kuwait completely, immediately and without condition.
> Kuwait's legitimate government must be restored.
> The security and stability of the Persian Gulf must be assured.
> And American citizens abroad must be protected.

These goals are not ours alone. They've been endorsed by the U.N. Security Council five times in as many weeks. Most countries share our concern for principle, and many have a stake in the stability of the Persian Gulf. This is not, as Saddam Hussein would have it, the United States against Iraq. It is Iraq against the world.

As you know, I've just returned from a very productive meeting with Soviet President [Mikhail] Gorbachev, and I am pleased that we are working together to build a new relationship. In Helsinki, our joint statement affirmed to the world our shared resolve to counter Iraq's threat to peace. Let me quote: "We are united in

---

Did You Know?

Genocide and Politicide

Genocide is the deliberate and systematic destruction of a people because of their ethnicity, religion, and or race. Politicide is the systematic destruction of a people for political or ideological reasons. Coined by Polish-Jewish legal scholar Rafael Lemkin just before World War II, *genocide* is a composite word from the Greek *genos*, meaning nation, and the Latin *-cide*, meaning killing. After World War II, the codification of genocide and other crimes against humanity became necessary. By 1948 the United Nations had passed the Convention on the Prevention and Punishment of the Crime of Genocide, and in more recent times the International criminal Court was created to deal with such issues. Even though genocide became an international crime, it has nevertheless been attempted on several occasions. In Cambodia in the late 1970s, the systematic destruction of at least a quarter of its population at the hands of the Khmer Rouge was termed politicide. In Rwanda in 1994, ethnic Tutsis suffered approximately a million deaths in three months of slaughter at the hands of their Hutu compatriots. In Bosnia, during one incident in Srebrenica (July 1995), approximately 8,000 Muslim males were put to death and 25,000 to 30,000 refugees were "cleansed" (expelled) by the Bosnian Serb army under the command of General Ratko Mladic. The most recent example of a genocide is in Darfur, which was declared a genocide by the United States in 2004, where the Sudanese Army and the Janjaweed militia have been deemed responsible for the deaths of a quarter million people through expulsion, starvation, and rape. While several Sudanese leaders, including the president of Sudan, have been issued arrest warrants, the Sudanese government claims the ICC has no jurisdiction in Sudan and refuses to comply. The conflict in Sudan continues to this day.

Did You Know?

The United States and the Peace Process in Arab-Israeli Relations

President George H. W. Bush called a conference in Madrid, Spain, in 1991 for direct negotiations between Arabs and Israelis, which led to the Oslo Accords two years later, in 1993. In 1994 the two leaders of Israel and Palestine were awarded the Nobel Peace Prize, but subsequently Yitzhak Rabin, the Israeli Prime Minister, was assassinated by a fundamentalist Jew and the peace process came to a halt. President Bill Clinton's efforts to restart the peace process seemed to succeed when the two parties signed the Wye River accord, which promised to implement the Oslo agreement. In the final days of the Clinton administration the two parties met, but the meeting did not go well and yielded no significant accomplishment. Soon afterward the government of Israel changed, and the hardline Israeli Prime Minister Ariel Sharon further harmed the situation with his actions, which helped reignite the Palestinian intifada (resistance). President George W. Bush last attempted to solve the Israeli-Palestinian problem with what he termed "the roadmap to peace," in which the Palestinians would eventually get statehood in exchange for recognizing Israel's right to exist. In part because the Bush administration was preoccupied with wars in Iraq and Afghanistan, the roadmap to peace led nowhere. The Israelis continue building settlements in the occupied territories, which, in turn, draws the ire of the Palestinians.

the belief that Iraq's aggression must not be tolerated. No peaceful international order is possible if larger states can devour their smaller neighbors."

Clearly, no longer can a dictator count on East-West confrontation to stymie concerted United Nations action against aggression.

A new partnership of nations has begun, and we stand today at a unique and extraordinary moment. The crisis in the Persian Gulf, as grave as it is, also offers a rare opportunity to move toward an historic period of cooperation. Out of these troubled times, our fifth objective—a **new world order**—can emerge: A new era—freer from the threat of terror, stronger in the pursuit of justice and more secure in the quest for peace. An era in which the nations of the world, east and west, north and south, can prosper and live in harmony.

A hundred generations have searched for this elusive path to peace, while a thousand wars raged across the span of human endeavor, and today that new world is struggling to be born. A world quite different from the one we've known. A world where the rule of law supplants the rule of the jungle. A world in which nations recognize the shared responsibility for freedom and justice. A world where the strong respect the rights of the weak.

This is the vision that I shared with President Gorbachev in Helsinki. He and the other leaders from Europe, the gulf and around the world understand that how we manage this crisis today could shape the future for generations to come.

. . .

"The Test We Face Is Great"

The test we face is great and so are the stakes. This is the first assault on the new world that we seek, the first test of our mettle. Had we not responded to this first provocation with clarity of purpose; if we do not continue to demonstrate our determination, it would be a signal to actual and potential despots around the world.

America and the world must defend common vital interests. And we will.
America and the world must support the rule of law. And we will.
America and the world must stand up to aggression. And we will.
And one thing more: in the pursuit of these goals, America will not be intimidated.

Vital issues of principle are at stake. Saddam Hussein is literally trying to wipe a country off the face of the Earth.

We do not exaggerate. Nor do we exaggerate when we say: Saddam Hussein will fail.

Vital economic interests are at risk as well. Iraq itself controls some 10 percent of the world's proven oil reserves. Iraq plus Kuwait controls twice that. An Iraq permitted to swallow Kuwait would have the economic and military power, as well as the

President George H. W. Bush talks with troops in Saudi Arabia on November 23, 1990, during Operation Desert Shield. (U.S. Department of Defense)

arrogance, to intimidate and coerce its neighbors—neighbors who control the lion's share of the world's remaining oil reserves. We cannot permit a resource so vital to be dominated by one so ruthless. And we won't.

Recent events have surely proven that there is no substitute for American leadership. In the face of tyranny, let no one doubt American credibility and reliability. Let no one doubt our staying power. We will stand by our friends. One way or another, the leader of Iraq must learn this fundamental truth.

From the outset, acting hand-in-hand with others, we've sought to fashion the broadest possible international response to Iraq's aggression. The level of world cooperation and condemnation of Iraq is unprecedented.

Armed forces from countries spanning four continents are there at the request of King Fahd of Saudi Arabia to deter and, if need be, to defend against attack. Muslims and non-Muslims, Arabs and non-Arabs, soldiers from many nations, stand shoulder-to-shoulder, resolute against Saddam Hussein's ambitions.

And we can now point to five United Nations Security Council resolutions that condemn Iraq's aggression. They call for Iraq's immediate and unconditional withdrawal, the restoration of Kuwait's legitimate government and categorically reject Iraq's cynical and self-serving attempt to annex Kuwait.

Finally, the United Nations has demanded the release of all foreign nationals held hostage against their will and in contravention of international law. It's a mockery of human decency to call these people "guests." They are hostages, and the whole world knows it.

Prime Minister Margaret Thatcher, a dependable ally, said it all: "We do not bargain over hostages. We will not stoop to the level of using human beings as bargaining [chips]. Ever."

. . .

I am hopeful—in fact, I am confident—the Congress will do what it should. And I can assure you that we in the executive branch will do our part.

In the final analysis, our ability to meet our responsibilities abroad depends upon political will and consensus at home. It's never easy in democracies, for we govern only with the consent of the governed. And although free people in a free society are bound to have their differences, Americans traditionally come together in times of adversity and challenge.

Once again, Americans have stepped forward to share a tearful goodbye with their families before leaving for a strange and distant shore. At this very moment, they serve together with Arabs, Europeans, Asians and Africans in defense of principle and the dream of a **new world order**. That is why they sweat and toil in the sand and the heat and the sun.

If they can come together under such adversity; if old adversaries like the Soviet Union and the United States can work in common cause, then surely we who are so fortunate to be in this great chamber—Democrats, Republicans, liberals, conservatives—can come together to fulfill our responsibilities here.

Thank you. Good night. And God bless the United States of America.

- **Document: President George H. W. Bush's Address to the Nation Announcing U.S. Military Action in Panama**
- **Date:** December 20, 1989
- **Significance:** In this speech, President George H. W. Bush explains why he authorized the U.S. invasion of Panama to remove and capture Manuel Noriega.
- **Source:** Address to the Nation Announcing United States Military Action in Panama, December 20, 1989/ George Bush Presidential Library and Museum.

My fellow citizens, last night I ordered U.S. military forces to Panama. No President takes such action lightly. This morning I want to tell you what I did and why I did it.

For nearly 2 years, the United States, nations of Latin America and the Caribbean have worked together to resolve the crisis in Panama. The goals of the United States have been to safeguard the lives of Americans, to defend democracy in Panama, to combat drug trafficking, and to protect the integrity of the Panama Canal treaty. Many attempts have been made to resolve this crisis through diplomacy and negotiations. All were rejected by the dictator of Panama, General Manuel Noriega, an indicted drug trafficker.

Last Friday, Noriega declared his military dictatorship to be in a state of war with the United States and publicly threatened the lives of Americans in Panama. The very next day, forces under his command shot and killed an unarmed American serviceman; wounded another; arrested and brutally beat a third American serviceman; and then brutally interrogated his wife, threatening her with sexual abuse. That was enough.

General Noriega's reckless threats and attacks upon Americans in Panama created an imminent danger to the 35,000 American citizens in Panama. As President, I have no higher obligation than to safeguard the lives of American citizens. And that is why I directed our Armed Forces to protect the lives of American citizens in Panama and to bring General Noriega to justice in the United States. I contacted the bipartisan leadership of Congress last night and informed them of this decision, and after taking this action, I also talked with leaders in Latin America, the Caribbean, and those of other U.S. allies.

At this moment, U.S. forces, including forces deployed from the United States last night, are engaged in action in Panama. The United States intends to withdraw the forces newly deployed to Panama as quickly as possible. Our forces have conducted themselves courageously and selflessly. And as Commander in Chief, I salute every one of them and thank them on behalf of our country.

Tragically, some Americans have lost their lives in defense of their fellow citizens, in defense of democracy. And my heart goes out to their families. We also regret and mourn the loss of innocent Panamanians.

The brave Panamanians elected by the people of Panama in the elections last May, President Guillermo Endara and Vice Presidents Calderon and Ford, have assumed the rightful leadership of their country. You remember those horrible pictures of newly elected Vice President Ford, covered head to toe with blood, beaten mercilessly by so-called "dignity battalions." Well, the United States today recognizes the democratically elected government of President Endara. I will send our Ambassador back to Panama immediately.

Key military objectives have been achieved. Most organized resistance has been eliminated, but the operation is not over yet: General Noriega is in hiding. And nevertheless, yesterday a dictator ruled Panama, and today constitutionally elected leaders govern.

I have today directed the Secretary of the Treasury and the Secretary of State to lift the economic sanctions with respect to the democratically elected government of Panama and, in cooperation with that government, to take steps to effect an

Did You Know?

The Powell Doctrine

The "Powell Doctrine" was enunciated by Colin Powell, who, as Chairman of the Joint Chiefs of Staff during President George H. W. Bush's administration, helped plan and execute the Panama invasion of 1989 and the Gulf War of 1991. The goal of the Powell Doctrine was not just to win wars but to nullify the "Vietnam Syndrome," the view that military success depended on domestic public support and that the American public would sour on military actions when there was a high level of casualties, thus making political leaders apprehensive when considering the use of military force. The Powell Doctrine advocated the projection of overwhelming American force—in troops and weaponry—to quickly and decisively defeat the enemy. Applied to the Gulf War, the Powell Doctrine is one reason the United States mobilized 400,000 troops and the international coalition contributed an additional 200,000 troops. After beginning with air strikes against Iraqi targets, land forces entered Kuwait, where they quickly pushed Iraqi forces out of Kuwait within 100 hours. The combination of a decisive victory, low troop casualties, and high levels of domestic public support was seen as proof that the Powell Doctrine had laid the Vietnam Syndrome to rest. Yet in 2003, when Powell was the Secretary of State under President George W. Bush, the Powell Doctrine was rejected by Secretary of Defense Donald Rumsfeld, who assured the American public that "regime change" in Iraq would be easy and would not require the large number of troops recommended by military leaders, such as General Anthony Zinni and others, who still supported the Powell Doctrine. The Iraqi regime was quickly toppled after the invasion in March 2003, but the post-invasion insurgency saw an increase in American casualties, which fueled a decline in public support for the war. Eventually, top-level officials criticized Rumsfeld for not deploying a sufficient number of troops to maintain security after the initial invasion.

orderly unblocking of Panamanian Government assets in the United States. I'm fully committed to implement the Panama Canal treaties and turn over the Canal to Panama in the year 2000. The actions we have taken and the cooperation of a new, democratic government in Panama will permit us to honor these commitments. As soon as the new government recommends a qualified candidate— Panamanian—to be Administrator of the Canal, as called for in the treaties, I will submit this nominee to the Senate for expedited consideration.

I am committed to strengthening our relationship with the democratic nations in this hemisphere. I will continue to seek solutions to the problems of this region through dialog and multilateral diplomacy. I took this action only after reaching the conclusion that every other avenue was closed and the lives of American citizens were in grave danger. I hope that the people of Panama will put this dark chapter of dictatorship behind them and move forward together as citizens of a democratic Panama with this government that they themselves have elected.

The United States is eager to work with the Panamanian people in partnership and friendship to rebuild their economy. The Panamanian people want democracy, peace, and the chance for a better life in dignity and freedom. The people of the United States seek only to support them in pursuit of these noble goals. Thank you very much.

- **Document:** START I
- **Date:** July 31, 1991
- **Significance:** The bilateral negotiation between the United States and the Soviet Union that started with Nixon in the 1970s entered a new cycle of life in the 1990s with the express agreement to reduce nuclear weaponry in both superpowers. The largest and most complex negotiation ever undertaken by the two powers resulted in two Strategic Arms Reduction Treaties (START I and START II; the latter never took effect).
- **Source:** U.S. Congress, Senate, Treaty on the Reduction and Limitation of Strategic Offensive Arms, July 31, 1991. S. Treaty Doc. No. 102-20.

TREATY BETWEEN
THE UNITED STATES OF AMERICA
AND
THE UNION OF SOVIET SOCIALIST REPUBLICS ON
THE REDUCTION AND
LIMITATION OF STRATEGIC OFFENSIVE ARMS

The United States of America and the Union of Soviet Socialist Republics, hereinafter referred to as the Parties,

Conscious that nuclear war would have devastating consequences for all humanity, that it cannot be won and must never be fought,

Convinced that the measures for the reduction and limitation of strategic offensive arms and the other obligations set forth in this Treaty will help to reduce the risk of outbreak of nuclear war and strengthen international peace and security,

Recognizing that the interests of the Parties and the interests of international security require the strengthening of strategic stability,

Mindful of their undertakings with regard to strategic offensive arms in Article VI of the Treaty on the Non-Proliferation of Nuclear Weapons of July 1, 1968; Article XI of the Treaty on the Limitation of Anti-Ballistic Missile Systems of May 26, 1972; and the Washington Summit Joint Statement of June 1, 1990, [ABA]

Have agreed as follows:

ARTICLE I

Each Party shall reduce and limit its strategic offensive arms in accordance with the provisions of this Treaty, and shall carry out the other obligations set forth in this Treaty and its Annexes, Protocols, and Memorandum of Understanding.

ARTICLE II

1. Each Party shall reduce and limit its ICBMs and ICBM launchers, SLBMs and SLBM launchers, heavy bombers, ICBM warheads, SLBM warheads, and heavy bomber armaments, so that seven years after entry into force of this Treaty and thereafter, the aggregate numbers, as counted in accordance with Article III of this Treaty, do not exceed:

    (a) 1600, for deployed ICBMs and their associated launchers, deployed SLBMs and their associated launchers, and deployed heavy bombers, including 154 for deployed heavy ICBMs and their associated launchers; [RF MOU, Section II] [US MOU, Section II] [Agreed State 33]

    (b) 6000, for warheads attributed to deployed ICBMs, deployed SLBMs, and deployed heavy bombers, [RF MOU, Section II] [US MOU, Section II] including: [Agreed State 33] [START II, Art. I, 3]

        (i)   4900, for warheads attributed to deployed ICBMs and deployed SLBMs; [RF MOU, Section II] [US MOU, Section II] [START II, Art. I,4] [Agreed State 33]

        (ii) 1100, for warheads attributed to deployed ICBMs on mobile launchers of ICBMs; [RF MOU, Section II]

        (iii) 1540, for warheads attributed to deployed heavy ICBMs. [phased heavy reductions] [RF MOU, Section II] ABA

2. Each Party shall implement the reductions pursuant to paragraph 1 of this Article in three phases, so that its strategic offensive arms do not exceed:

    (a) by the end of the first phase, that is, no later than 36 months after entry into force of this Treaty, and thereafter, the following aggregate numbers:

        (i) 2100, for deployed ICBMs and their associated launchers, deployed SLBMs and their associated launchers, and deployed heavy bombers;

        (ii) 9150, for warheads attributed to deployed ICBMs, deployed SLBMs, and deployed heavy bombers;

(iii) 8050, warheads attributed to deployed ICBMs and deployed SLBMs;

(b) by the end of the second phase, that is, no later than 60 months after entry into force of this Treaty, and thereafter, the following aggregate numbers:

(i)   1900, for deployed ICBMs and their associated launchers, deployed SLBMs and their associated launchers, and deployed heavy bombers;

(ii) 7950, for warheads attributed to deployed ICBMs, deployed SLBMs, and deployed heavy bombers;

(iii) 6750, warheads attributed to deployed ICBMs and deployed SLBMs;

(c) by the end of the third phase, that is, no later than 84 months after entry into force of this Treaty: the aggregate numbers provided for in paragraph 1 of this Article .ABA

3. Each Party shall limit the aggregate throw-weight [RF MOU, Section II] [US MOU Section II] of its deployed ICBMs [RF MOU, Section I] [US MOU Section I] and deployed SLBMs [RF MOU, Section I] [US MOU Section I] so that seven years after entry into force of this Treaty and thereafter such aggregate throw-weight does not exceed 3600 metric tons. ABA [Throw-weight Limits/Provisions for Types of ICBMs and SLBMs]

ARTICLE III

1. For the purposes of counting toward the maximum aggregate limits provided for in subparagraphs 1(a), 2(a)(i), and 2(b)(i) of Article II of this Treaty:

(a) Each deployed ICBM and its associated launcher shall be counted as one unit; each deployed SLBM and its associated launcher; shall be counted as one unit.

(b) Each deployed heavy bombers shall be counted as one unit. ABA

2. For the purposes of counting deployed ICBMs and their associated launchers and deployed SLBMs and their associated launchers

(a) Each deployed launcher of ICBMs and each deployed launcher of SLBMs shall be considered to contain one deployed ICBM or one deployed SLBM, respectively. ABA

(b) If a deployed ICBM has been removed from its launcher and another missile has not been installed in that launcher, such an ICBM removed from its launcher and located at that ICBM base shall continue to be considered to be contained in that launcher. ABA

(c) If a deployed SLBM has been removed from its launcher and another missile has not been installed in that launcher, such an SLBM removed from its launcher shall be considered to be contained in that launcher. Such an SLBM removed from its launcher shall be located only at a facility at which non-deployed SLBMs may be located pursuant to subparagraph 9 (a) of Article IV of this Treaty or be in movement to such a facility. ABA

. . .

ARTICLE IV

1. For ICBMs and SLBMs:

   (a) Each Party shall limit the aggregate number of non-deployed ICBMs for mobile launchers of ICBMs to no more than 250. Within this limit, the number of non-deployed ICBMs for rail-mobile launchers of ICBMs shall not exceed 125. [RF MOU, Section IV] [US MOU Section IV] [Agreed State 37]

   (b) Each Party shall limit the number of non-deployed ICBMs at a maintenance facility of an ICBM base for mobile launchers of ICBMs to no more than two ICBMs of each type specified for that ICBM base. Non-deployed ICBMs for mobile launchers of ICBMs located at a maintenance facility shall be stored separately from non-deployed mobile launchers of ICBMs located at that maintenance facility.

   (c) Each Party shall limit the number of non-deployed ICBMs and sets of ICBM emplacement equipment at an ICBM base for silo launchers of ICBMs to no more than:

      (i) two ICBMs of each type specified for that ICBM base and six sets of ICBM emplacement equipment for each type of ICBM specified for that ICBM base; or [RF MOU Annex A] [US MOU, Annex A]

      (ii) four ICBMs of each type specified for that ICBM base and two sets of ICBM emplacement equipment for each type of ICBM specified for that ICBM base. [RF MOU Annex A] [US MOU, Annex A]

   (d) Each Party shall limit the aggregate number of ICBMs and SLBMs located at test ranges to no more than 35 during the seven-year period after entry into force of this Treaty. Thereafter, the aggregate number of ICBMs and SLBMs located at test ranges shall not exceed 25. [RF MOU, Section IV] [US MOU Section IV] [Agreed State 37]

2. For ICBM launchers and SLBM launchers:

   (a) Each Party shall limit the aggregate number of non-deployed mobile launchers of ICBMs to no more than 110. Within this limit, the number of non-deployed rail-mobile launchers of ICBMs shall not exceed 18. [RF MOU, Section IV] [US MOU Section IV]

   (b) Each Party shall limit the number of non-deployed mobile launchers of ICBMs located at the maintenance facility of each ICBM base for mobile launchers of ICBMs to no more than two such ICBM launchers of each type of ICBM specified for that ICBM base. [RF MOU Annex A]

   (c) Each Party shall limit the number of non-deployed mobile launchers of ICBMs located at training facilities for ICBMs to no more than 40. Each such launcher may contain only a training model of a missile. Non-deployed mobile launchers of ICBMs that contain training models of missiles shall not be located outside a training facility. [RF MOU, Section IV] [US MOU Section IV]

   (d) Each Party shall limit the aggregate number of test launchers to no more than 45 during the seven-year period after entry into force of this Treaty.

Within this limit, the number of fixed test launchers shall not exceed 25, and the number of mobile test launchers shall not exceed 20. Thereafter, the aggregate number of test launchers shall not exceed 40. Within this limit, the number of fixed test launchers shall not exceed 20, and the number of mobile test launchers shall not exceed 20. [RF MOU, Section IV] [US MOU Section IV] [Agreed State 37(h)]

(e) Each Party shall limit the aggregate number of silo training launchers and mobile training launchers to no more than 60. ICBMs shall not be launched from training launchers. Each such launcher may contain only a training model of a missile. Mobile training launchers shall not be capable of launching ICBMs, and shall differ from mobile launchers of ICBMs and other road vehicles or railcars on the basis of differences that are observable by national technical means of verification. [Agreed State 13] [RF MOU, Section IV] [US MOU Section IV]

3. For heavy bombers and former heavy bombers:

(a) Each Party shall limit the aggregate number of heavy bombers equipped for non-nuclear armaments, former heavy bombers, and training heavy bombers to no more than 75. [category] [RF MOU, Section IV] [US MOU Section IV] [Agreed State 6] [Agreed State 12]

(b) Each Party shall limit the number of test heavy bombers to no more than 20. [category] [RF MOU, Section IV] [US MOU Section IV]

4. For ICBMs and SLBMs used for delivering objects into the upper atmosphere or space: [JCIC Joint State 21]

(a) Each Party shall limit the number of space launch facilities to no more than five, unless otherwise agreed. Space launch facilities shall not overlap ICBM bases. [RF MOU, Annex D] [US MOU Annex D]

(b) Each Party shall limit the aggregate number of ICBM launchers and SLBM launchers located at space launch facilities to no more than 20, unless otherwise agreed. Within this limit, the aggregate number of silo launchers of ICBMs and mobile launchers of ICBMs located at space launch facilities shall not exceed ten, unless otherwise agreed. [Agreed State 26] [Agreed State 37(h)]

(c) Each Party shall limit the aggregate number of ICBMs and SLBMs located at a space launch facility to no more than the number of ICBM launchers and SLBM launchers located at that facility. [Agreed State 37]

5. Each Party shall limit the number of transporter-loaders for ICBMs for road-mobile launchers of ICBMs located at each deployment area or test range to no more than two for each type of ICBM for road-mobile launchers of ICBMs that is attributed with one warhead and that is specified for that deployment area or test range, and shall limit the number of such transporter-loaders located outside deployment areas and test ranges to no more than six. The aggregate number of transporter-loaders for ICBMs for road-mobile launchers of ICBMs shall not exceed 30. [RF MOU, Section IV]

6. Each Party shall limit the number of ballistic missile submarines in dry dock within five kilometers of the boundary of each submarine base to no more than two.

. . .

ARTICLE V

1. Except as prohibited by the provisions of this Treaty, modernization and replacement of strategic offensive arms may be carried out.
2. Each Party undertakes not to:

    (a) produce, flight-test, or deploy heavy ICBMs of a new type, or increase the launch weight [RF MOU, Annex F] or throw-weight [RF MOU, Section I] of heavy ICBMs of an existing type;
    (b) produce, flight-test, or deploy heavy SLBMs;
    (c) produce, test, or deploy mobile launchers of heavy ICBMs;
    (d) produce, test, or deploy additional silo launchers of ICBMs of heavy ICBMs, except for silo launchers of heavy ICBMs that replace silo launchers of heavy ICBMs that have been eliminated in accordance with Section II of the Conversion or Elimination Protocol, provided that the limits provided for in Article II of this Treaty are not exceeded; [Agreed State 5]
    (e) convert launchers that are not launchers of heavy ICBMs into launchers of heavy ICBMs;
    (f) produce, test, or deploy launchers of heavy SLBMs;
    (g) reduce the number of warheads attributed to a heavy ICBM of an existing type.

3. Each Party undertakes not to deploy ICBMs other than in silo launchers of ICBMs, on road-mobile launchers of ICBMs, or on rail-mobile launchers of ICBMs. Each Party undertakes not to produce, test, or deploy ICBM launchers other than silo launchers of ICBMs, road-mobile launchers of ICBMs, or rail-mobile launchers of ICBMs.
4. Each Party undertakes not to deploy on a mobile launcher of ICBMs an ICBM of a type that was not specified as a type of ICBM for mobile launchers of ICBMs in accordance with paragraph 2 of Section VII of the Protocol on Notifications Relating to this Treaty, hereinafter referred to as the Notification Protocol, unless it is an ICBM to which no more than one warhead is attributed and the Parties have agreed within the framework of the Joint Compliance and Inspection Commission to permit deployment of such ICBMs on mobile launchers of ICBMs. A new type of ICBM for mobile launchers of ICBMs may cease to be considered to be a type of ICBM for mobile launchers of ICBMs if no ICBM of that type has been contained on, or flight-tested from, a mobile launcher of ICBMs.
5. Each Party undertakes not to deploy ICBM launchers of a new type of ICBM and not to deploy SLBM launchers of a new type of SLBM if such launchers are capable of launching ICBMs or SLBMs, respectively, of other types. ICBM launchers of existing types of ICBMs and SLBM launchers of existing types of

SLBMs shall be incapable, without conversion, of launching ICBMs or SLBMs, respectively, of other types. [Agreed State 16]

6. Each Party undertakes not to convert SLBMs into ICBMs for mobile launchers of ICBMs, or to load SLBMs on, or launch SLBMs from, mobile launchers of ICBMs.

7. Each Party undertakes not to produce, test, or deploy transporter-loaders other than transporter-loaders for ICBMs for road-mobile launchers of ICBMs attributed with one warhead.

8. Each Party undertakes not to locate deployed silo launchers of ICBMs outside ICBM bases for silo launchers of ICBMs.

9. Each Party undertakes not to locate soft-site launchers except at test ranges and space launch facilities. All existing soft-site launchers not at test ranges or space launch facilities shall be eliminated in accordance with the procedures provided for in the Conversion or Elimination Protocol no later than 60 days after entry into force of this Treaty. [Agreed State 27]

10. Each Party undertakes not to:

    (a) flight-test ICBMs or SLBMs of a retired or former type from other than test launchers specified for such use or launchers at space launch facilities. Except for soft-site launchers, test launchers specified for such use shall not be used to flight-test ICBMs or SLBMs of a type, any one of which is deployed; [III.10(c)]

    (b) produce ICBMs for mobile launchers of ICBMs of a retired type.

11. Each Party undertakes not to convert silos used as launch control centers into silo launchers of ICBMs. [Silo LCC Letters]

. . .

ARTICLE VI

1. Deployed road-mobile launchers of ICBMs and their associated missiles shall be based only in restricted areas. A restricted area shall not exceed five square kilometers in size and shall not overlap another restricted area. No more than ten deployed road-mobile launchers of ICBMs and their associated missiles may be based or located in a restricted area. A restricted area shall not contain deployed ICBMs for road-mobile launchers of ICBMs of more than one type of ICBM. [RF MOU Annex A] [Agreed State 19]

2. Each Party shall limit the number of fixed structures for road-mobile launchers of ICBMs within each restricted areas so that these structures shall not be capable of containing more road-mobile launchers of ICBMs than the number of road-mobile launchers of ICBMs specified for that restricted area. [RF MOU Annex A]

3. Each restricted area shall be located within a deployment area. A deployment area shall not exceed 125,000 square kilometers in size and shall not overlap another deployment area. A deployment area shall contain no more than one ICBM base for road-mobile launchers of ICBMs. [RF MOU Annex A]

4. Deployed rail-mobile launchers of ICBMs and their associated missiles shall be based only in rail garrisons. Each Party shall have no more than seven rail garrisons. No point on a portion of track located inside a rail garrison shall be more than 20 kilometers from any entrance/exit for that rail garrison. This

U.S. president George Bush and Soviet leader Mikhail Gorbachev sign the Strategic Arms Reduction Treaty (START) in Moscow in July 1991. Aimed at reducing the nuclear arsenal of the United States and the Soviet Union, the START negotiations succeeded the Strategic Arms Limitation Talks of the 1970s. (George Bush Library)

distance shall be measured along the tracks. A rail garrison shall not overlap another rail garrison. [RF MOU Annex A]

5. Each rail garrison shall have no more than two rail entrances/exits. Each such entrance/exit shall have no more than two separate sets of tracks passing through it (a total of four rails). [RF MOU Annex A]

6. Each Party shall limit the number of parking sites in each rail garrison to no more than the number of trains of standard configuration specified for that rail garrison. Each rail garrison shall have no more than five parking sites. [RF MOU Annex A] [RF MOU Annex F]

7. Each Party shall limit the number of fixed structures for rail-mobile launchers of ICBMs in each rail garrison to no more than the number of trains of standard configuration specified for that rail garrison. Each such structure shall contain no more than one train of standard configuration. [RF MOU Annex A] [RF MOU Annex F]

. . .

ARTICLE VII

1. Conversion and elimination of strategic offensive arms, fixed structures for mobile launchers of ICBMs, and facilities shall be carried out pursuant to this

Article and in accordance with procedures provided for in the Conversion or Elimination Protocol. Conversion and elimination shall be verified by national technical means of verification and by inspection as provided for in Articles IX and XI of this Treaty; in the Conversion or Elimination Protocol; and in the Protocol on Inspections and Continuous Monitoring Activities Relating to this Treaty, hereinafter referred to as the Inspection Protocol.

2. ICBMs for mobile launchers of ICBMs, ICBM launchers, SLBM launchers, heavy bombers, former heavy bombers, and support equipment shall be subject to the limitations provided for in this Treaty until they have been eliminated, or otherwise cease to be subject to the limitations provided for in this Treaty, in accordance with procedures provided for in the Conversion or Elimination Protocol. [Agreed State 11] [Agreed State 37] [Joint State Missile Production Technology]

3. ICBMs for silo launchers of ICBMs and SLBMs shall be subject to the limitations provided for in this Treaty until they have been eliminated by rendering them inoperable, precluding their use for their original purpose, using procedures at the discretion of the Party possessing the ICBMs or SLBMs.

4. The elimination of ICBMs for mobile launchers of ICBMs, mobile launchers of ICBMs, SLBM launchers, heavy bombers, and former heavy bombers [Agreed State 10] shall be carried out at conversion or elimination facilities, except as provided for in Sections VII and VIII of the Conversion or Elimination Protocol. Fixed launchers of ICBMs and fixed structures for mobile launchers of ICBMs subject to elimination shall be eliminated in situ. A launch canister [Launch Canister Letters] [Agreed State 20] remaining at a test range or ICBM base after the flight test of an ICBM for mobile launchers of ICBMs shall be eliminated in the open in situ, or at a conversion or elimination facility, in accordance with procedures provided for in the Conversion or Elimination Protocol. [Agreed State 37]

. . .

ARTICLE XI

1. For the purpose of ensuring verification of compliance with the provisions of this Treaty, each Party shall have the right to conduct inspections and continuous monitoring activities and shall conduct exhibitions pursuant to this Article and the Inspection Protocol. Inspections, continuous monitoring activities, and exhibitions shall be conducted in accordance with the procedures provided for in the Inspection Protocol and the Conversion or Elimination Protocol. [item of inspection] [size criteria] [Agreed State 36]

2. Each Party shall have the right to conduct baseline data inspections at facilities to confirm the accuracy of data on the numbers and types of items specified for such facilities in the initial exchange of data provided in accordance with paragraph 1 of Section I of the Notification Protocol. [facility inspections at] [Agreed State 10]

3. Each Party shall have the right to conduct data update inspections at facilities to confirm the accuracy of data on the numbers and types of items specified for such facilities in the notifications and regular exchanges of updated data

provided in accordance with paragraphs 2 and 3 of Section I of the Notification Protocol. [facility inspections at] [Agreed State 10]

4. Each Party shall have the right to conduct new facility inspections to confirm the accuracy of data on the numbers and types of items specified in the notifications of new facilities provided in accordance with paragraph 3 of Section I of the Notification Protocol. [facility inspections at]

5. Each Party shall have the right to conduct suspect-site inspections to confirm that covert assembly of ICBMs for mobile launchers of ICBMs or covert assembly of first stages of such ICBMs is not occurring. [facility inspections at] [RF MOU Annex I] [US MOU Annex I] [Joint State on Site Diagrams]

. . .

ARTICLE XII

1. To enhance the effectiveness of national technical means of verification, each Party shall, if the other Party makes a request in accordance with paragraph 1 of Section V of the Notification Protocol, carry out the following cooperative measures:

   (a) a display in the open of the road-mobile launchers of ICBMs located within restricted areas specified by the requesting Party. The number of road-mobile launchers of ICBMs based at the restricted areas specified in each such request shall not exceed ten percent of the total number of deployed road-mobile launchers of ICBMs of the requested Party, and such launchers shall be contained within one ICBM base for road-mobile launchers of ICBMs. For each specified restricted area, the roofs of fixed structures for road-mobile launchers of ICBMs shall be open for the duration of a display. The road-mobile launchers of ICBMs located within the restricted area shall be displayed either located next to or moved halfway out of such fixed structures; [RF MOU Annex A]

   (b) a display in the open of the rail-mobile launchers of ICBMs located at parking sites specified by the requesting Party. Such launchers shall be displayed by removing the entire train from its fixed structure and locating the train within the rail garrison. The number of rail-mobile launchers of ICBMs subject to display pursuant to each such request shall include all such launchers located at no more than eight parking sites, provided that no more than two parking sites may be requested within any one rail garrison in any one request. Requests concerning specific parking sites shall include the designation for each parking site as provided for in Annex A to the Memorandum of Understanding; and [RF MOU Annex A]

   (c) a display in the open of all heavy bombers and former heavy bombers located within one air base specified by the requesting Party, except those heavy bombers and former heavy bombers that are not readily movable due to maintenance or operations. Such heavy bombers and former heavy bombers shall be displayed by removing the entire airplane from its fixed structure, if any, and locating the airplane within the air base. Those heavy bombers and former heavy bombers at the air base specified by the requesting Party that are not readily movable due to maintenance or operations shall be specified by the requested Party in a notification provided in accordance with paragraph 2 of Section V of the Notification Protocol. Such a notification shall be provided no later than 12 hours after the request for display has been made.

2. Road-mobile launchers of ICBMs, rail-mobile launchers of ICBMs, heavy bombers, and former heavy bombers subject to each request pursuant to paragraph 1 of this Article shall be displayed in open view without using concealment measures. Each Party shall have the right to make seven such requests each year, but shall not request a display at any particular ICBM base for road-mobile launchers of ICBMs, any particular parking site, or any particular air base more than two times each year. A Party shall have the right to request, in any single request, only a display of road-mobile launchers of ICBMs, a display of rail-mobile launchers of ICBMs, or a display of heavy bombers and former heavy bombers. A display shall begin no later than 12 hours after the request is made and shall continue until 18 hours have elapsed from the time that the request was made. If the requested Party cannot conduct a display due to circumstances brought about by force majeure, it shall provide notification to the requesting Party in accordance with paragraph 3 of Section V of the Notification Protocol, and the display shall be cancelled. In such a case, the number of requests to which the requesting Party is entitled shall not be reduced.

3. A request for cooperative measures shall not be made for a facility that has been designated for inspection until such an inspection has been completed and the inspectors have departed the facility. A facility for which cooperative measures have been requested shall not be designated for inspection until the cooperative measures have been completed or until notification has been provided in accordance with paragraph 3 of Section V of the Notification Protocol.

ARTICLE XIII

1. Each Party shall have the right to conduct exercise dispersal of deployed mobile launchers of ICBMs and their associated missiles from restricted areas or rail garrisons. Such an exercise dispersal may involve either road-mobile launchers of ICBMs or rail-mobile launchers of ICBMs, or both road-mobile launchers of ICBMs and rail-mobile launchers of ICBMs. Exercise dispersals of deployed mobile launchers of ICBMs and their associated missiles shall be conducted as provided for below:

   (a) An exercise dispersal shall be considered to have begun as of the date and time specified in the notification provided in accordance with paragraph 11 of Section II of the Notification Protocol.

   (b) An exercise dispersal shall be considered to be completed as of the date and time specified in the notification provided in accordance with paragraph 12 of Section II of the Notification Protocol.

   (c) Those ICBM bases for mobile launchers of ICBMs specified in the notification provided in accordance with paragraph 11 of Section II of the Notification Protocol shall be considered to be involved in an exercise dispersal.

(d) When an exercise dispersal begins, deployed mobile launchers of ICBMs and their associated missiles engaged in a routine movement from a restricted area or rail garrison of an ICBM base for mobile launchers of ICBMs that is involved in such a dispersal shall be considered to be part of the dispersal.

(e) When an exercise dispersal begins, deployed mobile launchers of ICBMs and their associated missiles engaged in a relocation from a restricted area or rail garrisons of an ICBM base for mobile launchers of ICBMs that is involved in such a dispersal shall continue to be considered to be engaged in a relocation. Notification of the completion of the relocation shall be provided in accordance with paragraph 10 of Section II of the Notification Protocol, unless notification of the completion of the relocation was provided in accordance with paragraph 12 of Section II of the Notification Protocol.

(f) During an exercise dispersal, all deployed mobile launchers of ICBMs and their associated missiles that depart a restricted area or rail garrison of an ICBM base for mobile launchers of ICBMs involved in such a dispersal shall be considered to be part of the dispersal, except for such launchers and missiles that relocate to a facility outside their associated ICBM base during such a dispersal.

(g) An exercise dispersal shall be completed no later than 30 days after it begins.

(h) Exercise dispersals shall not be conducted:

  (i)   more than two times in any period of two calendar years;
  (ii) during the entire period of time provided for baseline data inspections;
  (iii) from a new ICBM base for mobile launchers of ICBMs until a new facility inspection has been conducted or until the period of time provided for such an inspection has expired; or
  (iv) from an ICBM base for mobile launchers of ICBMs that has been designated for a data update inspection or reentry vehicle inspection, until completion of such an inspection.
  (v)   If a notification of an exercise dispersal has been provided in accordance with paragraph 11 of Section II of the Notification Protocol, the other Party shall not have the right to designate for data update inspection or reentry vehicle inspection an ICBM base for mobile launchers of ICBMs involved in such a dispersal, or to request cooperative measures for such an ICBM base, until the completion of such a dispersal.

. . .

ARTICLE XIV

1. Each Party shall have the right to conduct operational dispersals of deployed mobile launchers of ICBMs and their associated missiles, ballistic missile submarines, and heavy bombers. There shall be no limit on the number and

duration of operational dispersals, and there shall be no limit on the number of deployed mobile launchers of ICBMs and their associated missiles, ballistic missile submarines, or heavy bombers involved in such dispersals. When an operational dispersal begins, all strategic offensive arms of a Party shall be considered to be part of the dispersal. Operational dispersals shall be conducted as provided for below: [Agreed State 7]

. . .

FOR THE UNITED STATES OF AMERICA: George Bush
President of the United States of America
FOR THE UNION OF SOVIET SOCIALIST REPUBLICS: M. Gorbachev
President of the Union of Soviet Socialist Republics

FURTHER READING

Gibbs, D. (2009) *First Do No Harm: Humanitarian Interventions and the Destruction of Yugoslavia*. Nashville, TN: Vanderbilt University Press.
Glenny, M. (2001) *The Balkans: Nationalism, War, and the Great Powers, 1804–1999*. New York: Penguin.
Gourevitch, P. (1999) *We Wish to Inform You That Tomorrow We Will Be Killed with Our Families: Stories from Rwanda*. New York: Picador.
Jensen, L. (1988) *Bargaining for National Security: The Postwar Disarmament Negotiations*. Columbia: University of South Carolina Press.
Johnstone, D. (2003) *Fool's Crusade: Yugoslavia, NATO, and Western Delusions*. New York: Monthly Review Press.
Kinzer, S. (2003) *All the Shah's Men: An American Coup and the Roots of Middle East Terror*. New York: John Wiley and Sons.
Kinzer, S. (2006) *Overthrow: America's Century of Regime Change from Hawaii to Iraq*. New York: Time Books.
Parenti, M. (2002) *To Kill a Nation: The Attack on Yugoslavia*. New York: Verso.
Smith, J. E. (1992) *George Bush's War*. New York: Henry Holt.

8

GEORGE W. BUSH: EMPIRE

INTRODUCTION

George W. Bush won the disputed 2000 election and entered the White House with little interest or experience in foreign policy. Setting a course for a more domestic-oriented presidency, Bush promised a more humble foreign policy, one that would not be involved in Clinton-like multilateralism or nation-building efforts. This changed on September 11, 2001, when 19 terrorists hijacked four domestic flights and used three of the jetliners to attack the Pentagon, outside of Washington, D.C., and the World Trade Center in New York City. (The fourth hijacked plane, bound for San Francisco, crashed in a field in southwestern Pennsylvania when passengers realized what was occurring and stormed the cockpit; the hijackers had diverted the flight toward Washington, D.C.) While the group behind the attacks, al Qaeda, was largely unknown to a reeling American public, it was well known to national security analysts because of its previous attacks on U.S. embassies and naval ships during the Clinton administration. The attacks of September 11, 2001, forced the Bush administration to focus on foreign policy, and it did so in ways that remain controversial.

The immediate response to 9/11 was to prepare for war in Afghanistan, the country that provided safe haven to al Qaeda leaders such as Osama bin Laden. Afghanistan was ruled by the Taliban, many of whom were given aid by the Reagan administration in the 1980s because they were seen as "freedom fighters" resisting the Soviet invasion. Operation "Enduring Freedom" began on October 7, 2001. With the United States leading a multinational coalition, including many NATO allies who joined the effort when NATO invoked Article 5 of its charter. Afghanistan was invaded, and the Taliban were quickly removed from power. The initial victories soon turned into a stalemate as the United States failed to find, capture, or kill Osama bin Laden, and many Taliban leaders escaped by retreating into Pakistan's northwest tribal regions, where they remain today. Nevertheless, President Bush declared victory in Afghanistan in his State of the Union address and, more boldly, he declared a "War on Terror" that would be undertaken on domestic and international fronts, seeking terrorists and the regimes that harbor them. In this War on Terror, President Bush said to the world, "you are either with us or you are against us."

As questions emerged regarding the fate of Taliban and al Qaeda fighters captured in Afghanistan, the Bush administration turned to some of its most controversial tactics. On November 13, 2001, President Bush issued a military order designating those detained by the United States in Afghanistan as "unlawful combatants," a term previously unknown in international law and key agreements such as the Geneva Conventions, and ordered their detention and prosecution in military commissions established by the U.S. military. In 2006, in *Hamdan v. Rumsfeld*, the U.S. Supreme Court declared these military commissions unconstitutional, but the U.S. Congress quickly authorized them in the Military Commissions Act of 2006. This act, however, was declared unconstitutional by the Supreme Court in 2008, in *Boumediene v. Bush*. Regardless of the domestic political wrangling, from 2001 to the present, most people detained by the U.S. military as unlawful combatants have been held in detention facilities at Baghram airbase in Afghanistan, Guantánamo Bay, Cuba, and other "black sites" around the world.

While some questioned the indefinite detention and treatment of unlawful combatants as a failure of the United States to adhere to human rights laws, especially if detainees were found innocent or were tortured, most politicians were in no mood to be "soft" in the fight against terrorism. The U.S. Congress quickly passed the USA PATRIOT Act of 2001. (The name is capitalized because it is an acronym for its official title: "Uniting and Strengthening America by Providing Appropriate Tools Required to Intercept and Obstruct Terrorism"; the act is more often referred to simply as the Patriot Act.) This law increased the power of the executive branch and federal agencies to combat terrorism by using techniques, such as data mining and electronic surveillance, that critics saw as a violation of civil liberties because the process lacked sufficient judicial oversight. In 2006 Congress extended the Patriot Act with some stronger protections for civil liberties.

As the Afghanistan war became a stalemate, the Taliban regrouped in Pakistan and started attacking U.S. positions in Afghanistan. Despite intelligence that located Osama bin Laden, the United States failed to capture him. At this point, the Bush administration sought to expand its War on Terror by focusing on Iraq. Saddam Hussein's regime, the Bush administration claimed, was actively supporting terrorists, had used weapons of mass destruction against its Kurdish population in the past, and possessed weapons of mass destruction that threatened regional and global peace and stability. The Persian Gulf War had left Hussein in power; this time, President Bush decided to force "regime change" in Iraq. Seeking proof of Iraq's weapons of mass destruction, the United States sent former Ambassador Joseph C. Wilson IV to Niger to find out whether Iraq had attempted to purchase low-grade uranium, or "yellowcake," in order to process it into weapons-grade material. Wilson reported back that the story was false, but after President Bush repeated the charge nearly a year later in his 2003 State of the Union address, Wilson published an op-ed article in the New York Times suggesting that the White House was manipulating intelligence to justify its policies. Shortly thereafter it was leaked to the press that Wilson's wife, Valerie Plame, worked for the CIA. Critics saw this illegal revelation as political retribution for undermining the Bush administration's claims. The scandal led to years of investigation into the source of the leak, resulting in the conviction of Lewis "Scooter" Libby, Vice President Cheney's chief of staff, on perjury charges. President Bush later commuted his sentence but elected not to pardon him, and questions remained about other sources of the leak.

After months of claiming that Iraq possessed weapons of mass destruction and implying that Saddam Hussein was involved in the 9/11 attacks, the Bush administration was ready to invade Iraq. There was enough domestic opposition, however, that in 2002 President Bush had to seek a U.S. congressional resolution for the use of force in Iraq. Administration officials gave several speeches in which they repeated their claims that Iraq possessed weapons of mass destruction and represented an imminent threat. Further, they justified a doctrine of "preemptive war" against Iraq on grounds that the United States should not wait for Iraq to use those weapons of mass destruction but should instead proactively intervene before they were used. This was dubbed the "one percent doctrine" after Vice President Cheney's assertion that even if there was only a 1 percent chance that a regime possessed weapons of mass destruction, the United States was justified in taking them out rather than waiting for them to be used against the United States or its allies.

The Bush administration also faced strong global opposition to an invasion of Iraq. Many countries wanted UN weapons inspectors to have more time to finish their work. The United States at first wanted to assuage these concerns and gave the UN inspections team more time to look for weapons of mass destruction in Iraq.

Having previously been expelled from Iraq for spying, the UN Verification and Inspection Team (UNMOVIC), led by Hans Blix, as well as the International Atomic Energy Agency (IAEA), led by Mohamed ElBaradei, concluded in 2003 that there was no evidence that Iraq possessed weapons of mass destruction.

The Bush administration made a last attempt to persuade the UN to authorize the use of force against Iraq with a now-famous presentation by Secretary of State Colin Powell. Rumored to be skeptical of an invasion but highly respected in domestic and international circles, Powell argued that the Iraqi regime did in fact possess weapons of mass destruction and actively supported terrorism. Finally, President Bush also gave a speech to the UN, in which he appealed to the international community for its support while also stating that when it came to defending itself against rogue nations, the United States did not need or seek anyone's approval. President Bush pieced together a "coalition of the willing," but this paled in comparison to the multinational coalition his father was able to assemble for the Persian Gulf War of 1991.

On March 19, 2003, the opening salvo of the war took place, with attacks on Dora farm, where Saddam Hussein was reported to be visiting his family. The air strikes failed to kill him or his sons. The U.S. strategy, famously called "shock and awe," aimed at decapitating the Iraqi leadership and bringing the war to a swift end. Within a month, U.S. and coalition forces were in Baghdad, and it seemed that Iraq would not be any more a threat in 2003 than it had been in 1991. However, with the Iraqi military command on the run and Saddam Hussein nowhere to be found, mass looting and rioting broke out in Baghdad and other cities while the U.S. military seemed unwilling to impose order. On May 1, 2003, President Bush was flown by a naval jet to the aircraft carrier USS *Abraham Lincoln* and famously declared that all major combat operations were over in Iraq and the U.S. was victorious.

In hindsight, this declaration was premature. Domestically, critics argued that the United States invaded with enough troops to win the war but not enough to keep the peace. The Bush administration assembled a Coalition Provisional Authority (CPA) to govern Iraq, but many who worked in it lacked any expertise regarding Iraqi or Middle Eastern politics. U.S. forces succeeded in killing Saddam Hussein's sons, and on December 13, 2003, found Saddam Hussein hiding near his birthplace in Tikrit. The CPA eventually transferred authority to an interim Iraqi president and established a timetable for future elections, but by then Iraq had imploded into a brutal civil war that was fueled by a Sunni insurgency, the disbanding of the Iraqi military, and the emergence of al Qaeda in Iraq, led by Abu Musab al-Zarqawi. Ironically, just as Dick Cheney predicted in 1991 when he was the Secretary of Defense, when the Iraqi regime was removed, a massive bloodletting and civil war between the Sunni minority and Shia majority ensued, this time with U.S. troops caught in the crossfire.

The search for weapons of mass destruction soon found nothing, and the mission in Iraq was redefined as an effort to bring democracy to Iraq, to serve as an example for the Middle East. These claims were undermined when in 2004 photographs of the humiliation and abuse of Iraqi detainees at the Abu Ghraib prison were made public. This scandal undermined U.S. claims of promoting democracy and human rights and was used to recruit new insurgents to fight the U.S. occupation.

As the Iraqi war descended into chaos, domestic and international critics of President Bush openly argued that the United States was engaged in an imperialist war to control oil reserves in the Middle East and that the search for weapons of mass destruction was only a pretext. The Bush administration found itself increasingly isolated but remained defiant, asserting that the invasion was the correct choice. As more U.S. troops were killed by insurgents, President Bush faced calls to withdraw troops. In his words, President Bush refused to "cut and run." Instead, in a last effort to bring stability, in 2007 President Bush authorized a "surge" that sent an additional 30,000 U.S. troops to help pacify the Iraq and create a stable climate for a political solution. As he left office, this strategy seemed to have worked. However, it also vindicated critics who in 2003 argued that the U.S. invasion should have involved 500,000 to 600,000 troops to prevent the outbreak of civil war after the initial invasion.

The war in Iraq diverted U.S. attention and resources away from the war in Afghanistan, which by the end of the Bush administration was facing a resurgent al Qaeda and Taliban. Further, the War on Terror led the Bush administration to become involved in several other nations, such as Pakistan, the Philippines, and Somalia, in order to battle regional Islamic terrorist groups that sought to expand the reach of al Qaeda. In a controversial move, the Bush administration expanded the "extraordinary rendition" program, a program initiated under the Clinton administration, by which the United States abducted, detained, and in some cases tortured suspected terrorists in third countries and secret CIA prisons. This policy, along with the ongoing detention of unlawful combatants at Guantánamo Bay, increasingly isolated the United States on the world stage. Critics saw these policies not just as violations of human rights but as politically counterproductive problems because they gave al Qaeda new recruitment tools.

Did You Know?

9/11 and NATO

The North Atlantic Treaty Organization (NATO) was an alliance among Canada, the United States, and several Western European countries to defend one another against communism. NATO was founded in 1949, when the enemy was the Soviet Union. After the collapse of the Berlin Wall and the dissolution of the Soviet Union, NATO remained—without an enemy, and, some argued, without a purpose. The 1990s were a particularly difficult time for NATO because of its lack of rationale and its expansion eastward, which was perceived as an aggressive move by Russia. In an attempt to shore up support and carve out an area of operation, NATO was used in the bombing of Serbia in 1999 during the Kosovo war, but questions regarding NATO's usefulness persisted.

On September 11, 2001, the United States was attacked in an unprecedented terrorist attack that killed approximately 3,000 people. For the first time in its history, NATO invoked Article 5 of its charter: An attack on a member is an attack on all members. In 2003, by a unanimous vote, NATO members approved the creation of a NATO force, the International Security Assistance Force, to participate in the war in Afghanistan. NATO has a 64,000-strong force in Afghanistan. The largest casualty figures, with the exception of those sustained by the United States, are those of the United Kingdom, Canada, and France.

- **Document: Public Law 107-40: Joint Resolution: Authorization for Use of Military Force**
- **Date:** September 18, 2001
- **Significance:** In this document, the president is given the authorization to use force against those who perpetrated the attacks of 9/11/2001, as well as against any regime that harbored them.
- **Source:** 107th Congress (2001–2002), S.J. Res. 23, Public Law 107-40.

JOINT RESOLUTION TO AUTHORIZE THE USE OF UNITED STATES ARMED FORCES AGAINST THOSE RESPONSIBLE FOR THE RECENT ATTACKS LAUNCHED AGAINST THE UNITED STATES

Whereas, on September 11, 2001, acts of treacherous violence were committed against the United States and its citizens; and

Whereas, such acts render it both necessary and appropriate that the United States exercise its rights to self-defense and to protect United States citizens both at home and abroad; and

Whereas, in light of the threat to the national security and foreign policy of the United States posed by these grave acts of violence; and

Whereas, such acts continue to pose an unusual and extraordinary threat to the national security and foreign policy of the United States; and

Whereas, the President has authority under the Constitution to take action to deter and prevent acts of international terrorism against the United States: Now, therefore, be it Resolved by the Senate and House of Representatives of the United States of America in Congress ...

SECTION 1. SHORT TITLE

This joint resolution may be cited as the "Authorization for Use of Military Force".

SEC. 2. AUTHORIZATION FOR USE OF UNITED STATES ARMED FORCES.

(a) In General. That the President is authorized to use all necessary and appropriate force against those nations, organizations, or persons he determines planned, authorized, committed, or aided the terrorist attacks that occurred on September 11, 2001, or harbored such organizations or persons, in order to prevent any future acts of international terrorism against the United States by such nations, organizations or persons.

(b) War Powers Resolution Requirements.

(1) Specific statutory authorization. Consistent with section 8(a)(1) of the War Powers Resolution, the Congress declares that this section is intended to constitute specific statutory authorization within the meaning of section 5(b) of the War Powers Resolution.

(2) Applicability of other requirements. Nothing in this resolution supercedes any requirement of the War Powers Resolution.

Approved September 18, 2001.
LEGISLATIVE HISTORY—S.J. Res. 23 (H.J. Res. 64):

- **Document: USA PATRIOT Act**
- **Date:** October 26, 2001
- **Significance:** This law significantly enhances the power of executive agencies and law enforcement in their fight against terror.

- **Source:** USA PATRIOT Act of 2001, Public Law 107-56 (October 26, 2001).

UNITING AND STRENGTHENING AMERICA BY PROVIDING APPROPRIATE TOOLS REQUIRED TO INTERCEPT AND OBSTRUCT TERRORISM (USA PATRIOT ACT) ACT 2001

Public Law 107-56
107th Congress

An Act To deter and punish terrorist acts in the United States and around the world, to enhance law enforcement investigatory tools, and for other purposes. Be it enacted by the Senate and House of Representatives of the United States of America in Congress assembled,

SECTION 1. SHORT TITLE AND TABLE OF CONTENTS
(a) Short Title. This Act may be cited as the "Uniting and Strengthening America by Providing Appropriate Tools Required to Intercept and Obstruct Terrorism (USA PATRIOT ACT) Act of 2001".

. . .

TITLE I—ENHANCING DOMESTIC SECURITY AGAINST TERRORISM
SEC. 101. COUNTERTERRORISM FUND

(a) Establishment; Availability. There is hereby established in the Treasury of the United States a separate fund to be known as the "Counterterrorism Fund", amounts in which shall remain available without fiscal year limitation—

(1) to reimburse any Department of Justice component for any costs incurred in connection with—

(A) reestablishing the operational capability of an office or facility that has been damaged or destroyed as the result of any domestic or international terrorism incident;

(B) providing support to counter, investigate, or prosecute domestic or international terrorism, including, without limitation, paying rewards in connection with these activities; and

Senator Patrick Leahy takes a photograph of President George W. Bush signing the USA Patriot Act during a ceremony in the White House on October 26, 2001. (Harry Hamburg/NY Daily News Archive via Getty Images)

(C) conducting terrorism threat assessments of Federal agencies and their facilities; and

(2) to reimburse any department or agency of the Federal Government for any costs incurred in connection with detaining in foreign countries individuals accused of acts of terrorism that violate the laws of the United States.

(b) No Effect on Prior Appropriations.—Subsection (a) shall not be construed to affect the amount or availability of any appropriation to the Counterterrorism Fund made before the date of the enactment of this Act.

. . .

SEC. 105. EXPANSION OF NATIONAL ELECTRONIC CRIME TASK FORCE INITIATIVE

The Director of the United States Secret Service shall take appropriate actions to develop a national network of electronic crime task forces, based on the New York Electronic Crimes Task Force model, throughout the United States, for the purpose of preventing, detecting, and investigating various forms of electronic crimes, including potential terrorist attacks against critical infrastructure and financial payment systems.

SEC. 106. PRESIDENTIAL AUTHORITY

Section 203 of the International Emergency Powers Act (50 U.S.C. 1702) is amended—

(1) in subsection (a)(1)—

(A) at the end of subparagraph (A) (flush to that subparagraph), by striking "; and" and inserting a comma and the following:

"by any person, or with respect to any property, subject to the jurisdiction of the United States";

(B) in subparagraph (B)—

    (i)   by inserting "block during the pendency of an investigation" after "investigate"; and

    (ii) by striking "interest;" and inserting "interest by any person, or with respect to any property, subject to the jurisdiction of the United States; and";

(C) by striking "by any person, or with respect to any property, subject to the jurisdiction of the United States"; and

(D) by inserting at the end the following:

"(C) when the United States is engaged in armed hostilities or has been attacked by a foreign country or foreign nationals, confiscate any property, subject to the jurisdiction of the United States, of any foreign person, foreign organization, or foreign country that he deter-mines has planned, authorized, aided, or engaged in such hostilities or attacks against the United States; and all right, title, and interest in any property so confiscated shall vest, when, as, and upon the terms directed by the President, in such agency or person as the President may designate from time to time, and upon such terms and conditions as the President may prescribe, such interest or property shall be held, used, administered, liquidated, sold, or otherwise dealt with in the interest of and for the benefit of the United States, and such desig-nated agency or person may perform any and all acts incident to the accomplishment or furtherance of these purposes."; and

(2) by inserting at the end the following:

"(c) Classified Information.—In any judicial review of a determina-tion made under this section, if the determination was based on clas-sified information (as defined in section 1(a) of the Classified Information Procedures Act) such information may be submitted to the reviewing court ex parte and in camera. This subsection does not confer or imply any right to judicial review.".

TITLE II—ENHANCED SURVEILLANCE PROCEDURES

SEC. 201. AUTHORITY TO INTERCEPT WIRE, ORAL, AND ELECTRONIC COMMUNICATIONS RELATING TO TERRORISM

. . .

SEC. 207. DURATION OF FISA SURVEILLANCE OF NON-UNITED STATES PERSONS WHO ARE AGENTS OF A FOREIGN POWER

(a) Duration.—

(1) Surveillance.—Section 105(e)(1) of the Foreign Intelligence Surveil-lance Act of 1978 (50 U.S.C. 1805(e)(1)) is amended by—

(A) inserting "(A)" after "except that"; and
(B) inserting before the period the following: ", and (B) an order under this Act for a surveillance targeted against an agent of a foreign power, as defined in section 101(b)(1)(A) may be for the period specified in the application or for 120 days, whichever is less".

(2) Physical Search.—Section 304(d)(1) of the Foreign Intelligence Sur-veillance Act of 1978 (50 U.S.C. 1824(d)(1)) is amended by—

(A) striking "forty-five" and inserting "90";
(B) inserting "(A)" after "except that"; and
(C) inserting before the period the following: ", and (B) an order under this section for a physical search targeted against an agent of a for-eign power as defined in section \101(b)(1)(A) may be for the period specified in the application or for 120 days, whichever is less".

(b) Extension.—

    (1) In general.—Section 105(d)(2) of the Foreign Intelligence Surveillance Act of 1978 (50 U.S.C. 1805(d)(2)) is amended by—

        (A) inserting "(A)" after "except that"; and

        (B) inserting before the period the following: ", and (B) an extension of an order under this Act for a surveillance targeted against an agent of a foreign power as defined in section 101(b)(1)(A) may be for a period not to exceed 1 year".

    (2) Defined term.—Section 304(d)(2) of the Foreign Intelligence Surveillance Act of 1978 (50 U.S.C. 1824(d)(2) is amended by inserting after "not a United States person," the following: "or against an agent of a foreign power as defined in section 101(b)(1)(A),".

. . .

SEC. 210. SCOPE OF SUBPOENAS FOR RECORDS OF ELECTRONIC COMMUNICATIONS

Section 2703(c)(2) of title 18, United States Code, as redesignated by section 212, is amended—

    (1) by striking "entity the name, address, local and long distance telephone toll billing records, telephone number or other subscriber number or identity, and length of service of a subscriber" and inserting the following: "entity the—

"(A) name;

"(B) address;

"(C) local and long distance telephone connection records, or records of session times and durations;

"(D) length of service (including start date) and types of service utilized;

"(E) telephone or instrument number or other subscriber number or identity, including any temporarily assigned network address; and

"(F) means and source of payment for such service (including any credit card or bank account number), of a subscriber"; and

    (2) by striking "and the types of services the subscriber or customer utilized,".

. . .

SEC. 215. ACCESS TO RECORDS AND OTHER ITEMS UNDER THE FOREIGN INTELLIGENCE SURVEILLANCE ACT

Title V of the Foreign Intelligence Surveillance Act of 1978 (50 U.S.C. 1861 et seq.) is amended by striking sections 501 through 503 and inserting the following:

"SEC. 501. ACCESS TO CERTAIN BUSINESS RECORDS FOR FOREIGN INTELLIGENCE AND INTERNATIONAL TERRORISM INVESTIGATIONS

"(a)(1) The Director of the Federal Bureau of Investigation or a designee of the Director (whose rank shall be no lower than Assistant Special Agent in Charge) may make an application for an order requiring the production of any tangible things (including books, records, papers, documents, and other items) for an investigation to protect against international terrorism or clandestine intelligence activities, provided that such investigation of a United States person is not conducted solely upon the basis of activities protected by the first amendment to the Constitution.

"(2) An investigation conducted under this section shall—

"(A) be conducted under guidelines approved by the Attorney General under Executive Order 12333 (or a successor order); and
"(B) not be conducted of a United States person solely upon the basis of activities protected by the first amendment to the Constitution of the United States.

"(b) Each application under this section—

"(1) shall be made to—

"(A) a judge of the court established by section 103(a); or
"(B) a United States Magistrate Judge under chapter 43 of title 28, United States Code, who is publicly designated by the Chief Justice of the United States to have the power to hear applications and grant orders for the production of tangible things under this section on behalf of a judge of that court; and

"(2) shall specify that the records concerned are sought for an authorized investigation conducted in accordance with subsection (a)(2) to obtain foreign intelligence information not concerning a United States person or to protect against international terrorism or clandestine intelligence activities.

"(c)(1) Upon an application made pursuant to this section, the judge shall enter an ex parte order as requested, or as modified, approving the release of records if the judge finds that the application meets the requirements of this section.

"(2) An order under this subsection shall not disclose that it is issued for purposes of an investigation described in subsection (a).

"(d) No person shall disclose to any other person (other than those persons necessary to produce the tangible things under this section) that the Federal Bureau of Investigation has sought or obtained tangible things under this section.

"(e) A person who, in good faith, produces tangible things under an order pursuant to this section shall not be liable to any other person for such production. Such production shall not be deemed to constitute a waiver of any privilege in any other proceeding or context."

. . .

TITLE III—INTERNATIONAL MONEY LAUNDERING ABATEMENT AND
ANTI-TERRORIST FINANCING ACT OF 2001

SEC. 301. SHORT TITLE

This title may be cited as the "International Money Laundering Abatement and
Financial Anti-Terrorism Act of 2001".

SEC. 302. FINDINGS AND PURPOSES

(a) Findings.—The Congress finds that—

(1) money laundering, estimated by the International Monetary Fund to
amount to between 2 and 5 percent of global gross domestic product, which
is at least $600,000,000,000 annually, provides the financial fuel that per-
mits transnational criminal enterprises to conduct and expand their operations to the detriment of the safety and security of American citizens;

(2) money laundering, and the defects in financial transparency on which
money launderers rely, are critical to the financing of global terrorism
and the provision of funds for terrorist attacks;

(3) money launderers subvert legitimate financial mechanisms and banking
relationships by using them as protective covering for the movement of
criminal proceeds and the financing of crime and terrorism, and, by so
doing, can threaten the safety of United States citizens and undermine
the integrity of United States financial institutions and of the global
financial and trading systems upon which prosperity and growth depend;

(4) certain jurisdictions outside of the United States that offer "offshore"
banking and related facilities designed to provide anonymity, coupled
with weak financial supervisory and enforcement regimes, provide
essential tools to disguise ownership and movement of criminal funds,
derived from, or used to commit, offenses ranging from narcotics trafficking, terrorism, arms smuggling, and trafficking in human beings, to
financial frauds that prey on law-abiding citizens;

(5) transactions involving such offshore jurisdictions make it difficult for
law enforcement officials and regulators to follow the trail of money
earned by criminals, organized international criminal enterprises, and
global terrorist organizations;

(6) correspondent banking facilities are one of the banking mechanisms susceptible in some circumstances to manipulation by foreign banks to permit the laundering of funds by hiding the identity of real parties in
interest to financial transactions;

(7) private banking services can be susceptible to manipulation by money
launderers, for example corrupt foreign government officials, particularly if those services include the creation of offshore accounts and
facilities for large personal funds transfers to channel funds into
accounts around the globe;

(8) United States anti-money laundering efforts are impeded by outmoded
and inadequate statutory provisions that make investigations, prosecutions, and forfeitures more difficult, particularly in cases in which money
laundering involves foreign persons, foreign banks, or foreign countries;

(9) the ability to mount effective counter-measures to international money launderers requires national, as well as bilateral and multilateral action, using tools specially designed for that effort; and

(10) the Basle Committee on Banking Regulation and Supervisory Practices and the Financial Action Task Force on Money Laundering, of both of which the United States is a member, have each adopted international anti-money laundering principles and recommendations.

(b) Purposes.—The purposes of this title are—

(1) to increase the strength of United States measures to prevent, detect, and prosecute international money laundering and the financing of terrorism;

(2) to ensure that—

   (A) banking transactions and financial relationships and the conduct of such transactions and relationships, do not contravene the purposes of subchapter II of chapter 53 of title 31, United States Code, section 21 of the Federal Deposit Insurance Act, or chapter 2 of title I of Public Law 91-508 (84 Stat. 1116), or facilitate the evasion of any such provision; and

   (B) the purposes of such provisions of law continue to be fulfilled, and such provisions of law are effectively and efficiently administered;

(3) to strengthen the provisions put into place by the Money Laundering Control Act of 1986 (18 U.S.C. 981 note), especially with respect to crimes by non-United States nationals and foreign financial institutions;

(4) to provide a clear national mandate for subjecting to special scrutiny those foreign jurisdictions, financial institutions operating outside of the United States, and classes of international transactions or types of accounts that pose particular, identifiable opportunities for criminal abuse;

(5) to provide the Secretary of the Treasury (in this title referred to as the "Secretary") with broad discretion, subject to the safeguards provided by the Administrative Procedure Act under title 5, United States Code, to take measures tailored to the particular money laundering problems presented by specific foreign jurisdictions, financial institutions operating outside of the United States, and classes of international transactions or types of accounts;

(6) to ensure that the employment of such measures by the Secretary permits appropriate opportunity for comment by affected financial institutions;

(7) to provide guidance to domestic financial institutions on particular foreign jurisdictions, financial institutions operating outside of the United States, and classes of international transactions that are of primary money laundering concern to the United States Government;

(8) to ensure that the forfeiture of any assets in connection with the antiterrorist efforts of the United States permitsfor adequate challenge consistent with providing due process rights;

(9) to clarify the terms of the safe harbor from civil liability for filing suspicious activity reports;

(10) to strengthen the authority of the Secretary to issue and administer geographic targeting orders, and to clarify that violations of such orders or any other requirement imposed under the authority contained in chapter 2 of title I of Public Law 91-508 and subchapters II and III of chapter 53 of title 31, United States Code, may result in criminal and civil penalties;

(11) to ensure that all appropriate elements of the financial services industry are subject to appropriate requirements to report potential money laundering transactions to proper authorities, and that jurisdictional disputes do not hinder examination of compliance by financial institutions with relevant reporting requirements;

(12) to strengthen the ability of financial institutions to maintain the integrity of their employee population; and

(13) to strengthen measures to prevent the use of the United States financial system for personal gain by corrupt foreign officials and to facilitate the repatriation of any stolen assets to the citizens of countries to whom such assets belong.

...

SEC. 371. BULK CASH SMUGGLING INTO OR OUT OF THE UNITED STATES

(a) Findings.—The Congress finds the following:

(1) Effective enforcement of the currency reporting requirements of subchapter II of chapter 53 of title 31, United States Code, and the regulations prescribed under such subchapter, has forced drug dealers and other criminals engaged in cash-based businesses to avoid using traditional financial institutions.

(2) In their effort to avoid using traditional financial institutions, drug dealers and other criminals are forced to move large quantities of currency in bulk form to and through the airports, border crossings, and other ports of entry where the currency can be smuggled out of the United States and placed in a foreign financial institution or sold on the black market.

(3) The transportation and smuggling of cash in bulk form may now be the most common form of money laundering, and the movement of large sums of cash is one of the most reliable warning signs of drug trafficking, terrorism, money laundering, racketeering, tax evasion and similar crimes.

(4) The intentional transportation into or out of the United States of large amounts of currency or monetary instruments, in a manner designed to circumvent the mandatory reporting provisions of subchapter II of chapter 53 of title 31, United States Code, is the equivalent of, and creates the same harm as, the smuggling of goods.

(5) The arrest and prosecution of bulk cash smugglers are important parts of law enforcement's effort to stop the laundering of criminal proceeds, but

the couriers who attempt to smuggle the cash out of the United States are typically low-level employees of large criminal organizations, and thus are easily replaced. Accordingly, only the confiscation of the smuggled bulk cash can effectively break the cycle of criminal activity of which the laundering of the bulk cash is a critical part.

(6) The current penalties for violations of the currency reporting requirements are insufficient to provide a deterrent to the laundering of criminal proceeds. In particular, in cases where the only criminal violation under current law is a reporting offense, the law does not adequately provide for the confiscation of smuggled currency. In contrast, if the smuggling of bulk cash were itself an offense, the cash could be confiscated as the corpus delicti of the smuggling offense.

(b) Purposes.—The purposes of this section are—

(1) to make the act of smuggling bulk cash itself a criminal offense;
(2) to authorize forfeiture of any cash or instruments of the smuggling offense; and
(3) to emphasize the seriousness of the act of bulk cash smuggling.

(c) Enactment of Bulk Cash Smuggling Offense.—Subchapter II of chapter 53 of title 31, United States Code, is amended by adding at the end the following:

"Sec. 5332. Bulk cash smuggling into or out of the United States

"(a) Criminal Offense.—

"(1) In general.—Whoever, with the intent to evade a currency reporting requirement under section 5316, knowingly conceals more than $10,000 in currency or other monetary instruments on the person of such individual or in any conveyance, article of luggage, merchandise, or other container, and transports or transfers or attempts to transport or transfer such currency or monetary instruments from a place within the United States to a place outside of the United States, or from a place outside the United States to a place within the United States, shall be guilty of a currency smuggling offense and subject to punishment pursuant to subsection (b).

"(2) Concealment on person.—For purposes of this section, the concealment of currency on the person of any individual includes concealment in any article of clothing worn by the individual or in any luggage, backpack, or other container worn or carried by such individual.

"(b) Penalty.—

"(1) Term of imprisonment.—A person convicted of a currency smuggling offense under subsection (a), or a conspiracy to commit such offense, shall be imprisoned for not more than 5 years.

"(2) Forfeiture.—In addition, the court, in imposing sentence under paragraph (1), shall order that the defendant forfeit to the United States, any property, real or personal, involved in the offense, and any property traceable to such property, subject to subsection (d) of this section.

"(3) Procedure.—The seizure, restraint, and forfeiture of property under this section shall be governed by section 413 of the Controlled Substances Act.

"(4) Personal money judgment.—If the property subject to forfeiture under paragraph (2) is unavailable, and the defendant has insufficient substitute property that may be forfeited pursuant to section 413(p) of the Controlled Substances Act, the court shall enter a personal money judgment against the defendant for the amount that would be subject to forfeiture.

"(c) Civil Forfeiture.—

"(1) In general.—Any property involved in a violation of subsection (a), or a conspiracy to commit such violation, and any property traceable to such violation or conspiracy, may be seized and, subject to subsection (d) of this section, forfeited to the United States.

"(2) Procedure.—The seizure and forfeiture shall be governed by the procedures governing civil forfeitures in money laundering cases pursuant to section 981(a)(1)(A) of title 18, United States Code.

"(3) Treatment of certain property as involved in the offense.—For purposes of this subsection and subsection (b), any currency or other monetary instrument that is concealed or intended to be concealed in violation of subsection (a) or a conspiracy to commit such violation, any article, container, or conveyance used, or intended to be used, to conceal or transport the currency or other monetary instrument, and any other property used, or intended to be used, to facilitate the offense, shall be considered property involved in the offense.".

. . .

SEC. 373. ILLEGAL MONEY TRANSMITTING BUSINESSES

(a) Scienter Requirement for Section 1960 Violation.—Section 1960 of title 18, United States Code, is amended to read as follows:

"Sec. 1960. Prohibition of unlicensed money transmitting businesses

"(a) Whoever knowingly conducts, controls, manages, supervises, irects, or owns all or part of an unlicensed money transmitting usiness, shall be fined in accordance with this title or imprisoned not ore than 5 years, or both.

"(b) As used in this section—

"(1) the term 'unlicensed money transmitting business' means a money transmitting business which affects interstate or foreign commerce in any manner or degree and—

"(A) is operated without an appropriate money transmitting license in a State where such operation is punishable as a misdemeanor or a felony under State law, whether or not the defendant knew that the operation was required to be licensed or that the operation was so punishable;

"(B) fails to comply with the money transmitting business registration requirements under section 5330 of title 31, United States Code, or regulations prescribed under such section; or

"(C) otherwise involves the transportation or transmission of funds that are known to the defendant to have been derived from a criminal offense or are intended to be used to be used to promote or support unlawful activity;

"(2) the term 'money transmitting' includes transferring funds on behalf of the public by any and all means including but not limited to transfers within this country or to locations abroad by wire, check, draft, facsimile, or courier; and

"(3) the term 'State' means any State of the United States, the District of Columbia, the Northern Mariana Islands, and any commonwealth, territory, or possession of the United States.".

(b) Seizure of Illegally Transmitted Funds.—Section 981(a)(1)(A) of itle 18, United States Code, is amended by striking 'or 1957' and inserting ', 1957 or 1960'.

(c) Clerical Amendment.—The table of sections for chapter 95 of title 18, United States Code, is amended in the item relating to section 1960 by striking 'illegal' and inserting 'unlicensed'.

. . .

SEC. 412. MANDATORY DETENTION OF SUSPECTED TERRORISTS; HABEAS CORPUS; JUDICIAL REVIEW

(a) In General.—The Immigration and Nationality Act (8 U.S.C. 1101 et seq.) is amended by inserting after section 236 the following:

"mandatory detention of suspected terrorists; habeas corpus; judicial review

"Sec. 236A. (a) Detention of Terrorist Aliens.—

"(1) Custody.—The Attorney General shall take into custody any alien who is certified under paragraph (3).

"(2) Release.—Except as provided in paragraphs (5) and (6), the Attorney General shall maintain custody of such an alien until the alien is removed from the United States. Except as provided in paragraph (6), such custody shall be maintained irrespective of any relief from removal for which the alien may be eligible, or any relief from removal granted the alien, until the Attorney General determines that the alien is no longer an alien who may be certified under paragraph (3). If the alien is finally determined not to be removable, detention pursuant to this subsection shall terminate.

"(3) Certification.—The Attorney General may certify an alien under this paragraph if the Attorney General has reasonable grounds to believe that the alien—

"(A) is described in section 212(a)(3)(A)(i), 212(a)(3)(A)(iii), 212(a)(3)(B), 237(a)(4)(A)(i), 237(a)(4)(A)(iii), or 237(a)(4)(B); or
"(B) is engaged in any other activity that endangers the national security of the United States.

"(4) Nondelegation.—The Attorney General may delegate the authority provided under paragraph (3) only to the Deputy Attorney General. The Deputy Attorney General may not delegate such authority.
"(5) Commencement of proceedings.—The Attorney General shall place an alien detained under paragraph (1) in removal proceedings, or shall charge the alien with a criminal offense, not later than 7 days after the commencement of such detention. If the requirement of the preceding sentence is not satisfied, the Attorney General shall release the alien.
"(6) Limitation on indefinite detention.—An alien detained solely under paragraph (1) who has not been removed under section 241(a)(1)(A), and whose removal is unlikely in the reasonably foreseeable future, may be detained for additional periods of up to six months only if the release of the alien will threaten the national security of the United States or the safety of the community or any person.
"(7) Review of certification.—The Attorney General shall review the certification made under paragraph (3) every 6 months. If the Attorney General determines, in the Attorney General's discretion, that the certification should be revoked, the alien may be released on such conditions as the Attorney General deems appropriate, unless such release is otherwise prohibited by law. The alien may request each 6 months in writing that the Attorney General reconsider the certification and may submit documents or other evidence in support of that request.

"(b) Habeas Corpus and Judicial Review.—

"(1) In general.—Judicial review of any action or decision relating to this section (including judicial review of the merits of a determination made under subsection (a)(3) or (a)(6)) is available exclusively in habeas corpus proceedings consistent with this subsection. Except as provided in the preceding sentence, no court shall have jurisdiction to review, by habeas corpus petition or otherwise, any such action or decision.
"(2) Application.—

"(A) In general.—Notwithstanding any other provision of law, including section 2241(a) of title 28, United States Code, habeas corpus proceedings described in paragraph (1) may be initiated only by an application filed with—"(i) the Supreme Court; "(ii) any justice of the Supreme Court; "(iii) any circuit judge of the United States Court of Appeals for the District of Columbia

Circuit; or "(iv) any district court otherwise having jurisdiction to entertain it.

"(B) Application transfer.—Section 2241(b) of title 28, United States Code, shall apply to an application for a writ of habeas corpus described in subparagraph (A).

"(3) Appeals.—Notwithstanding any other provision of law, including section 2253 of title 28, in habeas corpus proceedings described in paragraph (1) before a circuit or district judge, the final order shall be subject to review, on appeal, by the United States Court of Appeals for the District of Columbia Circuit. There shall be no right of appeal in such proceedings to any other circuit court of appeals.

"(4) Rule of decision.—The law applied by the Supreme Court and the United States Court of Appeals for the District of Columbia Circuit shall be regarded as the rule of decision in habeas corpus proceedings described in paragraph (1).

"(c) Statutory Construction.—The provisions of this section shall not be applicable to any other provision of this Act.".

(b) Clerical Amendment.—The table of contents of the Immigration and Nationality Act is amended by inserting after the item relating to section 236 the following:

"Sec. 236A. Mandatory detention of suspected terrorist; habeas corpus; judicial review.".

. . .

SEC. 414. VISA INTEGRITY AND SECURITY

(a) Sense of Congress Regarding the Need To Expedite Implementation of Integrated Entry and Exit Data System.—

(1) Sense of congress.—In light of the terrorist attacks perpetrated against the United States on September 11, 2001, it is the sense of the Congress that—

(A) the Attorney General, in consultation with the Secretary of State, should fully implement the integrated entry and exit data system for airports, seaports, and land border ports of entry, as specified in section 110 of the Illegal Immigration Reform and Immigrant Responsibility Act of 1996 (8 U.S.C. 1365a), with all deliberate speed and as expeditiously as practicable; and

(B) the Attorney General, in consultation with the Secretary of State, the Secretary of Commerce, the Secretary of the Treasury, and the Office of Homeland Security, should immediately begin establishing the Integrated Entry and Exit Data System Task Force, as described in section 3 of the Immigration and Naturalization Service Data Management Improvement Act of 2000 (Public Law 106-215).

(2) Authorization of appropriations.—There is authorized to be appropriated such sums as may be necessary to fully implement the system described in paragraph (1)(A).

(b) Development of the System.—In the development of the integrated entry and exit data system under section 110 of the Illegal Immigration Reform and Immigrant Responsibility Act of 1996 (8 U.S.C. 1365a), the Attorney General and the Secretary of State shall particularly focus on—

(1) the utilization of biometric technology; and
(2) the development of tamper-resistant documents readable at ports of entry.

(c) Interface With Law Enforcement Databases.—The entry and exit data system described in this section shall be able to interface with law enforcement databases for use by Federal law enforcement to identify and detain individuals who pose a threat to the national security of the United States.

(d) Report on Screening Information.—Not later than 12 months after the date of enactment of this Act, the Office of Homeland Security shall submit a report to Congress on the information that is needed from any United States agency to effectively screen visa applicants and applicants for admission to the United States to identify those affiliated with terrorist organizations or those that pose any threat to the safety or security of the United States, including the type of information currently received by United States agencies and the regularity with which such information is transmitted to the Secretary of State and the Attorney General.

. . .

SEC. 416. FOREIGN STUDENT MONITORING PROGRAM

(a) Full Implementation and Expansion of Foreign Student Visa Monitoring Program Required.—The Attorney General, in consultation with the Secretary of State, shall fully implement and expand the program established by section 641(a) of the Illegal Immigration Reform and Immigrant Responsibility Act of 1996 (8 U.S.C. 1372(a)).

(b) Integration With Port of Entry Information.—For each alien with respect to whom information is collected under section 641 of the Illegal Immigration Reform and Immigrant Responsibility Act of 1996 (8 U.S.C. 1372), the Attorney General, in consultation with the Secretary of State, shall include information on the date of entry and port of entry.

(c) Expansion of System To Include Other Approved Educational Institutions.—Section 641 of the Illegal Immigration Reform and Immigrant Responsibility Act of 1996 (8 U.S.C.1372) is amended—

(1) in subsection (a)(1), subsection (c)(4)(A), and subsection (d)(1) (in the text above subparagraph (A)), by inserting ", other approved educational institutions," after "higher education" each place it appears;
(2) in subsections (c)(1)(C), (c)(1)(D), and (d)(1)(A), by inserting ", or other approved educational institution," after "higher education" each place it appears;

(3) in subsections (d)(2), (e)(1), and (e)(2), by inserting ", other approved educational institution," after "higher education" each place it appears; and

(4) in subsection (h), by adding at the end the following new paragraph:

"(3) Other approved educational institution.—The term 'other approved educational institution' includes any air flight school, language training school, or vocational school, approved by the Attorney General, in consultation with the Secretary of Education and the Secretary of State, under subparagraph (F), (J), or (M) of section 101(a)(15) of the Immigration and Nationality Act.".

(d) Authorization of Appropriations.—There is authorized to be appropriated to the Department of Justice $36,800,000 for the period beginning on the date of enactment of this Act and ending on January 1, 2003, to fully implement and expand prior to January 1, 2003, the program established by section 641 (a) of the Illegal Immigration Reform and Immigrant Responsibility Act of 1996 (8 U.S.C. 1372(a)).

. . .

TITLE V—REMOVING OBSTACLES TO INVESTIGATING TERRORISM
SEC. 501. ATTORNEY GENERAL'S AUTHORITY TO PAY REWARDS TO COMBAT TERRORISM

(a) Payment of Rewards To Combat Terrorism.—Funds available to the Attorney General may be used for the payment of rewards pursuant to public advertisements for assistance to the Department of Justice to combat terrorism and defend the Nation against terrorist acts, in accordance with procedures and regulations established or issued by the Attorney General.

(b) Conditions.—In making rewards under this section—

(1) no such reward of $250,000 or more may be made or offered without the personal approval of either the Attorney General or the President;

(2) the Attorney General shall give written notice to the Chairmen and ranking minority members of the Committees on Appropriations and the Judiciary of the Senate and of the House of Representatives not later than 30 days after the approval of a reward under paragraph (1);

(3) any executive agency or military department (as defined, respectively, in sections 105 and 102 of title 5, United States Code) may provide the Attorney General with funds for the payment of rewards;

(4) neither the failure of the Attorney General to authorize a payment nor the amount authorized shall be subject to judicial review; and

(5) no such reward shall be subject to any per- or aggregate reward spending limitation established by law, unless that law expressly refers to this section, and no reward paid pursuant to any such offer shall count toward any such aggregate reward spending limitation.

. . .

SEC. 507. DISCLOSURE OF EDUCATIONAL RECORDS

Section 444 of the General Education Provisions Act (20 U.S.C. 1232g), is amended by adding after subsection (i) a new subsection (j) to read as follows:

"(j) Investigation and Prosecution of Terrorism.—

"(1) In general.—Notwithstanding subsections (a) through (i) or any provision of State law, the Attorney General (or any Federal officer or employee, in a position not lower than an Assistant Attorney General, designated by the Attorney General) may submit a written application to a court of competent jurisdiction for an ex parte order requiring an educational agency or institution to permit the Attorney General (or his designee) to—

"(A) collect education records in the possession of the educational agency or institution that are relevant to an authorized investigation or prosecution of an offense listed in section 2332b(g)(5)(B) of title 18 United States Code, or an act of domestic or international terrorism as defined in section 2331 of that title; and

"(B) for official purposes related to the investigation or prosecution of an offense described in paragraph (1)(A), retain, disseminate, and use (including as evidence at trial or in other administrative or judicial proceedings) such records, consistent with such guidelines as the Attorney General, after consultation with the Secretary, shall issue to protect confidentiality.

"(2) Application and approval.—

"(A) In general.—An application under paragraph (1) shall certify that there are specific and articulable facts giving reason to believe that the education records are likely to contain information described in paragraph (1)(A).

"(B) The court shall issue an order described in paragraph (1) if the court finds that the application for the order includes the certification described in subparagraph (A).

"(3) Protection of educational agency or institution.—An educational agency or institution that, in good faith, produces education records in accordance with an order issued under this subsection shall not be liable to any person for that production.

"(4) Record-keeping.—Subsection (b)(4) does not apply to education records subject to a court order under this subsection.".

. . .

TITLE VIII—STRENGTHENING THE CRIMINAL LAWS AGAINST TERRORISM

SEC. 801. TERRORIST ATTACKS AND OTHER ACTS OF VIOLENCE AGAINST MASS TRANSPORTATION SYSTEMS

Chapter 97 of title 18, United States Code, is amended by adding at the end the following:

"Sec. 1993. Terrorist attacks and other acts of violence against mass transportation systems

"(a) General Prohibitions.—Whoever willfully—

"(1) wrecks, derails, sets fire to, or disables a mass transportation vehicle or ferry;

"(2) places or causes to be placed any biological agent or toxin for use as a weapon, destructive substance, or destructive device in, upon, or near a mass transportation vehicle or ferry, without previously obtaining the permission of the mass transportation provider, and with intent to endanger the safety of any passenger or employee of the mass transportation provider, or with a reckless disregard for the safety of human life;

"(3) sets fire to, or places any biological agent or toxin for use as a weapon, destructive substance, or destructive device in, upon, or near any garage, terminal, structure, supply, or facility used in the operation of, or in support of the operation of, a mass transportation vehicle or ferry, without previously obtaining the permission of the mass transportation provider, and knowing or having reason to know such activity would likely derail, disable, or wreck a mass transportation vehicle or ferry used, operated, or employed by the mass transportation provider;

"(4) removes appurtenances from, damages, or otherwise impairs the operation of a mass transportation signal system, including a train control system, centralized dispatching system, or rail grade crossing warning signal without authorization from the mass transportation provider;

"(5) interferes with, disables, or incapacitates any dispatcher, driver, captain, or person while they are employed in dispatching, operating, or maintaining a mass transportation vehicle or ferry, with intent to endanger the safety of any passenger or employee of the mass transportation provider, or with a reckless disregard for the safety of human life;

"(6) commits an act, including the use of a dangerous weapon, with the intent to cause death or serious bodily injury to an employee or passenger of a mass transportation provider or any other person while any of the foregoing are on the property of a mass transportation provider;

"(7) conveys or causes to be conveyed false information, knowing the information to be false, concerning an attempt or alleged attempt being made or to be made, to do any act which would be a crime prohibited by this subsection; or

"(8) attempts, threatens, or conspires to do any of the aforesaid acts, shall be fined under this title or imprisoned not more than twenty years, or both, if such act is committed, or in the case of a threat or conspiracy such act would be committed, on, against, or affecting a mass transportation provider engaged in or affecting interstate or foreign commerce, or if in the course of committing such act, that person travels or communicates across a State line in order to commit such act, or transports materials across a State line in aid of the commission of such act.

"(b) Aggravated Offense.—Whoever commits an offense under subsection (a) in a circumstance in which—

"(1) the mass transportation vehicle or ferry was carrying a passenger at the time of the offense; or

"(2) the offense has resulted in the death of any person, shall be guilty of an aggravated form of the offense and shall be fined under this title or imprisoned for a term of years or for life, or both.

"(c) Definitions.—In this section—

"(1) the term 'biological agent' has the meaning given to that term in section 178(1) of this title;

"(2) the term 'dangerous weapon' has the meaning given to that term in section 930 of this title;

"(3) the term 'destructive device' has the meaning given to that term in section 921(a)(4) of this title;

"(4) the term 'destructive substance' has the meaning given to that term in section 31 of this title;

"(5) the term 'mass transportation' has the meaning given to that term in section 5302(a)(7) of title 49, United States Code, except that the term shall include schoolbus, charter, and sightseeing transportation;

"(6) the term 'serious bodily injury' has the meaning given to that term in section 1365 of this title;

"(7) the term 'State' has the meaning given to that term in section 2266 of this title; and

"(8) the term 'toxin' has the meaning given to that term in section 178(2) of this title.".

(f) Conforming Amendment.—The analysis of chapter 97 of title 18, United States Code, is amended by adding at the end:

"1993. Terrorist attacks and other acts of violence against mass transportation systems.".

SEC. 802. DEFINITION OF DOMESTIC TERRORISM

(a) Domestic Terrorism Defined.—Section 2331 of title 18, United States Code, is amended—

(1) in paragraph (1)(B)(iii), by striking "by assassination or kidnapping" and inserting "by mass destruction, assassination, or kidnapping";

(2) in paragraph (3), by striking "and";

(3) in paragraph (4), by striking the period at the end and inserting "; and"; and

(4) by adding at the end the following:

"(5) the term 'domestic terrorism' means activities that—

"(A) involve acts dangerous to human life that are a violation of the criminal laws of the United States or of any State;

"(B) appear to be intended— "(i) to intimidate or coerce a civilian population; "(ii) to influence the policy of a government by intimidation or coercion; or"(iii) to affect the conduct of a government by mass destruction, assassination, or kidnapping; and

"(C) occur primarily within the territorial jurisdiction of the United States.".

(b) Conforming Amendment.—Section 3077(1) of title 18, United States Code, is amended to read as follows:

"(1) 'act of terrorism' means an act of domestic or international terrorism as defined in section 2331;".

SEC. 803. PROHIBITION AGAINST HARBORING TERRORISTS

(a) In General.—Chapter 113B of title 18, United States Code, is amended by adding after section 2338 the following new section:

"Sec. 2339. Harboring or concealing terrorists

"(a) Whoever harbors or conceals any person who he knows, or has reasonable grounds to believe, has committed, or is about to commit, an offense under section 32 (relating to destruction of aircraft or aircraft facilities), section 175 (relating to biological weapons), section 229 (relating to chemical weapons), section 831 (relating to nuclear materials), paragraph (2) or (3) of section 844(f) (relating to arson and bombing of government property risking or causing injury or death), section 1366(a) (relating to the destruction of an energy facility), section 2280 (relating to violence against maritime navigation), section 2332a (relating to weapons of mass destruction), or section 2332b (relating to acts of terrorism transcending national boundaries) of this title, section 236(a) (relating to sabotage of nuclear facilities or fuel) of the Atomic Energy Act of 1954 (42 U.S.C. 2284(a)), or section 46502 (relating to aircraft piracy) of title 49, shall be fined under this title or imprisoned not more than ten years, or both.".

"(b) A violation of this section may be prosecuted in any Federal judicial district in which the underlying offense was committed, or in any other Federal judicial district as provided by law.".

(b) Technical Amendment.—The chapter analysis for chapter 113B of title 18, United States Code, is amended by inserting after the item for section 2338 the following:

"2339. Harboring or concealing terrorists.".

SEC. 804. JURISDICTION OVER CRIMES COMMITTED AT U.S. FACILITIES ABROAD

Section 7 of title 18, United States Code, is amended by adding at the end the following:

"(9) With respect to offenses committed by or against a national of the United States as that term is used in section 101 of the Immigration and Nationality Act—

"(A) the premises of United States diplomatic, consular, military or other United States Government missions or entities in foreign States, including the buildings, parts of buildings, and land appurtenant or ancillary thereto or used for purposes of those missions or entities, irrespective of ownership; and

"(B) residences in foreign States and the land appurtenant or ancillary thereto, irrespective of ownership, used for purposes of those missions or entities or used by United States personnel assigned to those missions or entities.

Nothing in this paragraph shall be deemed to supersede any treaty or international agreement with which this paragraph conflicts. This paragraph does not apply with respect to an offense committed by a person described in section 3261(a) of this title.".

. . .

SEC. 808. DEFINITION OF FEDERAL CRIME OF TERRORISM

Section 2332b of title 18, United States Code, is amended—

(1) in subsection (f), by inserting "and any violation of section 351(e), 844(e), 844(f)(1), 956(b), 1361, 1366(b), 1366(c), 1751(e), 2152, or 2156 of this title," before "and the Secretary"; and

(2) in subsection (g)(5)(B), by striking clauses (i) through (iii) and inserting the following:

"(i) section 32 (relating to destruction of aircraft or aircraft facilities), 37 (relating to violence at international airports), 81 (relating to arson within special maritime and territorial jurisdiction), 175 or 175b (relating to biological weapons), 229 (relating to chemical weapons), subsection (a), (b), (c), or (d) of section 351 (relating to congressional, cabinet, and Supreme Court assassination and kidnaping), 831 (relating to nuclear materials), 842(m) or (n) (relating to plastic explosives), 844(f)(2) or (3) (relating to arson and bombing of Government property risking or causing death), 844(i) (relating to arson and bombing of property used in interstate commerce), 930(c) (relating to killing or attempted killing during an attack on a Federal facility with a dangerous weapon), 956(a)(1) (relating to conspiracy to murder, kidnap, or maimpersons abroad), 1030(a)(1) (relating to protection of computers), 1030(a)(5)(A)(i) resulting in damage as defined in 1030(a)(5)(B)(ii) through (v) (relating to protection of computers), 1114 (relating to killing or attempted killing of officers and employees of the United States), 1116 (relating to murder or manslaughter of foreign officials, official guests, or internationally protected persons), 1203 (relating to hostage taking), 1362 (relating to destruction of communication lines, stations, or systems), 1363 (relating to injury to buildings or property within special maritime and territorial jurisdiction of the United States), 1366(a) (relating to destruction of an energy facility), 1751(a), (b), (c), or (d) (relating to Presidential and Presidential staff assassination and kidnaping), 1992 (relating to wrecking trains), 1993 (relating to terrorist attacks and other acts of violence against mass transportation systems), 2155 (relating to destruction of national defense materials, premises, or utilities), 2280 (relating to violence against maritime navigation), 2281 (relating to violence against maritime fixed platforms), 2332 (relating to certain homicides and other violence against United States nationals occurring outside of the United States), 2332a (relating to use of weapons of mass destruction), 2332b (relating to acts of terrorism transcending national boundaries), 2339 (relating to harboring terrorists), 2339A (relating to providing material support to terrorists), 2339B (relating to providing material support to terrorist organizations), or 2340A (relating to torture) of this title; "(ii) section 236 (relating to sabotage of nuclear facilities or fuel) of the Atomic Energy Act of 1954 (42 U.S.C. 2284); or "(iii) section 46502 (relating to aircraft piracy), the second sentence of section 46504 (relating to assault on a flight crew with a dangerous weapon), section 46505(b)(3) or (c) (relating to explosive or incendiary devices, or endangerment of human life by means of weapons, on aircraft), section 46506 if homicide or attempted homicide is involved (relating to application of certain criminal laws to acts on aircraft), or section 60123(b) (relating to destruction of interstate gas or hazardous liquid pipeline facility) of title 49.".

SEC. 809. NO STATUTE OF LIMITATION FOR CERTAIN TERRORISM OFFENSES

(a) In General.—Section 3286 of title 18, United States Code, is amended to read as follows:

"Sec. 3286. Extension of statute of limitation for certain terrorism offenses

"(a) Eight-Year Limitation.—Notwithstanding section 3282, no person shall be prosecuted, tried, or punished for any noncapital offense involving a violation of any provision listed in section 2332b(g)(5)(B), or a violation of section 112, 351(e), 1361, or 1751(e) of this title, or section 46504, 46505, or 46506 of title 49, unless the indictment is found or the information is instituted within 8 years after the offense was committed. Notwithstanding the preceding sentence, offenses listed in section 3295 are subject to the statute of limitations set forth in that section.

"(b) No Limitation.—Notwithstanding any other law, an indictment may be found or an information instituted at any time without limitation for any offense listed in section 2332b(g)(5)(B), if the commission of such offense resulted in, or created a forseeable risk of, death or serious bodily injury to another person.".

(b) Application.—The amendments made by this section shall apply to the prosecution of any offense committed before, on, or after the date of the enactment of this section.

SEC. 810. ALTERNATE MAXIMUM PENALTIES FOR TERRORISM OFFENSES

(a) Arson.—Section 81 of title 18, United States Code, is amended in the second undesignated paragraph by striking "not more than twenty years" and inserting "for any term of years or for life".

(b) Destruction of an Energy Facility.—Section 1366 of title 18, United States Code, is amended—

(1) in subsection (a), by striking "ten" and inserting "20"; and
(2) by adding at the end the following:

"(d) Whoever is convicted of a violation of subsection (a) or (b) that has resulted in the death of any person shall be subject to imprisonment for any term of years or life.".

(c) Material Support to Terrorists.—Section 2339A(a) of title 18, United States Code, is amended—

   (1) by striking "10" and inserting "15"; and
   (2) by striking the period and inserting ", and, if the death of any person results, shall be imprisoned for any term of years or for life.".

(d) Material Support to Designated Foreign Terrorist Organizations.—Section 2339B(a)(1) of title 18, United States Code, is amended—

   (1) by striking "10" and inserting "15"; and
   (2) by striking the period after "or both" and inserting ", and, if the death of any person results, shall be imprisoned for any term of years or for life.".

(e) Destruction of National-Defense Materials.—Section 2155(a) of title 18, United States Code, is amended—

   (1) by striking "ten" and inserting "20"; and
   (2) by striking the period at the end and inserting ", and, if death results to any person, shall be imprisoned for any term of years or for life.".

(f) Sabotage of Nuclear Facilities or Fuel.—Section 236 of the Atomic Energy Act of 1954 (42 U.S.C. 2284), is amended—

   (1) by striking "ten" each place it appears and inserting "20";
   (2) in subsection (a), by striking the period at the end and inserting ", and, if death results to any person, shall be imprisoned for any term of years or for life."; and
   (3) in subsection (b), by striking the period at the end and inserting ", and, if death results to any person, shall be imprisoned for any term of years or for life.".

(g) Special Aircraft Jurisdiction of the United States.—Section 46505(c) of title 49, United States Code, is amended—

   (1) by striking "15" and inserting "20"; and
   (2) by striking the period at the end and inserting ", and, if death results to any person, shall be imprisoned for any term of years or for life.".

(h) Damaging or Destroying an Interstate Gas or Hazardous Liquid Pipeline Facility.—Section 60123(b) of title 49, United States Code, is amended—

   (1) by striking "15" and inserting "20"; and
   (2) by striking the period at the end and inserting ", and, if death results to any person, shall be imprisoned for any term of years or for life.".

SEC. 811. PENALTIES FOR TERRORIST CONSPIRACIES

(a) Arson.—Section 81 of title 18, United States Code, is amended in the first undesignated paragraph—

(1) by striking ", or attempts to set fire to or burn"; and

(2) by inserting "or attempts or conspires to do such an act," before "shall be imprisoned".

(b) Killings in Federal Facilities.—Section 930(c) of title 18, United States Code, is amended—

(1) by striking "or attempts to kill";

(2) by inserting "or attempts or conspires to do such an act," before "shall be punished"; and

(3) by striking "and 1113" and inserting "1113, and 1117".

(c) Communications Lines, Stations, or Systems.—Section 1362 of title 18, United States Code, is amended in the first undesignated paragraph—

(1) by striking "or attempts willfully or maliciously to injure or destroy"; and

(2) by inserting "or attempts or conspires to do such an act," before "shall be fined".

(d) Buildings or Property Within Special Maritime and Territorial Jurisdiction.—Section 1363 of title 18, United States Code, is amended—

(1) by striking "or attempts to destroy or injure"; and

(2) by inserting "or attempts or conspires to do such an act," before "shall be fined" the first place it appears.

(e) Wrecking Trains.—Section 1992 of title 18, United States Code, is amended by adding at the end the following:

"(c) A person who conspires to commit any offense defined in this section shall be subject to the same penalties (other than the penalty of death) as the penalties prescribed for the offense, the commission of which was the object of the conspiracy.".

(f) Material Support to Terrorists.—Section 2339A of title 18, United States Code, is amended by inserting "or attempts or conspires to do such an act," before "shall be fined".

(g) Torture.—Section 2340A of title 18, United States Code, is amended by adding at the end the following:

"(c) Conspiracy.—A person who conspires to commit an offense under this section shall be subject to the same penalties (other than the penalty of death) as the penalties prescribed for the offense, the commission of which was the object of the conspiracy.".

(h) Sabotage of Nuclear Facilities or Fuel.—Section 236 of the Atomic Energy Act of 1954 (42 U.S.C. 2284), is amended—

(1) in subsection (a)—

(A) by striking ", or who intentionally and willfully attempts to destroy or cause physical damage to";

      (B) in paragraph (4), by striking the period at the end and inserting a comma; and

      (C) by inserting "or attempts or conspires to do such an act," before "shall be fined"; and

  (2) in subsection (b)—

      (A) by striking "or attempts to cause"; and

      (B) by inserting "or attempts or conspires to do such an act," before "shall be fined".

(i) Interference with Flight Crew Members and Attendants.—Section 46504 of title 49, United States Code, is amended by inserting "or attempts or conspires to do such an act," before "shall be fined".

(j) Special Aircraft Jurisdiction of the United States.—Section 46505 of title 49, United States Code, is amended by adding at the end the following:

"(e) Conspiracy.—If two or more persons conspire to violate subsection (b) or (c), and one or more of such persons do any act to effect the object of the conspiracy, each of the parties to such conspiracy shall be punished as provided in such subsection.".

(k) Damaging or Destroying an Interstate Gas or Hazardous Liquid Pipeline Facility.—Section 60123(b) of title 49, United States Code, is amended—

  (1) by striking ",or attempting to damage or destroy,"; and

  (2) by inserting ",or attempting or conspiring to do such an act," before "shall be fined".

- **Document: Military Order on Detention, Treatment, and Trial of Certain Non-Citizens**
- **Date:** November 13, 2001
- **Significance:** In this executive order President Bush denies the status of "prisoner of war" for people taken into custody in Afghanistan. He authorized them to be held in a specially built prison at the Guantánamo Bay naval facility, on the island of Cuba, making them the responsibility of the Secretary of Defense, who was given additional powers.
- **Source:** 66 FR 57833, November 16, 2001.

Detention, Treatment, and Trial of Certain Non-Citizens in the War Against Terrorism

By the authority vested in me as President and as Commander in Chief of the Armed Forces of the United States by the Constitution and the laws of the United States of America, including the Authorization for Use of Military Force Joint

Resolution (Public Law 107-40, 115 Stat. 224) and sections 821 and 836 of title 10, United States Code, it is hereby ordered as follows:

Section 1. Findings.

(a) International terrorists, including members of al Qaida, have carried out attacks on United States diplomatic and military personnel and facilities abroad and on citizens and property within the United States on a scale that has created a state of armed conflict that requires the use of the United States Armed Forces.

(b) In light of grave acts of terrorism and threats of terrorism, including the terrorist attacks on September 11, 2001, on the headquarters of the United States Department of Defense in the national capital region, on the World Trade Center in New York, and on civilian aircraft such as in Pennsylvania, I proclaimed a national emergency on September 14, 2001 (Proc. 7463, Declaration of National Emergency by Reason of Certain Terrorist Attacks).

(c) Individuals acting alone and in concert involved in international terrorism possess both the capability and the intention to undertake further terrorist attacks against the United States that, if not detected and prevented, will cause mass deaths, mass injuries, and massive destruction of property, and may place at risk the continuity of the operations of the United States Government.

U.S. military police escort a detainee to his cell at the naval base at Guantanamo Bay, Cuba, on January 11, 2002. (U.S. Department of Defense)

(d) The ability of the United States to protect the United States and its citizens, and to help its allies and other cooperating nations protect their nations and their citizens, from such further terrorist attacks depends in significant part upon using the United States Armed Forces to identify terrorists and those who support them, to disrupt their activities, and to eliminate their ability to conduct or support such attacks.

(e) To protect the United States and its citizens, and for the effective conduct of military operations and prevention of terrorist attacks, it is necessary for individuals subject to this order pursuant to section 2 hereof to be detained, and, when tried, to be tried for violations of the laws of war and other applicable laws by military tribunals.

(f) Given the danger to the safety of the United States and the nature of international terrorism, and to the extent provided by and under this order, I find consistent with section 836 of title 10, United States Code, that it is not practicable to apply in military commissions under this order the principles of law and the rules of evidence generally recognized in the trial of criminal cases in the United States district courts.

(g) Having fully considered the magnitude of the potential deaths, injuries, and property destruction that would result from potential acts of terrorism against the United States, and the probability that such acts will occur, I have determined that an extraordinary emergency exists for national defense purposes, that this emergency constitutes an urgent and compelling government interest, and that issuance of this order is necessary to meet the emergency.

Sec. 2. Definition and Policy.

(a) The term "individual subject to this order" shall mean any individual who is not a United States citizen with respect to whom I determine from time to time in writing that:

(1) there is reason to believe that such individual, at the relevant times,

    (i)   is or was a member of the organization known as al Qaida;

    (ii) has engaged in, aided or abetted, or conspired to commit, acts of international terrorism, or acts in preparation therefor, that have caused, threaten to cause, or have as their aim to cause, injury to or adverse effects on the United States, its citizens, national security, foreign policy, or economy; or

    (iii) has knowingly harbored one or more individuals described in subparagraphs (i) or (ii) of subsection 2(a)(1) of this order;

and

(2) it is in the interest of the United States that such individual be subject to this order.

(b) It is the policy of the United States that the Secretary of Defense shall take all necessary measures to ensure that any individual subject to this order is detained in accordance with section 3, and, if the individual is to be tried, that such individual is tried only in accordance with section 4.

(c) It is further the policy of the United States that any individual subject to this order who is not already under the control of the Secretary of Defense but who is under the control of any other officer or agent of the United States or any State shall, upon delivery of a copy of such written determination to such officer or agent, forthwith be placed under the control of the Secretary of Defense.

Sec. 3. Detention Authority of the Secretary of Defense. Any individual subject to this order shall be—

(a) detained at an appropriate location designated by the Secretary of Defense outside or within the United States;
(b) treated humanely, without any adverse distinction based on race, color, religion, gender, birth, wealth, or any similar criteria;
(c) afforded adequate food, drinking water, shelter, clothing, and medical treatment;
(d) allowed the free exercise of religion consistent with the requirements of such detention; and
(e) detained in accordance with such other conditions as the Secretary of Defense may prescribe.

Sec. 4. Authority of the Secretary of Defense Regarding Trials of Individuals Subject to this Order.

(a) Any individual subject to this order shall, when tried, be tried by military commission for any and all offenses triable by military commission that such individual is alleged to have committed, and may be punished in accordance with the penalties provided under applicable law, including life imprisonment or death.
(b) As a military function and in light of the findings in section 1, including subsection (f) thereof, the Secretary of Defense shall issue such orders and regulations, including orders for the appointment of one or more military commissions, as may be necessary to carry out subsection (a) of this section.
(c) Orders and regulations issued under subsection (b) of this section shall include, but not be limited to, rules for the conduct of the proceedings of military commissions, including pretrial, trial, and post-trial procedures, modes of proof, issuance of process, and qualifications of attorneys, which shall at a minimum provide for—

(1) military commissions to sit at any time and any place, consistent with such guidance regarding time and place as the Secretary of Defense may provide;
(2) a full and fair trial, with the military commission sitting as the triers of both fact and law;
(3) admission of such evidence as would, in the opinion of the presiding officer of the military commission (or instead, if any other member of the commission so requests at the time the presiding officer renders that opinion, the opinion of the commission rendered at that time by a

majority of the commission), have probative value to a reasonable person;

(4) in a manner consistent with the protection of information classified or classifiable under Executive Order 12958 of April 17, 1995, as amended, or any successor Executive Order, protected by statute or rule from unauthorized disclosure, or otherwise protected by law, (A) the handling of, admission into evidence of, and access to materials and information, and (B) the conduct, closure of, and access to proceedings;

(5) conduct of the prosecution by one or more attorneys designated by the Secretary of Defense and conduct of the defense by attorneys for the individual subject to this order;

(6) conviction only upon the concurrence of two-thirds of the members of the commission present at the time of the vote, a majority being present;

(7) sentencing only upon the concurrence of two-thirds of the members of the commission present at the time of the vote, a majority being present; and

(8) submission of the record of the trial, including any conviction or sentence, for review and final decision by me or by the Secretary of Defense if so designated by me for that purpose.

Sec. 5. Obligation of Other Agencies to Assist the Secretary of Defense.

Departments, agencies, entities, and officers of the United States shall, to the maximum extent permitted by law, provide to the Secretary of Defense such assistance as he may request to implement this order.

Sec. 6. Additional Authorities of the Secretary of Defense.

(a) As a military function and in light of the findings in section 1, the Secretary of Defense shall issue such orders and regulations as may be necessary to carry out any of the provisions of this order.

(b) The Secretary of Defense may perform any of his functions or duties, and may exercise any of the powers provided to him under this order (other than under section 4(c)(8) hereof) in accordance with section 113(d) of title 10, United States Code.

Sec. 7. Relationship to Other Law and Forums.

(a) Nothing in this order shall be construed to—

(1) authorize the disclosure of state secrets to any person not otherwise authorized to have access to them;

(2) limit the authority of the President as Commander in Chief of the Armed Forces or the power of the President to grant reprieves and pardons; or

(3) limit the lawful authority of the Secretary of Defense, any military commander, or any other officer or agent of the United States or of any State to detain or try any person who is not an individual subject to this order.

(b) With respect to any individual subject to this order—

   (1) military tribunals shall have exclusive jurisdiction with respect to offenses by the individual; and

   (2) the individual shall not be privileged to seek any remedy or maintain any proceeding, directly or indirectly, or to have any such remedy or proceeding sought on the individual's behalf, in (i) any court of the United States, or any State thereof, (ii) any court of any foreign nation, or (iii) any international tribunal.

(c) This order is not intended to and does not create any right, benefit, or privilege, substantive or procedural, enforceable at law or equity by any party, against the United States, its departments, agencies, or other entities, its officers or employees, or any other person.

(d) For purposes of this order, the term "State" includes any State, district, territory, or possession of the United States.

(e) I reserve the authority to direct the Secretary of Defense, at any time hereafter, to transfer to a governmental authority control of any individual subject to this order. Nothing in this order shall be construed to limit the authority of any such governmental authority to prosecute any individual for whom control is transferred.

Sec. 8. Publication.

This order shall be published in the Federal Register.
GEORGE W. BUSH
THE WHITE HOUSE,
November 13, 2001

- **Document: President George W. Bush: "Axis of Evil" Speech**
- **Date:** January 29, 2002
- **Significance:** In his first State of the Union address to the nation after the tragic events of 9/11/2001, President Bush reviewed progress in the War on Terror but also hinted that the United States might be interested in overthrowing other regional regimes, such as Iraq's, by claiming that they belong to an "Axis of Evil" comprising Iraq, Iran, and North Korea.
- **Source:** George W. Bush, *Public Papers of the Presidents of the United States: George Bush, 2002*, Book I. Washinton, D.C.: GPO, 2002, pp. 129–136.

Did You Know?

PNAC

The Project for a New American Century (PNAC) is a prominent foreign policy think tank formed in the 1997 to oppose what it saw as the timidity and drift of President Clinton's foreign policy. Its founding members included future Bush administration officials, such as Donald Rumsfeld, Dick Cheney, and Paul Wolfowitz; prominent scholars, such as Francis Fukuyama; and intellectuals, such as Bill Kristol. PNAC's stated goal is to restore a "Reaganite" foreign policy of "military strength and moral clarity" by increasing military spending, challenging hostile regimes, promoting economic and political freedom, and accepting responsibility for America's "unique" role in defending a world order that is friendly to U.S. interests and values. PNAC famously called for the invasion of Iraq and the removal of Saddam Hussein from power. When President George W. Bush was elected, many PNAC members found themselves in positions of decision-making power within the White House and Pentagon, where they were able to carry out their goal of regime change in Iraq.

Think tanks such as PNAC are influential in U.S. politics for two reasons. First, they offer more academically oriented policy proposals that either defend or criticize the president's party. And second, the party out of power frequently uses think tanks not just to criticize the sitting president but to formulate policy positions in preparation for when their party wins the presidency.

Thank you very much. Mr. Speaker, Vice President Cheney, members of Congress, distinguished guests, fellow citizens: As we gather tonight, our nation is at war, our economy is in recession, and the civilized world faces unprecedented dangers. Yet the state of our Union has never been stronger.

We last met in an hour of shock and suffering. In four short months, our nation has comforted the victims, begun to rebuild New York and the Pentagon, rallied a great coalition, captured, arrested, and rid the world of thousands of terrorists, destroyed Afghanistan's terrorist training camps, saved a people from starvation, and freed a country from brutal oppression. (Applause.)

The American flag flies again over our embassy in Kabul. Terrorists who once occupied Afghanistan now occupy cells at Guantanamo Bay. And terrorist leaders who urged followers to sacrifice their lives are running for their own.

America and Afghanistan are now allies against terror. We'll be partners in rebuilding that country. And this evening we welcome the distinguished interim leader of a liberated Afghanistan: Chairman Hamid Karzai.

The last time we met in this chamber, the mothers and daughters of Afghanistan were captives in their own homes, forbidden from working or going to school. Today women are free, and are part of Afghanistan's new government. And we welcome the new Minister of Women's Affairs, Doctor Sima Samar.

Our progress is a tribute to the spirit of the Afghan people, to the resolve of our coalition, and to the might of the United States military. When I called our troops into action, I did so with complete confidence in their courage and skill. And tonight, thanks to them, we are winning the war on terror. The man and women of our Armed Forces have delivered a message now clear to every enemy of the United States: Even 7,000 miles away, across oceans and continents, on mountaintops and in caves—you will not escape the justice of this nation.

For many Americans, these four months have brought sorrow, and pain that will never completely go away. Every day a retired firefighter returns to Ground Zero, to feel closer to his two sons who died there. At a memorial in New York, a little boy left his football with a note for his lost father: Dear Daddy, please take this to heaven. I don't want to play football until I can play with you again some day.

Last month, at the grave of her husband, Michael, a CIA officer and Marine who died in Mazur-e-Sharif, Shannon Spann said these words of farewell: "Semper Fi, my love." Shannon is with us tonight.

Shannon, I assure you and all who have lost a loved one that our cause is just, and our country will never forget the debt we owe Michael and all who gave their lives for freedom.

Our cause is just, and it continues. Our discoveries in Afghanistan confirmed our worst fears, and showed us the true scope of the task ahead. We have seen the depth of our enemies' hatred in videos, where they laugh about the loss of innocent life. And the depth of their hatred is equaled by the madness of the destruction they design. We have found diagrams of American nuclear power plants and public water facilities, detailed instructions for making chemical weapons, surveillance maps of American cities, and thorough descriptions of landmarks in America and throughout the world.

What we have found in Afghanistan confirms that, far from ending there, our war against terror is only beginning. Most of the 19 men who hijacked planes on September the 11th were trained in Afghanistan's camps, and so were tens of thousands of others. Thousands of dangerous killers, schooled in the methods of murder, often supported by outlaw regimes, are now spread throughout the world like ticking time bombs, set to go off without warning.

Thanks to the work of our law enforcement officials and coalition partners, hundreds of terrorists have been arrested. Yet, tens of thousands of trained terrorists are still at large. These enemies view the entire world as a battlefield, and we must pursue them wherever they are. So long as training camps operate, so long as nations harbor terrorists, freedom is at risk. And America and our allies must not, and will not, allow it.

Our nation will continue to be steadfast and patient and persistent in the pursuit of two great objectives. First, we will shut down terrorist camps, disrupt terrorist plans, and bring terrorists to justice. And, second, we must prevent the terrorists and regimes who seek chemical, biological or nuclear weapons from threatening the United States and the world.

Our military has put the terror training camps of Afghanistan out of business, yet camps still exist in at least a dozen countries. A terrorist underworld—including groups like Hamas, Hezbollah, Islamic Jihad, Jaish-i-Mohammed—operates in remote jungles and deserts, and hides in the centers of large cities.

While the most visible military action is in Afghanistan, America is acting elsewhere. We now have troops in the Philippines, helping to train that country's armed forces to go after terrorist cells that have executed an American, and still hold hostages. Our soldiers, working with the Bosnian government, seized terrorists who were plotting to bomb our embassy. Our Navy is patrolling the coast of Africa to block the shipment of weapons and the establishment of terrorist camps in Somalia.

My hope is that all nations will heed our call, and eliminate the terrorist parasites who threaten their countries and our own. Many nations are acting forcefully. Pakistan is now cracking down on terror, and I admire the strong leadership of President Musharraf.

But some governments will be timid in the face of terror. And make no mistake about it: If they do not act, America will.

Our second goal is to prevent regimes that sponsor terror from threatening America or our friends and allies with weapons of mass destruction. Some of these regimes have been pretty quiet since September the 11th. But we know their true nature. North Korea is a regime arming with missiles and weapons of mass destruction, while starving its citizens.

Iran aggressively pursues these weapons and exports terror, while an unelected few repress the Iranian people's hope for freedom.

Iraq continues to flaunt its hostility toward America and to support terror. The Iraqi regime has plotted to develop anthrax, and nerve gas, and nuclear weapons for over a decade. This is a regime that has already used poison gas to murder thousands of its own citizens—leaving the bodies of mothers huddled over their dead children. This is a regime that agreed to international inspections—then kicked out the inspectors. This is a regime that has something to hide from the civilized world.

States like these, and their terrorist allies, constitute an axis of evil, arming to threaten the peace of the world. By seeking weapons of mass destruction, these regimes pose a grave and growing danger. They could provide these arms to terrorists, giving them the means to match their hatred. They could attack our allies or attempt to blackmail the United States. In any of these cases, the price of indifference would be catastrophic.

We will work closely with our coalition to deny terrorists and their state sponsors the materials, technology, and expertise to make and deliver weapons of mass

During his first State of the Union address on January 29, 2002, U.S. president George W. Bush characterized Iran, Iraq, and North Korea as an "axis of evil." (AP Photo/Susan Walsh)

destruction. We will develop and deploy effective missile defenses to protect America and our allies from sudden attack. (Applause.) And all nations should know: America will do what is necessary to ensure our nation's security.

We'll be deliberate, yet time is not on our side. I will not wait on events, while dangers gather. I will not stand by, as peril draws closer and closer. The United States of America will not permit the world's most dangerous regimes to threaten us with the world's most destructive weapons. (Applause.)

Our war on terror is well begun, but it is only begun. This campaign may not be finished on our watch—yet it must be and it will be waged on our watch.

We can't stop short. If we stop now—leaving terror camps intact and terror states unchecked—our sense of security would be false and temporary. History has called America and our allies to action, and it is both our responsibility and our privilege to fight freedom's fight. (Applause.)

Our first priority must always be the security of our nation, and that will be reflected in the budget I send to Congress. My budget supports three great goals for America: We will win this war; we'll protect our homeland; and we will revive our economy.

September the 11th brought out the best in America, and the best in this Congress. And I join the American people in applauding your unity and resolve. (Applause.) Now Americans deserve to have this same spirit directed toward addressing problems here at home. I'm a proud member of my party—yet as we act to win the war, protect our people, and create jobs in America, we must act, first and foremost, not as Republicans, not as Democrats, but as Americans. (Applause.)

It costs a lot to fight this war. We have spent more than a billion dollars a month—over $30 million a day—and we must be prepared for future operations. Afghanistan proved that expensive precision weapons defeat the enemy and spare innocent lives, and we need more of them. We need to replace aging aircraft and make our military more agile, to put our troops anywhere in the world quickly and safely. Our men and women in uniform deserve the best weapons, the best equipment, the best training—and they also deserve another pay raise. (Applause.)

My budget includes the largest increase in defense spending in two decades—because while the price of freedom and security is high, it is never too high. Whatever it costs to defend our country, we will pay. (Applause.)

The next priority of my budget is to do everything possible to protect our citizens and strengthen our nation against the ongoing threat of another attack. Time and distance from the events of September the 11th will not make us safer unless we act on its lessons. America is no longer protected by vast oceans. We are protected from attack only by vigorous action abroad, and increased vigilance at home.

My budget nearly doubles funding for a sustained strategy of homeland security, focused on four key areas: bioterrorism, emergency response, airport and border security, and improved intelligence. We will develop vaccines to fight anthrax and other deadly diseases. We'll increase funding to help states and communities train and equip our heroic police and firefighters. (Applause.) We will improve intelligence collection and sharing, expand patrols at our borders, strengthen the security of air travel, and use technology to track the arrivals and departures of visitors to the United States. (Applause.)

Homeland security will make America not only stronger, but, in many ways, better. Knowledge gained from bioterrorism research will improve public health. Stronger police and fire departments will mean safer neighborhoods. Stricter border enforcement will help combat illegal drugs. (Applause.) And as government works to better secure our homeland, America will continue to depend on the eyes and ears of alert citizens.

A few days before Christmas, an airline flight attendant spotted a passenger lighting a match. The crew and passengers quickly subdued the man, who had been trained by al Qaeda and was armed with explosives. The people on that plane were alert and, as a result, likely saved nearly 200 lives. And tonight we welcome and thank flight attendants Hermis Moutardier and Christina Jones. (Applause.)

Once we have funded our national security and our homeland security, the final great priority of my budget is economic security for the American people. (Applause.) To achieve these great national objectives—to win the war, protect the homeland, and revitalize our economy—our budget will run a deficit that will be small and short-term, so long as Congress restrains spending and acts in a fiscally responsible manner. (Applause.) We have clear priorities and we must act at home with the same purpose and resolve we have shown overseas: We'll prevail in the war, and we will defeat this recession. (Applause.)

. . .

None of us would ever wish the evil that was done on September the 11th. Yet after America was attacked, it was as if our entire country looked into a mirror and saw our better selves. We were reminded that we are citizens, with obligations to each other, to our country, and to history. We began to think less of the goods we can accumulate, and more about the good we can do.

For too long our culture has said, "If it feels good, do it." Now America is embracing a new ethic and a new creed: "Let's roll." In the sacrifice of soldiers, the fierce brotherhood of firefighters, and the bravery and generosity of ordinary citizens, we have glimpsed what a new culture of responsibility could look like. We want to be a nation that serves goals larger than self. We've been offered a unique opportunity, and we must not let this moment pass.

My call tonight is for every American to commit at least two years—4,000 hours over the rest of your lifetime—to the service of your neighbors and your nation. Many are already serving, and I thank you. If you aren't sure how to help, I've got a good place to start. To sustain and extend the best that has emerged in America, I invite you to join the new USA Freedom Corps. The Freedom Corps will focus on three areas of need: responding in case of crisis at home; rebuilding our communities; and extending American compassion throughout the world.

One purpose of the USA Freedom Corps will be homeland security. America needs retired doctors and nurses who can be mobilized in major emergencies;

volunteers to help police and fire departments; transportation and utility workers well-trained in spotting danger.

Our country also needs citizens working to rebuild our communities. We need mentors to love children, especially children whose parents are in prison. And we need more talented teachers in troubled schools. USA Freedom Corps will expand and improve the good efforts of AmeriCorps and Senior Corps to recruit more than 200,000 new volunteers.

And America needs citizens to extend the compassion of our country to every part of the world. So we will renew the promise of the Peace Corps, double its volunteers over the next five years—(applause)—and ask it to join a new effort to encourage development and education and opportunity in the Islamic world.

This time of adversity offers a unique moment of opportunity—a moment we must seize to change our culture. Through the gathering momentum of millions of acts of service and decency and kindness, I know we can overcome evil with greater good. And we have a great opportunity during this time of war to lead the world toward the values that will bring lasting peace.

All fathers and mothers, in all societies, want their children to be educated, and live free from poverty and violence. No people on Earth yearn to be oppressed, or aspire to servitude, or eagerly await the midnight knock of the secret police.

If anyone doubts this, let them look to Afghanistan, where the Islamic "street" greeted the fall of tyranny with song and celebration. Let the skeptics look to Islam's own rich history, with its centuries of learning, and tolerance and progress. America will lead by defending liberty and justice because they are right and true and unchanging for all people everywhere.

No nation owns these aspirations, and no nation is exempt from them. We have no intention of imposing our culture. But America will always stand firm for the non-negotiable demands of human dignity: the rule of law; limits on the power of the state; respect for women; private property; free speech; equal justice; and religious tolerance.

America will take the side of brave men and women who advocate these values around the world, including the Islamic world, because we have a greater objective than eliminating threats and containing resentment. We seek a just and peaceful world beyond the war on terror.

In this moment of opportunity, a common danger is erasing old rivalries. America is working with Russia and China and India, in ways we have never before, to achieve peace and prosperity. In every region, free markets and free trade and free societies are proving their power to lift lives. Together with friends and allies from Europe to Asia, and Africa to Latin America, we will demonstrate that the forces of terror cannot stop the momentum of freedom.

The last time I spoke here, I expressed the hope that life would return to normal. In some ways, it has. In others, it never will. Those of us who have lived through these challenging times have been changed by them. We've come to know truths that we will never question: evil is real, and it must be opposed. Beyond all differences of race or creed, we are one country, mourning together and facing danger together. Deep in the American character, there is honor, and it is stronger than cynicism. And many have discovered again that even in tragedy—especially in tragedy—God is near.

In a single instant, we realized that this will be a decisive decade in the history of liberty, that we've been called to a unique role in human events. Rarely has the world faced a choice more clear or consequential.

Our enemies send other people's children on missions of suicide and murder. They embrace tyranny and death as a cause and a creed. We stand for a different choice, made long ago, on the day of our founding. We affirm it again today. We choose freedom and the dignity of every life.

Steadfast in our purpose, we now press on. We have known freedom's price. We have shown freedom's power. And in this great conflict, my fellow Americans, we will see freedom's victory.

Thank you all. May God bless.

- • **Document:** Joint Resolution to Authorize the Use of United States Armed Forces Against Iraq
- • **Date:** October 16, 2002
- • **Significance:** To reinforce decisions made by the UN Security Council, President George W. Bush secured from Congress an authorization for the use of force against Iraq.
- • **Source:** Authorization for Use of Military Force Against Iraq Resolution of 2002. Public Law 107-243, U.S. Statutes at Large, 116 (2002):1498.

Whereas in 1990 in response to Iraq's war of aggression against and illegal occupation of Kuwait, the United States forged a coalition of nations to liberate Kuwait and its people in order to defend the national security of the United States and enforce United Nations Security Council resolutions relating to Iraq;

Whereas after the liberation of Kuwait in 1991, Iraq entered into a United Nations sponsored cease-fire agreement pursuant to which Iraq unequivocally agreed, among other things, to eliminate its nuclear, biological, and chemical weapons programs and the means to deliver and develop them, and to end its support for international terrorism;

Whereas the efforts of international weapons inspectors, United States intelligence agencies, and Iraqi defectors led to the discovery that Iraq had large stockpiles of chemical weapons and a large scale biological weapons program, and that Iraq had an advanced nuclear weapons development program that was much closer to producing a nuclear weapon than intelligence reporting had previously indicated;

Whereas Iraq, in direct and flagrant violation of the cease-fire, attempted to thwart the efforts of weapons inspectors to identify and destroy Iraq's weapons of mass destruction stockpiles and development capabilities, which finally resulted in the withdrawal of inspectors from Iraq on October 31, 1998;

Whereas in 1998 Congress concluded that Iraq's continuing weapons of mass destruction programs threatened vital United States interests and international peace and security, declared Iraq to be in "material and unacceptable breach of its international obligations" and urged the President "to take appropriate action, in accordance with the Constitution and relevant laws of the United States, to bring Iraq into compliance with its international obligations" (Public Law 105-235);

Whereas Iraq both poses a continuing threat to the national security of the United States and international peace and security in the Persian Gulf region and remains in material and unacceptable breach of its international obligations by, among other things, continuing to possess and develop a significant chemical and biological weapons capability, actively seeking a nuclear weapons capability, and supporting and harboring terrorist organizations;

Whereas Iraq persists in violating resolutions of the United Nations Security Council by continuing to engage in brutal repression of its civilian population thereby threatening international peace and security in the region, by refusing to release, repatriate, or account for non-Iraqi citizens wrongfully detained by Iraq, including an American serviceman, and by failing to return property wrongfully seized by Iraq from Kuwait;

Whereas the current Iraqi regime has demonstrated its capability and willingness to use weapons of mass destruction against other nations and its own people;

Whereas the current Iraqi regime has demonstrated its continuing hostility toward, and willingness to attack, the United States, including by attempting in 1993 to assassinate former President Bush and by firing on many thousands of occasions on United States and Coalition Armed Forces engaged in enforcing the resolutions of the United Nations Security Council;

Whereas members of al Qaida, an organization bearing responsibility for attacks on the United States, its citizens, and interests, including the attacks that occurred on September 11, 2001, are known to be in Iraq;

Whereas Iraq continues to aid and harbor other international terrorist organizations, including organizations that threaten the lives and safety of American citizens;

Whereas the attacks on the United States of September 11, 2001 underscored the gravity of the threat posed by the acquisition of weapons of mass destruction by international terrorist organizations;

Whereas Iraq's demonstrated capability and willingness to use weapons of mass destruction, the risk that the current Iraqi regime will either employ those weapons to launch a surprise attack against the United States or its Armed Forces or provide them to international terrorists who would do so, and the extreme magnitude of harm that would result to the United States and its citizens from such an attack, combine to justify action by the United States to defend itself;

Whereas United Nations Security Council Resolution 678 authorizes the use of all necessary means to enforce United Nations Security Council Resolution 660 and subsequent relevant resolutions and to compel Iraq to cease certain activities that threaten international peace and security, including the development of weapons of mass destruction and refusal or obstruction of United Nations weapons inspections in violation of United Nations Security Council Resolution 687, repression of its civilian population in violation of United Nations Security Council Resolution 688, and threatening its neighbors or United Nations operations in Iraq in violation of United Nations Security Council Resolution 949;

Whereas Congress in the Authorization for Use of Military Force Against Iraq Resolution (Public Law 102-1) has authorized the President "to use United States Armed Forces pursuant to United Nations Security Council Resolution 678 (1990) in order to achieve implementation of Security Council Resolutions 660, 661, 662, 664, 665, 666, 667, 669, 670, 674, and 677";

Whereas in December 1991, Congress expressed its sense that it "supports the use of all necessary means to achieve the goals of United Nations Security Council Resolution 687 as being consistent with the Authorization of Use of Military Force Against Iraq Resolution (Public Law 102-1)," that Iraq's repression of its civilian population violates United Nations Security Council Resolution 688 and "constitutes a continuing threat to the peace, security, and stability of the Persian Gulf region," and that Congress, "supports the use of all necessary means to achieve the goals of United Nations Security Council Resolution 688";

Whereas the Iraq Liberation Act (Public Law 105-338) expressed the sense of Congress that it should be the policy of the United States to support efforts to remove from power the current Iraqi regime and promote the emergence of a democratic government to replace that regime;

Whereas on September 12, 2002, President Bush committed the United States to "work with the United Nations Security Council to meet our common challenge" posed by Iraq and to "work for the necessary resolutions," while also making clear that "the Security Council resolutions will be enforced, and the just demands of peace and security will be met, or action will be unavoidable";

Whereas the United States is determined to prosecute the war on terrorism and Iraq's ongoing support for international terrorist groups combined with its development of weapons of mass destruction in direct violation of its obligations under the 1991 cease-fire and other United Nations Security Council resolutions make clear that it is in the national security interests of the United States and in furtherance of the war on terrorism that all relevant United Nations Security Council resolutions be enforced, including through the use of force if necessary;

Whereas Congress has taken steps to pursue vigorously the war on terrorism through the provision of authorities and funding requested by the President to take the necessary actions against international terrorists and terrorist organizations, including those nations, organizations or persons who planned, authorized, committed or aided the terrorist attacks that occurred on September 11, 2001 or harbored such persons or organizations;

Whereas the President and Congress are determined to continue to take all appropriate actions against international terrorists and terrorist organizations, including those nations, organizations or persons who planned, authorized, committed or aided the terrorist attacks that occurred on September 11, 2001, or harbored such persons or organizations;

Whereas the President has authority under the Constitution to take action in order to deter and prevent acts of international terrorism against the United States, as Congress recognized in the joint resolution on Authorization for Use of Military Force (Public Law 107-40); and

Whereas it is in the national security of the United States to restore international peace and security to the Persian Gulf region;

. . .

PRESIDENTIAL DETERMINATION

In connection with the exercise of the authority granted in subsection (a) to use force the President shall, prior to such exercise or as soon thereafter as may be feasible, but no later than 48 hours after exercising such authority, make available to the Speaker of the House of Representatives and the President pro tempore of the Senate his determination that

(1) reliance by the United States on further diplomatic or other peaceful means alone either (A) will not adequately protect the national security of the United States against the continuing threat posed by Iraq or (B) is not likely to lead to enforcement of all relevant United Nations Security Council resolutions regarding Iraq, and

(2) acting pursuant to this resolution is consistent with the United States and other countries continuing to take the necessary actions against international terrorists and terrorist organizations, including those nations, organizations or persons who planned, authorized, committed or aided the terrorists attacks that occurred on September 11, 2001.

(c) WAR POWERS RESOLUTION REQUIREMENTS.—

(1) SPECIFIC STATUTORY AUTHORIZATION.—Consistent with section 8 (a)(1) of the War Powers Resolution, the Congress declares that this section is intended to constitute specific statutory authorization within the meaning of section 5(b) of the War Powers Resolution.

(2) APPLICABILITY OF OTHER REQUIREMENTS.—Nothing in this resolution supersedes any requirement of the War Powers Resolution.

SEC. 4. REPORTS TO CONGRESS

(a) The President shall, at least once every 60 days, submit to the Congress a report on matters relevant to this joint resolution, including actions taken pursuant to the exercise of authority granted in section 2 and the status of planning for efforts that are expected to be required after such actions are completed, including those actions described in section 7 of Public Law 105-338 (the Iraq Liberation Act of 1998).

(b) To the extent that the submission of any report described in subsection (a) coincides with the submission of any other report on matters relevant to this joint resolution otherwise required to be submitted to Congress pursuant to the reporting requirements of Public Law 93-148 (the War Powers Resolution), all such reports may be submitted as a single consolidated report to the Congress.

(c) To the extent that the information required by section 3 of Public Law 102-1 is included in the report required by this section, such report shall be considered as meeting the requirements of section 3 of Public Law 102-1.

. . .

Approved October 16, 2002.
LEGISLATIVE HISTORY—H.J. Res. 114 (S.J. Res. 45) (S.J. Res. 46):

- **Document: Executive Order 13425: Trial of Alien Unlawful Enemy Combatants by Military Commission**
- **Date:** February 14, 2007
- **Significance:** This executive order orders the prisoners of war the United States held outside of the jurisdiction of U.S. courts to be tried by military commissions rather than civilian courts.
- **Source:** *Federal Register*, Vol. 72, No. 33 (February 20, 2007), pp. 7737.

By the authority vested in me as President by the Constitution and the laws of the United States of America, including the Military Commissions Act of 2006 (Public Law 109-366), the Authorization for the Use of Military Force (Public Law 107-40), and section 948 (b) of title 10, United States Code, it is hereby ordered as follows:

Section 1. Establishment of Military Commissions

There are hereby established military commissions to try alien unlawful enemy combatants for offenses triable by military commission as provided in chapter 47A of title 10.

Sec. 2. Definitions

As used in this order:

(a) "unlawful enemy combatant" has the meaning provided for that term in section 948a(1) of title 10; and

(b) "alien" means a person who is not a citizen of the United States.

Sec. 3. Supersedure

This order supersedes any provision of the President's Military Order of November 13, 2001 (66 Fed. Reg. 57,833), that relates to trial by military commission, specifically including:

(a) section 4 of the Military Order; and

(b) any requirement in section 2 of the Military Order, as it relates to trial by military commission, for a determination of:

(i) reason to believe specified matters; or

(ii) the interest of the United States.

Sec. 4. General Provisions

(a) This order shall be implemented in accordance with applicable law and subject to the availability of appropriations.

    (b) The heads of executive departments and agencies shall provide such information and assistance to the Secretary of Defense as may be necessary to implement this order and chapter 47A of title 10.

    (c) This order is not intended to, and does not, create any right or benefit, substantive or procedural, enforceable at law or in equity by any party against the United States, its departments, agencies, entities, officers, employees, or agents, or any other person.

- **Document: Executive Order 13440 Regarding Detainee Interrogation**
- **Date:** July 20, 2007
- **Significance:** Although President Bush claimed that the United States did not torture its prisoners of war or those designated to be unlawful combatants, his administration reviewed the Geneva Conventions in such a way as to allow for "harsh" interrogation techniques that provided cover, according to critics, for torture by another name.
- **Source:** *Federal Register*, Vol. 72, No. 141 (July 24, 2007), pp. 40707.

Interpretation of the Geneva Conventions Common Article 3 as Applied to a Program of Detention and Interrogation Operated by the Central Intelligence Agency

By the authority vested in me as President and Commander in Chief of the Armed Forces by the Constitution and the laws of the United States of America, including the Authorization for Use of Military Force (Public Law 107-40), the Military Commissions Act of 2006 (Public Law 109-366), and section 301 of title 3, United States Code, it is hereby ordered as follows:

Section 1. General Determinations.

    (a) The United States is engaged in an armed conflict with al Qaeda, the Taliban, and associated forces. Members of al Qaeda were responsible for the attacks on the United States of September 11, 2001, and for many other terrorist attacks, including against the United States, its personnel, and its allies throughout the world. These forces continue to fight the United States and its allies in Afghanistan, Iraq, and elsewhere, and they continue to plan additional acts of terror throughout the world. On February 7, 2002, I determined for the United States that members of al Qaeda, the Taliban, and associated forces are unlawful enemy combatants who are not entitled to the protections that the Third Geneva Convention provides to prisoners of war. I hereby reaffirm that determination.

    (b) The Military Commissions Act defines certain prohibitions of Common Article 3 for United States law, and it reaffirms and reinforces the authority of the President to interpret the meaning and application of the Geneva Conventions.

Sec. 2. Definitions. As used in this order:

(a) "Common Article 3" means Article 3 of the Geneva Conventions.
(b) "Geneva Conventions" means:

   (i) the Convention for the Amelioration of the Condition of the Wounded and Sick in Armed Forces in the Field, done at Geneva August 12, 1949 (6 UST 3114);
   (ii) the Convention for the Amelioration of the Condition of Wounded, Sick and Shipwrecked Members of Armed Forces at Sea, done at Geneva August 12, 1949 (6 UST 3217);
   (iii) the Convention Relative to the Treatment of Prisoners of War, done at Geneva August 12, 1949 (6 UST 3316); and (iv) the Convention Relative to the Protection of Civilian Persons in Time of War, done at Geneva August 12, 1949 (6 UST 3516).

(c) "Cruel, inhuman, or degrading treatment or punishment" means the cruel, unusual, and inhumane treatment or punishment prohibited by the Fifth, Eighth, and Fourteenth Amendments to the Constitution of the United States.

Sec. 3. Compliance of a Central Intelligence Agency Detention and Interrogation Program with Common Article 3.

(a) Pursuant to the authority of the President under the Constitution and the laws of the United States, including the Military Commissions Act of 2006, this order interprets the meaning and application of the text of Common Article 3 with respect to certain detentions and interrogations, and shall be treated as authoritative for all purposes as a matter of United States law, including satisfaction of the international obligations of the United States. I hereby determine that Common Article 3 shall apply to a program of detention and interrogation operated by the Central Intelligence Agency as set forth in this section. The requirements set forth in this section shall be applied with respect to detainees in such program without adverse distinction as to their race, color, religion or faith, sex, birth, or wealth.
(b) I hereby determine that a program of detention and interrogation approved by the Director of the Central Intelligence Agency fully complies with the obligations of the United States under Common Article 3, provided that:

   (i) the conditions of confinement and interrogation practices of the program do not include:

      (A) torture, as defined in section 2340 of title 18, United States Code; (B) any of the acts prohibited by section 2441(d) of title 18, United States Code, including murder, torture, cruel or inhuman treatment, mutilation or maiming, intentionally causing serious bodily injury, rape, sexual assault or abuse, taking of hostages, or performing of biological experiments; (C) other acts of violence serious enough to be considered comparable to murder, torture, mutilation, and cruel or inhuman treatment, as defined in section

2441(d) of title 18, United States Code; (D) any other acts of cruel, inhuman, or degrading treatment or punishment prohibited by the Military Commissions Act (subsection 6(c) of Public Law 109-366) and the Detainee Treatment Act of 2005 (section 1003 of Public Law 109-148 and section 1403 of Public Law 109-163); (E) willful and outrageous acts of personal abuse done for the purpose of humiliating or degrading the individual in a manner so serious that any reasonable person, considering the circumstances, would deem the acts to be beyond the bounds of human decency, such as sexual or sexually indecent acts undertaken for the purpose of humiliation, forcing the individual to perform sexual acts or to pose sexually, threatening the individual with sexual mutilation, or using the individual as a human shield; or (F) acts intended to denigrate the religion, religious practices, or religious objects of the individual;

(ii) the conditions of confinement and interrogation practices are to be used with an alien detainee who is determined by the Director of the Central Intelligence Agency:

(A) to be a member or part of or supporting al Qaeda, the Taliban, or associated organizations; and (B) likely to be in possession of information that:

(1) could assist in detecting, mitigating, or preventing terrorist attacks, such as attacks within the United States or against its Armed Forces or other personnel, citizens, or facilities, or against allies or other countries cooperating in the war on terror with the United States, or their armed forces or other personnel, citizens, or facilities; or (2) could assist in locating the senior leadership of al Qaeda, the Taliban, or associated forces;

(iii) the interrogation practices are determined by the Director of the Central Intelligence Agency, based upon professional advice, to be safe for use with each detainee with whom they are used; and (iv) detainees in the program receive the basic necessities of life, including adequate food and water, shelter from the elements, necessary clothing, protection from extremes of heat and cold, and essential medical care.

(c) The Director of the Central Intelligence Agency shall issue written policies to govern the program, including guidelines for Central Intelligence Agency personnel that implement paragraphs (i)(C), (E), and (F) of subsection 3(b) of this order, and including requirements to ensure:

(i) safe and professional operation of the program; (ii) the development of an approved plan of interrogation tailored for each detainee in the program to be interrogated, consistent with subsection 3(b)(iv) of this order; (iii) appropriate training for interrogators and all personnel operating the program; (iv) effective monitoring of the program, including with respect to medical matters, to ensure the safety of those in the program; and (v) compliance with applicable law and this order.

Sec. 4. Assignment of Function. With respect to the program addressed in this order, the function of the President under section 6©(3) of the Military Commissions Act of 2006 is assigned to the Director of National Intelligence.

Sec. 5. General Provisions. (a) Subject to subsection (b) of this section, this order is not intended to, and does not, create any right or benefit, substantive or procedural, enforceable at law or in equity, against the United States, its departments, agencies, or other entities, its officers or employees, or any other person.

(b) Nothing in this order shall be construed to prevent or limit reliance upon this order in a civil, criminal, or administrative proceeding, or otherwise, by the Central Intelligence Agency or by any individual acting on behalf of the Central Intelligence Agency in connection with the program addressed in this order.

George W. Bush
THE WHITE HOUSE,
July 20, 2007.

FURTHER READING

Galbraith. P. (2007) *The End of Iraq: How American Incompetence Created a War Without End*. New York: Simon and Schuster

Hersh, S. (2004) *Chain of Command: The Road from 9/11 to Abu Ghraib*. New York: HarperCollins.

Mann, J. (2004) *The Rise of the Vulcans: The History of Bush's War Cabinet*. New York: Viking.

National Commission on Terrorist Attacks on the United States. (2004) *The 9/11 Commission Report: Final Report of the National Commission on Terrorist Attacks on the United States*. Washington, DC: USGPO.

Packer, G. (2005) *The Assassin's Gate: America in Iraq*. New York: Farrar, Straus & Giroux.

Ricks, T. (2006) *Fiasco: The American Military Adventure in Iraq*. New York: Penguin.

Woodward, B. (2002) *Bush at War*. New York: Simon and Schuster.

Woodward, B. (2004) *Plan of Attack*. New York: Simon and Schuster.

Woodward, B. (2007) *State of Denial: Bush at War, Part III*. New York: Simon and Schuster.

9

BARACK OBAMA: LIBERAL REALISM

INTRODUCTION

President Bush finished his second term with some of the lowest approval ratings of any modern U.S. president. Additionally, during his last years in office the United States was held in low esteem even by traditional allies, who never warmed to Bush's unilateralism and whose citizens were weary of the wars in Iraq and Afghanistan, the mistreatment of detainees at Guantánamo Bay, and U.S. foot-dragging on issues such as global climate change. The election of 2008 gave American voters the chance to elect a new president who could reestablish U.S. global standing and carve out new post-Bush foreign policies even though the United States was actively fighting two wars, not to mention an ongoing War on Terror.

In the 2008 presidential election, Americans had a choice between Republican Senator John McCain of Arizona and Democratic Senator Barack Obama of Illinois. A decorated Vietnam veteran, former prisoner of war, and long-time member of the U.S. Congress, Senator McCain supported the 2003 invasion of Iraq and was one of the few senators who strongly encouraged and supported President Bush's 2007 troop surge even while criticizing the Bush policies of detainee treatment and torture. With a reputation as a "maverick," McCain campaigned on a platform of national security, emphasizing his vast experience and knowledge in foreign affairs. To balance his ticket, and perhaps in the hopes of winning some votes from women who were disappointed that Senator Hillary Clinton failed to secure the Democratic nomination, McCain chose Alaska Governor Sarah Palin as his running mate. This decision was initially seen as a stroke of political genius, but as the campaign neared November Palin's gaffes and obvious inexperience in key areas of domestic and foreign policy began to hamper McCain's chances.

By contrast, Senator Obama was a relative newcomer on the national political stage. Obama was elected to the U.S. Senate in 2004, but as an Illinois state senator he publicly opposed the Iraq invasion as an unnecessary diversion from the war in Afghanistan. Obama secured the Democratic nomination after a hard-fought contest with Hillary Clinton, President Bill Clinton's wife and senator from New York, by appealing to anti-war voters in the primaries and by suggesting that Clinton's vote to authorize the use of force in the Iraq war illustrated that experience did not necessarily equal good judgment. It was, he famously argued, a time for change, both from the policies of President Bush and also from a recycling of the Clinton political dynasty. McCain's chances were hurt when the U.S. economy took a sharp downturn into a severe recession only a few days after he had announced that the "fundamentals of the economy are strong," a claim that Obama's campaign constantly repeated in order to portray McCain as out of touch and offering only a continuation of failed Bush economic policies. To compensate for the fact that he had little foreign policy experience, candidate Obama selected Senator Joseph Biden of Delaware as his running mate, in part because of Biden's wide-ranging experience in matters of foreign policy. Obama emerged victorious in a historic election, both because of record turnout and because he became the first African American to be elected president of the United States.

Upon taking office, President Obama moved quickly to make his mark on U.S. foreign policy. Early on, he issued an executive order banning the use of torture by the United States and announced he would close the detention facilities at Guantánamo Bay within one year. It was helpful that the Bush administration had already decided to review some of the detainees' cases, allowing some to return to their home countries for lack of evidence or because they were determined not to pose a security threat. Nevertheless, the roughly 300 detainees that remained at Guantánamo Bay were alleged to be the "worst of the worst." Of particular interest was the case of 17 Uyghur detainees who had been apprehended in Afghanistan and were held at Guantánamo Bay for over six years. With no evidence to justify detaining them, but without sufficient guarantees from China that their rights as members of a Muslim ethnic minority would be respected, the Obama administration was ordered by a U.S. federal court to release them. Faced with the possibility of a public furor over Guantánamo detainees set free in the United States, the Obama administration claimed they had no right to live in the United States and arranged for their relocation to the Bahamas and the Pacific island nation of Palau.

As the first year of President Obama's term neared its end, Attorney General Eric Holder announced that some of the Guantánamo Bay detainees would be brought to trial in a U.S. district court in New York City. This decision was praised by many Democrats, who argued that U.S. federal courts had successfully prosecuted terrorist suspects before and that such a case would renew the United States' image as a champion of justice under the law, but it was roundly criticized by Republicans, who feared that such a trial would allow terrorists such as Khalid Sheikh Mohamed to use the venue for propaganda purposes and potentially be freed on a technicality. President Obama also admitted that he would not be able to meet the one-year deadline to close Guantánamo Bay due to the difficulty of finding a suitable site to relocate the remaining detainees. Despite Republican attempts to block the relocation of detainees to American soil, by December 2009 the Obama administration had identified a vacant state prison in Illinois as its choice for the relocation of Guantánamo detainees, a decision welcomed by Democrats in Illinois for the money and jobs it would bring to the state.

In other policy areas, President Obama sought to renew U.S. leadership in the world and repair its tarnished image. Vowing to reach out to the Muslim world and renew the Middle East peace process, which had withered under the Bush administration, Obama visited the Middle East and gave an historic speech at Cairo University in Egypt. In this speech, Obama reiterated that the United States would renew the peace process between Israel and the Palestinians and argued that the United States was not engaged in a war on Islam but only against those who use terrorism. He added that Middle Eastern nations must modernize, democratize, and respect the rights of women and religious minorities as well as reject the vile stereotypes about Jewish people that were repeated by leaders such as Iran's president. And he reiterated that while the United States had no intention of indefinitely occupying Iraq, it had a responsibility to help it transition to a stable democracy before withdrawing its troops. Although the speech drew some domestic criticism from Republicans, who accused Obama of appeasement, it drew high marks from world leaders, especially those from Arab and Muslim nations who sought more evenhanded treatment from the United States.

While Obama made progress in finalizing a withdrawal date for U.S. combat troops from Iraq, many suggested that the wheels of this decision had been set in motion at the end of the Bush administration. Regarding the war in Afghanistan, within the first year of his presidency, Obama twice increased the number of U.S. combat troops, despite the fact that many fellow Democrats urged him to bring

U.S. troops home before Afghanistan became another Vietnam. The withdrawal of troops from Iraq and a renewed focus on Afghanistan was consistent with Obama's campaign platform assertion that Iraq was a war of choice but Afghanistan was a war of necessity. In May 2009 Obama replaced the military command in Afghanistan and ordered a troop increase. Then, in December 2009, after conducting a lengthy review of U.S. goals in Afghanistan and waiting for the dust to settle after a corrupt election in which President Hamid Karzai was reelected, President Obama ordered a surge of 30,000 troops to help bring security to Afghan citizens by fighting a resurgent Taliban and al Qaeda. He also set a timetable for withdrawal of U.S. troops on grounds that it would signal that the U.S. commitment was not open-ended and would put pressure on Afghan leaders to take control of their country's fate. This decision was criticized by some on the political left as wasting lives and resources by propping up a corrupt government, praised by centrists as a sensible and prudent strategy, and criticized by Republicans who supported the troop increase but opposed any semblance of a timeline for withdrawal. While the administration hoped to repeat the success of Bush's 2007 troop surge in Iraq, many worried that Afghanistan was more like Vietnam than Iraq. Given these decisions in his first year in office, President Obama clearly established his "ownership" of both the Iraq and Afghanistan wars as well as the War on Terror.

Ironically, President Obama made the decision to escalate the U.S. involvement in the Afghanistan war only weeks after he won the Nobel Peace Prize for 2009. In a controversial decision, the Nobel committee awarded Obama the Peace Prize not for his accomplishments but for his promise to bring hope, revive diplomacy, and promote multilateralism over unilateralism. In his acceptance speech, Obama himself admitted that his résumé was long on goals but short on accomplishments. And paradoxically, while accepting the Peace Prize, Obama's speech reflected a Reaganesque realism regarding the necessity of just war and a Bush-like admission that there is "evil" in the world that must be confronted. Such a robust defense of just war, realism, and military strength in the pursuit of peace from a U.S. President who campaigned on an anti-war platform won Obama some praise even from stalwart Republicans such as Newt Gingrich.

Some tentative results from President Obama's multilateralism and opening toward the Muslim world were seen in the second year of his tenure, when the nation of Tunisia erupted in anger against its authoritarian president, mainly because of rising unemployment and food prices. Zine al-Abidine Ben Ali had ruled Tunisia since 1987, "winning" his last three elections with 99% of the vote. President Obama made it clear where he stood in regard to the upheaval in Tunisia in his second State of the Union address, in January 2011, saying, "And we saw that same desire to be free in Tunisia, where the will of the people proved more powerful than the writ of a dictator. And tonight, let us be clear: The United States of America stands with the people of Tunisia, and supports the democratic aspirations of all people."

Before the ink was dry on his speech, however, the president of the United States found himself caught "flatfooted" when the nation of Egypt, following the successful revolt of Tunisia, rose against their own president, Hosni Mubarak, a longtime U.S. ally and the recipient a large sums of aid yearly. Egypt was no Tunisia, and everyone in Washington, D.C., and the rest of the world understood this. Egypt is the largest Arab nation in the world, a nation that recognizes the state of Israel and is a key player in the peace process in the Middle East. As protests in the Middle East spread from Tunisia and Egypt to countries such as Bahrain, Syria, and Libya in the "Arab Spring" of 2011, the Obama administration and its critics have sought to balance a strong defense of democratic values and human rights in the Middle East with a desire for regional stability.

Beyond these foreign policy areas, the Obama administration has tried to revive the peace process in the Middle East Peace and pledged to hit the "restart" button with Russia after United States–Russia relations soured in the last years of the Bush administration. President Obama has also visited China, a country that is important not just for foreign policy reasons but for domestic and economic reasons, given that China owns billions of dollars of U.S. bonds and investments and remains the United States' largest trading partner.

Finally, Obama's diplomatic skills and multilateralism are being tested in two additional foreign policy areas. First, despite claims that its nuclear program is for peaceful domestic energy production, there is growing evidence and concern that Iran is seeking to build a nuclear weapon. Given that Iran also has rocket delivery systems with which to threaten Israel, the United States is working feverishly with allies and with the UN to prevent this potential from coming to fruition and to ensure that Iran's intentions remain peaceful. This task is made all the more difficult given that Iran's President Mahmoud Ahmadinejad won reelection in a rigged election in the summer of 2009, after which Iranian security forces brutally suppressed reformers who were peacefully protesting in the streets.

Second, the United States seems ready to rejoin the global effort to proactively reduce carbon emissions and seriously address global climate change. In December 2009, the diplomatic and multilateral approach of the Obama administration was put to the test at the global climate summit in Copenhagen, Denmark. Obama himself issued a challenge that the time for talk was over, and the time had come to make serious and enforceable changes. Time will tell if a renewed emphasis on diplomacy and multilateralism will yield success. What is clear, however, is that Obama has set a foreign policy course that has revitalized the image of the United States as a global leader. By fusing together high ideals of diplomacy, multilateralism, and peace with a willingness to deploy and use military force, whether in Afghanistan or against pirates off the coast of Somalia, President Obama is establishing a "liberal realist" approach to foreign policy.

- **Document: Executive Order for the Closure of Guantánamo Bay Detention Facilities**
- **Date:** January 22, 2009
- **Significance:** As a candidate, Senator Obama promised to close the detention facilities at the naval base at Guantánamo Bay, Cuba. Upon his victory and inauguration as president, he moved quickly to sign an executive order to close the prison facilities. Nevertheless, into his third year in office, they remain open.
- **Source:** *Federal Register*, Vol. 74, No. 16 (January 27,), p. 4897.

Closure of Guantánamo Detention Facilities

EXECUTIVE ORDER—REVIEW AND DISPOSITION OF INDIVIDUALS DETAINED AT THE GUANTÁNAMO BAY NAVAL BASE AND CLOSURE OF DETENTION FACILITIES

By the authority vested in me as President by the Constitution and the laws of the United States of America, in order to effect the appropriate disposition of individuals currently detained by the Department of Defense at the Guantánamo Bay Naval Base (Guantánamo) and promptly to close detention facilities at Guantánamo, consistent with the national security and foreign policy interests of the United States and the interests of justice, I hereby order as follows:

. . .

Sec. 2. Findings.

(a) Over the past 7 years, approximately 800 individuals whom the Department of Defense has ever determined to be, or treated as, enemy combatants have been detained at Guantánamo. The Federal Government has moved more than 500 such detainees from Guantánamo, either by returning them to their home country or by releasing or transferring them to a third country. The Department of Defense has determined that a number of the individuals currently detained at Guantánamo are eligible for such transfer or release.

(b) Some individuals currently detained at Guantánamo have been there for more than 6 years, and most have been detained for at least 4 years. In view of the significant concerns raised by these detentions, both within the United States and internationally, prompt and appropriate disposition of the individuals currently detained at Guantánamo and closure of the facilities in which they are detained would further the national security and foreign policy interests of the United States and the interests of justice. Merely closing the facilities without promptly determining the appropriate disposition of the individuals detained would not adequately serve those interests. To the extent practicable, the prompt and appropriate disposition of the individuals detained at Guantánamo should precede the closure of the detention facilities at Guantánamo.

(c) The individuals currently detained at Guantánamo have the constitutional privilege of the writ of habeas corpus. Most of those individuals have filed petitions for a writ of habeas corpus in Federal court challenging the lawfulness of their detention.

(d) It is in the interests of the United States that the executive branch undertake a prompt and thorough review of the factual and legal bases for the continued

President Barack Obama, accompanied by Vice President Joe Biden, and retired military members, gestures in the Oval Office of the White House where he was signing an executive order and a presidential directive aimed at closing the Guantanamo Bay detention center, January 22, 2009. (P Photo/J. Scott Applewhite)

detention of all individuals currently held at Guantánamo, and of whether their continued detention is in the national security and foreign policy interests of the United States and in the interests of justice. The unusual circumstances associated with detentions at Guantánamo require a comprehensive interagency review.

(e) New diplomatic efforts may result in an appropriate disposition of a substantial number of individuals currently detained at Guantánamo.

(f) Some individuals currently detained at Guantánamo may have committed offenses for which they should be prosecuted. It is in the interests of the United States to review whether and how any such individuals can and should be prosecuted.

(g) It is in the interests of the United States that the executive branch conduct a prompt and thorough review of the circumstances of the individuals currently detained at Guantánamo who have been charged with offenses before military commissions pursuant to the Military Commissions Act of 2006, Public Law 109-366, as well as of the military commission process more generally.

Sec. 3. Closure of Detention Facilities at Guantánamo. The detention facilities at Guantánamo for individuals covered by this order shall be closed as soon as practicable, and no later than 1 year from the date of this order. If any individuals covered by this order remain in detention at Guantánamo at the time of closure of those detention facilities, they shall be returned to their home country, released, transferred to a third country, or transferred to another United States detention facility in a manner consistent with law and the national security and foreign policy interests of the United States.

Sec. 4. Immediate Review of All Guantánamo Detentions.

. . .

(c) *Operation of Review.* The duties of the Review participants shall include the following:

(1) *Consolidation of Detainee Information.* The Attorney General shall, to the extent reasonably practicable, and in coordination with the other Review participants, assemble all information in the possession of the Federal Government that pertains to any individual currently detained at Guantánamo and that is relevant to determining the proper disposition of any such individual. All executive branch departments and agencies shall promptly comply with any request of the Attorney General to provide information in their possession or control pertaining to any such individual. The Attorney General may seek further information relevant to the Review from any source.

(2) *Determination of Transfer.* The Review shall determine, on a rolling basis and as promptly as possible with respect to the individuals currently detained at Guantánamo, whether it is possible to transfer or release the individuals consistent with the national security and foreign policy interests of the United States and, if so, whether and how the Secretary of Defense may effect their transfer or release. The Secretary of Defense, the Secretary of State, and, as appropriate, other Review participants shall work to effect promptly the release or transfer of all individuals for whom release or transfer is possible.

(3) *Determination of Prosecution.* In accordance with United States law, the cases of individuals detained at Guantánamo not approved for release or transfer shall be evaluated to determine whether the Federal Government should seek to prosecute the detained individuals for any offenses they may have committed, including whether it is feasible to prosecute such individuals before a court established pursuant to Article III of the United States Constitution, and the Review participants shall in turn take the necessary and appropriate steps based on such determinations.

(4) *Determination of Other Disposition.* With respect to any individuals currently detained at Guantánamo whose disposition is not achieved under paragraphs (2) or (3) of this subsection, the Review shall select lawful means, consistent with the national security and foreign policy interests of the United States and the interests of justice, for the disposition of such individuals. The appropriate authorities shall promptly implement such dispositions.

(5) *Consideration of Issues Relating to Transfer to the United States.* The Review shall identify and consider legal, logistical, and security issues relating to the potential transfer of individuals currently detained at Guantánamo to facilities within the United States, and the Review participants shall work with the Congress on any legislation that may be appropriate.

Sec. 5. Diplomatic Efforts. The Secretary of State shall expeditiously pursue and direct such negotiations and diplomatic efforts with foreign governments as are necessary and appropriate to implement this order.

Sec. 6. Humane Standards of Confinement. No individual currently detained at Guantánamo shall be held in the custody or under the effective control of any officer, employee, or other agent of the United States Government, or at a facility owned, operated, or controlled by a department or agency of the United States, except in conformity with all applicable laws governing the conditions of such confinement, including Common Article 3 of the Geneva Conventions. The Secretary of Defense shall immediately undertake a review of the conditions of detention at Guantánamo to ensure full compliance with this directive. Such review shall be completed within 30 days and any necessary corrections shall be implemented immediately thereafter.

Sec. 7. Military Commissions. The Secretary of Defense shall immediately take steps sufficient to ensure that during the pendency of the Review described in section 4 of this order, no charges are sworn, or referred to a military commission under the Military Commissions Act of 2006 and the Rules for Military Commissions, and that all proceedings of such military commissions to which charges have been referred but in which no judgment has been rendered, and all proceedings pending in the United States Court of Military Commission Review, are halted.

. . .

BARACK OBAMA
THE WHITE HOUSE,
January 22, 2009.

- **Document: Executive Order on Lawful Interrogations**
- **Date:** January 22, 2009
- **Significance:** As in the case of Guantánamo Bay detention facilities, President Obama issued an executive order rescinding the Bush administration's interpretation of the Geneva Conventions, which it claimed allowed for enhanced interrogation techniques. This executive order fulfills one of Obama's campaign promises to clearly state and ensure that the United States does not torture, reflecting his belief that torture is wrong as well as counterproductive to U.S. interests.
- **Source:** *Federal Register*, Vol. 74, No. 16 (January 27, 2009), p. 4891.

Ensuring Lawful Interrogations

EXECUTIVE ORDER—ENSURING LAWFUL INTERROGATIONS

By the authority vested in me by the Constitution and the laws of the United States of America, in order to improve the effectiveness of human intelligence gathering, to promote the safe, lawful, and humane treatment of individuals in United States custody and of United States personnel who are detained in armed conflicts, to ensure compliance with the treaty obligations of the United States, including the Geneva Conventions, and to take care that the laws of the United States are faithfully executed, I hereby order as follows:

Section 1. Revocation. Executive Order 13440 of July 20, 2007, is revoked. All executive directives, orders, and regulations inconsistent with this order, including but not limited to those issued to or by the Central Intelligence Agency (CIA) from September 11, 2001, to January 20, 2009, concerning detention or the interrogation of detained individuals, are revoked to the extent of their inconsistency with this order. Heads of departments and agencies shall take all necessary steps to ensure that all directives, orders, and regulations of their respective departments or agencies are consistent with this order. Upon request, the Attorney General shall provide guidance about which directives, orders, and regulations are inconsistent with this order.

Sec. 2. Definitions. As used in this order:

. . .

Sec. 4. Prohibition of Certain Detention Facilities, and Red Cross Access to Detained Individuals.

(a) CIA Detention. The CIA shall close as expeditiously as possible any detention facilities that it currently operates and shall not operate any such detention facility in the future.

(b) International Committee of the Red Cross Access to Detained Individuals. All departments and agencies of the Federal Government shall provide the International Committee of the Red Cross with notification of, and timely access to, any individual detained in any armed conflict in the custody or under the effective control of an officer, employee, or other agent of the United States Government or detained within a facility owned, operated, or controlled by a department or agency of the United States Government, consistent with Department of Defense regulations and policies.

Sec. 5. Special Interagency Task Force on Interrogation and Transfer Policies.

(a) Establishment of Special Interagency Task Force. There shall be established a Special Task Force on Interrogation and Transfer Policies (Special Task Force) to review interrogation and transfer policies.

(b) Membership. The Special Task Force shall consist of the following members, or their designees:

  (i) the Attorney General, who shall serve as Chair;
  (ii) the Director of National Intelligence, who shall serve as Co-Vice-Chair;
  (iii) the Secretary of Defense, who shall serve as Co-Vice-Chair;
  (iv) the Secretary of State;
  (v) the Secretary of Homeland Security;
  (vi) the Director of the Central Intelligence Agency;
  (vii) the Chairman of the Joint Chiefs of Staff; and

  (viii) other officers or full-time or permanent part time employees of the United States, as determined by the Chair, with the concurrence of the head of the department or agency concerned.

(c) Staff. The Chair may designate officers and employees within the Department of Justice to serve as staff to support the Special Task Force. At the request of the Chair, officers and employees from other departments or agencies may serve on the Special Task Force with the concurrence of the head of the department or agency that employ such individuals. Such staff must be officers or full-time or permanent part-time employees of the United States. The Chair shall designate an officer or employee of the Department of Justice to serve as the Executive Secretary of the Special Task Force.

(d) Operation. The Chair shall convene meetings of the Special Task Force, determine its agenda, and direct its work. The Chair may establish and direct subgroups of the Special Task Force, consisting exclusively of members of the Special Task Force, to deal with particular subjects.

(e) Mission. The mission of the Special Task Force shall be:

  (i) to study and evaluate whether the interrogation practices and techniques in Army Field Manual 2 22.3, when employed by departments or agencies outside the military, provide an appropriate means of acquiring the intelligence necessary to protect the Nation, and, if warranted, to recommend any additional or different guidance for other departments or agencies; and
  (ii) to study and evaluate the practices of transferring individuals to other nations in order to ensure that such practices comply with the domestic laws, international obligations, and policies of the United States and do

not result in the transfer of individuals to other nations to face torture or otherwise for the purpose, or with the effect, of undermining or circumventing the commitments or obligations of the United States to ensure the humane treatment of individuals in its custody or control.

(f) Administration. The Special Task Force shall be established for administrative purposes within the Department of Justice and the Department of Justice shall, to the extent permitted by law and subject to the availability of appropriations, provide administrative support and funding for the Special Task Force.

(g) Recommendations. The Special Task Force shall provide a report to the President, through the Assistant to the President for National Security Affairs and the Counsel to the President, on the matters set forth in subsection (d) within 180 days of the date of this order, unless the Chair determines that an extension is necessary.

(h) Termination. The Chair shall terminate the Special Task Force upon the completion of its duties.

Sec. 6. Construction with Other Laws. Nothing in this order shall be construed to affect the obligations of officers, employees, and other agents of the United States Government to comply with all pertinent laws and treaties of the United States governing detention and interrogation, including but not limited to: the Fifth and Eighth Amendments to the United States Constitution; the Federal torture statute, 18 U.S.C. 2340 2340A; the War Crimes Act, 18 U.S.C. 2441; the Federal assault statute, 18 U.S.C. 113; the Federal maiming statute, 18 U.S.C. 114; the Federal "stalking" statute, 18 U.S.C. 2261A; articles 93, 124, 128, and 134 of the Uniform Code of Military Justice, 10 U.S.C. 893, 924, 928, and 934; section 1003 of the Detainee Treatment Act of 2005, 42 U.S.C. 2000dd; section 6(c) of the Military Commissions Act of 2006, Public Law 109 366; the Geneva Conventions; and the Convention Against Torture. Nothing in this order shall be construed to diminish any rights that any individual may have under these or other laws and treaties. This order is not intended to, and does not, create any right or benefit, substantive or procedural, enforceable at law or in equity against the United States, its departments, agencies, or other entities, its officers or employees, or any other person.

BARACK OBAMA
THE WHITE HOUSE,
January 22, 2009

- **Document: Remarks of President Barack Obama in Cairo, Egypt: "A New Beginning"**
- **Date**: June 4, 2009
- **Significance:** In his effort to repair U.S. relations in the Muslim world, President Obama delivered a speech in Cairo, Egypt, in which he sought to convince Muslims that the United States is not engaging in a crusade against their religion. He also took the opportunity to

challenge Muslim countries to pursue democratic reforms and
promote civil society, tolerance, and rights for women.

- **Source:** Barack Obama, "Remarks by the President on a New Beginning." The White House. http://www.whitehouse.gov/the_press
  _office/Remarks-by-the-President-at-Cairo-University-6-04-09/.

I am honored to be in the timeless city of Cairo, and to be hosted by two
remarkable institutions. For over a thousand years, Al-Azhar has stood as a beacon
of Islamic learning, and for over a century, Cairo University has been a source of
Egypt's advancement. Together, you represent the harmony between tradition
and progress. I am grateful for your hospitality, and the hospitality of the people
of Egypt. I am also proud to carry with me the goodwill of the American people,
and a greeting of peace from Muslim communities in my country: assalaamu
alaykum.

We meet at a time of tension between the United States and Muslims around the
world—tension rooted in historical forces that go beyond any current policy debate.
The relationship between Islam and the West includes centuries of co-existence and
cooperation, but also conflict and religious wars. More recently, tension has been fed
by colonialism that denied rights and opportunities to many Muslims, and a Cold
War in which Muslim-majority countries were too often treated as proxies without
regard to their own aspirations. Moreover, the sweeping change brought by moder-
nity and globalization led many Muslims to view the West as hostile to the traditions of Islam.

Violent extremists have exploited these tensions in a small but potent minority of
Muslims. The attacks of September 11th, 2001 and the continued efforts of these
extremists to engage in violence against civilians has led some in my country to view
Islam as inevitably hostile not only to America and Western countries, but also to
human rights. This has bred more fear and mistrust.

So long as our relationship is defined by our differences, we will empower those
who sow hatred rather than peace, and who promote conflict rather than the cooperation that can help all of our people achieve justice and prosperity. This cycle
of suspicion and discord must end.

I have come here to seek a new beginning between the United States and Muslims around the world; one based upon mutual interest and mutual respect; and
one based upon the truth that America and Islam are not exclusive, and need not
be in competition. Instead, they overlap, and share common principles—principles
of justice and progress; tolerance and the dignity of all human beings.

I do so recognizing that change cannot happen overnight. No single speech can
eradicate years of mistrust, nor can I answer in the time that I have all the complex
questions that brought us to this point. But I am convinced that in order to move
forward, we must say openly the things we hold in our hearts, and that too often
are said only behind closed doors. There must be a sustained effort to listen to each
other; to learn from each other; to respect one another; and to seek common ground.
As the Holy Koran tells us, "Be conscious of God and speak always the truth." That
is what I will try to do—to speak the truth as best I can, humbled by the task before

us, and firm in my belief that the interests we share as human beings are far more powerful than the forces that drive us apart.

. . .

Moreover, freedom in America is indivisible from the freedom to practice one's religion. That is why there is a mosque in every state of our union, and over 1,200 mosques within our borders. That is why the U.S. government has gone to court to protect the right of women and girls to wear the hijab, and to punish those who would deny it.

So let there be no doubt: Islam is a part of America. And I believe that America holds within her the truth that regardless of race, religion, or station in life, all of us share common aspirations—to live in peace and security; to get an education and to work with dignity; to love our families, our communities, and our God. These things we share. This is the hope of all humanity.

Of course, recognizing our common humanity is only the beginning of our task. Words alone cannot meet the needs of our people. These needs will be met only if we act boldly in the years ahead; and if we understand that the challenges we face are shared, and our failure to meet them will hurt us all.

. . .

Make no mistake: we do not want to keep our troops in Afghanistan. We seek no military bases there. It is agonizing for America to lose our young men and women. It is costly and politically difficult to continue this conflict. We would gladly bring every single one of our troops home if we could be confident that there were not violent extremists in Afghanistan and Pakistan determined to kill as many Americans as they possibly can. But that is not yet the case.

That's why we're partnering with a coalition of forty-six countries. And despite the costs involved, America's commitment will not weaken. Indeed, none of us should tolerate these extremists. They have killed in many countries. They have killed people of different faiths—more than any other, they have killed Muslims. Their actions are irreconcilable with the rights of human beings, the progress of nations, and with Islam. The Holy Koran teaches that whoever kills an innocent, it is as if he has killed all mankind; and whoever saves a person, it is as if he has saved all mankind. The enduring faith of over a billion people is so much bigger than the narrow hatred of a few. Islam is not part of the problem in combating violent extremism—it is an important part of promoting peace.

We also know that military power alone is not going to solve the problems in Afghanistan and Pakistan. That is why we plan to invest $1.5 billion each year over the next five years to partner with Pakistanis to build schools and hospitals, roads and businesses, and hundreds of millions to help those who have been displaced. And that is why we are providing more than $2.8 billion to help Afghans develop their economy and deliver services that people depend upon.

Let me also address the issue of Iraq. Unlike Afghanistan, Iraq was a war of choice that provoked strong differences in my country and around the world. Although I believe that the Iraqi people are ultimately better off without the tyranny of Saddam

Hussein, I also believe that events in Iraq have reminded America of the need to use diplomacy and build international consensus to resolve our problems whenever possible. Indeed, we can recall the words of Thomas Jefferson, who said: "I hope that our wisdom will grow with our power, and teach us that the less we use our power the greater it will be."

Today, America has a dual responsibility: to help Iraq forge a better future—and to leave Iraq to Iraqis. I have made it clear to the Iraqi people that we pursue no bases, and no claim on their territory or resources. Iraq's sovereignty is its own. That is why I ordered the removal of our combat brigades by next August. That is why we will honor our agreement with Iraq's democratically-elected government to remove combat troops from Iraqi cities by July, and to remove all our troops from Iraq by 2012. We will help Iraq train its Security Forces and develop its economy. But we will support a secure and united Iraq as a partner, and never as a patron.

And finally, just as America can never tolerate violence by extremists, we must never alter our principles. 9/11 was an enormous trauma to our country. The fear and anger that it provoked was understandable, but in some cases, it led us to act contrary to our ideals. We are taking concrete actions to change course. I have unequivocally prohibited the use of torture by the United States, and I have ordered the prison at Guantanamo Bay closed by early next year.

So America will defend itself respectful of the sovereignty of nations and the rule of law. And we will do so in partnership with Muslim communities which are also threatened. The sooner the extremists are isolated and unwelcome in Muslim communities, the sooner we will all be safer.

The second major source of tension that we need to discuss is the situation between Israelis, Palestinians and the Arab world.

America's strong bonds with Israel are well known. This bond is unbreakable. It is based upon cultural and historical ties, and the recognition that the aspiration for a Jewish homeland is rooted in a tragic history that cannot be denied.

Around the world, the Jewish people were persecuted for centuries, and anti-Semitism in Europe culminated in an unprecedented Holocaust. Tomorrow, I will visit Buchenwald, which was part of a network of camps where Jews were enslaved, tortured, shot and gassed to death by the Third Reich. Six million Jews were killed—more than the entire Jewish population of Israel today. Denying that fact is baseless, ignorant, and hateful. Threatening Israel with destruction—or repeating vile stereotypes about Jews—is deeply wrong, and only serves to evoke in the minds of Israelis this most painful of memories while preventing the peace that the people of this region deserve.

On the other hand, it is also undeniable that the Palestinian people—Muslims and Christians—have suffered in pursuit of a homeland. For more than sixty years they have endured the pain of dislocation. Many wait in refugee camps in the West Bank, Gaza, and neighboring lands for a life of peace and security that they have never been able to lead. They endure the daily humiliations—large and small—that come with occupation. So let there be no doubt: the situation for the Palestinian people is intolerable. America will not turn our backs on the legitimate Palestinian aspiration for dignity, opportunity, and a state of their own.

For decades, there has been a stalemate: two peoples with legitimate aspirations, each with a painful history that makes compromise elusive. It is easy to point fingers—for Palestinians to point to the displacement brought by Israel's founding, and for Israelis to point to the constant hostility and attacks throughout its history

President Barack Obama's speech at Cairo University on June 4, 2009 was widely broadcast across the Islamic world. (AP Photo/ J. Scott Applewhite)

from within its borders as well as beyond. But if we see this conflict only from one side or the other, then we will be blind to the truth: the only resolution is for the aspirations of both sides to be met through two states, where Israelis and Palestinians each live in peace and security.

That is in Israel's interest, Palestine's interest, America's interest, and the world's interest. That is why I intend to personally pursue this outcome with all the patience that the task requires. The obligations that the parties have agreed to under the Road Map are clear. For peace to come, it is time for them—and all of us—to live up to our responsibilities.

Palestinians must abandon violence. Resistance through violence and killing is wrong and does not succeed. For centuries, black people in America suffered the lash of the whip as slaves and the humiliation of segregation. But it was not violence that won full and equal rights. It was a peaceful and determined insistence upon the ideals at the center of America's founding. This same story can be told by people from South Africa to South Asia; from Eastern Europe to Indonesia. It's a story with a simple truth: that violence is a dead end. It is a sign of neither courage nor power to shoot rockets at sleeping children, or to blow up old women on a bus. That is not how moral authority is claimed; that is how it is surrendered.

Now is the time for Palestinians to focus on what they can build. The Palestinian Authority must develop its capacity to govern, with institutions that serve the needs of its people. Hamas does have support among some Palestinians, but they also have responsibilities. To play a role in fulfilling Palestinian aspirations, and to unify the

Palestinian people, Hamas must put an end to violence, recognize past agreements, and recognize Israel's right to exist.

At the same time, Israelis must acknowledge that just as Israel's right to exist cannot be denied, neither can Palestine's. The United States does not accept the legitimacy of continued Israeli settlements. This construction violates previous agreements and undermines efforts to achieve peace. It is time for these settlements to stop.

Israel must also live up to its obligations to ensure that Palestinians can live, and work, and develop their society. And just as it devastates Palestinian families, the continuing humanitarian crisis in Gaza does not serve Israel's security; neither does the continuing lack of opportunity in the West Bank. Progress in the daily lives of the Palestinian people must be part of a road to peace, and Israel must take concrete steps to enable such progress.

Finally, the Arab States must recognize that the Arab Peace Initiative was an important beginning, but not the end of their responsibilities. The Arab-Israeli conflict should no longer be used to distract the people of Arab nations from other problems. Instead, it must be a cause for action to help the Palestinian people develop the institutions that will sustain their state; to recognize Israel's legitimacy; and to choose progress over a self-defeating focus on the past.

America will align our policies with those who pursue peace, and say in public what we say in private to Israelis and Palestinians and Arabs. We cannot impose peace. But privately, many Muslims recognize that Israel will not go away. Likewise, many Israelis recognize the need for a Palestinian state. It is time for us to act on what everyone knows to be true.

Too many tears have flowed. Too much blood has been shed. All of us have a responsibility to work for the day when the mothers of Israelis and Palestinians can see their children grow up without fear; when the Holy Land of three great faiths is the place of peace that God intended it to be; when Jerusalem is a secure and lasting home for Jews and Christians and Muslims, and a place for all of the children of Abraham to mingle peacefully together as in the story of Isra, when Moses, Jesus, and Mohammed (peace be upon them) joined in prayer.

The third source of tension is our shared interest in the rights and responsibilities of nations on nuclear weapons.

This issue has been a source of tension between the United States and the Islamic Republic of Iran. For many years, Iran has defined itself in part by its opposition to my country, and there is indeed a tumultuous history between us. In the middle of the Cold War, the United States played a role in the overthrow of a democratically-elected Iranian government. Since the Islamic Revolution, Iran has played a role in acts of hostage-taking and violence against U.S. troops and civilians. This history is well known. Rather than remain trapped in the past, I have made it clear to Iran's leaders and people that my country is prepared to move forward. The question, now, is not what Iran is against, but rather what future it wants to build.

It will be hard to overcome decades of mistrust, but we will proceed with courage, rectitude and resolve. There will be many issues to discuss between our two countries, and we are willing to move forward without preconditions on the basis of mutual respect. But it is clear to all concerned that when it comes to nuclear weapons, we have reached a decisive point. This is not simply about America's interests.

It is about preventing a nuclear arms race in the Middle East that could lead this region and the world down a hugely dangerous path.

I understand those who protest that some countries have weapons that others do not. No single nation should pick and choose which nations hold nuclear weapons. That is why I strongly reaffirmed America's commitment to seek a world in which no nations hold nuclear weapons. And any nation—including Iran—should have the right to access peaceful nuclear power if it complies with its responsibilities under the nuclear Non-Proliferation Treaty. That commitment is at the core of the Treaty, and it must be kept for all who fully abide by it. And I am hopeful that all countries in the region can share in this goal.

The fourth issue that I will address is democracy.

I know there has been controversy about the promotion of democracy in recent years, and much of this controversy is connected to the war in Iraq. So let me be clear: no system of government can or should be imposed upon one nation by any other.

That does not lessen my commitment, however, to governments that reflect the will of the people. Each nation gives life to this principle in its own way, grounded in the traditions of its own people. America does not presume to know what is best for everyone, just as we would not presume to pick the outcome of a peaceful election. But I do have an unyielding belief that all people yearn for certain things: the ability to speak your mind and have a say in how you are governed; confidence in the rule of law and the equal administration of justice; government that is transparent and doesn't steal from the people; the freedom to live as you choose. Those are not just American ideas, they are human rights, and that is why we will support them everywhere.

There is no straight line to realize this promise. But this much is clear: governments that protect these rights are ultimately more stable, successful and secure. Suppressing ideas never succeeds in making them go away. America respects the right of all peaceful and law-abiding voices to be heard around the world, even if we disagree with them. And we will welcome all elected, peaceful governments—provided they govern with respect for all their people.

This last point is important because there are some who advocate for democracy only when they are out of power; once in power, they are ruthless in suppressing the rights of others. No matter where it takes hold, government of the people and by the people sets a single standard for all who hold power: you must maintain your power through consent, not coercion; you must respect the rights of minorities, and participate with a spirit of tolerance and compromise; you must place the interests of your people and the legitimate workings of the political process above your party. Without these ingredients, elections alone do not make true democracy.

The fifth issue that we must address together is religious freedom.

Islam has a proud tradition of tolerance. We see it in the history of Andalusia and Cordoba during the Inquisition. I saw it firsthand as a child in Indonesia, where devout Christians worshiped freely in an overwhelmingly Muslim country. That is the spirit we need today. People in every country should be free to choose and live their faith based upon the persuasion of the mind, heart, and soul. This tolerance is essential for religion to thrive, but it is being challenged in many different ways.

Among some Muslims, there is a disturbing tendency to measure one's own faith by the rejection of another's. The richness of religious diversity must be upheld—

whether it is for Maronites in Lebanon or the Copts in Egypt. And fault lines must be closed among Muslims as well, as the divisions between Sunni and Shia have led to tragic violence, particularly in Iraq.

Freedom of religion is central to the ability of peoples to live together. We must always examine the ways in which we protect it. For instance, in the United States, rules on charitable giving have made it harder for Muslims to fulfill their religious obligation. That is why I am committed to working with American Muslims to ensure that they can fulfill zakat.

Likewise, it is important for Western countries to avoid impeding Muslim citizens from practicing religion as they see fit—for instance, by dictating what clothes a Muslim woman should wear. We cannot disguise hostility towards any religion behind the pretence of liberalism.

Indeed, faith should bring us together. That is why we are forging service projects in America that bring together Christians, Muslims, and Jews. That is why we welcome efforts like Saudi Arabian King Abdullah's Interfaith dialogue and Turkey's leadership in the Alliance of Civilizations. Around the world, we can turn dialogue into Interfaith service, so bridges between peoples lead to action—whether it is combating malaria in Africa, or providing relief after a natural disaster.

The sixth issue that I want to address is women's rights.

I know there is debate about this issue. I reject the view of some in the West that a woman who chooses to cover her hair is somehow less equal, but I do believe that a woman who is denied an education is denied equality. And it is no coincidence that countries where women are well-educated are far more likely to be prosperous.

Now let me be clear: issues of women's equality are by no means simply an issue for Islam. In Turkey, Pakistan, Bangladesh and Indonesia, we have seen Muslim-majority countries elect a woman to lead. Meanwhile, the struggle for women's equality continues in many aspects of American life, and in countries around the world.

Our daughters can contribute just as much to society as our sons, and our common prosperity will be advanced by allowing all humanity—men and women—to reach their full potential. I do not believe that women must make the same choices as men in order to be equal, and I respect those women who choose to live their lives in traditional roles. But it should be their choice. That is why the United States will partner with any Muslim-majority country to support expanded literacy for girls, and to help young women pursue employment through micro-financing that helps people live their dreams.

Finally, I want to discuss economic development and opportunity.

. . .

It is easier to start wars than to end them. It is easier to blame others than to look inward; to see what is different about someone than to find the things we share. But we should choose the right path, not just the easy path. There is also one rule that lies at the heart of every religion—that we do unto others as we would have them do unto us. This truth transcends nations and peoples—a belief that isn't new; that isn't black or white or brown; that isn't Christian, or Muslim or Jew. It's a belief that pulsed in the cradle of civilization, and that still beats in the heart of billions. It's a faith in other people, and it's what brought me here today.

We have the power to make the world we seek, but only if we have the courage to make a new beginning, keeping in mind what has been written.

The Holy Koran tells us, "O mankind! We have created you male and a female; and we have made you into nations and tribes so that you may know one another."

The Talmud tells us: "The whole of the Torah is for the purpose of promoting peace."

The Holy Bible tells us, "Blessed are the peacemakers, for they shall be called sons of God."

The people of the world can live together in peace. We know that is God's vision. Now, that must be our work here on Earth. Thank you. And may God's peace be upon you.

- **Document: President Obama's Speech at West Point Regarding His Afghanistan Policy**
- **Date:** December 2, 2009
- **Significance:** In this speech President Obama significantly alters the course of military policy regarding the war in Afghanistan. After waiting for the results of national elections in Afghanistan and after conducting a lengthy, thorough review process, President Obama authorized an increase in the number of troops but also set conditions and a timeframe for withdrawing U.S. forces.
- **Source:** Barack Obama, "Remarks by the President in Address to the Nation on the Way Forward in Afghanistan and Pakistan." The White House. http://www.whitehouse.gov/the-press-office/remarks -president-address-nation-way-forward-afghanistan-and-pakistan.

Thank you. Please be seated.

Good evening. To the United States Corps of Cadets, to the men and women of our armed services, and to my fellow Americans, I want to speak to you tonight about our effort in Afghanistan, the nature of our commitment there, the scope of our interests, and the strategy that my administration will pursue to bring this war to a successful conclusion.

It's an extraordinary honor for me to do so here at West Point, where so many men and women have prepared to stand up for our security and to represent what is finest about our country.

To address these important issues, it's important to recall why America and our allies were compelled to fight a war in Afghanistan in the first place.

We did not ask for this fight. On September 11, 2001, 19 men hijacked four airplanes and used them to murder nearly 3,000 people. They struck at our military and economic nerve centers. They took the lives of innocent men, women, and children without regard to their faith or race or station.

Were it not for the heroic actions of passengers on board one of those flights, they could have also struck at one of the great symbols of our democracy in Washington and killed many more.

As we know, these men belonged to al-Qaeda, a group of extremists who have distorted and defiled Islam, one of the world's great religions, to justify the slaughter of innocents. al-Qaeda's base of operations was in Afghanistan, where they were harbored by the Taliban, a ruthless, repressive and radical movement that seized control of that country after it was ravaged by years of Soviet occupation and civil war and after the attention of America and our friends had turned elsewhere.

Just days after 9/11, Congress authorized the use of force against al-Qaeda and those who harbored them, an authorization that continues to this day. The vote in the Senate was 98-0; the vote in the House was 420-1.

For the first time in its history, the North Atlantic Treaty Organization invoked Article 5, the commitment that says an attack on one member nation is an attack on all. And the United Nations Security Council endorsed the use of all necessary steps to respond to the 9/11 attacks. America, our allies, and the world were acting as one to destroy al-Qaeda's terrorist network and to protect our common security.

Under the banner of this domestic unity and international legitimacy—and only after the Taliban refused to turn over Osama bin Laden—we sent our troops into Afghanistan.

Within a matter of months, al-Qaeda was scattered and many of its operatives were killed. The Taliban was driven from power and pushed back on its heels. A place that had known decades of fear now had reason to hope.

At a conference convened by the U.N., a provisional government was established under President Hamid Karzai. And an International Security Assistance Force was established to help bring a lasting peace to a war-torn country.

Then, in early 2003, the decision was made to wage a second war in Iraq. The wrenching debate over the Iraq war is well-known and need not be repeated here. It's enough to say that, for the next six years, the Iraq war drew the dominant share of our troops, our resources, our diplomacy, and our national attention, and that the decision to go into Iraq caused substantial rifts between America and much of the world.

Today, after extraordinary costs, we are bringing the Iraq war to a responsible end. We will remove our combat brigades from Iraq by the end of next summer and all of our troops by the end of 2011. That we are doing so is a testament to the character of the men and women in uniform.

Thanks to their courage, grit and perseverance, we have given Iraqis a chance to shape their future, and we are successfully leaving Iraq to its people.

But while we have achieved hard-earned milestones in Iraq, the situation in Afghanistan has deteriorated. After escaping across the border into Pakistan in 2001 and 2002, al-Qaeda's leadership established a safe haven there. Although a legitimate government was elected by the Afghan people, it's been hampered by corruption, the drug trade, an under-developed economy, and insufficient security forces.

Over the last several years, the Taliban has maintained common cause with al-Qaeda, as they both seek an overthrow of the Afghan government. Gradually, the Taliban has begun to control additional swaths of territory in Afghanistan, while engaging in increasingly brazen and devastating acts of terrorism against the Pakistani people.

Now, throughout this period, our troop levels in Afghanistan remained a fraction of what they were in Iraq. When I took office, we had just over 32,000 Americans serving in Afghanistan compared to 160,000 in Iraq at the peak of the war.

Commanders in Afghanistan repeatedly asked for support to deal with the reemergence of the Taliban, but these reinforcements did not arrive. And that's why, shortly after taking office, I approved a long-standing request for more troops.

After consultations with our allies, I then announced a strategy recognizing the fundamental connection between our war effort in Afghanistan and the extremist safe havens in Pakistan. I set a goal that was narrowly defined as disrupting, dismantling, and defeating al-Qaeda and its extremist allies, and pledged to better coordinate our military and civilian efforts.

Since then, we've made progress on some important objectives. High-ranking al-Qaeda and Taliban leaders have been killed, and we've stepped up the pressure on al-Qaeda worldwide.

In Pakistan, that nation's army has gone on its largest offensive in years. In Afghanistan, we and our allies prevented the Taliban from stopping a presidential election, and although it was marred by fraud, that election produced a government that is consistent with Afghanistan's laws and constitution.

Yet huge challenges remain: Afghanistan is not lost, but for several years, it has moved backwards. There's no imminent threat of the government being overthrown, but the Taliban has gained momentum. Al-Qaeda has not reemerged in Afghanistan in the same numbers as before 9/11, but they retain their safe havens along the border. And our forces lack the full support they need to effectively train and partner with Afghan security forces and better secure the population.

Our new commander in Afghanistan, General McChrystal, has reported that the security situation is more serious than he anticipated. In short, the status quo is not sustainable.

As cadets, you volunteered for service during this time of danger. Some of you have fought in Afghanistan. Some of you will deploy there. As your commander-in-chief, I owe you a mission that is clearly defined and worthy of your service.

And that's why, after the Afghan voting was completed, I insisted on a thorough review of our strategy.

Now, let me be clear: There has never been an option before me that called for troop deployments before 2010, so there has been no delay or denial of resources necessary for the conduct of the war during this review period. Instead, the review has allowed me to ask the hard questions and to explore all the different options, along with my national security team, our military, and civilian leadership in Afghanistan, and our key partners.

And given the stakes involved, I owed the American people and our troops no less.

This review is now complete. And as commander-in-chief, I have determined that it is in our vital national interest to send an additional 30,000 U.S. troops to Afghanistan.

After 18 months, our troops will begin to come home. These are the resources that we need to seize the initiative, while building the Afghan capacity that can allow for a responsible transition of our forces out of Afghanistan.

I do not make this decision lightly. I opposed the war in Iraq precisely because I believe that we must exercise restraint in the use of military force and always consider the long-term consequences of our actions.

We have been at war now for eight years, at enormous cost in lives and resources. Years of debate over Iraq and terrorism have left our unity on national security issues in tatters and created a highly polarized and partisan backdrop for this effort. And having just experienced the worst economic crisis since the Great Depression, the American people are understandably focused on rebuilding our economy and putting people to work here at home.

Most of all, I know that this decision asks even more of you, a military that, along with your families, has already borne the heaviest of all burdens.

As president, I have signed a letter of condolence to the family of each American who gives their life in these wars. I have read the letters from the parents and spouses of those who deployed. I've visited our courageous wounded warriors at Walter Reed. I've traveled to Dover to meet the flag-draped caskets of 18 Americans returning home to their final resting place.

I see firsthand the terrible wages of war. If I did not think that the security of the United States and the safety of the American people were at stake in Afghanistan, I would gladly order every single one of our troops home tomorrow.

So, no, I do not make this decision lightly. I make this decision because I am convinced that our security is at stake in Afghanistan and Pakistan. This is the epicenter of violent extremism practiced by al-Qaeda. It is from here that we were attacked on 9/11, and it is from here that new attacks are being plotted as I speak.

This is no idle danger, no hypothetical threat. In the last few months alone, we have apprehended extremists within our borders who were sent here from the border region of Afghanistan and Pakistan to commit new acts of terror. And this danger will only grow if the region slides backwards and al-Qaeda can operate with impunity.

We must keep the pressure on al-Qaeda. And to do that, we must increase the stability and capacity of our partners in the region.

Of course, this burden is not ours alone to bear. This is not just America's war. Since 9/11, al-Qaeda's safe havens have been the source of attacks against London and Amman and Bali. The people and governments of both Afghanistan and Pakistan are endangered. And the stakes are even higher within a nuclear-armed Pakistan, because we know that al-Qaeda and other extremists seek nuclear weapons, and we have every reason to believe that they would use them.

These facts compel us to act along with our friends and allies. Our overarching goal remains the same: to disrupt, dismantle and defeat al-Qaeda in Afghanistan and Pakistan and to prevent its capacity to threaten America and our allies in the future.

To meet that goal, we will pursue the following objectives within Afghanistan. We must deny al-Qaeda a safe haven. We must reverse the Taliban's momentum and deny it the ability to overthrow the government. And we must strengthen the capacity of Afghanistan's security forces and government, so that they can take lead responsibility for Afghanistan's future.

We will meet these objectives in three ways. First, we will pursue a military strategy that will break the Taliban's momentum and increase Afghanistan's capacity over the next 18 months.

The 30,000 additional troops that I'm announcing tonight will deploy in the first part of 2010, the fastest possible pace, so that they can target the insurgency and secure key population centers. They'll increase our ability to train competent Afghan security forces and to partner with them so that more Afghans can get into the fight. And they will help create the conditions for the United States to transfer responsibility to the Afghans.

Because this is an international effort, I've asked that our commitment be joined by contributions from our allies. Some have already provided additional troops, and we're confident that there will be further contributions in the days and weeks ahead.

Our friends have fought and bled and died alongside us in Afghanistan. And now we must come together to end this war successfully. For what's at stake is not simply a test of NATO's credibility; what's at stake is the security of our allies and the common security of the world.

Now, taken together, these additional American and international troops will allow us to accelerate handing over responsibility to Afghan forces and allow us to begin the transfer of our forces out of Afghanistan in July of 2011. Just as we have done in Iraq, we will execute this transition responsibly, taking into account conditions on the ground.

We'll continue to advise and assist Afghanistan's security forces to ensure that they can succeed over the long haul. But it will be clear to the Afghan government—and, more importantly, to the Afghan people—that they will ultimately be responsible for their own country.

Second, we will work with our partners, the United Nations, and the Afghan people to pursue a more effective civilian strategy so that the government can take advantage of improved security. This effort must be based on performance. The days of providing a blank check are over.

President Karzai's inauguration speech sent the right message about moving in a new direction. And going forward, we will be clear about what we expect from those who receive our assistance.

We'll support Afghan ministries, governors, and local leaders that combat corruption and deliver for the people. We expect those who are ineffective or corrupt to be held accountable. And we will also focus our assistance in areas such as agriculture that can make an immediate impact in the lives of the Afghan people.

Now, the people of Afghanistan have endured violence for decades. They've been confronted with occupation by the Soviet Union, and then by foreign al-Qaeda fighters who used Afghan land for their own purposes.

So tonight, I want the Afghan people to understand: America seeks an end to this era of war and suffering. We have no interest in occupying your country. We will support efforts by the Afghan government to open the door to those Taliban who abandon violence and respect the human rights of their fellow citizens. And we will seek a partnership with Afghanistan grounded in mutual respect, to isolate those who destroy, to strengthen those who build, to hasten the day when our troops will leave, and to forge a lasting friendship in which America is your partner and never your patron.

Third, we will act with the full recognition that our success in Afghanistan is inextricably linked to our partnership with Pakistan. We're in Afghanistan to prevent a cancer from once again spreading through that country. But this same cancer has also taken root in the border region of Pakistan. And that's why we need a strategy that works on both sides of the border.

In the past, there have been those in Pakistan who've argued that the struggle against extremism is not their fight and that Pakistan is better off doing little or seeking accommodation with those who use violence.

But in recent years, as innocents have been killed from Karachi to Islamabad, it has become clear that it is the Pakistani people who are the most endangered by extremism. Public opinion has turned. The Pakistani army has waged an offensive in Swat and South Waziristan, and there is no doubt that the United States and Pakistan share a common enemy.

In the past, we too often defined our relationship with Pakistan narrowly. And those days are over.

Moving forward, we are committed to a partnership with Pakistan that is built on a foundation of mutual interest, mutual respect, and mutual trust. We will strengthen Pakistan's capacity to target those groups that threaten our countries and have made it clear that we cannot tolerate a safe haven for terrorists whose location is known and whose intentions are clear.

America is also providing substantial resources to support Pakistan's democracy and development. We are the largest international supporter for those Pakistanis displaced by the fighting. And going forward, the Pakistan people must know: America will remain a strong supporter of Pakistan's security and prosperity long after the guns have fallen silent so that the great potential of its people can be unleashed.

These are the three core elements of our strategy: a military effort to create the conditions for a transition; a civilian surge that reinforces positive action; and an effective partnership with Pakistan.

And I recognize there are a range of concerns about our approach. So let me briefly address a few of the more prominent arguments that I've heard and which I take very seriously.

First, there are those who suggest that Afghanistan is another Vietnam. They argue that it cannot be stabilized and we're better off cutting our losses and rapidly withdrawing. I believe this argument depends on a false reading of history.

Unlike Vietnam, we are joined by a broad coalition of 43 nations that recognizes the legitimacy of our action. Unlike Vietnam, we are not facing a broad-based popular insurgency. And most importantly, unlike Vietnam, the American people were viciously attacked from Afghanistan and remain a target for those same extremists who are plotting along its border.

To abandon this area now and to rely only on efforts against al-Qaeda from a distance would significantly hamper our ability to keep the pressure on al-Qaeda and create an unacceptable risk of additional attacks on our homeland and our allies.

Second, there are those who acknowledge that we can't leave Afghanistan in its current state, but suggest that we go forward with the troops that we already have, but this would simply maintain a status quo in which we muddle through and permit a slow deterioration of conditions there. It would ultimately prove more costly and prolong our stay in Afghanistan, because we would never be able to generate the conditions needed to train Afghan security forces and give them the space to take over.

Finally, there are those who oppose identifying a timeframe for our transition to Afghan responsibility. Indeed, some call for a more dramatic and open-ended escalation of our war effort, one that would commit us to a nation-building project of up to a decade. I reject this course because it sets goals that are beyond what can be achieved at a reasonable cost and what we need to achieve to secure our interests.

Furthermore, the absence of a timeframe for transition would deny us any sense of urgency in working with the Afghan government. It must be clear that Afghans will have to take responsibility for their security and that America has no interest in fighting an endless war in Afghanistan.

As president, I refuse to set goals that go beyond our responsibility, our means, or our interests. And I must weigh all of the challenges that our nation faces. I don't have the luxury of committing to just one.

Indeed, I'm mindful of the words of President Eisenhower, who, in discussing our national security, said, "Each proposal must be weighed in the light of a broader consideration: the need to maintain balance in and among national programs."

Over the past several years, we have lost that balance. We failed to appreciate the connection between our national security and our economy. In the wake of an economic crisis, too many of our neighbors and friends are out of work and struggle to pay the bills. Too many Americans are worried about the future facing our children.

Meanwhile, competition within the global economy has grown more fierce, so we can't simply afford to ignore the price of these wars.

All told, by the time I took office, the cost of the wars in Iraq and Afghanistan approached a trillion dollars. And going forward, I am committed to addressing these costs openly and honestly. Our new approach in Afghanistan is likely to cost us roughly $30 billion for the military this year, and I'll work closely with Congress to address these costs as we work to bring down our deficit.

But as we end the war in Iraq and transition to Afghan responsibility, we must rebuild our strength here at home. Our prosperity provides a foundation for our power. It pays for our military; it underwrites our diplomacy; it taps the potential of our people and allows investment in new industry; and it will allow us to compete in this century as successfully as we did in the last.

That's why our troop commitment in Afghanistan cannot be open-ended: because the nation that I'm most interested in building is our own.

Now, let me be clear. None of this will be easy. The struggle against violent extremism will not be finished quickly, and it extends well beyond Afghanistan and Pakistan. It will be an enduring test of our free society and our leadership in the world. And unlike the great power conflicts and clear lines of division that defined the 20th century, our effort will involve disorderly regions, failed states, diffuse enemies.

So as a result, America will have to show our strength in the way that we end wars and prevent conflict, not just how we wage wars. We'll have to be nimble and precise in our use of military power. Where Al Qaida and its allies attempt to establish a foothold—whether in Somalia or Yemen or elsewhere—they must be confronted by growing pressure and strong partnerships.

And we can't count on military might alone. We have to invest in our homeland security, because we can't capture or kill every violent extremist abroad. We have to improve and better coordinate our intelligence so that we stay one step ahead of shadowy networks.

We will have to take away the tools of mass destruction. And that's why I've made it a central pillar of my foreign policy to secure loose nuclear materials from terrorists, to stop the spread of nuclear weapons, and to pursue the goal of a world without them, because every nation must understand that true security will never come from an endless race for ever more destructive weapons. True security will come for those who reject them.

We'll have to use diplomacy, because no one nation can meet the challenges of an interconnected world acting alone. I've spent this year renewing our alliances and forging new partnerships. And we have forged a new beginning between America and the Muslim world, one that recognizes our mutual interest in breaking a cycle of conflict and that promises a future in which those who kill innocents are isolated by those who stand up for peace and prosperity and human dignity.

And, finally, we must draw on the strength of our values, for the challenges that we face may have changed, but the things that we believe in must not. That's why we must promote our values by living them at home, which is why I've prohibited torture and will close the prison at Guantanamo Bay.

And we must make it clear to every man, woman and child around the world who lives under the dark cloud of tyranny that America will speak out on behalf of their human rights and tend for the light of freedom and justice and opportunity and respect for the dignity of all peoples. That is who we are; that is the source, the moral source of America's authority.

Since the days of Franklin Roosevelt and the service and sacrifice of our grandparents and great-grandparents, our country has borne a special burden in global affairs. We have spilled American blood in many countries on multiple continents. We have spent our revenue to help others rebuild from rubble and develop their own economies. We have joined with others to develop an architecture of institutions—from the United Nations to NATO to the World Bank—that provide for the common security and prosperity of human beings.

We have not always been thanked for these efforts, and we have at times made mistakes. But more than any other nation, the United States of America has underwritten global security for over six decades, a time that, for all its problems, has seen walls come down, and markets open, and billions lifted from poverty, unparalleled scientific progress, and advancing frontiers of human liberty.

For unlike the great powers of old, we have not sought world domination. Our union was founded in resistance to oppression. We do not seek to occupy other nations. We will not claim another nation's resources or target other peoples because their faith or ethnicity is different from ours.

What we have fought for, what we continue to fight for is a better future for our children and grandchildren. And we believe that their lives will be better if other peoples' children and grandchildren can live in freedom and access opportunity.

As a country, we're not as young—and perhaps not as innocent—as we were when Roosevelt was president. Yet we are still heirs to a noble struggle for freedom. And now we must summon all of our might and moral suasion to meet the challenges of a new age.

In the end, our security and leadership does not come solely from the strength of our arms. It derives from our people, from the workers and businesses who will rebuild our economy; from the entrepreneurs and researchers who will pioneer new industries; from the teachers that will educate our children and the service of those who work in our communities at home; from the diplomats and Peace Corps volunteers who spread hope abroad; and from the men and women in uniform who are part of an unbroken line of sacrifice that has made government of the people, by the people, and for the people a reality on this Earth.

This vast and diverse citizenry will not always agree on every issue, nor should we. But I also know that we as a country cannot sustain our leadership nor navigate the momentous challenges of our time if we allow ourselves to be split asunder by the same rancor and cynicism and partisanship that has in recent times poisoned our national discourse.

It's easy to forget that, when this war began, we were united, bound together by the fresh memory of a horrific attack and by the determination to defend our homeland and the values we hold dear. I refuse to accept the notion that we cannot summon that unity again. I believe ...

I believe with every fiber of my being that we, as Americans, can still come together behind a common purpose, for our values are not simply words written into parchment. They are a creed that calls us together and that has carried us through the darkest of storms as one nation, as one people.

America, we are passing through a time of great trial. And the message that we send in the midst of these storms must be clear: that our cause is just, our resolve unwavering. We will go forward with the confidence that right makes might and with the commitment to forge an America that is safer, a world that is more secure, and a future that represents not the deepest of fears but the highest of hopes.

Thank you, God bless you, and God bless the United States of America.

Thank you very much.

- **Document: President Obama's Nobel Peace Prize Remarks**
- **Date:** December 11, 2009
- **Significance**: The Nobel Committee awarded President Obama the Nobel Peace Prize for 2009. Many saw this decision as an indirect criticism of President Bush's policies more than a recognition of President Obama's accomplishments. Indeed, after not even serving a full year as president, Obama himself admitted that his list of accomplishments was relatively short. Ironically, his acceptance speech is as much a defense of a just war theory as it was a defense of peace. The speech was given soon after President Obama decided to send 30,000 additional U.S. troops to Afghanistan, and the speech provides justifications for this decision.
- **Source:** Barack Obama, "Remarks by the President at the Acceptance of the Nobel Peace Prize." The White House. http://www.whitehouse .gov/the-press-office/remarks-president-acceptance-nobel-peace-prize.

Your Majesties, Your Royal Highnesses, distinguished members of the Norwegian Nobel Committee, citizens of America, and citizens of the world:

I receive this honor with deep gratitude and great humility. It is an award that speaks to our highest aspirations—that for all the cruelty and hardship of our world, we are not mere prisoners of fate. Our actions matter, and can bend history in the direction of justice.

And yet I would be remiss if I did not acknowledge the considerable controversy that your generous decision has generated. (Laughter.) In part, this is because I am at the beginning, and not the end, of my labors on the world stage. Compared to some of the giants of history who've received this prize—Schweitzer and King; Marshall and Mandela—my accomplishments are slight. And then there are the men and women around the world who have been jailed and beaten in the pursuit of justice; those who toil in humanitarian organizations to relieve suffering; the unrecognized millions whose quiet acts of courage and compassion inspire even the most hardened cynics. I cannot argue with those who find these men and women—some known, some obscure to all but those they help—to be far more deserving of this honor than I.

But perhaps the most profound issue surrounding my receipt of this prize is the fact that I am the Commander-in-Chief of the military of a nation in the midst of two wars. One of these wars is winding down. The other is a conflict that America did

Did You Know?

Presidents and Nobel Peace Prizes

Four U.S. presidents have won the Nobel Peace Prize—three while in office and one after leaving office. Teddy Roosevelt won the Peace Prize in 1906 in recognition for many diplomatic accomplishments, including his role in facilitating the end of the Russo-Japanese War in 1905. Woodrow Wilson won in 1919 for his role in founding the League of Nations, even though the United States did not join. In 2002, the Nobel Committee awarded the Peace Prize to Jimmy Carter "for his decades of untiring effort to find peaceful solutions to international conflicts, to advance democracy and human rights, and to promote economic and social development." And in 2009, Barack Obama won, according to the Nobel Committee, "for his extraordinary efforts to strengthen international diplomacy and cooperation between peoples." Other U.S. officials and diplomats have won the Nobel Peace Prize, including Vice President Al Gore, Henry Kissinger, Ralph Bunche, Cordell Hull, and George C. Marshall.

not seek; one in which we are joined by 42 other countries—including Norway—in an effort to defend ourselves and all nations from further attacks.

Still, we are at war, and I'm responsible for the deployment of thousands of young Americans to battle in a distant land. Some will kill, and some will be killed. And so I come here with an acute sense of the costs of armed conflict—filled with difficult questions about the relationship between war and peace, and our effort to replace one with the other.

Now these questions are not new. War, in one form or another, appeared with the first man. At the dawn of history, its morality was not questioned; it was simply a fact, like drought or disease—the manner in which tribes and then civilizations sought power and settled their differences.

And over time, as codes of law sought to control violence within groups, so did philosophers and clerics and statesmen seek to regulate the destructive power of war. The concept of a "just war" emerged, suggesting that war is justified only when certain conditions were met: if it is waged as a last resort or in self-defense; if the force used is proportional; and if, whenever possible, civilians are spared from violence.

. . .

But the world must remember that it was not simply international institutions—not just treaties and declarations—that brought stability to a post-World War II world. Whatever mistakes we have made, the plain fact is this: The United States of America has helped underwrite global security for more than six decades with the blood of our citizens and the strength of our arms. The service and sacrifice of our men and women in uniform has promoted peace and prosperity from Germany to Korea, and enabled democracy to take hold in places like the Balkans. We have borne this burden not because we seek to impose our will. We have done so out of enlightened self-interest—because we seek a better future for our children and grandchildren, and we believe that their lives will be better if others' children and grandchildren can live in freedom and prosperity.

So yes, the instruments of war do have a role to play in preserving the peace. And yet this truth must coexist with another—that no matter how justified, war promises human tragedy. The soldier's courage and sacrifice is full of glory, expressing devotion to country, to cause, to comrades in arms. But war itself is never glorious, and we must never trumpet it as such.

So part of our challenge is reconciling these two seemingly irreconcilable truths—that war is sometimes necessary, and war at some level is an expression of human folly. Concretely, we must direct our effort to the task that President Kennedy called for long ago. "Let us focus," he said, "on a more practical, more attainable peace, based not on a sudden revolution in human nature but on a gradual evolution in human institutions." A gradual evolution of human institutions.

What might this evolution look like? What might these practical steps be?

To begin with, I believe that all nations—strong and weak alike—must adhere to standards that govern the use of force. I—like any head of state—reserve the right to act unilaterally if necessary to defend my nation. Nevertheless, I am convinced that adhering to standards, international standards, strengthens those who do, and isolates and weakens those who don't.

The world rallied around America after the 9/11 attacks, and continues to support our efforts in Afghanistan, because of the horror of those senseless attacks and the recognized principle of self-defense. Likewise, the world recognized the need to confront Saddam Hussein when he invaded Kuwait—a consensus that sent a clear message to all about the cost of aggression.

Furthermore, America—in fact, no nation—can insist that others follow the rules of the road if we refuse to follow them ourselves. For when we don't, our actions appear arbitrary and undercut the legitimacy of future interventions, no matter how justified.

And this becomes particularly important when the purpose of military action extends beyond self-defense or the defense of one nation against an aggressor. More and more, we all confront difficult questions about how to prevent the slaughter of civilians by their own government, or to stop a civil war whose violence and suffering can engulf an entire region.

I believe that force can be justified on humanitarian grounds, as it was in the Balkans, or in other places that have been scarred by war. Inaction tears at our conscience and can lead to more costly intervention later. That's why all responsible nations must embrace the role that militaries with a clear mandate can play to keep the peace.

America's commitment to global security will never waver. But in a world in which threats are more diffuse, and missions more complex, America cannot act alone. America alone cannot secure the peace. This is true in Afghanistan. This is true in failed states like Somalia, where terrorism and piracy is joined by famine and human suffering. And sadly, it will continue to be true in unstable regions for years to come.

The leaders and soldiers of NATO countries, and other friends and allies, demonstrate this truth through the capacity and courage they've shown in Afghanistan. But in many countries, there is a disconnect between the efforts of those who serve and the ambivalence of the broader public. I understand why war is not popular, but I also know this: The belief that peace is desirable is rarely enough to achieve it. Peace requires responsibility. Peace entails sacrifice. That's why NATO continues to be indispensable. That's why we must strengthen U.N. and regional peacekeeping, and not leave the task to a few countries. That's why we honor those who return home from peacekeeping and training abroad to Oslo and Rome; to Ottawa and Sydney; to Dhaka and Kigali—we honor them not as makers of war, but of wagers—but as wagers of peace.

Let me make one final point about the use of force. Even as we make difficult decisions about going to war, we must also think clearly about how we fight it. The Nobel Committee recognized this truth in awarding its first prize for peace to Henry Dunant—the founder of the Red Cross, and a driving force behind the Geneva Conventions.

Where force is necessary, we have a moral and strategic interest in binding ourselves to certain rules of conduct. And even as we confront a vicious adversary that abides by no rules, I believe the United States of America must remain a standard bearer in the conduct of war. That is what makes us different from those whom we fight. That is a source of our strength. That is why I prohibited torture. That is why I ordered the prison at Guantanamo Bay closed. And that is why I have reaffirmed America's commitment to abide by the Geneva Conventions. We lose ourselves when we compromise the very ideals that we fight to defend. (Applause.) And we honor— we honor those ideals by upholding them not when it's easy, but when it is hard.

I have spoken at some length to the question that must weigh on our minds and our hearts as we choose to wage war. But let me now turn to our effort to avoid such tragic choices, and speak of three ways that we can build a just and lasting peace.

First, in dealing with those nations that break rules and laws, I believe that we must develop alternatives to violence that are tough enough to actually change behavior— for if we want a lasting peace, then the words of the international community must mean something. Those regimes that break the rules must be held accountable. Sanctions must exact a real price. Intransigence must be met with increased pressure—and such pressure exists only when the world stands together as one.

One urgent example is the effort to prevent the spread of nuclear weapons, and to seek a world without them. In the middle of the last century, nations agreed to be bound by a treaty whose bargain is clear: All will have access to peaceful nuclear power; those without nuclear weapons will forsake them; and those with nuclear weapons will work towards disarmament. I am committed to upholding this treaty. It is a centerpiece of my foreign policy. And I'm working with President Medvedev to reduce America and Russia's nuclear stockpiles.

But it is also incumbent upon all of us to insist that nations like Iran and North Korea do not game the system. Those who claim to respect international law cannot avert their eyes when those laws are flouted. Those who care for their own security cannot ignore the danger of an arms race in the Middle East or East Asia. Those who seek peace cannot stand idly by as nations arm themselves for nuclear war.

The same principle applies to those who violate international laws by brutalizing their own people. When there is genocide in Darfur, systematic rape in Congo, repression in Burma—there must be consequences. Yes, there will be engagement; yes, there will be diplomacy—but there must be consequences when those things fail. And the closer we stand together, the less likely we will be faced with the choice between armed intervention and complicity in oppression.

This brings me to a second point—the nature of the peace that we seek. For peace is not merely the absence of visible conflict. Only a just peace based on the inherent rights and dignity of every individual can truly be lasting.

It was this insight that drove drafters of the Universal Declaration of Human Rights after the Second World War. In the wake of devastation, they recognized that if human rights are not protected, peace is a hollow promise.

And yet too often, these words are ignored. For some countries, the failure to uphold human rights is excused by the false suggestion that these are somehow Western principles, foreign to local cultures or stages of a nation's development. And within America, there has long been a tension between those who describe themselves as realists or idealists—a tension that suggests a stark choice between the narrow pursuit of interests or an endless campaign to impose our values around the world.

I reject these choices. I believe that peace is unstable where citizens are denied the right to speak freely or worship as they please; choose their own leaders or assemble without fear. Pent-up grievances fester, and the suppression of tribal and religious identity can lead to violence. We also know that the opposite is true. Only when Europe became free did it finally find peace. America has never fought a war against a democracy, and our closest friends are governments that protect the rights of their citizens. No matter how callously defined, neither America's interests—nor the world's—are served by the denial of human aspirations.

So even as we respect the unique culture and traditions of different countries, America will always be a voice for those aspirations that are universal. We will bear witness to the quiet dignity of reformers like Aung Sang Suu Kyi; to the bravery of Zimbabweans who cast their ballots in the face of beatings; to the hundreds of thousands who have marched silently through the streets of Iran. It is telling that the leaders of these governments fear the aspirations of their own people more than the power of any other nation. And it is the responsibility of all free people and free nations to make clear that these movements—these movements of hope and history—they have us on their side.

Let me also say this: The promotion of human rights cannot be about exhortation alone. At times, it must be coupled with painstaking diplomacy. I know that engagement with repressive regimes lacks the satisfying purity of indignation. But I also know that sanctions without outreach—condemnation without discussion—can carry forward only a crippling status quo. No repressive regime can move down a new path unless it has the choice of an open door.

In light of the Cultural Revolution's horrors, Nixon's meeting with Mao appeared inexcusable—and yet it surely helped set China on a path where millions of its citizens have been lifted from poverty and connected to open societies. Pope John Paul's engagement with Poland created space not just for the Catholic Church, but for labor leaders like Lech Walesa. Ronald Reagan's efforts on arms control and embrace of perestroika not only improved relations with the Soviet Union, but empowered dissidents throughout Eastern Europe. There's no simple formula here. But we must try as best we can to balance isolation and engagement, pressure and incentives, so that human rights and dignity are advanced over time.

Third, a just peace includes not only civil and political rights—it must encompass economic security and opportunity. For true peace is not just freedom from fear, but freedom from want.

It is undoubtedly true that development rarely takes root without security; it is also true that security does not exist where human beings do not have access to enough food, or clean water, or the medicine and shelter they need to survive. It does not exist where children can't aspire to a decent education or a job that supports a family. The absence of hope can rot a society from within.

And that's why helping farmers feed their own people—or nations educate their children and care for the sick—is not mere charity. It's also why the world must come together to confront climate change. There is little scientific dispute that if we do nothing, we will face more drought, more famine, more mass displacement—all of which will fuel more conflict for decades. For this reason, it is not merely scientists and environmental activists who call for swift and forceful action—it's military leaders in my own country and others who understand our common security hangs in the balance.

Agreements among nations. Strong institutions. Support for human rights. Investments in development. All these are vital ingredients in bringing about the evolution that President Kennedy spoke about. And yet, I do not believe that we will have the will, the determination, the staying power, to complete this work without something more—and that's the continued expansion of our moral imagination; an insistence that there's something irreducible that we all share.

As the world grows smaller, you might think it would be easier for human beings to recognize how similar we are; to understand that we're all basically seeking the same things; that we all hope for the chance to live out our lives with some measure of happiness and fulfillment for ourselves and our families.

. . .

Let us live by their example. We can acknowledge that oppression will always be with us, and still strive for justice. We can admit the intractability of deprivation, and still strive for dignity. Clear-eyed, we can understand that there will be war, and still strive for peace. We can do that—for that is the story of human progress; that's the hope of all the world; and at this moment of challenge, that must be our work here on Earth.

Thank you very much.

- **Document: The NEW START Treaty**
- **Date:** April 8, 2010 (signed in Prague)
- **Significance**: The NEW START Treaty represents the latest step in the bilateral agreements between the United States and Russia. The bilateral relations of the two nations were dominated by a rivalry in the area of nuclear weapons during the Cold War. The previous treaty had ended in 2009. New START was ratified by the U.S. Congress in December 2010 and by Russia's parliament in January 2011.
- **Source:** U.S. Department of State. Treaty Between the United States of America and the Russian Federation on Measures for the Further Reduction and Limitation of Strategic Offensive Arms. http://www.state.gov/documents/organization/140035.pdf.

TREATY BETWEEN THE UNITED STATES OF AMERICA AND THE RUSSIAN FEDERATION ON MEASURES FOR THE FURTHER REDUCTION AND LIMITATION OF STRATEGIC OFFENSIVE ARMS

The United States of America and the Russian Federation, hereinafter referred to as the Parties, Believing that global challenges and threats require new approaches to interaction across the whole range of their strategic relations,

Working therefore to forge a new strategic relationship based on mutual trust, openness, predictability, and cooperation,

Desiring to bring their respective nuclear postures into alignment with this new relationship, and endeavoring to reduce further the role and importance of nuclear weapons,

Committed to the fulfillment of their obligations under Article VI of the Treaty on the Non-Proliferation of Nuclear Weapons of July 1, 1968, and to the achievement of the historic goal of freeing humanity from the nuclear threat,

Expressing strong support for on-going global efforts in non-proliferation,

Seeking to preserve continuity in, and provide new impetus to, the step-by-step process of reducing and limiting nuclear arms while maintaining the safety and security of their nuclear arsenals, and with a view to expanding this process in the future, including to a multilateral approach,

Guided by the principle of indivisible security and convinced that measures for the reduction and limitation of strategic offensive arms and the other obligations set forth in this Treaty will enhance predictability and stability, and thus the security of both Parties,

Recognizing the existence of the interrelationship between strategic offensive arms and strategic defensive arms, that this interrelationship will become more important as strategic nuclear arms are reduced, and that current strategic defensive arms do not undermine the viability and effectiveness of the strategic offensive arms of the Parties,

Mindful of the impact of conventionally armed ICBMs and SLBMs on strategic stability,

Taking into account the positive effect on the world situation of the significant, verifiable reduction in nuclear arsenals at the turn of the 21st century,

Desiring to create a mechanism for verifying compliance with the obligations under this Treaty, adapted, simplified, and made less costly in comparison to the Treaty Between the United States of America and the Union of Soviet Socialist Republics on the Reduction and Limitation of Strategic Offensive Arms of July 31, 1991, hereinafter referred to as the START Treaty,

Recognizing that the START Treaty has been implemented by the Republic of Belarus, the Republic of Kazakhstan, the Russian Federation, Ukraine, and the United States of America, and that the reduction levels envisaged by the START Treaty were achieved,

Deeply appreciating the contribution of the Republic of Belarus, the Republic of Kazakhstan, and Ukraine to nuclear disarmament and to strengthening international peace and security as non-nuclear-weapon states under the Treaty on the Non-Proliferation of Nuclear Weapons of July 1, 1968,

Welcoming the implementation of the Treaty Between the United States of America and the Russian Federation on Strategic Offensive Reductions of May 24, 2002,

Did You Know?

From the "Bush Doctrine" to the "Obama Doctrine"

The "Bush Doctrine" took shape after 9/11/01 when President Bush asserted that other countries are "with us or against us" in the War on Terror. Later, the doctrine was refined to justify preemptive strikes by the United States against any country suspected of possessing weapons of mass destruction. If allies were "unwilling" to join the United States, the Bush Doctrine was carried out unilaterally if necessary. While it has not been clearly stated as an official "doctrine," in Barack Obama's first year in office, there was a lively debate around what some have called the "Obama Doctrine." Some clearly see an Obama Doctrine that emphasizes multilateralism, alliance-building, diplomacy, and even engagement with hostile regimes. For instance, in Strasbourg, France, President Obama noted that it is "always harder to forge true partnerships and sturdy alliances than to act alone." Defenders of the Obama Doctrine argue that it emphasizes multilateralism and diplomacy, which were neglected by President George W. Bush and in turn isolated the United States even from its historical allies. On the other hand, critics of the Obama Doctrine see it as naïve, weak, overly apologetic, unwilling to stand up to hostile regimes in North Korea and Iran, and ineffective in promoting U.S. global leadership and American interests. In actuality, while President Obama emphasizes diplomacy more than President George W. Bush, he has so far carried out a moderately "realist" foreign policy by continuing the military policies set forth by President Bush in Iraq, deciding in favor of a troop surge in Afghanistan, and increasing the number of "drone" attacks on terrorists hiding in Pakistan. At the very least, the Obama Doctrine emphasizes a different tone and style of foreign policy when compared to the Bush Doctrine.

U.S. president Barack Obama and Russian president Dmitry Medvedev sign the New START treaty in Prague, April 8, 2010. (AP Photo/Alex Brandon)

Have agreed as follows:

Article I

1. Each Party shall reduce and limit its strategic offensive arms in accordance with the provisions of this Treaty and shall carry out the other obligations set forth in this Treaty and its Protocol.
2. Definitions of terms used in this Treaty and its Protocol are provided in Part One of the Protocol.

Article II

1. Each Party shall reduce and limit its ICBMs and ICBM launchers, SLBMs and SLBM launchers, heavy bombers, ICBM warheads, SLBM warheads, and heavy bomber nuclear armaments, so that seven years after entry into force of this Treaty and thereafter, the aggregate numbers, as counted in accordance with Article III of this Treaty, do not exceed:

   (a) 700, for deployed ICBMs, deployed SLBMs, and deployed heavy bombers;
   (b) 1550, for warheads on deployed ICBMs, warheads on deployed SLBMs, and nuclear warheads counted for deployed heavy bombers;
   (c) 800, for deployed and non-deployed ICBM launchers, deployed and non-deployed SLBM launchers, and deployed and non-deployed heavy bombers.

2. Each Party shall have the right to determine for itself the composition and structure of its strategic offensive arms.

Article III

1. For the purposes of counting toward the aggregate limit provided for in subparagraph l(a) of Article I1 of this Treaty:

    (a) Each deployed ICBM shall be counted as one. (b) Each deployed SLBM shall be counted as one. (c) Each deployed heavy bomber shall be counted as one.

2. For the purposes of counting toward the aggregate limit provided for in subparagraph l(b) of Article I1 of this Treaty:

    (a) For ICBMs and SLBMs, the number of warheads shall be the number of reentry vehicles emplaced on deployed ICBMs and on deployed SLBMs.
    (b) One nuclear warhead shall be counted for each deployed heavy bomber.

3. For the purposes of counting toward the aggregate limit provided for in subparagraph l(c) of Article I1 of this Treaty:

    (a) Each deployed launcher of ICBMs shall be counted as one.
    (b) Each non-deployed launcher of ICBMs shall be counted as one.
    (c) Each deployed launcher of SLBMs shall be counted as one.
    (d) Each non-deployed launcher of SLBMs shall be counted as one.
    (e) Each deployed heavy bomber shall be counted as one.
    (f) Each non-deployed heavy bomber shall be counted as one.

4. For the purposes of this Treaty, including counting ICBMs and SLBMs:

    (a) For ICBMs or SLBMs that are maintained, stored, and transported as assembled missiles in launch canisters, an assembled missile of a particular type, in its launch canister, shall be considered to be an ICBM or SLBM of that type.
    (b) For ICBMs or SLBMs that are maintained, stored, and transported as assembled missiles without launch canisters, an assembled missile of a particular type shall be considered to be an ICBM or SLBM of that type.
    (c) For ICBMs or SLBMs that are maintained, stored, and transported in stages, the first stage of an ICBM or SLBM of a particular type shall be considered to be an ICBM or SLBM of that type.
    (d) Each launch canister shall be considered to contain an ICBM or SLBM from the time it first leaves a facility at which an ICBM or SLBM is installed in it, until an ICBM or SLBM has been launched from it, or until an ICBM or SLBM has been removed from it for elimination. A launch canister shall not be considered to contain an ICBM or SLBM if it contains a training model of a missile or has been placed on static display. Launch canisters for ICBMs or SLBMs of a particular type shall be distinguishable from launch canisters for ICBMs or SLBMs of a different type.

5. Newly constructed strategic offensive arms shall begin to be subject to this Treaty as follows:

   (a) an ICBM, when it first leaves a production facility;
   (b) a mobile launcher of ICBMs, when it first leaves a production facility;
   (c) a silo launcher of ICBMs, when the silo door is first installed and closed;
   (d) an SLBM, when it first leaves a production facility;
   (e) an SLBM launcher, when the submarine on which that launcher is installed is first launched;
   (f) a heavy bomber equipped for nuclear armaments, when its airframe is first brought out of the shop, plant, or building in which components of such a heavy bomber are assembled to produce complete airframes; or when its airframe is first brought out of the shop, plant, or building in which existing bomber airframes are converted to such heavy bomber airframes.

6. ICBMs, SLBMs, ICBM launchers, SLBM launchers, and heavy bombers shall cease to be subject to this Treaty in accordance with Parts Three and Four of the Protocol to this Treaty. ICBMs or SLBMs of an existing type shall cease to be subject to this Treaty if all ICBM or SLBM launchers of a type intended for such ICBMs or SLBMs have been eliminated or converted in accordance with Part Three of the Protocol to this Treaty.

7. For the purposes of this Treaty:

   (a) A missile of a type developed and tested solely to intercept and counter objects not located on the surface of the Earth shall not be considered to be a ballistic missile to which the provisions of this Treaty apply.
   (b) Within the same type, a heavy bomber equipped for nuclear armaments shall be distinguishable from a heavy bomber equipped for non-nuclear armaments.
   (c) Heavy bombers of the same type shall cease to be subject to this Treaty or to the limitations thereof when the last heavy bomber equipped for nuclear armaments of that type is eliminated or converted, as appropriate, to a heavy bomber equipped for non-nuclear armaments in accordance with Part Three of the Protocol to this Treaty.

8. As of the date of signature of this Treaty:

   (a) Existing types of ICBMs are:

       (i) for the United States of America, the Minuteman 11, Minuteman 111, and Peacekeeper;
       (ii) for the Russian Federation, the RS-12M, RS-12M2, RS-18, RS-20, and RS-24.

   (b) Existing types of SLBMs are:

       (i) for the Russian Federation, the RSM-50, RSM-52, RSM-54, and RSM-56;
       (ii) for the United States of America, the Trident 11.

(c) Existing types of heavy bombers are:

   (i) for the United States of America, the B-52G, B- 52H, B-IB, and B-2A;
   (ii) for the Russian Federation, the Tu-95MS and Tu-160.

(d) Existing types of ICBM launchers and SLBM launchers are:

   (i) for the Russian Federation, ICBM launchers RS-12M, RS-12M2, RS-18, RS-20, and RS-24; SLBM launchers RSM-50, RSM-52, RSM-54, and RSM-56;
   (ii) for the United States of America, ICBM launchers Minuteman 11, Minuteman 111, and Peacekeeper; the SLBM launchers Trident 11.

Article IV

1. Each Party shall base:

   (a) deployed launchers of ICBMs only at ICBM bases;
   (b) deployed heavy bombers only at air bases.

2. Each Party shall install deployed launchers of SLBMs only on ballistic missile submarines.
3. Each Party shall locate:

   (a) non-deployed launchers of ICBMs only at ICBM bases, production facilities, ICBM loading facilities, repair facilities, storage facilities, conversion or elimination facilities, training facilities, test ranges, and space launch facilities. Mobile launchers of prototype ICBMs shall not be located at maintenance facilities of ICBM bases;
   (b) non-deployed ICBMs and non-deployed SLBMs only at, as appropriate, submarine bases, ICBM or SLBM loading facilities, maintenance facilities, repair facilities for ICBMs or SLBMs, storage facilities for ICBMs or SLBMs, conversion or elimination facilities for ICBMs or SLBMs, test ranges, space launch facilities, and production facilities. Prototype ICBMs and prototype SLBMs, however, shall not be located at maintenance facilities of ICBM bases or at submarine bases.

4. Non-deployed ICBMs and non-deployed SLBMs as well as non-deployed mobile launchers of ICBMs may be in transit. Each Party shall limit the duration of each transit between facilities to no more than 30 days.
5. Test launchers of ICBMs or SLBMs may be located only at test ranges.
6. Training launchers maybe located only at ICBM bases, training facilities, and test ranges. The number of silo training launchers located at each ICBM base for silo launchers of ICBMs shall not exceed one for each type of ICBM specified for that ICBM base.
7. Each Party shall limit the number of test heavy bombers to no more than ten.

8. Each Party shall base test heavy bombers only at heavy bomber flight test centers. Non-deployed heavy bombers other than test heavy bombers shall be located only at repair facilities or production facilities for heavy bombers.

9. Each Party shall not carry out at an air base joint basing of heavy bombers equipped for nuclear armaments and heavy bombers equipped for non-nuclear armaments, unless otherwise agreed by the Parties.

10. Strategic offensive arms shall not be located at eliminated facilities except during their movement through such facilities and during visits of heavy bombers at such facilities.

11. Strategic offensive arms subject to this Treaty shall not be based outside the national territory of each Party. The obligations provided for in this paragraph shall not affect the Parties' rights in accordance with generally recognized principles and rules of international law relating to the passage of submarines or flights of aircraft, or relating to visits of submarines to ports of third States. Heavy bombers may be temporarily located outside the national territory, notification of which shall be provided in accordance with Part Four of the Protocol to this Treaty.

Article V

1. Subject to the provisions of this Treaty, modernization and replacement of strategic offensive arms may be carried out.

2. When a Party believes that a new kind of strategic offensive arm is emerging, that Party shall have the right to raise the question of such a strategic offensive arm for consideration in the Bilateral Consultative Commission.

3. Each Party shall not convert and shall not use ICBM launchers and SLBM launchers for placement of missile defense interceptors therein. Each Party further shall not convert and shall not use launchers of missile defense interceptors for placement of ICBMs and SLBMs therein. This provision shall not apply to ICBM launchers that were converted prior to signature of this Treaty for placement of missile defense interceptors therein.

Article VI

1. Conversion, elimination, or other means for removal from accountability of strategic offensive arms and facilities shall be carried out in accordance with Part Three of the Protocol to this Treaty.

2. Notifications related to conversion, elimination, or other means for removal from accountability shall be provided in accordance with Parts Three and Four of the Protocol to this Treaty.

3. Verification of conversion or elimination in accordance with this Treaty shall be carried out by:

   (a) national technical means of verification in accordance with Article X of this Treaty; and

   (b) inspection activities as provided for in Article XI of this Treaty.

Article VII

1. A database pertaining to the obligations under this Treaty shall be created in accordance with Parts Two and Four of the Protocol to this Treaty. Categories of data for this database are set forth in Part Two of the Protocol to this Treaty.
2. Each Party shall notify the other Party about changes in data and shall provide other notifications in a manner provided for in Part Four of the Protocol to this Treaty.
3. Each Party shall use the Nuclear Risk Reduction Centers in order to provide and receive notifications, unless otherwise provided for in this Treaty.
4. Each Party may provide additional notifications on a voluntary basis, in addition to the notifications specified in paragraph 2 of this Article, if it deems this necessary to ensure confidence in the fulfillment of obligations assumed under this Treaty.
5. The Parties shall hold consultations within the framework of the Bilateral Consultative Commission on releasing to the public data and information obtained during the implementation of this Treaty. The Parties shall have the right to release to the public such data and information following agreement thereon within the framework of the Bilateral Consultative Commission. Each Party shall have the right to release to the public data related to its respective strategic offensive arms.
6. Geographic coordinates relating to data provided for in Part Two of the Protocol to this Treaty, unique identifiers, site diagrams of facilities provided by the Parties pursuant to this Treaty, as well as coastlines and waters diagrams provided by the Parties pursuant to this Treaty shall not be released to the public unless otherwise agreed by the Parties within the framework of the Bilateral Consultative Commission.
7. Notwithstanding paragraph 5 of this Article, the aggregate numbers of deployed ICBMs, deployed SLBMs, and deployed heavy bombers; the aggregate numbers of warheads on deployed ICBMs, deployed SLBMs, and nuclear warheads counted for deployed heavy bombers; and the aggregate numbers of deployed and non- deployed ICBM launchers, deployed and non-deployed SLBM launchers, and deployed and non-deployed heavy bombers, may be released to the public by the Parties.

Article VIII

In those cases in which one of the Parties determines that its actions may lead to ambiguous situations, that Party shall take measures to ensure the viability and effectiveness of this Treaty and to enhance confidence, openness, and predictability concerning the reduction and limitation of strategic offensive arms. Such measures may include, among other things, providing information in advance on activities of that Party associated with deployment or increased readiness of strategic offensive arms, to preclude the possibility of misinterpretation of its actions by the other Party. This information shall be provided through diplomatic or other channels.

. . .

Article XVI

This Treaty shall be registered pursuant to article 102 of the charter of the United Nations.
Done at Prague, this eighth of April 2010, in two originals, each in English and Russian languages, both text equally authentic.
For the President of the United States:
BARACK OBAMA

For the Russian Federation
DIMITRY MEDVEDEV

FURTHER READING

Cooke, J. G., and J. S. Morrison, eds. (2009) *Africa Policy Beyond the Bush Years: Critical Choices for the Obama Administration.* Washington, DC: Center for Strategic & International Studies.

Kagan, R. (2009) *The Return of History and the End of Dreams.* New York: Vintage.

Lowenthal, A. F., T. J. Piccone, and L. Whitehead, eds. (2009) *The Obama Administration and the Americas: Agenda for Change.* Washington, DC: Brookings Institution Press.

O'Hanlon, M. E. (2009) *Budgeting for Hard Power: Defense and Security Spending under Barack Obama.* Washington, DC: Brookings Institution Press.

Renshon, S. A. (2009) *National Security in the Obama Administration: Reassessing the Bush Doctrine.* New York: Routledge.

Sanger, D. E. (2010) *The Inheritance: The World Obama Confronts and the Challenges to American Power.* New York: Harmony Books.

Zakaria, F. (2009) *The Post-American World.* New York: W. W. Norton & Company.

AFTERWORD

This book has taken a historical rather than a thematic approach to understanding U.S. foreign policy. While tracing the arc of American foreign policy across time, we have nevertheless made reference to some of these themes, such as economics, trade, and nuclear disarmament. In fact, some of these themes seem to hold the key when trying to understand the current and future course of U.S. foreign policy. The United States stands at the apex of its global power. It is the undisputed military and economic superpower on the world stage. But several questions are being debated: Can the United States sustain its dominance in world affairs? If so, for how long? Will the United States be challenged by emerging economic and military powers such as China? Will the United States fall victim to overextension and overreach? Given these and other questions, scholars and pundits are currently assessing global politics to predict what the future will hold for U.S. foreign policy. Some question whether the United States is in decline and foresee a continuation of U.S. global dominance. Others argue that while the United States will not be able to remain dominant forever; it may be in the early stages of decline as a global superpower.

To conclude this book, we will offer an overview of these debates so that readers can ponder and debate what the future will hold for U.S. foreign policy and America's place in the world.

THE UNIPOLAR MOMENT

In an influential *Foreign Affairs* article in 1990, Charles Krauthammer argued that the United States was enjoying a "unipolar moment," given its unrivaled position as the sole military superpower. Despite this military might, however, for the better part of the 1990s the United States remained committed to internationalism and eschewed the temptation to unilaterally impose its will. Some suggested that despite its power, the United States was in a state of drift (Lieven 2008).

After the collapse of the Berlin Wall and the demise of the Soviet Union, the United States stood alone as the world's sole superpower. In the United States, conservatives and realists such as Ronald Reagan were given credit for winning the "Cold War." Reagan's successor, however, was not known as a unilateralist. Despite the U.S. invasion of Panama and the arrest of General Manuel Noriega, President George H. W. Bush was more of an internationalist, and as such, he preferred to pursue the Persian Gulf War by building an international alliance and working through international organizations such as the UN. For those who subscribed to Krauthammer's position, such an approach was disappointing. Among those who disagreed with President Bush's decision not to prosecute the Persian Gulf War to its logical conclusion by removing Saddam Hussein from power in Iraq were members of his own cabinet, such as Secretary of Defense Dick Cheney and his Undersecretary of Defense Paul Wolfowitz.

As we now know, Cheney, Wolfowitz, and others who became known as the "Vulcans" would become influential actors in the future administration of President George W. Bush (Mann 2004). Many of them would also openly criticize the multilateralism and nation-building preferred by President Bill Clinton. Along with groups such as the think tank Project for a New American Century (PNAC), they accused Clinton of squandering the unipolar moment by not acting decisively and unilaterally to promote U.S. interests around the world.

The attacks of September 11, 2001, resulted in a dramatic shift in the posture, goals, and methods of U.S. foreign policy. Indeed, they provided a decisive moment in which the United States could work with allies to attack the regime that provided safe harbor to al Qaeda but also use its ideological and military clout to pursue unilateral goals such as the War on Terror and even the war with Iraq in 2003, which was supported by a nominal "coalition of the willing." Moreover, during this quintessential unipolar moment, the United States all but ignored the United Nations, especially when questions were raised about the justifiability of invading a sovereign country, albeit one with a spotty track record of complying with the UN charter.

In the ultimate unipolar statement, President Bush told the world "you are either with us or against us" in the War on Terror, and he argued that the United States would not seek anyone's permission to defend itself from threats. (In the Spring of 2011, President Obama authorized a successful operation that killed Osama bin Laden who was living in a compound in Pakistan.) Moreover, from 2004 until 2006 an insurgency raged in Iraq, thwarting U.S. efforts to establish a stable democracy. It was not until the end of the Bush administration that the 2007 surge, which took advantage of an indigenous movement to isolate the insurgents, began to pay off. At the same time, however, the U.S. economy slid into a recession, led by foreclosures, bankruptcies, and the speculative practices of Wall Street investment banks, which had enjoyed several years of lax regulation. As the U.S. economy slowed down, so, too, did the global economy. Suddenly, commentators started to consider these events as signaling the end of the unipolar moment and the decline of the United States as the preeminent global power (Ferguson 2010).

FOREIGN POLICY CONUNDRUMS

The United States faces two difficult paradoxes regarding its conduct of foreign policy, (1) the paradox of security, and (2) the paradox of ideology. The first paradox is extremely important, considering that most people measure power in terms of military capabilities, something that has been termed "hard power." If this hard power is in decline, clearly the United States is in decline. However, hard power is not understood simply in terms of military equipment or soldiers on the ground but also in terms of economic indicators, research and development, and intellectual resources that enable the United States to construct its military–intelligence apparatus. It is also known that when foreign policy is closely linked with military policy, the United States may fall into a "security trap" (Ikenberry 2008). This security trap is an expression of the effects of relative power, in which the United States is only powerful and safe when it is the global superpower, while every move by another state to close the military gap between itself and the United States is seen as a decline of power for the United States.

Put in terms of the Bush Doctrine, the duty to protect the American people and U.S. interests requires that military power be used preemptively and proactively:

> It is an enduring American principle that this duty obligates the government to anticipate and counter threats, using all elements of national power, before the threats can do grave damage. The greater the threat, the greater is the risk of inaction—and the more compelling the case for taking anticipatory action to defend ourselves, even if uncertainty remains as to the time and place of the enemy's attack. There are few greater threats than a terrorist attack with WMD.
>
> To forestall or prevent such hostile acts by our adversaries, the United States will, if necessary, act preemptively in exercising our inherent right of self-defense. The United States will not resort to force in all cases to preempt emerging threats. Our preference is that nonmilitary actions succeed. And no country should ever use preemption as a pretext for aggression (Bush 2002).

By pursuing such a policy, by which the United States will do whatever is necessary to keep itself safe, President Bush inadvertently set up the security trap. While the United States acted to secure its interests and keep itself safely above all other nations in terms of military and economic capacity, the rest of the world started to balk at what it saw as American "cowboy" attitudes.

Even though President Obama has extended a friendly hand to the Middle East, U.S. policy in the region is unlikely to change. The more the United States worries about its security and acts unilaterally and heavy-handedly, the more the nation invites the scorn of the world and a race to replace it as a global hegemon. This leads to situations such as the paradox of unrealized power in Afghanistan, where, even though the United States is fighting with forces far superior to those of the Taliban, it has so far failed to make any progress in creating a stable state or stopping the resurgence of the Taliban and al Qaeda. Although the war in Afghanistan is a work in progress, President Obama's decision to send an additional 30,000 troops to Afghanistan was seen as an admission that the United States was losing the war. (In June 2011, President Obama announced plans to eventually draw down this troop surge by the end of the summer of 2012.) Despite its military and economic might, there is no guarantee that "hard power" guarantees success.

Second, the paradox of ideology only enhances the negative impact of the security trap because it eliminates possible solutions from policymakers' options and skews the understanding of conflicts the United States is involved in. The paradox of ideology represents the domestic side of U.S. foreign policymaking; it argues that the more the

United States is convinced of the superiority of its own political system of liberalism, the less democratically it acts with respect to pursuing foreign policy. The U.S. public has convinced itself that the United States has only the noblest of intentions in terms of foreign policy, and when people around the world fail to see this, both American politicians and the general public react with a righteous indignation that elicits a Jacksonian response to foreign policy. To deny or even question the intentions of U.S. foreign policy, which are taken to be inherently noble, is to side with the terrorists, just as honest criticism of the U.S. invasion of Iraq was equated with defending dictators such as Saddam Hussein. This paradox of ideology supports unilateralist responses to complicated international crises, and when unintended consequences or long-term planning questions are raised, they are discounted as evidence of a lack of resolve.

If the United States is indeed a Wilsonian "liberal empire," the United States benefits by ensuring its own security, but the world benefits because it extends the reach of capitalism and democracy. Pursuing this unilaterally, however, can breed resentment even among allies. However, preserving U.S. influence by multilateral means is seen by realists as a sign of weakness. For instance, President Obama's strategy of peeling off some Taliban who can be channeled into political institutions in order to isolate and hunt down the hardcore Taliban and al Qaeda members who cannot be reconciled may be a smart strategy, but it is one that critics see as dangerous and a sign of weakness. And attempts to promote multilateral solutions to global problems such as climate change bring criticism that such efforts amount to a surrender of American sovereignty to international commissions. Moreover, suggestions that the United States is losing its economic or military status to an emerging China, as the next superpower, are rejected as premature defeatism that ignores the ingenuity Americans can exercise to stay on top.

The dominant position of the United States on the world stage can be defended either unilaterally or multilaterally, and it can be defended on the basis of the hard power of military and economic might. However, without friends and allies, such an approach is self-isolating and perhaps even self-defeating if it means that the United States squanders valuable resources on sustaining a military that is unable to adapt to new security threats that could be addressed through creative diplomatic solutions. Finally, purely military and security approaches to foreign policy risk squandering opportunities to use "soft power" to remind people around the world of the culture, values, and ideals that still make the United States a beacon of freedom and liberty for so many.

FURTHER READING

Bush, G. (2002) National Security Strategy, available at: http://georgewbush-whitehouse.archives.gov/nsc/nss/2002/

Chomsky, N. (2004) *Hegemony or Survival: America's Quest for Global Domination*. New York: Henry Holt.

Ferguson, N. (2010) "Decline and Fall: When the American Empire Goes, It Is Likely to go Quickly," *Foreign Affairs*, Vol. 89, No. 2, March/April, pp. 18–32.

Ikenberry, G. J. (2008) "America's Security Trap," in Cox M. and Stokes D. *US Foreign Policy*, Oxford: Oxford University Press, pp. 421–432.

Kagan, R. (2004) "American Crisis of Legitimacy," *Foreign Affairs*, 8(2) (March/April), 2–18.

Lieven, A. (2008) "The Future of US Foreign Policy." In Cox, M., and D. Stokes, *US Foreign Policy* (pp. 432–450). Oxford: Oxford University Press.

Mc Dougall, W. A. (1997) *Promised Land, Crusader State: The American Encounter with the World since 1776*. Boston: Houghton Mifflin.

SELECTED RESOURCES

HANDBOOKS, CHRONOLOGIES, AND BIBLIOGRAPHIES

Beisner, R., and K. Hanson, eds. (2003) *American Foreign Relations since 1600: A Guide to the Literature*, 2d ed. Santa Barbara: ABC-CLIO.
Prepared under the auspices of the Society for Historians of American Foreign Relations. The third edition (2007) is available as an electronic publication.

Bemis, S., and G. Griffin, eds. (1935; reprint, 1951) *Guide to the Diplomatic History of the United States, 1775–1921*. Washington, DC: USGPO.
Despite its age, this work, chiefly in bibliographical essay format, is still valuable, chiefly for its Part II, which covers government documents and other primary sources.

Brune, L., ed. (2003) *Chronological History of U.S. Foreign Relations*, 2d ed. 3 vols. New York: Routledge.
Year-by-year coverage from 1776 to 2002; considered an essential reference.

Europa World Year Book (1959–) Europa Publications, ed. Milton Park, Abingdon, Oxon.: Routledge
Comprehensive handbook profiling some 1900 international organizations and all of the world's nations, as well as territories and other possessions. Country profiles begin with an introductory survey essay covering recent political history, economic affairs, constitution and government, and characteristic regional and international cooperation. A statistical survey presents demographics, economic sectors, finance, infrastructure, and more. Finally, there is a directory with contact information for governmental and other public officials, political parties and political and development organizations, the judiciary, diplomatic representation, religious bodies, the media, trade and industry groups, and educational, scientific, and cultural institutions. *Europa Year Book* and the publisher's nine *Europa Regional Surveys of the World* are available as a subscription online product, Europa World Plus (http://www.europaworld.com/pub/about).

Goehlert, R., and E. Hoffmeister, eds. (1986) *The Department of State and American Diplomacy: A Bibliography*. New York: Garland.
Entries are unannotated. Focuses tightly on the Department of State and its conduct of diplomacy; there are sections on geographical studies and on biographies of secretaries and other officials.

Haines, G., and J. S. Walker, eds. (1981) *American Foreign Relations: A Historiographical Review.* Westport, CT: Greenwood Press.
  Essays on the state of historiography in particular areas of U.S. diplomatic history from the country's foundation to the 1980s.

Langer, W., and H. Armstrong et al., eds. (1933–1976) *Foreign Affairs Bibliography: A Selected and Annotated List of Books on International Relations.* Various publishers.
  Prepared under the auspices of the Council on Foreign Relations; remains an important resource. Topical, geographical, and historical sections.

Mugridge, I., ed. (1982) *United States Foreign Relations under Washington and Adams: A Guide to the Literature and Sources.* New York: Garland.
  Annotated entries on some 400 of the chief primary and secondary sources.

Urdang, L. (1996) *The Timetables of American History,* updated ed. New York: Simon & Schuster.
  Presents a chronology of American history in parallel columns covering history and politics, arts, science and technology, and other developments.

DICTIONARIES AND ENCYCLOPEDIAS

Berridge, G., and A. James, eds. (2004) *A Dictionary of Diplomacy,* 2nd ed. New York: Palgrave.
  Covers legal terms in addition to the specialized vocabulary of diplomacy; entries on international events and important figures.

DeConde, A., R. Burns, and F. Logevall, eds. (2002) *Encyclopedia of American Foreign Policy,* 2nd ed. 3 vols. New York: Charles Scribner's Sons.
  Thoroughly revised edition of DeConde's three-volume *Encyclopedia of American Foreign Policy: Studies of the Principal Movements and Ideas* (1978), with more than 40 new essays.

Findling, J., ed. (1989) *Dictionary of American Diplomatic History,* 2nd ed. New York: Greenwood.
  Brief entries with bibliographies. Strong emphasis on biography.

Jentleson, B., and T. Paterson, eds. (1997) *Encyclopedia of U.S Foreign Relations.* 4 vols. New York: Oxford University Press.
  Prepared under the auspices of the Council of Foreign Relations. One thousand entries by scholars and specialists covering American diplomatic history from its foundations. Includes an excellent chronology.

BOOKS

Ambrose, S., and D. Brinkley. (2011) *Rise to Globalism: American Foreign Policy since 1938,* 9th ed. New York: Penguin.
Alden, E., and F. Schurmann. (1990) *Why We Need Ideologies in American Foreign Policy: Democratic Politics and World Order.* Berkeley, CA: Institute of International Studies, University of California.
Bacevich, A. (2002) *American Empire: The Realities and Consequences of U.S. Diplomacy.* Cambridge, MA: Harvard University Press.
Bamford, J. (2004) *A Pretext for War: 9/11, Iraq, and the Abuse of America's Intelligence Agencies.* New York: Doubleday.
Barber, B. (2003) *Fear's Empire: War, Terrorism and Democracy.* New York: Norton.
Barnet, R. (1972) *Roots of War: The Men and Institutions Behind U.S. Foreign Policy.* New York: Atheneum.

Beisner, R. (1986) *From the Old Diplomacy to the New, 1865–1900*. Arlington Heights, IL: H. Davidson.

Berman, L. (2001) *No Peace, No Honor: Nixon, Kissinger and Betrayal in Vietnam*. New York: Free Press.

Beschloss, M. (2002) *The Conquerors: Roosevelt, Truman and the Destruction of Hitler's Germany, 1941–1945*. New York: Simon & Schuster.

Blank, S. (2008) *Towards a New Russia Policy*. Carlisle, PA: U.S. Army War College, Strategic Studies Institute.

Boot, M. (2002) *The Savage Wars of Peace: Small Wars and the Rise off American Power*. New York: Basic Books.

Bradford, J., ed. (1993) *Crucible of Empire: The Spanish-American War and Its Aftermath*. Annapolis: Naval Institute Press.

Brzezinski, Z., and Scowcroft, B. (2008) *America and the World: Conversations on the Future of American Foreign Policy*. New York: Basic Books.

Calhoun, C., F. Cooper, and K. Moore. (2006) *Lessons of Empire: Imperial Histories and American Power*. New York: The New Press.

Chua, A. (2007) *Day of Empire: How Hyperpowers Rise to Global Dominance—and Why They Fail*. New York: Anchor.

Cohen, W., ed. (1993) *The Cambridge History of American Foreign Relations*. 4 vols. Cambridge, UK: Cambridge University Press. Includes a bibliographic essay.

Cole, W. (1995) *Determinism and American Foreign Relations during the Franklin D. Roosevelt Era*. Lanham, MD: University Press of America.

Cooley, J. (2005) *An Alliance Against Babylon: The U.S., Israel, and Iraq*. Ann Arbor, MI: Pluto Press.

Costigliola, F. (1984) *Awkward Dominion: American Political, Economic, and Cultural Relations with Europe, 1919–1933*. Ithaca, NY: Cornell University Press.

Cox, M., and D. Stokes. (2008) *U.S. Foreign Policy*. New York: Oxford University Press.

Daadler, I., and Lindsay J. (2005) *America Unbound: The Bush Revolution in Foreign Policy*. Hoboken, NJ: John Wiley and Sons.

David, S. (1991) *Choosing Sides: Alignment and Realignment in the Third World*. Baltimore, MD: The Johns Hopkins University Press.

DeConde, A. (1962, repr. 1975) *The American Secretary of State: An Interpretation*. Westport, CT: Greenwood Press.

DeConde, A. (1992) *Ethnicity, Race, and American Foreign Policy: A History*. Boston: Northeastern Univ. Press.

DeConde, A. (2000) *Presidential Machismo: Executive Authory, Military Intervention, and Foreign Relations*. Boston: Northeastern University Press.

Doyle, M. (1986) *Empires*. Ithaca, NY: Cornell University Press.

Fairbank, J. (1979) *The United States and China*, 4th ed. Cambridge, MA: Harvard University Press.

Ferguson, N. (2002) *Empire: The Rise and Demise of the British World Order and the Lessons for Global Power*. New York: Basic Books.

Ferguson, N. (2004) *Colossus: The Rise and Fall of the American Empire*. New York: Penguin.

Foner, P. (1972) *The Spanish-Cuban-American War and the Birth of American Imperialism, 1895–1902*. New York: Monthly Review Press.

Frieden, J., D. Lake, and K. Schultz. (2009) *World Politics: Interests, Interactions, Institutions*. New York: W. W. Norton.

Gacek, C. (1994). *The Logic of Force: The Dilemma of Limited War in American Foreign Policy*. New York: Columbia University Press.

Gaddis, J. (1982) *Strategies of Containment: A Critical Appraisal of Postwar American National Security Policy*. New York: Oxford University Press.

Gaddis, J. L. (1989) *The Long Peace: Inquiries in the History of the Cold War*. Oxford: Oxford University Press.

Gaddis, J. L. (2005) *The Cold War: A New History*. New York: Penguin.

George, A. (1992) *Forceful Persuasion: Coercive Diplomacy as an Alternative to War*. Washington, DC: United States Institute of Peace.

Gibney, F. (1992) *The Pacific Century: America and Asia in a Changing World*. New York: Macmillan.

Greenberg, A. (2005) *Manifest Manhood and the Antebellum American Empire*. Cambridge: Cambridge University Press.

Haas, R. (1999) *Intervention: The Use of American Military Force in the Post-Cold War World*, rev. ed. Washington: Brookings Institution.

Hagan, K. (1973) *American Gunboat Diplomacy and the Old Navy, 1877–1889*. Westport, CT: Greenwood Press.

Halper, S., and Clarke, J. (2004) *America Alone: The Neo-Conservatives and the Global Order*. Cambridge: Cambridge University Press.

Held, D., and Koening-Archibugi, M. (2004) *American Power in the 21st Century*. Cambridge, UK: Polity Press.

Hendrikson, R. (2002) *The Clinton Wars: The Constitution, Congress and War Powers*. Nashville: Vanderbilt University Press.

Herring, G. (1983) *The Secret Diplomacy of the Vietnam War: The Negotiating Volumes of the Pentagon Papers*. Austin: University of Texas Press.

Herring, G. (2008) *From Colony to Superpower: U.S. Foreign Relations since 1776*. Oxford: Oxford University Press.

Hersh, S. (1983) *The Price of Power: Kissinger in the Nixon White House*. New York: Summit.

Hilsman, R. (1967) *To Move a Nation: The Politics of Foreign Policy in the Administration of John F. Kennedy*. Garden City, NY: Doubleday.

Hinsley, F. (1967) *Power and the Pursuit of Peace: Theory and Practice in the History of Relations Between States*. London: Cambridge University Press.

Hoff, J. (2008) *A Faustian Foreign Policy from Woodrow Wilson to George W. Bush: Dreams of Perfectability*. Cambridge: Cambridge University Press.

Hogan, M. (1987) *The Marshall Plan: America, Britain, and the Reconstruction of Europe, 1947–1952*. Cambridge: Cambridge University Press.

Hogan, M., ed. (1999) *The Ambiguous Legacy: U.S. Foreign Relations in the "American Century."* Cambridge: Cambridge University Press.

Hogan, M., ed. (2000) *Paths to Power: The Historiography of American Foreign Relations to 1941*. Cambridge: Cambridge University Press.

Hogan, M., and T. Paterson, eds. (1991) *Explaining the History of American Foreign Relations*. Cambridge: Cambridge University Press.

Hoxie, F., R. Hoffman, and P. Albert (1999) *Native Americans and the Early Republic*. Charlottesville, VA: University Press of Virginia. [Published for the United States Capitol Historical Society.]

Hunt, M. (1987) *Ideology and U.S. Foreign Policy*. New Haven, CT: Yale University Press.

Huntington, S. (1996) *The Clash of Civilizations and the Remaking of World Order*. New York: Simon & Schuster.

Hymans, J. (2006) *The Psychology of Nuclear Proliferation: Identity, Emotions, and Foreign Policy*. London: Cambridge University Press.

Ikenberry, G. J. (1995) *American Foreign Policy: Theoretical Essays*, 2nd ed. New York: HarperCollins College Publishers.

Jensen, L. (1988) *Bargaining for National Security: The Postwar Disarmament Negotiations*. Columbia: University of South Carolina Press.

Johnson, C. (2004) *Blowback: The Cost and Consequences of American Empire*, 2nd ed. New York: Holt.

Johnson, C. (2004) *The Sorrows of Empire: Militarism, Secrecy, and the End of the Republic*. New York: Owl Books.

Johnson, C. (2007) *Nemesis: The Last Days of the Republic*. New York: Metropolitan Books.

Johnson, C. (2010) *Dismantling the Empire: America's Last Best Hope*. New York: Metropolitan Books.

Johnson, R. (1995) *The Peace Progressives and American Foreign Relations*. Cambridge, MA: Harvard University Press.

Jones, H., ed. (1992) *Safeguarding the Republic: Essays and Documents in American Foreign Relations, 1890–1991*. New York: McGraw-Hill.

Kaiser, D. (2000) *American Tragedy: Kennedy, Johnson, and the Origins of the Vietnam War*. Cambridge, MA: Belknap Press of Harvard University Press.

Kaplan, L. (1987) *Entangling Alliances with None: American Foreign Policy in the Age of Jefferson*. Kent, OH: Kent State University Press.

Katzenstein, P., ed. (1996) *The Culture of National Security: Identity and Norms in World Politics*. New York: Columbia University Press.

Kaufman, S., R. Little, and W. Wohlforth, eds. (2007) *The Balance of Power in World History*. New York: Palgrave Macmillan.

Kennan, G. (1951) *American Diplomacy, 1900–1950*. Chicago: University of Chicago.

Kennedy, P. (1987) *The Rise and the Fall of the Great Powers*. New York: Random House.

Keohane, R. (1986) *Neorealism and Its Critics*. New York: Columbia University Press.

Keohane, R. (2005) *After Hegemony: Cooperation and Discord in the World Political Economy*. Princeton, NJ: Princeton University Press.

Keynes, J. M. (1920) *The Economic Consequences of the Peace*. New York: Harcourt Brace.

Kindleberger, C. (1986) *The World in Depression: 1929–1939*. Berkeley: University of California Press.

Kissinger, H. (2001) *Does America Need a Foreign Policy? Towards a Diplomacy for the 21st Century*. New York: Touchstone.

Kissinger, H. (1994) *Diplomacy*. New York: Simon & Schuster.

Knock, T. (1992) *To End All Wars: Woodrow Wilson and the Quest for a New World Order*. New York: Oxford University Press.

Kolko, G. (1968; reprint, 1990) *The Politics of War: The World and United States Foreign Policy, 1943–1945*. New York, Pantheon.

Kolko, G. (1969) *The Roots of American Foreign Policy: An Analysis of Power and Purpose*. Boston: Beacon Press.

Kolko, J., and G. Kolko. (1972) *The Limits of Power: The World and United States Foreign Policy, 1945–1954*. New York: Harper & Row.

Kunz, D., ed. (1994) *The Diplomacy of the Crucial Decade: American Foreign Relations During the 1960s*. New York: Columbia University Press.

LaFeber, W. (2004) *America, Russia, and the Cold War, 1945–2002*, 9th ed. Boston: McGraw-Hill.

LaFeber, W. (1994) *The American Age: United States Foreign Policy at Home and Abroad since 1750*, 2nd ed. 2 vols. New York: Norton.

Lieven, A. (2004) *America Right or Wrong: An Anatomy of American Nationalism*. Oxford: Oxford University Press.

Leuchtenburg, W. (1997) *The FDR Years*. New York: Columbia University Press.

Link, A. (1954) *Woodrow Wilson and the Progressive Era, 1910–1917*. New York: Harper.

Lowenthal, M. (2008) *Intelligence: From Secrets to Policy*. Washington, DC: CQ Press.

Lucas, E. (2008) *The New Cold War: Putin's Russia and the Threat to the West*. New York: Palgrave Macmillan.

Malik, H. (2008) *U.S. Relations with Afghanistan and Pakistan: The Imperial Dimension*. New York: Oxford University Press.

Mandelbaum, M (2003) *The Ideas That Conquered the World: Peace, Democracy, and the Free Markets in the Twenty First Century*. New York: Public Affairs.

Mann, J. (2009) *The Rebellion of Ronald Reagan: A History of the End of the Cold War*. New York: Penguin.

Martel, G., ed. (1994) *American Foreign Relations Reconsidered, 1890–1993*. London: Routledge.

Mayer, J. (2008) *The Dark Side: The Inside Story of How the War on Terror Turned into a War on American Ideals*. New York: Anchor Books.

McDougall, W. (1997) *Promised Land, Crusader State: The American Encounter with the World since 1776*. Boston: Houghton Mifflin.

McMahon, R. *The Limits of Empire: The United States and Southeast Asia since World War II*. New York: Columbia University Press.

Mearsheimer, J. (2003) *The Tragedy of Great Power Politics*. New York: W. W. Norton.

Micklethwait, J., and Wooldridge, A. (2004) *The Right Nation: Conservative Power in America*. New York: The Penguin Press.

Miscamble, W. (2007) *From Roosevelt to Truman: Potsdam, Hiroshima, and the Cold War*. Cambridge: Cambridge University Press.

Musicant, I. (1990) *The Banana Wars: A History of United States Military Intervention in Latin America from the Spanish-American War to the Invasion of Panama*. New York: Macmillan.

National Commission on Terrorist Attacks on the United States. (2004) *The 9/11 Commission Report: Final Report of the National Commission on Terrorist Attacks on the United States*. Washington, DC: USGPO.

Nye, J. (2002) *The Paradox of American Power: Why the World's Only Superpower Can't Go It Alone*. Oxford: Oxford University Press.

Odom, W. (2003) *Fixing Intelligence: For a More Secure America*. New Haven, CT: Yale University Press.

Odom, W. and Dujarric, R. (2004) *America's Inadvertent Empire*. New Heaven, CT: Yale University Press.

Paterson, T., J. G. Clifford, and K. Hagan. (1999) *American Foreign Relations*, 5th ed. 2 vols. Boston: Houghton Mifflin.

Paul, T., J. Wirtz, and M. Fortmann. (2004) *Balance of Power: Theory and Practice in the 21st Century*. Palo Alto, CA: Stanford University Press.

Powers, S. (2003) *A Problem from Hell: America and the Age of Genocide*. London: Harper.

Prados, J. (2006) *Safe for Democracy: The Secret Wars of the CIA*. Chicago: Ivan Dee.

Rashid, A. (2008) *Descent into Chaos: The United States and the Failure of Nation Building in Pakistan, Afghanistan, and Central Asia*. New York: Viking.

Renshon, S. A. (2010) *National Security in the Obama Administration: Reassessing the Bush Doctrine*. Milton Park, Abington, Oxon.: Routledge.

Richelson, J. (2007) *The U.S. Intelligence Community*. New York: Westview Press.

Roberts, J. (1995) *Putting Foreign Policy to Work: The Role of Organized Labor in American Foreign Relations, 1932–1941*. New York: Garland.

Rose, G. (2010) *How Wars End: Why We Always Fight the Last Battle: A History of American Intervention from World War I to Afghanistan*. New York: Simon & Schuster.

Rosenau, J. (1990) *Turbulence in World Politics*. Princeton, NJ: Princeton University Press.

Rosenberg, E. (1999) *Financial Missionaries to the World: The Politics and Culture of Dollar Diplomacy, 1900–1930*. Cambridge: Harvard University Press.

Sanger, D. (2009) *The Inheritance: The World Obama Confronts and the Challenges to American Power*. New York: Harmony Books.

Schlesinger, A. (1973) *The Imperial Presidency*. New York: Mariner Books.

Schoonover, T. (1991) *The United States in Central America, 1860–1911: Episodes of Social Imperialism and Imperial Rivalry in the World System*. Durham, NC: Duke University Press.

Schoultz, L. (1998) *Beneath the United States: A History of U.S. Policy Toward Latin America*. Cambridge, MA: Harvard University Press.

Shulsky, A., and G. Schmitt. (2002) *Silent Warfare: Understanding the World of Intelligence*. Dulles,VA: Brasseys.

Sloan, S. R. (2010) *Permanent Alliance? NATO and the Transatlantic Bargain from Truman to Obama*. New York: Continuum.

Snyder, G. (2007) *Alliance Politics*. New York: Cornell University Press.

Stephanson, A. (1989) *Kennan and the Art of Foreign Policy*. Cambridge, MA: Harvard University Press.

Tebbel, John. *America's Great Patriotic War with Spain: Mixed Motives, Lies and Racism in Cuba and the Philippines, 1893–1915*. Manchester Center, VT: Marshall Jones, 1996.

Thompson, N. (2009) *The Hawk and the Dove: Paul Nitze, George Kennan, and the History of the Cold War*. New York: Henry Holt & Co.

Vasquez, J., and C. Elman. (2002) *Realism and the Balancing of Power: A New Debate*. New York: Prentice Hall.

Walt, S. (1990) *Origins of Alliances*. Ithaca: Cornell University Press.

Waltz, K. (2010) *Theory of International Politics*. Long Grove, IL: Waveland Press.

Westad, O. A. (2007) *The Global Cold War: Third World Interventions and the Making of Our Times*. Cambridge: Cambridge University Press.

White, P. (1970) *The Critical Years: American Foreign Policy, 1793–1823*. New York: Wiley.
Young. M. (1991) *The Vietnam Wars, 1945–1990*. New York: Harper Collins.

WEB SITES

CIA, World Fact Book: Afghanistan. https://www.cia.gov/library/publications/the-world
-factbook/geos/af.html.
American Foreign Policy Council. http://www.afpc.org/home/index.

INDEX

About the Authors

AKIS KALAITZIDIS is an associate professor of political science at the University of Central Missouri. He is the author of *Europe's Greece: A Giant in the Making* (2009) and coauthor of *Immigration: A Documentary and Reference Guide* (Greenwood Press, 2008).

GREGORY W. STREICH is a professor of political science at the University of Central Missouri. He is the author of *Justice Beyond "Just Us": Dilemmas of Time, Place, and Difference in American Politics* (2011). Dr. Streich has written extensively on democratic theory, justice, and national identity.